The 200 Stagecoach Bus Handbook

British Bus Publishing

Body codes used in the Bus Handbook series:

Type:
A   Articulated vehicle
B   Bus, either single-deck or double-deck
BC   Interurban - high-back seated bus
C   Coach
M   Minibus with design capacity of 16 seats or less
N   Low-floor bus (*Niederflur*), either single-deck or double-deck
O   Open-top bus (CO = convertible - PO = partial open-top)

Seating capacity is then shown. For double-decks the upper deck quantity is followed by the lower deck.

Door position:-
C   Centre entrance/exit
D   Dual doorway.
F   Front entrance/exit
R   Rear entrance/exit (no distinction between doored and open)
T   Three or more access points

Equipment:-
L	Lift for wheelchair	TV	Training vehicle.
M	Mail compartment	RV	Used as tow bus or engineers' vehicle.
T	Toilet		

Allocation:-
t   Training bus
u   out of service - maintenance or seasonal requirement
w   Vehicle is withdrawn and awaiting disposal.

e.g. - B32/28F is a double-deck bus with thirty-two seats upstairs, twenty-eight down and a front entrance/exit.
       N43D is a low-floor bus with two or more doorways.

Re-registrations:-
Where a vehicle has gained new index marks the details are listed at the end of each fleet showing the current mark, followed in sequence by those previously carried starting with the original mark.

Regional books in the series:
The North East Bus Handbook
The Yorkshire Bus Handbook
The North West Bus Handbook
The East Midlands Bus Handbook
The West Midlands Bus Handbook
The Eastern Bus Handbook
The London Bus Handbook
The South East Bus Handbook
The South West Bus Handbook
The Scottish Bus Handbook
The Welsh Bus Handbook
The Ireland & Islands Bus Handbook

Annual books are produced for the major groups:
The Stagecoach Bus Handbook
The First Bus Handbook
The Arriva Bus Handbook
The Go-Ahead Bus Handbook
The National Express Handbook (bi-annual)
Some editions for earlier years are available. Please contact the publisher.

Associated series:
The Hong Kong Bus Handbook
The Malta Bus Handbook
The Leyland Lynx Handbook
The Model Bus Handbook
The Postbus Handbook
The Overall Advertisment Bus Handbook - Volume 1
The Toy & Model Bus Handbook - Volume 1 - Early Diecasts
The Fire Brigade Handbook (fleet list of each local authority fire brigade)
The Fire Brigade Handbook - Special Appliances Volume 1
The Fire Brigade Handbook - Special Appliances Volume 2
The Police Range Rover Handbook

The 2005 Stagecoach Bus Handbook

The 2005 Stagecoach Bus Handbook is the twelfth edition of this volume dedicated to the various bus fleets of Stagecoach Holdings, both within the United Kingdom and its operations in New Zealand.

Although this book has been produced with the encouragement of, and in co-operation with, Stagecoach management, it is not an official Stagecoach fleet list and the vehicles included are subject to variation, particularly as new vehicle deliveries lead to older vehicles being 'cascaded' to other subsidiaries. Some vehicles listed are no longer in regular use on service but are retained for special purposes or preserved by the company. The services operated and the allocation of vehicles to subsidiary companies are subject to variation at any time, although accurate at the time of going to print. The contents are correct to mid-January 2005.

Quality photographs for inclusion in the series are welcome, for which a fee is payable. Unfortunately the publishers cannot accept responsibility for any loss and request you show your name on each picture or slide.

To keep the fleet information up to date we recommend the Ian Allan publication, *Buses*, published monthly, or for more detailed information, the PSV Circle monthly news sheets. The writer and publisher would be glad to hear from readers should any information be available which corrects or enhances that given in this publication.

Principal Editors: Stuart Martin; Bill Potter and David Donati.

Acknowledgments:
We are grateful to Keith Grimes, Adrian Havlin, Nigel Hunt, Tom Johnson, Malcolm Jones, Colin Lloyd, Malcolm Tranter, Tony Wilson, the PSV Circle and the Management and officials of Stagecoach Group and their operating companies for their kind assistance and co-operation in the compilation of this book.

The front cover photo and frontispiece are by Tony Wilson. Rear cover pictures are by Mark Lyons.

ISBN 1 904875 05 X
Published by British Bus Publishing Ltd
16 St Margaret's Drive, Wellington, Telford, TF1 3PH

Telephone: 01952 255669 - Facsimile 01952 222397 - www.britishbuspublishing.co.uk
© British Bus Publishing Ltd, January 2005

Contents

During the course of a vehicle's life there are many occasions when, for a variety of reasons, it is considered desirable to move it from one depot to another, and from one fleet to another. The Bus Handbook series is interested primarily in vehicles and features bus fleets, irrespective of the operator's disc that may be displayed. To aid the management of Stagecoach vehicles the identification of the vehicles was consolidated into a single series in January 2003. While many options were considered, the most appropriate seemed to organise the numbers to allow vehicles of similar type to be numbered together. To avoid input errors with leading zeros, no vehicle was numbered below 10000. Leyland and Volvo Olympians have been separated as have low and standard floor vehicles. The result will allow the transfer of vehicles between depots and management units to be undertaken more easily. Buses are now allocated numbers as they are ordered, the number being retained thoughtout the vehicle's life, including time with training and other ancillary duties.

Several of the initial low-height batch of Dennis Tridents have now been refurbished for use in provincial fleets. Illustrating the batch is 17073, T673KPU, which is one of seven now based at Lewes and is seen operating along the Marine Drive in Saltdean. *Mark Lyons*

Stagecoach

Stagecoach Group plc is a leading operator of buses and trains in the UK and overseas. This Bus Handbook details the bus and coach fleets of UK Bus and Overseas Bus though, for Coach USA, only the operation centres are listed.

Stagecoach can trace its roots back to a small self-drive caravan and caravanette rental business that was formed in Perth in 1976. Trading as Gloagtrotter (later GT Coaches), the business expanded a couple of years later to include minibus private hire under the original partnership of Ann Gloag, now one of the Non-Executive Directors of Stagecoach Group, and her husband, Robin. Her brother, Brian Souter, (an accountant by profession), is now Chief Executive, having joined the fledgling organisation in 1980 just prior to its starting regular long distance services at which time the Stagecoach name, suggested jointly by Ann and David, their brother, was adopted. This move into regular services was made possible by coach deregulation, introduced in the 1980 Transport Act.

Stagecoach was born out of deregulation and matured through privatisation. The freedom of deregulation and the opportunities of privatisation have facilitated the rapid growth of Stagecoach.

The first service began in October 1980, an overnight run from Dundee to London. Subsequently further legs were added that brought in Aberdeen and Glasgow to form a network of coach services within Scotland and running south of the border to London via Manchester and Birmingham. The quality of vehicle provided on these services quickly improved, exotic foreign double-deck coaches in a bright livery becoming the norm from 1982 onwards, in marked contrast to the traditional single-deck coaches with a rather dowdy image used by their main competitor - Scottish Bus Group.

In December 1982 Mrs Gloag's husband left the business and set up his own company trading as Highwayman Coaches at Errol, near Perth. In tandem with the coach service expansion, a number of school contracts had been secured. These were operated primarily with second-hand Bristol Lodekkas and, by the mid 1980s, Stagecoach was the largest operator of that type, with a fleet of over twenty. In December 1980 Stagecoach took its first step into regular bus service operation when the Perth to Errol route of A & C McLennan of Spittalfield was taken over. It was this route which five years later was to see the birth of the 'Provincial Routemaster Revival' that Stagecoach started when it introduced Routemasters between Perth and Errol in the spring of 1985. In the early 1980s a number of other Scottish coach operations were absorbed into Stagecoach including Adamson & Low of Edinburgh and Bennetts of Kilwinning in Ayrshire, although both were subsequently disposed of. After a period of consolidation, a further expansion into local bus services was achieved when, in November 1985, the remaining business of McLennan's of Spittalfield was purchased. This gave the Stagecoach company a significant presence in the Tayside region and, most importantly, McLennan's extensive workshops and engineering facilities at Spittalfield which were needed to maintain the ever-growing express coach fleet.

The 1985 Transport Act resulted in the deregulation of bus services outside of London. As implementation of the Act drew near, Stagecoach prepared its plans for a major expansion in the bus market. A new company was formed called Magic Bus, and on 26th October 1986 it commenced operating a number of services in Glasgow. The vehicles used were primarily Routemasters and these vehicles reintroduced conductor operation to the city. At the same time there was some expansion of services in Tayside, with Stagecoach taking over commercially a number of rural routes left for the tendering process by Strathtay Scottish, including the routes north of Perth to Aberfeldy and Pitlochry.

With established operations in Tayside and Glasgow, and an extensive network of express services, the Stagecoach team considered for the first time acquiring operators outside its native

Scotland, and took an interest in the pending privatisation of National Bus Company's subsidiaries. An unsuccessful bid for City of Oxford did not deter the directors who turned their attention to Hampshire Bus. Directors Brian Souter and Ann Gloag, together with their uncle Fraser McColl and the General Manager of Hampshire Bus, formed a new holding company, Skipburn Limited. Hampshire Bus, together with Pilgrim Coaches, was successfully purchased on 2nd April 1987. The new owners did not waste time in rationalising their new acquisition, with Pilgrim Coaches, which had been loss-making from the outset, closing down on 26th April 1987. By 3rd October, the Southampton area operations had been sold to Southern Vectis who formed a new company, trading as Solent Blue Line, to operate the routes. The residual Hampshire Bus operation continues as part of the Stagecoach South company with depots at Andover, Basingstoke and Winchester.

In 1987 Derek Scott joined the board as Finance Director, and subsequently played a key role in shaping the growth of the group before taking a back seat in the post of company secretary since 1996. While still digesting Hampshire Bus, the Stagecoach board turned its attention to the acquisition of a second NBC subsidiary. This time Cumberland was the target and, following a successful offer, Stagecoach took control of Cumberland Motor Services on 23rd July 1987. The Cumberland operations were based at Whitehaven with depots in Carlisle, Penrith, Keswick, Workington and Millom. The new owners quickly recast the Carlisle city network and introduced crew-operated Routemasters. The Cumberland company acquired a number of its competitors during 1988 including Yeowart's of Whitehaven and Kirkpatrick of Brigham, near Cockermouth. Barry Hinkley who later became the Engineering Director joined Stagecoach with the acquisition. Another board member to arrive in 1987 was Brian Cox who, in December, succeeded Dawson Williams at Hampshire Bus.

In July 1987 the McColl interests in Skipburn were acquired by a new holding company, Stagecoach Holdings (renamed Stagecoach Group in August 2001). However, further expansion of the group was still being sought. Under the NBC privatisation rules any purchaser could acquire only three subsidiaries. However, Hampshire Bus and Pilgrim Coaches had been classed as one unit, Cumberland a second and, therefore, Stagecoach was able to acquire United Counties as its third NBC company. The area of operation encompassed Bedford, Corby, Huntingdon, Kettering and Northampton and was the group's first presence in the Midlands. As with Cumberland, it was not long before the potential of Routemasters was realised and the Corby and Bedford networks received a fleet of these vehicles soon after the Stagecoach acquisition.

In December 1988 Ewan Brown CBE joined the board of directors in a non-executive capacity. Being a Merchant Banker by profession, and a former non-executive director of the Scottish Transport Group, he brought valuable skills and knowledge to the management team.

Up to this point the Stagecoach Group had acquired three NBC companies. All were operating a typical mix of National Bus Company standard vehicles that primarily consisted of Leyland Nationals and Leopards, and Bristol VRTs. Additionally, the fleet in Scotland was mainly secondhand Routemasters and Bristol Lodekkas together with Volvo B58 and Neoplan coaches for the express network. Vehicles in Scotland were in the then standard Stagecoach livery of white with blue, red and mustard (later to become orange) stripes and it was decided that in order to provide flexibility and enable vehicles to be transferred between fleets, all vehicles in the group would be painted in this corporate style. Very quickly the new livery began to appear on all three English fleets.

New vehicle purchases had to be made in order that the bus companies could maintain and develop their business into the 1990s and early purchases of Alexander-bodied Mercedes 709 minibuses and Olympians were to be a portent of large numbers of vehicles of these types in years to come. The importance of investing in new vehicles, and its consequent increase in patronage and reduction of maintenance costs, has continued.

The most significant event of 1988 was the private placing of a quantity of Stagecoach shares with institutional investors. This raised £5 million and set the financial scene for Stagecoach to

Stagecoach retains ownership of a number of historical buses and coaches, several used in service on special occasions or loaned to museums. HDV639E is a Bristol MW6G with Eastern Coach Works body and carries Bluebird livery. Bluebird was granted the Royal Warrant for services to the Royal Family with vehicles at Ballater now displaying the Royal Coat of Arms. Fleet numbers towards the end of the type series have been allocated, this coach being 59939. *Phillip Stephenson*

develop into a major force within the bus industry. It was also a sign of things to come, with the planned Stock Market flotation five years later.

1989 saw the first Stagecoach acquisition overseas when, in March of that year, it purchased a 51% share in United Transport Malawi Limited from United Transport International, a British Electric Traction (BET) subsidiary.

The vehicles operated in Africa were somewhat strange to British eyes with large numbers of ERF Trailblazer and Leyland Victory single deckers, all built to meet the rough African conditions where much mileage is run on dirt roads. Full details of the vehicles with pictures can be found in the mid 1990s editions of this Handbook. Stagecoach sold the operation in 1997 though some of the double-deck buses were returned for operation in Greater Manchester.

Having ventured into Africa, Stagecoach soon returned to the acquisition trail in England. East Midland Motor Services had been sold to its management by NBC, but in April 1989 the management decided to sell its entire share holding, Stagecoach being the purchaser. The operation was conducted under East Midland, Mansfield & District, and Rainworth Travel names in the East Midlands area, and in addition there were two Frontrunner operations, one based in Essex and the other in north-west Derbyshire and eastern Greater Manchester. The Frontrunner South East operation was quickly sold on to Ensign Bus of Purfleet while Ribble absorbed the Derbyshire/Manchester operation. This left the East Midland management to concentrate on its own territory and soon its coaching operations were consolidated into Rainworth Travel which was renamed Midland Travel. The bus operations were based in Worksop, Chesterfield and Mansfield and, as with other acquisitions, former London Routemasters were again tried, this time in Mansfield where Routemaster operation lasted until 1991. In May 1993 the Midland Travel coaching operation was sold to Skills of Nottingham.

Only a matter of days after the East Midland acquisition, a further company was acquired from its management. Ribble Motor Services Limited, based in the north-west of England, had also been bought by its management team and had subsequently purchased, from United Transport, the Bee Line Buzz Company - a large minibus operation based in Manchester, together with the Zippy minibus operation based in Preston.

Having added two major bus companies in North West England to one it already owned, Stagecoach embarked upon a reorganisation and rationalisation of its interests in the area. The Barrow-in-Furness municipal undertaking had been in financial difficulties for some time, following heavy competition with Ribble, and its services and depot were acquired in May 1989. For operational control reasons, and to align with county boundaries, Ribble's South Cumbrian and Lake District operations were transferred to Cumberland Motor Services, which also took control in Barrow. In September of 1989 Ribble sold its Bee Line Buzz subsidiary and some of its own Ribble Manchester operations to the Drawlane Group though it retained the Preston-based Zippy minibuses. Ribble remained to concentrate on the central Lancashire area and Bolton.

Despite the activity in England there were still changes taking place in Scotland during 1989. On 19th June new bus services in and around the cities of Perth and Dundee were introduced, primarily in competition with Strathtay Scottish, whose managing director, Neil Renilson was recruited by the group at the same time. This new network was branded Perth Panther and, after a prolonged period of competition, in which both operators used Routemasters on Perth City services, Strathtay closed their Crieff depot and operations in 1991 and their Perth depot and operations in the summer of 1993.

Perhaps the most surprising development of 1989 was the decision by Stagecoach to sell the express coach operations that had been the genesis of the company. On 4th August 1989 the company announced the sale of its express network to National Express who re-branded the operation as Caledonian Express. With this sale Stagecoach clearly indicated that it was to concentrate on local bus operations in future. The Scottish operations saw further expansion when Inverness Traction was purchased from receivership in November. Inverness Traction had been competing with Highland Scottish on town services in Inverness since 1987. Stagecoach placed this Inverness operation under the Magicbus and Perth Panther management, and renamed the Magicbus company Stagecoach Scotland Ltd as the holding company. All of these operations were carving out their market through head-to-head competition with established state-owned operators, whereas in England established operators had been purchased, and competitive pressures were the other way round.

The south coast of England was not neglected either. In August 1989 the management of Southdown decided to sell out to Stagecoach. This brought a sixth former NBC subsidiary into the fold and Stagecoach then acquired, in October, the operations of Portsmouth City Bus from Southampton City Bus who held 75% and a workers' co-operative which owned the remaining 25%. In December 1989 Hastings and District was added when the management sold the company, which it had bought from NBC.

In 1990 there was expansion overseas with the purchase of Gray Coach Lines of Toronto, Canada. This brought to the Stagecoach Group an extensive network of express coach services throughout eastern Canada together with Niagara Falls sightseeing tours and the Toronto City/Airport express coach service. The venture proved to be unsuccessful in financial terms and the Group's interest in Gray Coach Lines was sold to Greyhound Lines of Canada in December 1992, but not before a number of Stagecoach Scotland Bristol FLFs had been transferred for sightseeing tour work.

One result of the large expansion on the south coast of England was an inquiry by the Monopolies and Mergers Commission. The DTI subsequently instructed Stagecoach to divest themselves of Portsmouth City Bus, and this operation was later sold to Transit Holdings in January 1991. The South of England subsidiaries that remained were then restructured and consolidated in April 1992 when a new company, Stagecoach South Limited, was given overall control of Hastings Buses, Southdown and Hampshire Bus. As part of the reorganisation

The 2005 Stagecoach Bus Handbook

Southdown was split into two operating companies, Sussex Coastline Buses and South Coast Buses, the latter also taking in Hastings Buses. The Southdown name was discontinued, and South Coast Buses operating from Eastbourne and Hastings with Coastline Buses trading from Chichester, Havant and Worthing.

Following on from the privatisation of NBC, the Government decided to extend privatisation to the Scottish Bus Group. It was decreed that any one purchaser could acquire only two companies and Stagecoach completed its quota with the purchase of Bluebird Northern and Fife Scottish during the first half of 1991. Bluebird was acquired in March and its archaic legal company name of Northern Scottish Omnibuses Ltd was quickly changed to Bluebird Buses Ltd. Bluebird was placed under common management with Stagecoach Scotland Ltd and its fleet renumbered into a single series.

By July 1991 the Fife company was also under the Stagecoach umbrella, and in the autumn of 1991 Stagecoach Scotland further expanded when it took over the remaining Inverness and Easter Ross area operations from Highland, adding some 30 extra buses to the Inverness Traction fleet, plus the former Highland depot at Tain.

With two former SBG companies now under its wing, plus the Perth and Inverness operations, Stagecoach had established a strong presence on the eastern side of Scotland. In line with Stagecoach policy the corporate colours started to appear on the newly-acquired fleets and fleet renewal commenced, primarily involving Alexander-bodied Mercedes minibuses and Leyland Olympians. There were also transfers north of the border of vehicles from the English companies, which resulted in some unfamiliar types of vehicle being introduced into Scotland, especially ECW-bodied Bristol VRTs. The VRT had been despised by SBG with all its initial examples being exchanged for NBC-owned Bristol FLFs.

November 1991 saw further expansion in Africa following BET's decision to divest itself of local bus operations throughout the world and Stagecoach saw potential in acquiring its Kenya operations to add to those of Malawi, though all the African interests have now been sold.

There is one company in the Stagecoach Group that plays a not insignificant part in the UK transport system as a whole, but operates no buses. National Transport Tokens was formed in the 1970s to manufacture and distribute concessionary travel tokens to various bodies, mostly local authorities and a minority shareholding came to Stagecoach with the purchase of Ribble in April 1989. The aluminium tokens produced by National Transport Tokens are accepted by a variety of operators in lieu of cash fares, including bus companies, taxi firms and rail services. Stagecoach bought a controlling interest in the company in March 1992 and its headquarters were moved from Manchester to Preston and, more recently, Blackburn.

It came as a significant surprise in April 1992 when Stagecoach decided to sell another of its initial operations. Having disposed of the express network the deal was now to sell the Glasgow-based Magicbus operation to recently privatised Kelvin Central Buses. The vehicles transferred included some newly-delivered Dennis Darts and a substantial number of Bristol VRTs and Routemasters, and Kelvin acquired the Glasgow depot. The Magicbus name and Stagecoach livery continued in use with Kelvin Central until 1993 as part of the deal.

1992 also saw further expansion of the southern fleet when Stagecoach acquired Alder Valley's operations based at depots in Aldershot, Alton and Hindhead. Alder Valley had been through a particularly disturbed time having had a number of owners since privatisation from NBC and suffering from subsequent fragmentation. The operation acquired by Stagecoach was placed under the Stagecoach South umbrella and is operated under the brand name Hants & Surrey.

Having seen the deregulation and privatisation process in the United Kingdom the Wellington municipal authority in New Zealand decided to embark on a similar course of action. In October 1992 the Wellington City Transport undertaking was privatised and Stagecoach was the successful bidder. There are three companies involved: Wellington City Transport, with a depot at Kilbirnie and an outstation at Karori; Cityline Auckland based at Papakura and Cityline Hutt Valley with depots at Lower Hutt and Stokes Valley. With its new undertaking, Stagecoach gained experience of operating MAN and Hino vehicles and, more interestingly, electric traction. The Wellington City Transport fleet contains over seventy Volvo trolleybuses while Wellington City Transport's share in Harbour City Cable Car Limited resulted in Stagecoach having an operating interest in this funicular railway for a short time.

Overseas developments in 1992 were not confined to Africa and New Zealand. For some time Stagecoach had held a stake in Speedybus Enterprises Limited of Hong Kong, whose primary functions were to sell advertising space on double deckers it supplied to Chinese municipal bus companies, and to import vehicles to China through Hong Kong. Speedybus also supplied Hong Kong double deckers to Stagecoach Malawi. In 1992 Stagecoach Hong Kong Ltd was formed to tender for bus services in Hong Kong, and to gain an operating base in the colony. Speedybus was primarily a bus dealer and bus advertising contractor rather than an operator. Stagecoach's 50% interest was sold in 1993. In 1994 the company commenced operating services on two commuter routes with five Volvo B10Ms. These vehicles were almost the same as the Stagecoach standard Alexander PS-bodied Volvo B10Ms except for their length and that they were fitted with air conditioning to cope with the humid Hong Kong climate. In 1995 six tri-axle Volvo Olympians joined the operation and a second residents' route was introduced. The Hong Kong operations were sold in the summer of 1996 after attempts to enlarge the business through the tendering/franchising process had been unsuccessful.

In the spring of 1993 Lancaster City Council expressed an intention to sell its municipal bus undertaking, much of the network comprising joint services with Ribble. As Ribble already had a substantial presence in Lancaster and the surrounding area, Stagecoach was not expected to be a bidder for the operation. However, in order to protect its interests in the area, Ribble registered many of Lancaster City's routes and subsequently the City Council decided to liquidate their undertaking, selling the depot and some twelve buses to Ribble during 1993. Because of this acquisition Ribble was able to close its own, smaller, depot in Morecambe and move into the former council depot in Heysham, which it retained until new facilities were opened in 2000.

Expansion in the south of England continued in 1993 when the management of East Kent sold their company. This is yet another former NBC subsidiary that was originally purchased by a management team. Again the new acquisition was placed under the control of Stagecoach South. In 1994 four Dennis low-floor vehicles with Berkhof bodies were allocated to South's fleet for the Canterbury Park and Ride service, these being the first such vehicles in the Stagecoach Group with more of the type delivered during 1996 for a Greater Manchester PTE contract.

While the Government had not legislated for the privatisation of municipal bus companies, a number of councils took the opportunity to sell before the end of 1993 to allow all of the income from the sale to be used on other projects. The proportion for reallocation was later reduced to 75% if sold before 31st March 1997.

Grimsby Cleethorpes Transport was jointly owned by the Boroughs of Grimsby and Cleethorpes and the two councils decided to sell the undertaking through a competitive tendering process and Stagecoach were the successful bidder. The deal was completed in November 1993 and brought the Stagecoach livery to South Humberside. It was this acquisition that brought Les Warnford, the then Grimsby MD, into the group. Today Les is the UK Bus Division's MD. The vehicles acquired were of a typical municipal nature and included substantial numbers of Dennis Dominators and Lances. The last of the five Lances delivered in 1993 was painted into Stagecoach livery before delivery.

The 1000th new bus to join Stagecoach was handed over to Ann Gloag and Brian Souter on the opening day of Coach & Bus 93; this was a Volvo B6 destined for United Counties. The order for new vehicles for delivery in 1995 was the largest annual order for buses in the UK since privatisation began in the 1980s. Purchasing policy continued to be based on Volvo double-deck and single-deck chassis together with Mercedes-Benz minibuses, though during 1995 Dennis started to supply their Dart and Javelin in significant numbers. Alexander, with assembly plants in Scotland and Northern Ireland, were the preferred bus body builder with Plaxton as the coach body supplier. Some vehicles were bodied by Northern Counties when destined to be for the Group's provincial operations.

December 1993 saw a further major acquisition by Stagecoach. Western Travel Ltd was formed on the privatisation of the Cheltenham and Gloucester company from NBC. Cheltenham and Gloucester operates in both the cities in its title together with services in Swindon and the Cotswolds based on Stroud. Western Travel itself went on the acquisition trail as part of the NBC privatisation process and acquired the Midland Red South company which brought with it operations in Leamington Spa, Nuneaton, Rugby, Stratford-upon-Avon and Warwick. Western Travel had also secured the eastern part of the National Welsh operation trading as Red & White, adding operations around the Red & White historical base of Monmouthshire and the eastern valleys of South Wales. A further 650 vehicles were added to the Stagecoach Group with this purchase, the first being painted into corporate colours in December 1993.

1993 also saw the company become listed on the London Stock Exchange. The successful share flotation attracted much publicity and the proceeds gave the group access to considerable additional funds with which to expand. Some 20,000 (over 90%) of Stagecoach's UK employees became shareholders. A significant addition to the management team in 1993 was Keith Cochrane, who was appointed company secretary and group financial controller. He later became group finance director in 1996 and in February 2000 he succeeded Mike Kinski as group chief executive. At 35, Keith Cochrane was one of the youngest CEOs of larger listed UK companies, though he left the company in 2002.

1994 saw the bus industry's consolidation accelerate and Stagecoach's development move into the larger metropolitan markets in which it previously had limited operations. The year opened with the launch of Stagecoach Manchester at the end of January. Although a division of Ribble, it traded separately under its own brand name on the long established 192 route from central Manchester to Hazel Grove south of Stockport. Originally set up as a unit with sixteen B6s, rapid passenger growth called for more and larger vehicles, and the year finished with 23 B10Ms allocated to the route. In the autumn of 1995 this operation, with the vehicles, was sold to EYMS Group Ltd who also operated south Manchester services through their Finglands subsidiary.

The first full scale acquisition of 1994 was Western Scottish, a former SBG company, which was owned by its management and employees. Western is based at Ayr with other depots at Cumnock, Dumfries, Kilmarnock and Stranraer, and a number of sub-depots both on the mainland and on the Isle of Arran. Shortly after acquisition the legal company name was changed to Western Buses Limited.

In July 1994 Busways Travel Services Ltd became a subsidiary company of Stagecoach. Busways Travel Services Ltd was a private limited company established by the Transport Act 1985 to acquire the bus undertaking of Tyne and Wear Passenger Transport Executive.

Busways commenced trading in October 1986 under the ownership of the PTA, though its origins can be found in the municipal transport undertakings in Newcastle upon Tyne, South Shields and Sunderland, and also the private companies acquired in 1973 (Armstrong Galley) and 1975 (Economic). In May 1989 a management/employee buyout was successfully completed. The management of ten purchased 51% of the shares while 49% were purchased for employees through an ESOP. The Tyne and Wear Omnibus Company Ltd was acquired in November 1989 and in August 1993 Busways acquired a majority shareholding in Wellcome Passenger Transport Ltd.

With a fleet of 590 buses and coaches Busways provided mainly urban local bus services in the Newcastle upon Tyne, South Shields and Sunderland areas whose combined population is approximately a million. Because of the strength of the Busways brand names in the local market the group agreed that Busways should retain its distinctive liveries once Busways joined the group and the presentation of trading names was revised to include reference to group membership. However, during 1995 corporate livery was introduced following a local employee decision after market research showed the group livery to have a more modern image.

Also in the summer of 1994, Stagecoach announced its intention to buy a 20% share in Mainline, the former South Yorkshire PTE bus operation based on Sheffield, Doncaster and

Rotherham. In October, however, the Office of Fair Trading decided to investigate this purchase the result being a requirement for Stagecoach to divest its interest. While a sale to FirstGroup was agreed, an appeal against the principle of forced divestment was made but subsequently lost in the London courts.

The breakthrough into London bus operation was achieved in September 1994 with the purchase of London Buses' subsidiaries East London and Selkent as part of the privatisation of the capital's red bus fleets. In the case of East London this returned Stagecoach operations to that area of the city following the disposal of East Midland's Frontrunner South East in 1989 to Ensign Bus of Purfleet. Both companies run local suburban services in their respective areas of London as well as trunk routes into the central area. East London's fleet comprised 600 buses operating out of depots at Leyton, Barking, East Ham and Stratford, while Selkent's had 450 buses operating from depots at Bromley, Catford, Plumstead and Orpington, the latter since closed as a result of the Roundabout network tender losses. Roger Bowker joined the group in September 1994 and continued to run the London operation for Stagecoach until seconded to Swebus and later to Coach USA, where today he is Senior VP responsible for the largest (North East) region.

Further expansion in the urban areas of the north-east of England followed a few weeks later with the acquisition of Cleveland Transit early in October, and along with it 51% of the share capital of formerly troubled Kingston upon Hull City Transport. The remaining 49% of Kingston upon Hull City transport owned by the ESOP was also acquired. Days later, Darlington City Transport, which had been experiencing financial problems for some time, ceased trading after Busways established a competing network of services in the town, and with it the birth of Stagecoach Darlington. In the middle of the following month Hartlepool Transport joined Stagecoach in an agreed sale. Hartlepool, also based in the county of Cleveland, employed some 145 staff and operated 68 vehicles. In 1995 the management of the Darlington operation was transferred from Busways to Cleveland Transit.

November 1994 was planned to see the return of Stagecoach into Glasgow with the introduction of Stagecoach Glasgow, a 60-vehicle quality operation, in similar fashion to the Manchester unit. However, two days before Stagecoach Glasgow was due to commence operations, Strathclyde Buses announced they would sell 20% of their shares to Stagecoach in a similar style deal to the Mainline share exchange, and the Stagecoach Glasgow operation, staff and 18 Volvo B10Ms passed to SBL. Like the Mainline operation, this holding attracted the attention of the Monopolies and Mergers Commission who, after investigation, instructed divestment. A legal appeal was lost in July 1996, although the DTI agreed in an out of court settlement not to seek any undertakings against Stagecoach in Strathclyde (apart from separate undertakings in respect of A1 services in Ayrshire) or South Yorkshire.

Further expansion in 1995 commenced in January with the acquisition of A1 Service. This was a complex sale in that Ayrshire Bus Owners was the last Scottish co-operative bus company and was owned by nine separate family members. Stagecoach took 75 vehicles with the purchase, not all constituent members sold all their vehicles, and Stagecoach declined to purchase some of the most elderly vehicles. Because of this and an urgent need to replace many of those acquired, Leyland Titans and Bristol VRs were transferred from other companies to ensure operational needs were met. During the year no less than 21 new Volvo Olympians and many modern mid-life vehicles were placed with this operation to replace the very elderly A1 fleet, which had been the subject of a Traffic Commissioner's maintenance hearing and warning shortly prior to the sale to Stagecoach.

Despite the small scale of this operation the Secretary of State for Trade and Industry directed the Monopolies and Mergers Commission to inquire into the purchase. Much criticism of the MMC was voiced over this inquiry as each investigation costs the taxpayer a considerable amount of money and consumes valuable management time and energy. It was widely commented on at the time that often larger acquisitions by other groups were being cleared without referral. In November the report was published allowing the retention of the operation providing certain conditions on fares and service levels were adhered to.

June 1995 saw the announcement of a joint venture with Montagu Private Equity to buy part of Rodoviária de Lisboa, the main operator in and around the Portuguese capital. The main towns served were Cascais, Estoril and Sintra, with the 900mm gauge Sintra tram operation included though this has subsequently returned to municipal operation. In 2001 the Portuguese operations was sold.

In New Zealand Stagecoach acquired the operations of Cesta Travel in Wellington, which brought one additional vehicle to the fleet and Stokes Valley Coaches of Upper Hutt. The Runcimans Motors business was also acquired with bus services taken into the Cityline Hutt Valley operation initially while the remaining contract and hire business was acquired subsequently, retaining a local identity.

In July 1995 Stagecoach confirmed the acquisition of ailing Chesterfield Transport following an Extraordinary General Meeting at which 99% of Chesterfield's employees voted in favour of the take over. The Chesterfield operation was placed under East Midland management, who moved its local depot to the former municipal's Stonegravels depot. This acquisition too became the subject of a Monopolies and Mergers Commission enquiry with vehicle repainting delayed pending the outcome. Meanwhile ten much-travelled B10Ms were transferred in from Ribble. This purchase was found to be in the public interest and cleared during 1996 allowing the fleet to be renumbered and brought together.

October brought Coach and Bus 95 at which four Stagecoach buses were exhibited by various suppliers. Mercedes-Benz displayed the 800th 709D for the group, destined for Cumberland. On the Northern Counties stand was the last of 52 Volvo Olympians destined for Selkent, all of which are now in provincial fleets. Also in red livery was an Alexander-bodied Dennis Dart for East London but the main Stagecoach attraction was the Volvo B10L demonstrator for the group. After the show it operated in the Fife fleet for a year alongside new B10Ms and featured the Säffle-designed body built by Alexander as its Ultra model.

The investment in new vehicles continued during 1995 with some 627 new vehicles delivered in the year ending 30th April, and at Coach and Bus 95 substantial corporate orders were announced totaling over 1000 buses for delivery during 1996. 1996 was another year of outstanding growth with pre-tax profits up 34% despite adverse weather and fuel duty increases. In Scotland, Bluebird was granted the Royal Warrant for services to the Royal Family with vehicles at Ballater now displaying the Royal Coat of Arms. Western Buses saw the greatest change with many services revised and new routes introduced, including several Stagecoach Express interurban services providing links from the centres of operation to Glasgow and Edinburgh. Fife introduced the first articulated coaches on its service to and from Glasgow and further articulated coaches built by Plaxton entered service with other fleets. In November 1996 Bluebird won the prestigious Bus Company of the year award, at a ceremony in London where the Managing Director, Neil Renilson, received the award from the then Minister of Transport, John Watts.

The north-west of England saw the acquisition of GM Buses South (now Stagecoach Manchester) in February after several months of speculation. Also in the north-west, Ribble secured the Hyndburn operations during September; the services to be provided from several Ribble depots as the purchase did not include the Hyndburn operation buildings in Accrington.

The Midlands fleets were joined by Cambus in 1995 and the administration of Cambus and Chesterfield Transport were integrated into East Midland at Chesterfield. The MMC report presented to Parliament in 1996 noted that Chesterfield Transport could have collapsed if Stagecoach had not made the merger offer. Following the merger with Cambus undertakings were agreed with the Department of Trade that the divestment of the Huntingdon depot and Milton Keynes operations of Cambus would be made and this took place the following year.

In the west of England two operations units were in operation, Stagecoach West and Stagecoach Devon the latter acquired from Transit Holdings in February 1996. All three divisions of Stagecoach West (Cheltenham & Gloucester, Midland Red South and Red & White) received new single deck buses and minibuses during the year with the Volvo B10Ms being devoted to the important corridors of Nuneaton-Coventry, Cheltenham-Gloucester and Newport-Tredegar. The

Devon operation was formed by the amalgamation into one company with two operational divisions of Exeter and Torbay, the latter acquiring open-top Bristol VRs to re-instate regular big-bus services in the Torquay area. 185 vehicles were delivered to Stagecoach South in 1996, some 25% of the fleet strength. Stagecoach South also received Titans from Selkent as part of a group policy to cascade urban vehicles to lighter duties at mid-life and help minimise whole-life costs.

During March 1996 the small Hong Kong operation was sold, the B10Ms moving to New Zealand while the Olympians remained in the colony, passing to Citybus.

The group was awarded a seven-year franchise for South West Trains in December 1995 and took over operations in February 1996. SWT operates urban and main-line passenger rail services from London Waterloo to over 200 stations principally in south-west London, Surrey, Hampshire and Dorset using 1022 vehicles, mainly electric multiple units and all the Class 159 diesel rail-cars. One of the early developments was the introduction of bus/rail feeder services between Romsey-Winchester and Bordon-Liphook using buses initially provided by East London though operated by Stagecoach South. The Isle of Wight rail line franchise was also awarded to Stagecoach during 1996.

August 1996 saw the acquisition of Porterbrook Leasing Company MEBO Limited, one of three railway rolling stock leasing operators (ROSCO). Control of this operation was sold to Abbey National in April 2000 at a substantial profit to the group.

Swebus was acquired on 2nd October, though the announcement that Stagecoach was the preferred bidder was made several weeks earlier and this operation was sold in 1999. The Swebus fleet was detailed in the 1999 edition of this book.

Some 625 vehicles were ordered for 1997 delivery for Stagecoach's British fleets In the year to April 1998 turnover increased by 20% to £1,381 million, the results reflecting the first full year contributions from Porterbrook and Swebus, an improved performance from South West Trains as well as further growth within the UK bus division. This growth was attributed to organic passenger growth of 1.6% achieved mostly through ticket initiatives and innovative network planning. On 30th April 1998, Stagecoach announced Mike Kinski's appointment as Group Chief Executive with Brian Souter continuing as Executive Chairman. The 1998 vehicle delivery for the UK bus division included the first from MAN with Oxford (acquired from Transit Holdings in July the previous year) and Manchester introducing the low floor examples, while Jonckheere became the preferred supplier of coach bodywork supplying examples for both luxury and interurban duties.

1998 also saw Stagecoach focus on improving customer service and the development of integrated public transport, particularly around Prestwick airport, the Supertram services in Sheffield and to connect with Virgin Trains (where Stagecoach acquired a 49% interest in October).

The Overseas Bus Division saw expansion in New Zealand when the 600-vehicle Yellow Bus Company and Fuller's Ferries were acquired. These were consolidated into the existing operations. Fuller's Ferries operate nine vessels on routes between Auckland and surrounding islands.

As 1998 drew towards its close the South China Morning Post reported that Stagecoach had commenced negotiations to purchase a substantial holding in Hong Kong Citybus from China Paint, acquiring control in March 1999. Citybus operate approximately 110 franchised routes with more than 950 buses. The network is governed by two franchises. The Hong Kong island franchise covers the routes within Hong Kong island and cross harbour routes to Kowloon. The Chek Lap Kok airport franchise covers routes to the airport from Hong Kong island and Tung Chung, a new town on Lantau Island. The company also operates non-franchised services on residential routes and when acquired ran five long-haul routes between Hong Kong and the southern part of Guangdong province, though these ceased in 2000. On 7th May, the group acquired 45% of Hong Kong Kwoon Chung (Chongqing) Bus Investments which has been placed under Citybus control. This operation involved three metropolitan routes in mainland China.

Turnover grew a further 15% across all the business in 1999 and the new vehicle programme for 1999 included 16 Volvo B10M coaches for National Express contracts with Jonckheere bodywork; two Plaxton MPDs for Western Scottish; 100 10-metre Dennis Dart SLF bodied by Plaxton (66) and Alexander; 106 MAN 18.220 low floor buses with Alexander ALX300 bodywork and a further 172 Dennis Tridents with Alexander bodywork, the majority to 'London' specification. The continued investment in new buses brought the average age of the fleet to seven years, one of the lowest in the industry.

On 14th June 1999 the group announced it proposed to acquire Coach USA. At the time of purchase, Coach USA was the largest provider of motorcoach charter and sightseeing services and one of the largest non-municipal providers of commuter and transit services in USA. This purchase introduced the North American Bus Division into the group structure. Coach USA conducts operations throughout the United States and parts of Canada with operating locations in over 120 cities. Coach USA operates approximately 9500 buses, coaches and taxicabs. Since May 1996 the company had increased its size through the purchase of over 70 motorcoach and taxicab businesses.

To partly fund Coach USA it was decided to sell the Swebus operation during 1999, thus reducing the group's European presence in favour of North America.

To end the twentieth century, the UK Bus Division ordered 731 buses for delivery during the year 2000. These comprised a further 60 MAN/Alexander ALX300 buses, 158 Dennis Trident/Alexander ALX400 and 5 Dennis Tridents/Plaxton President. The rest were Dennis Darts with 29 receiving ALX200 bodywork, 66 being the SPD variant supplied by Plaxton with the balance of 53 being supplied in varying lengths of the Plaxton Pointer.

In April 2000 the group sold the rail leasing company Porterbrook to Abbey National. Much time was spent on the rail division during the year with new proposals for the extension of the South West Trains franchise along with Virgin-Stagecoach proposals for the East Coast Main Line. Brian Hinkley left the Board in July 2000 being replaced on the Board by Graham Eccles from the rail industry. Graham was latterly MD of Network South Central but a joint bid between Stagecoach and his management team was unsuccessful when the franchise was awarded to Connex. Graham then left NSC to work exclusively for Stagecoach on other franchise bids (winning Island Line and helping with the Virgin joint venture) and acted as MD of South West Trains, before becoming its chairman in 2000.

Brian Cox, an Executive Director of Stagecoach Group was appointed full time Executive Chairman of the UK Bus division with Les Warneford as Managing Director for the whole division. The new structure includes twelve operating companies reduced from nineteen. The new structure was to deliver both a stronger centre based in Perth, with the companies supported by a new information technology system for the division. Fuel Saver tickets aimed at moving people from cars onto buses is one of the main initiatives of the launch. The group used the opportunity to introduce a new corporate styling, its first change in twenty years, which started to appear on new buses from 2001. Changes to styling involved a new interior scheme and the introduction of Lazzerini Practico seats with a new mid blue moquette that incorporates the new logo. A 'London' version of the scheme was adapted to meet the tendering requirements though it retains the family look all aimed at a new drive to attract people onto the buses.

In 2001 the bus operations at four depots in East Lancashire were sold to Blazefield Holdings, while contract renewals in London had taken the share of TfL routes to 16%.

New vehicle deliveries for 2001 and 2002 were mostly destined for the London operations with planned to cascades the provinces. In 2001 these comprised 176 Alexander-bodied Dennis Tridents along with 110 Dennis Darts with Alexander bodywork of varying lengths with more of the same types for 2002. The provincial needs met by a further fifty MAN 18.220 buses with ALX300 bodywork in 2001 and a further fifty are expected soon. Optare Solo minibuses for Midland Red and Lancashire and Excel midibuses for East Midlands were a new departure and these joined a single 8.5 metre Dart for Devon.

The new millennium saw much change to the UK rail network. Consequent to the accident at Hatfield, major disruption occurred to the whole service network. Stagecoach remained firmly committed to rebuilding the confidence of passengers to deliver a modern, efficient and safe railway. Its two principal operations, South West Trains and Virgin Rail Group have seen much investment in new units. Stagecoach was granted preferred bidder status for a franchise for South West Trains and placed a £1 billion order for new rolling stock the first of which are now arriving in the UK having been built and tested on the continent before delivery to the UK through the tunnel. At Virgin the new Voyager and Pendelino trains are now in service.

Stagecoach believe their Kick Start proposal for targeted funding, successfully implemented in New Zealand and trialed in the group's town of Perth in Scotland, can benefit communities across the country, delivering more comprehensive bus services, reduced congestion, better value for the taxpayer, with important environmental and social inclusion benefits.

Kick Start is now being promoted to the UK Government. Both partners recognised that bus priority measures alone were insufficient to develop rapid organic passenger growth. The New Zealand system incorporates Transfund, a government established central funding body, which makes payments to regional councils to enable authorities to contract bus operators to introduce service increases short-term investment over three years to fund public transport improvements until they attract sufficient new passengers to make these services sustainable. The majority of Kick Start projects have arisen from ideas for service improvements developed by bus operators and then submitted to regional councils.

As a result the New Zealand fleet has been increased significantly and a further sixty buses are on order. For UK Bus, 2003 saw new fleet numbers applied to the vehicles. The new scheme took an intelligent approach to the single fleet scheme and allows greater flexibility in fleet management and swifter transfers between operations. Most types may be identified from their first two digits with last three reflecting their number or index mark where possible.

Megabus.com, Stagecoach's web-based low-cost intercity bus and coach service, now covers 30 cities across the UK. By the end of 2004, the service had carried around 1.5million passengers. Since the launch of the first service between Oxford and London in August 2003, new long-distance routes have been added to the network, which is now covered with a fleet of around 60 double-decker buses, coaches and articulated vehicles. Stagecoach placed a £6.5m order for 25 89 seat double-decker Neoplan Skyliners in the autumn of 2004 and the first of these are now in service. The new vehicles are being used to increase the quality of the megabus.com product on long-distance routes to and from London, and for future expansion plans.

In October 2004, Stagecoach launched a major UK-wide marketing campaign to get more people to travel by bus. The £250,000 campaign uses detailed customer research techniques pioneered by the supermarket giants to encourage people to get out of their cars and onto public transport. Stagecoach expects to target up to 20% of its bus networks over the next two years, with a major focus on mothers and commuters. Detailed geodemographic research, similar to that used by the retail sector, is being undertaken by Stagecoach to focus on people whose lifestyle is most suited to switching to bus travel. A new telemarketing unit set up at the company's headquarters in Perth will concentrate a new town or city every six weeks. The team discusses prospective passengers' current travel choices, their satisfaction with existing bus services and offers seven days free travel to encourage them to try the bus.

In additon to five Enviro 300 buses currently entering service, a further 120 Tridents, Fifty Optare Solo buses and a further 120 Darts form part of the 2005 order, all for provincial depots. Options are held on further quantities should further Kick-Start schemes develop.

Stagecoach UK Depots

East Scotland:	**ES**	Northampton		NN
Aberdeen	AN	Peterborough		PE
Aberhill	AL	**South Midlands:**		**SM**
Banchory	BJ	Banbury		BB
Buchan (Fraserburgh, Peterhead)	FH	Leamington		LE
Cowdenbeath	CJ	Nuneaton		NU
Dunfermline	DE	Oxford		OX
Glenrothes	GS	Rugby		RU
Inverness	IS	Witney		WY
Moray (Elgin, Macduff)	BQ			
Perth	PH	**London:**		**LN**
St Andrews	SA	Barking		BK
West Scotland:	**WS**	Bow		BW
		Bromley		TB
Ardrossan	AS	Catford		TL
Arran	AA	Leyton		T
Ayr	AY	Plumstead		PD
Cumnock	CC	North Street, Romford		NS
Dumfries	DS	Stratford		SD
Dunoon	DU	Upton Park		U
Glasgow	GW	Waterden Road		WD
Kilmarnock	KK			
Rothesay	RO	**South East:**		**SE**
Stranraer	SR	Aldershot		AT
North East:	**NE**	Andover		AR
		Ashford		AD
Darlington	DA	Basingstoke		BE
Hartlepool	HP	Canterbury		CA
Slatyford, Newcastle	SY	Chichester		CR
South Shields	SS	Dover		DO
Stockton	SC	Folkestone		FO
Sunderland	SU	Hastings		HS
Walkergate, Newcastle	WA	Lewes		LS
North West:	**NW**	Portsmouth		PM
		Thanet		TH
Barrow	BA	Winchester		WI
Carlisle	CE	Worthing		WG
Chorley	CY	**South West:**		**SW**
Kendal	KL			
Lillyhall	LL	Exeter		EX
Morecambe	ME	Exmouth		EH
Preston	PR	Paignton		PN
Manchester:	**MA**	Torquay		TQ
Glossop	GP	**Wales:**		**WX**
Hyde Road, Manchester	HE			
Princess Road, Manchester	PS	Aberdare		AE
Charles Street, Stockport	CS	Brynmawr		BR
Stockport (Daw Bank)	ST	Caerphilly		CL
		Chepstow		CW
East Midlands:	**EM**	Cwmbran		CN
Chesterfield	CH	Merthyr Tydfil		MR
Grimsby	GY	Pontypool		PY
Hull	HL	Porth		PT
Mansfield	MD	**West:**		**WW**
Worksop	WP			
East:	**EA**	Cheltenham		CT
		Gloucester		GR
Bedford	BD	Ross-on-Wye		RY
Cambridge	CB	Stroud		SZ
Corby	CX	Swindon		SN
Kettering	KG			

Stagecoach UK *Depot Codes - code order*

Arran	AA	Morecambe	ME
Ashford	AD	Merthyr Tydfil	MR
Aberdare	AE	Northampton	NN
Aberhill	AL	North Street, Romford	NS
Aberdeen	AN	Nuneaton	NU
Andover	AR	Oxford	OX
Ardrossan	AS	Plumstead	PD
Aldershot	AT	Peterborough	PE
Ayr	AY	Perth	PH
Barrow	BA	Portsmouth	PM
Banbury	BB	Paignton	PN
Bedford	BD	Preston	PR
Basingstoke	BE	Princess Road, Manchester	PS
Banchory	BJ	Porth	PT
Barking	BK	Pontypool	PY
Brynmawr	BR	Rothesay	RO
Elgin / Macduff (Moray)	BQ	Rugby	RU
Bow	BW	Ross-on-Wye	RY
Canterbury	CA	St Andrews	SA
Cambridge	CB	Sussex Bus	SB
Cumnock	CC	Stockton	SC
Carlisle	CE	Stratford	SD
Chesterfield	CH	Swindon	SN
Cowdenbeath	CJ	Stranraer	SR
Caerphilly	CL	South Shields	SS
Cwmbran	CN	Stockport (Daw Bank)	ST
Chichester	CR	Sunderland	SU
Charles Street, Stockport	CS	Slatyford, Newcastle	SY
Cheltenham	CT	Stroud	SZ
Chepstow	CW	Leyton	T
Corby	CX	Bromley	TB
Chorley	CY	Thanet	TH
Darlington	DA	Catford	TL
Dunfermline	DE	Torquay	TQ
Dover	DO	Upton Park	U
Dumfries	DS	Walkergate, Newcastle	WA
Dunoon	DU	Waterden Road	WD
Exmouth	EH	Worthing	WG
Exeter	EX	Winchester	WI
Fraserburgh / Peterhead (Buchan)	FH	Worksop	WP
Folkestone	FO	Witney	WY
Glossop	GP		
Gloucester	GR		
Glenrothes	GS	**Company codes:**	
Glasgow	GW	East	EA
Grimsby	GY	East Midlands	EM
Hyde Road, Manchester	HE	East Scotland	ES
Hull	HL	London	LN
Hartlepool	HP	Manchester	MA
Hastings	HS	North East	NE
Inverness	IS	North West	NW
Kettering	KG	South East	SE
Kilmarnock	KK	South Midlands	SM
Kendal	KL	South West	SW
Leamington	LE	West Scotland	WS
Lillyhall	LL	West	WW
Lewes	LS	Wales	WX
Mansfield	MD		

Stagecoach London operates the first and the last Titans delivered to London Buses. The original, T1 now 10001 has reverted to its former red livery, while 11125, B125WUV, is currently with South East and carries the latest colours. It is seen at Wisley supporting Cobham Bus Museum's annual vehicle rally. *Mark Lyons*

| 10001 | NSu | THX401S | Leyland Titan TNLXB2RRSp | Park Royal | | | B44/26D | 1978 |

10005-10246

Leyland Titan TNLXB2RRSp — Park Royal — B44/26D — 1978-80

| 10005 | AY | WYV5T | 10056 | ME | WYV56T | 10208 | KK | CUL208V | 10236 | WSu | EYE236V |
| 10029 | AY | WYV29T | 10179 | NWu | CUL179V | 10209 | AY | CUL209V | 10246 | DS | EYE246V |

10252	AY	GYE252W	Leyland Titan TNLXB2RR	PR/Leyland	B44/29D	1981
10254	KL	GYE254W	Leyland Titan TNLXB2RR	PR/Leyland	O44/29F	1981
10281	KL	GYE281W	Leyland Titan TNLXB2RR	PR/Leyland	O44/29F	1981
10285	ME	KYN285X	Leyland Titan TNLXB2RR	Leyland	B44/29D	1981

10311-10542

Leyland Titan TNLXB2RR — Leyland — B44/27F* — 1981-82 — *10512 is O44/27F

10311	ME	KYV311X	10348	TH	KYV348X	10469	CC	KYV469X	10512	CEw	KYV512X
10334	ME	KYV334X	10410	SR	KYV410X	10473	AS	KYV473X	10542	CN	KYV542X
10340	ME	KYV340X	10462	AS	KYV462X	10492	CN	KYV492X

10555-10665

Leyland Titan TNLXB2RR — Leyland — B44/27F — 1982

10555	BQ	NUW555Y	10577	BQ	NUW577Y	10592	CN	NUW592Y	10622	ESu	NUW622Y
10560	BQ	NUW560Y	10585	KK	NUW585Y	10593	FH	NUW593Y	10626	BQ	NUW626Y
10562	BQ	NUW562Y	10586	FH	NUW586Y	10601	BQ	NUW601Y	10646	CN	NUW646Y
10566	ESw	NUW566Y	10587	BQ	NUW587Y	10602	CN	NUW602Y	10651	CN	NUW651Y
10571	FH	NUW571Y	10589	CN	NUW589Y	10615	BQ	NUW615Y	10665	CN	NUW665Y
10574	ESw	NUW574Y	10591	FH	NUW591Y	10619	CN	NUW619Y

10684-10802

Leyland Titan TNLXB2RR — Leyland — B44/27F — 1982-83

10684	ME	OHV684Y	10700	WSu	OHV700Y	10729	ME	OHV729Y	10762	SR	OHV762Y
10686	ME	OHV686Y	10702	CN	OHV702Y	10738	ME	OHV738Y	10802	ESu	OHV802Y
10699	ME	OHV699Y	10728	CE	OHV728Y	10751	BQ	OHV751Y

10825-10999

Leyland Titan TNLXB2RR — Leyland — B44/29F — 1983-84

10825	ESw	A825SUL	10866	WSu	A866SUL	10921	AN	A921SYE	10976	CC	A976SYE
10843	KK	A843SUL	10874	CC	A874SUL	10922	AN	A922SYE	10996	ESu	A996SYE
10855	ME	A855SUL	10905	CN	A905SYE	10950	KK	A950SYE	10999	AY	A999SYE
10858	AN	A858SUL

11007-11076   Leyland Titan TNLXB2RR   Leyland   B44/29F   1984

11032	CC	A632THV	**11045**	KK	A645THV	**11076**	AY	A76THX

11081	KL	B81WUV	Leyland Titan TNLXB2RR	Leyland	O44/26F	1984
11083	WSu	B83WUV	Leyland Titan TNLXB2RR	Leyland	O44/26F	1984
11084	ESw	B84WUV	Leyland Titan TNLXB2RR	Leyland	B44/29F	1984
11091	KL	B91WUV	Leyland Titan TNLXB2RR	Leyland	O44/26F	1984
11092	WSu	B92WUV	Leyland Titan TNLXB2RR	Leyland	O44/26F	1984
11093	ESu	NIB5233	Leyland Titan TNLXB2RR	Leyland	O44/26F	1984
11100	KL	NIB5232	Leyland Titan TNLXB2RR	Leyland	O44/29F	1984
11106	PH	NIB5455	Leyland Titan TNLXB2RR	Leyland	B44/29F	1984
11110	KL	RIB4309	Leyland Titan TNLXB2RR	Leyland	B44/29F	1984
11114	PH	NIB4138	Leyland Titan TNLXB2RR	Leyland	B44/29F	1984
11116	AN	B116WUV	Leyland Titan TNLXB2RR	Leyland	B44/29F	1984
11119	ESu	B119WUV	Leyland Titan TNLXB2RR	Leyland	B44/29F	1984
11122	AN	B122WUV	Leyland Titan TNLXB2RR	Leyland	B44/29F	1984
11125	CAu	B125WUV	Leyland Titan TNLXB2RR	Leyland	B44/29F	1984

12060	WSu	EDS50A	AEC Routemaster R2RH	Park Royal	B36/28R	1960
12107	ESu	LDS201A	AEC Routemaster 2R2RH	Park Royal	B36/24R	1963

12272-12492   AEC Routemaster R2RH1   Park Royal   B40/32R   1965-66

12286	EMu	CUV286C	**12435**	EMu	JJD435D				**12493**	NWu	JJD493D
12303	EMu	CUV303C	12437	EMu	JJD437D	12462	EMu	JJD462D	12495	CEw	JJD495D
12392	LNu	JJD392D	12444	WSu	JJD444D	12470	CEw	JJD470D	12496	EMu	JJD496D
12399	EMu	JJD399D	12450	EMu	JJD450D	12481	EMu	JJD481D	12550	WSu	JJD550D
12429	CEw	JJD429D	12451	CEw	JJD451D	12488	CEw	JJD488D	12592	CEw	JJD592D

12607-12760   AEC Routemaster R2RH1   Park Royal   B40/32R   1967-68.

12607	EMu	NML607E	**12642**	NWu	NML642E	12671	NWu	SMK671F	**12748**	CEw	SMK748F
12624	NWu	NML624E	12657	NWu	NML657E	12709	NWu	SMK709F	12749	NWu	SMK749F
12639	EMu	NML639E	12665	LNu	SMK665F	12738	EMu	SMK738F	12760	NSu	SMK760F
12641	NWu	NML641E									

During 2004 the last of the Routemaster routes in London operated by Stagecoach were converted to low-floor buses. The vehicles that remain are in store pending transfers for possible further duties elsewhere. During the year, 12665, SMK665F, was repainted into provincial colours and is seen during the 50th anniversary run in London. The bus has also been involved with other promotional activities.
Mark Lyons

2004 saw more of the re-imported Olympians latterly used in Hong Kong enter service in Manchester. Pictured entering Piccadilly on route 216 is 13505, C44HNF. Magic Bus, provide low fares and can now be found in Manchester, Newcastle and Glasgow. *Phillip Stephenson*

13022-13033
Leyland Olympian ONLX/1R Northern Counties B43/30F 1983-84

13022	CE	A22HNC	13026	CX	A26ORJ	13027	PSt	A27ORJ	13028	PSt	A28ORJ

13121-13236
Leyland Olympian ONLXB/1R Northern Counties B43/30F* 1984-86 *13198/214 are BC43/26F

13121	MAw	B121TVU	13176	PS	C176YBA	13198	MAu	C198YBA	13215	PS	C215CBU
13122	MAw	B122TVU	13178	MAu	C178YBA	13205	MAu	C205CBU	13221	HE	C221CBU
13165	MAu	C165YBA	13181	MAu	C181YBA	13207	HEt	C207CBU	13224	HE	C224CBU
13166	MAw	C166YBA	13185	MAu	C185YBA	13208	PS	C208CBU	13226	HE	C226ENE
13170	HE	C170YBA	13191	PS	C191YBA	13210	HE	C210CBU	13234	PS	C234ENE
13173	MAu	C173YBA	13193	HE	C193YBA	13212	HE	C212CBU	13236	HEt	C236EVU
13174	PS	C174YBA	13195	HE	C195YBA	13214	MAu	C214CBU			

13255-13277
Leyland Olympian ONLXB/1R Northern Counties BC43/26F 1986-87

13255	HE	C255FRJ	13260	HEt	D260JVR	13272	HEt	D272JVR	13277	HE	D277JVR

13282-13304
Leyland Olympian ONLXB/1RZ Northern Counties B43/30F* 1988-89 *13291 is BC43/25F

13282	HE	F282DRJ	13291	HE	F291DRJ	13296	PR	F296DRJ	13300	HE	F300DRJ
13283	HE	F283DRJ	13294	HE	F294DRJ	13297	CE	F297DRJ	13301	HE	F301DRJ
13285	HE	F285DRJ	13295	HE	F295DRJ	13298	HE	F298DRJ	13304	HE	F304DRJ
13289	HE	F289DRJ									

13502-13519
Leyland Olympian ON6LXCT/5RV Alexander RH B73/45FT 1987 KMB, Hong Kong, 2003

13502	HE	C160HBA	13507	HE	C169HBA	13512	HE	C152HBA	13516	HE	C156HBA
13503	HE	C42HNF	13508	HE	C168HBA	13513	HE	C38HNF	13517	HE	C50HNF
13504	HE	C43HNF	13509	HE	C45HNF	13514	HE	C157HBA	13518	HE	C158HBA
13505	HE	C44HNF	13510	HE	C46HNF	13515	HE	C166HBA	13519	HE	C49HNF
13506	HE	C170HBA	13511	HE	C167HBA						

13601-13615
Leyland Olympian ON3R49C18Z4 Alexander RH BC53/41FT 1990 Citybus, Hong Kong, 2003

13601	SN	BIW4977	13605	NE	SJI4558	13609	LN	J701HMY	13613	SE	J939MHC
13602	AN	WLT416	13606	LN	J702HMY	13610	WX	JSK492	13614	SM	J166UNH
13603	AN	VLT37	13607	LN	J703HMY	13611	WX	OSK784	13615	SM	J167UNH
13604	WX	331HWD	13608	LN	J734HNY	13612	SE	J938MHC			

13616-13654 — Leyland Olympian ON3R49C18Z4 Alexander RH — BC53/41F — 1990 — Citybus, Hong Kong, 2004

13616	PS	G189YRJ	13626	SM	H41GBD	13636	LN	G128HGX	13646	NE	H463EJR
13617	LN	H445EGU	13627	WX	HIL8410	13637	--		13647	MAu	H606LNA
13618	LN	H522FRP	13628	MAu		13638	--		13648	WW	J515WAX
13619	WX	511OHU	13629	PS	H495LNA	13639	MAu	H604LNA	13649	MAu	H607LNA'
13620	ES	H723KDY	13630	NE	H493LNA	13640	--		13650	MAu	
13621	ES	H724KDY	13631	NE	H492LNA	13641	--		13651	MAu	H603CNA
13622	ES	H725KDY	13632	EM	H778VHL	13642	MAu		13652	NE	H462EJR
13623	PS	H494LNA	13633	NE	G127HGX	13643	HE	G280YRJ	13653	AN	J925FPS
13624	WX	TSU638	13634	SE	H764KDY	13644	MAu	G278YRJ	13654	MA	J688TNF
13625	SM	H511FRP	13635	SE	H763KDY	13645	WW	H51SKG			

14000	BD	F110NES	Leyland Olympian ON6LXCT/5RZ	Alexander RL	B66/44F	1989
14005	NN	ARP605X	Leyland Olympian ONLXB/1R	Eastern Coach Works	B45/32F	1981

14020-14049 — Leyland Olympian ONLXB/2RZ — Alexander RL — B51/36F* — 1988-89 — *14035-49 are B51/34F

14020	BD	F620MSL	14027	KG	F627MSL	14034	BD	F634MSP	14043	KG	G643EVV
14021	BD	F621MSL	14028	KG	F628MSL	14035	BD	F635YRP	14045	KG	G645EVV
14022	BD	F622MSL	14029	KG	F629MSL	14036	BD	F636YRP	14046	KG	G646EVV
14023	BD	F623MSL	14030	BD	F630MSL	14038	BD	F638YRP	14047	NN	G647EVV
14024	BD	F624MSL	14032	BD	F632MSL	14040	BD	G640EVV	14048	NN	G648EVV
14025	KG	F625MSL	14033	KG	F633MSL	14042	BD	G642EVV	14049	NN	G649EVV
14026	KG	F626MSL									

14054	KG	H654VVV	Leyland Olympian ON2R56G13Z4	Alexander RL	B51/34F	1990

14055-14070 — Leyland Olympian ON2R50G13Z4 — Northern Counties Palatine — B47/29F — 1992

14055	KG	K655UNH	14059	KG	K659UNH	14063	KG	K663UNH	14068	KG	K668UNH
14056	KG	K656UNH	14060	KG	K660UNH	14064	KG	K664UNH	14069	KG	K669UNH
14057	KG	K657UNH	14061	KG	K661UNH	14067	KG	K667UNH	14070	KG	K670UNH
14058	KG	K658UNH	14062	KG	K662UNH						

14138	LS	A138MRN	Leyland Olympian ONLXB/1R	Eastern Coach Works	B45/32F	1984
14170	SEw	C170ECK	Leyland Olympian ONLXB/1R	Eastern Coach Works	BC42/30F	1985
14179	CX	C179ECK	Leyland Olympian ONLXB/1R	Eastern Coach Works	BC42/30F	1985

14180-14189 — Leyland Olympian ON2R56G16Z4 — Alexander RL — BC51/31F — 1989

14180	SC	G180JHG	14183	NEu	G183JHG	14186	DA	G186JHG	14188	BA	G188JHG
14181	SC	G181JHG	14184	DA	G184JHG	14187	BA	G187JHG	14189	SC	G189JHG
14182	SC	G182JHG	14185	SC	G185JHG						

14191-14197 — Leyland Olympian ON2R56G16Z4 — Alexander RL — BC51/36F* — 1990 — *14193/5-7 are B51/34F

14191	HP	H191WFR	14193	BA	H193WFR	14195	PR	H195WFR	14197	CY	H197WFR
14192	SC	H192WFR	14194	HP	H194WFR	14196	CY	H196WFR			

14198-14210 — Leyland Olympian ON2R56G13Z4 — Alexander RL — BC43/27F — 1991

14198	NEu	J198HFR	14202	ME	J202HFR	14205	ME	J205HFR	14208	ME	J208HFR
14199	PR	J199HFR	14203	LL	J203HFR	14206	ME	J206HFR	14209	ME	J209HFR
14201	ME	J201HFR	14204	ME	J204HFR	14207	ME	J207HFR	14210	ME	J210HFR

14229-14235 — Leyland Olympian ON2R50G13Z4 — Alexander RL — BC43/27F — 1992

14229	CEw	K129DAO	14231	CEw	K131DAO	14233	LL	K133DAO	14235	ME	K135DAO
14230	CEw	K130DAO	14232	CE	K132DAO	14234	LL	K134DAO			

14239	AN	WLT727	Leyland Olympian ONLXCT/3RZ	Alexander RL	BC55/41F	1989
14240	AN	WLT794	Leyland Olympian ONLXCT/3RZ	Alexander RL	BC55/41F	1989

14243-14251 — Leyland Olympian ONLXB/2RZ — Alexander RL — B51/36F — 1988

14243	PR	F803FAO	14246	BA	F806FAO	14248	KL	F808FAO	14250	BA	F810FAO
14244	BA	F804FAO	14247	BA	F807FAO	14249	BA	F809FAO	14251	CEw	F811FAO
14245	BA	F805FAO									

While Magic Bus is used for low-cost local services, the megabus.com name has been introduced for low-cost express services. During 2004 these grew to cover much of the country, principally using coaches and coach-seated double-decks, many latterly used by Citybus in Hong Kong. Illustrating a standard Olympian lettered for the Dundee to Glasgow service is 14337, G337KKW, though it was operating the M8 route when seen. *Mark Doggett*

14252-14259   Leyland Olympian ON2R56G13Z4 Alexander RL   B51/34F   1990

| 14252 | KL | H112SAO | 14254 | CY | H114SAO | 14256 | BA | H116SAO | 14258 | LL | H118SAO |
| 14253 | KL | H113SAO | 14255 | LL | H115SAO | 14257 | LL | H117SAO | 14259 | ME | H119SAO |

14260-14267   Leyland Olympian ON2R56G13Z4 Alexander RL   BC47/27F   1991

| 14260 | PR | J120AAO | 14262 | HE | J122AAO | 14264 | SN | J124XHH | 14266 | BA | J126XHH |
| 14261 | PR | J121AAO | 14263 | SN | J123XHH | 14265 | PR | J125XHH | 14267 | BA | J127XHH |

| 14268 | CE | K128DAO | Leyland Olympian ON2R50G13Z4 Alexander RL | | | BC43/27F | 1992 | | | |

14271-14275   Leyland Olympian ONLXB/2RZ   Alexander RL   B51/36F   1990

| 14271 | SN | G101AAD | 14273 | GR | G103AAD | 14274 | SZ | G104AAD | 14275 | SZ | G105AAD |
| 14272 | SN | G102AAD | | | | | | | | | |

| 14281 | SWu | UWW3X | Leyland Olympian ONLXB/1R | Roe | | O47/29F | 1982 | | | |

14282-14294   Leyland Olympian ONLXB/1R   Roe   B47/29F   1982-83

14282	SZ	JHU899X	14287	SN	LWS35Y	14291	GR	LWS39Y	14293	SZ	LWS41Y
14283	SN	UWW7X	14288	SZ	LWS36Y	14292	GR	LWS40Y	14294	GR	NTC132Y
14286	SZ	LWS34Y	14289	GR	LWS37Y						

14303-14335   Leyland Olympian ONLXB/1R   Eastern Coach Works   B45/32F   1981-86

| 14303 | EMu | NHL303X | 14319 | MD | A319XWG | 14324 | MD | A324AKU | 14335 | MD | C335HWJ |
| 14314 | ESw | A314XWG | | | | | | | | | |

14337-14343   Leyland Olympian ON6LXB/2RZ   Alexander RL   BC51/31F   1989

| 14337 | GW | G337KKW | 14339 | MD | G339KKW | 14341 | HL | G341KKW | 14343 | MD | G343KKW |
| 14338 | AN | G338KKW | 14340 | MD | G340KKW | 14342 | MD | G342KKW | | | |

New to London, before spending some time at Oxford, most of the remaining FYM batch of Olympians are now to be found in Warwickshire. Illustrating the type is 14386, D136FYM, which was on school duty when seen.
Mark Doggett

14344-14353

Leyland Olympian ON2R56G13Z4 Alexander RL BC51/31F* 1990-91 *14349-53 are BC47/27F

14344	MD	H344SWA	14347	MD	H347SWA	14350	MD	J350XET	14352	MD	J352XET
14345	MD	H345SWA	14348	MD	H348SWA	14351	MD	J351XET	14353	MD	J353XET
14346	MD	H346SWA	14349	MD	J349XET						

14354-14358

Leyland Olympian ON2R50G13Z4 Northern Counties Palatine B47/29F 1992

| 14354 | MD | K354DWJ | 14356 | MD | K356DWJ | 14357 | MD | K357DWJ | 14358 | MD | K358DWJ |
| 14355 | MD | K355DWJ | | | | | | | | | |

14359-14363

Leyland Olympian ON2R50G13Z4 Alexander RL BC43/27F 1992

| 14359 | HL | K359DWJ | 14361 | HL | K361DWJ | 14362 | HL | K362DWJ | 14363 | HL | K363DWJ |
| 14360 | HL | K360DWJ | | | | | | | | | |

14367-14392

Leyland Olympian ONLXB/1RH Eastern Coach Works B42/29F 1986

14367	WWu	C116CHM	14374	RU	D124FYM	14378	LE	D128FYM	14386	NU	D136FYM
14369	LE	C119CHM	14375	LE	D125FYM	14381	RU	D131FYM	14387	RU	D137FYM
14371	RU	C121CHM	14377	LE	D127FYM	14382	NU	D132FYM	14392	AS	D142FYM
14373	LE	D123FYM									

14408	PH	K508ESS	Leyland Olympian ON2R50G13Z4	Alexander RL		BC43/27F	1992	
14409	PH	K509ESS	Leyland Olympian ON2R50G13Z4	Alexander RL		BC43/27F	1992	
14410	FH	K510ESS	Leyland Olympian ON2R50G13Z4	Alexander RL		BC43/27F	1992	
14411	CC	K511ESS	Leyland Olympian ON2R50G13Z4	Alexander RL		BC43/27F	1992	
14412	AY	C800HCS	Leyland Olympian ONLXB/1R	Eastern Coach Works		B45/32F	1986	A1 Service, 1995
14415	AS	K515ESS	Leyland Olympian ON2R50G13Z4	Alexander RL		BC43/27F	1992	
14418	FH	K518ESS	Leyland Olympian ON2R50G13Z4	Alexander RL		BC43/27F	1992	

14444-14458

Leyland Olympian ONLXB/1R Alexander RL B45/32F* 1983-85 *14444 is BC41/29F

| 14444 | ESw | A44FRS | 14452 | PH | B352LSO | 14455 | FH | B355LSO | 14457 | PH | B357LSO |
| 14448 | ESw | B348LSO | 14454 | KK | B354LSO | 14456 | ESu | B356LSO | 14458 | PH | B358LSO |

Stagecoach's Magic Bus operation in Glasgow uses mostly Olympians and includes 14522, F149XCS, an example new to A1 Service at Ardrossan. *Billy Nicol*

14462-14472

		Leyland Olympian ONLXB/1RV	Alexander RL			B47/30F*	1986	14462 are BC43/27F
14462	GW	C462SSO	**14468**	PH	C468SSO	**14471**	PH	GSO1V	**14472**	CX	C472SSO
14467	PH	C467SSO	**14469**	PH	C469SSO						

14462	GW	C462SSO
14467	PH	C467SSO
14468	PH	C468SSO
14469	PH	C469SSO
14471	PH	GSO1V
14472	CX	C472SSO

14476-14488

Leyland Olympian ONLXB/1RV — Alexander RL — BC43/27F — 1987

14476	BD	GSO6V
14477	BD	GSO7V
14479	BD	D379XRS
14482	KG	D382XRS
14483	BD	D383XRS
14484	BD	D384XRS
14485	AS	D385XRS
14486	PH	D386XRS
14487	PH	D387XRS
14488	PH	D388XRS

14490	IS	J120XHH	Leyland Olympian ON2R56G13Z4	Alexander RL	BC47/27F	1991
14491	IS	J121XHH	Leyland Olympian ON2R56G13Z4	Alexander RL	BC47/27F	1991
14492	IS	J122XHH	Leyland Olympian ON2R56G13Z4	Alexander RL	BC47/27F	1991
14493	NN	J620GCR	Leyland Olympian ON2R56G13Z4	Alexander RL	B51/34F	1991
14494	NN	J621GCR	Leyland Olympian ON2R56G13Z4	Alexander RL	B51/34F	1991
14495	NN	J622GCR	Leyland Olympian ON2R56G13Z4	Alexander RL	B51/34F	1991

14496-14499

Leyland Olympian ON2R56G13Z4 — Alexander RL — BC47/27F — 1992

14496	AS	J196YSS
14497	FH	J197YSS
14498	GW	J198YSS
14499	PH	J199YSS

14500	GR	E500LFL	Leyland Olympian ONLXCT/1RH	Optare	BC43/27F	1988
14501	GR	E501LFL	Leyland Olympian ONLXCT/1RH	Optare	BC43/27F	1988
14502	GR	E502LFL	Leyland Olympian ONLXCT/1RH	Optare	BC43/27F	1988

14506-14517

Leyland Olympian ONLXB/1RZ — Northern Counties — B45/30F — 1989

14506	CB	F506NJE
14507	CB	F507NJE
14508	CB	F508NJE
14509	CB	F509NJE
14510	BD	F510NJE
14511	BD	F511NJE
14512	BD	F512NJE
14513	CB	F513NJE
14514	CB	F514NJE
14515	LE	F515NJE
14516	LE	F516NJE
14517	LE	F517NJE

14520	CX	F41XCS	Leyland Olympian ONCL10/1RZ	Leyland	B47/31F	1989	A1 Service, 1995
14521	GW	F524WSJ	Leyland Olympian ONCL10/1RZ	Leyland	B47/31F	1989	A1 Service, 1995
14522	GW	F149XCS	Leyland Olympian ONCL10/1RZ	Leyland	B47/31F	1989	A1 Service, 1995
14523	CB	H473CEG	Leyland Olympian ON2R50G13Z4	Leyland	B47/31F	1990	
14524	CB	H474CEG	Leyland Olympian ON2R50G13Z4	Leyland	B47/31F	1990	
14525	CB	H475CEG	Leyland Olympian ON2R50G13Z4	Leyland	B47/31F	1990	

The large batch of Olympians delivered to Busways in the mid-1980s is now spread widely across the depots. Many of those in Newcastle and Glasgow carry the blue Magic Bus livery, while corporate colours are applied elsewhere. Seen heading for Castlemilk is Glasgow's 14608, C608LFT. *Mark Doggett*

14601-14665

Leyland Olympian ONLXB/1R   Alexander RH   B45/31F   1985-86

14601	GW	C601LFT	14618	SC	C618LFT	14634	HL	C634LFT	14650	GW	C650LFT
14602	GW	C602LFT	14619	GW	C619LFT	14635	HL	C635LFT	14651	HP	C651LFT
14603	GW	C603LFT	14621	HL	C621LFT	14636	SC	C636LFT	14653	GW	C653LFT
			14622	GW	C622LFT	14638	GW	C638LFT	14654	GW	C654LFT
14605	DA	C605LFT	14623	GW	C623LFT	14639	HP	C639LFT	14655	SC	C655LFT
14608	GW	C608LFT	14624	SN	C624LFT	14640	WSw	C640LFT	14656	GW	C656LFT
14609	SN	C609LFT	14625	GW	C625LFT	14641	GW	C641LFT	14657	GW	C657LFT
14610	SZ	C610LFT	14626	GW	C626LFT	14642	WSw	C642LFT	14658	SC	C658LFT
14611	DA	C611LFT	14627	GW	C627LFT	14643	HL	C643LFT	14659	GW	C659LFT
14612	GW	C612LFT	14628	GW	C628LFT	14644	HL	C644LFT	14661	SC	C661LFT
14613	NEw	C613LFT	14629	GW	C629LFT	14645	DA	C645LFT	14662	GW	C662LFT
14614	DA	C614LFT	14630	HL	C630LFT	14646	DA	C646LFT	14663	GW	C663LFT
14615	SC	C615LFT	14631	CX	C631LFT	14647	GW	C647LFT	14664	HL	C664LFT
14616	GW	C616LFT	14632	HL	C632LFT	14648	HP	C648LFT	14665	HL	C665LFT
14617	SC	C617LFT	14633	SC	C633LFT	14649	HL	C649LFT			

14667-14676

Leyland Olympian ON2R50C13Z4   Northern Counties Palatine   B47/30F   1990-91

14667	NEu	H667BNL	14670	SC	H670BNL	14673	SU	H673BNL	14675	SC	H675BNL
14668	WA	H668BNL	14671	SC	H671BNL	14674	SU	H674BNL	14676	WA	H676BNL
14669	WA	H669BNL	14672	SU	H672BNL						

14701-14708

Leyland Olympian ON2R50G13Z4   Alexander RL   B47/32F   1992

14701	AL	J801WFS	14703	AL	J803WFS	14705	AL	J805WFS	14707	CJ	J807WFS
14702	AL	J802WFS	14704	AL	J804WFS	14706	PH	J806WFS	14708	BD	J808WFS

14709-14725

Leyland Olympian ON2R50G13Z4   Alexander RL   B47/32F   1992

14709	BD	K709ASC	14715	TH	K715ASC	14719	CJ	K719ASC	14723	CJ	K723ASC
14710	BD	K710ASC	14716	TH	K716ASC	14720	AL	K720ASC	14724	DE	K724ASC
14713	BD	K713ASC	14717	BE	K717ASC	14721	CJ	K721ASC	14725	CJ	K725ASC
14714	LS	K714ASC	14718	CJ	K718ASC	14722	CJ	K722ASC			

East Kent's batch of Northern Counties-bodied Olympians from 1990 is still operating in the area. Pictured heading for Park Farm is 14809, H809BKK. *Dave Heath*

14801-14810
Leyland Olympian ON2R56C16Z4 Northern Counties · B51/34F · 1990

14801	HS	H801BKK	14804	HS	H804BKK	14807	CA	H807BKK
14802	HS	H802BKK	14805	HS	H805BKK	14808	CA	H808BKK
14803	AD	H803BKK	14806	AD	H806BKK			

14801	HS	H801BKK	14804	HS	H804BKK
14809	AD	H809BKK
14810	TH	H810BKK

14811	FO	J811NKK	Leyland Olympian ON2R50C13Z4 Northern Counties	B47/30F	1992
14812	FO	J812NKK	Leyland Olympian ON2R50C13Z4 Northern Counties	B47/30F	1992
14813	FO	J813NKK	Leyland Olympian ON2R50C13Z4 Northern Counties	B47/30F	1992
14814	FO	J814NKK	Leyland Olympian ON2R50C13Z4 Northern Counties	B47/30F	1992

14815-14819
Leyland Olympian ON2R56G13Z4 Alexander RL · B51/34F · 1990

14815	TH	H815CBP	14817	WG	H817CBP	14818	CR	H818CBP
14816	WI	H816CBP				14819	TH	H819CBP

14821-14830
Leyland Olympian ON2R50C13Z4 Northern Counties · B47/30F · 1993

14821	FO	K821TKP	14824	TH	K824TKP	14827	TH	L827BKK	14829	AD	L829BKK
14822	FO	K822TKP	14825	FO	K825TKP	14828	AD	L828BKK	14830	AD	L830BKK
14823	TH	K823TKP	14826	TH	L826BKK			

14901-14925
Leyland Olympian ONLXB/1RH Northern Counties · B43/30F · 1988

14901	HL	E901KYR	14909	HL	E909KYR	14918	HL	E918KYR	14924	HL	E924KYR
14908	HL	E908KYR	14912	HL	E912KYR	14922	HL	E922KYR	14925	HL	E925KYR

14932	RU	B912ODU	Leyland Olympian ONLXB/1R	Eastern Coach Works	B45/32F	1984
14935	CX	C962XVC	Leyland Olympian ONLXB/1RH	Eastern Coach Works	BC42/29F	1985
14937	CX	C964XVC	Leyland Olympian ONLXB/1RH	Eastern Coach Works	BC42/29F	1985

14942-14947
Leyland Olympian ONLXB/1R Eastern Coach Works · B45/32F · 1983

14942	RU	A542HAC	14943	RU	A543HAC	14944	RU	A544HAC	14947	KG	A547HAC

14951-14956
Leyland Olympian ON2R56G13Z4 Alexander RL · B51/36F · 1988

14951	BE	F601MSL	14953	WI	F603MSL	14955	WI	F605MSL	14956	BE	F606MSL
14952	BE	F602MSL	14954	BE	F604MSL			

14957-14964 — Leyland Olympian ON2R56G13Z4 — Alexander RL — BC51/31F — 1989

| 14957 | AN | G807RTS | 14959 | AN | G809RTS | 14962 | AN | G212SSL | 14964 | FH | G214SSL |
| 14958 | GR | G808RTS | 14960 | AT | G210SSL | 14963 | AN | G213SSL | | | |

14970	CR	J720GAP	Leyland Olympian ON2R56G13Z4	Alexander RL	BC47/27F	1992
14971	CR	J721GAP	Leyland Olympian ON2R56G13Z4	Alexander RL	BC47/27F	1992
14972	CR	J722GAP	Leyland Olympian ON2R56G13Z4	Alexander RL	BC47/27F	1992
14973	WI	J623GCR	Leyland Olympian ON2R56G13Z4	Alexander RL	B47/30F	1991
14974	AR	J624GCR	Leyland Olympian ON2R56G13Z4	Alexander RL	B47/30F	1991

14975-14984 — Leyland Olympian ON2R56G13Z4 — Alexander RL — B51/34F — 1990

14975	CR	G705TCD	14978	CA	G708TCD	14981	DO	G701TCD	14983	DO	G703TCD
14976	CA	G706TCD	14979	DO	G709TCD	14982	CA	G702TCD	14984	DO	G704TCD
14977	CA	G707TCD	14980	CA	G710TCD						

14985-14990 — Leyland Olympian ON2R50G13Z4 — Alexander RL — BC43/27F — 1992

| 14985 | AT | K235NHC | 14987 | BE | K237NHC | 14989 | BE | K239NHC | 14990 | BE | K240NHC |
| 14986 | AR | K236NHC | 14988 | AT | K238NHC | | | | | | |

| 15011 | MAu | B911TVR | Dennis Dominator DDA1003 | Northern Counties | B43/32F | 1985 |
| 15023 | HEt | B23TVR | Dennis Dominator DDA1003 | Northern Counties | B43/32F | 1985 |

15031-15040 — Dennis Dominator DDA2033 — Northern Counties Palatine — B43/29F — 1991

15031	PS	H131GVM	15034	PS	H134GVM	15037	PS	H137GVM	15039	PS	H139GVM
15032	PS	H132GVM	15035	PS	H135GVM	15038	PS	H138GVM	15040	PS	H140GVM
15033	PS	H133GVM	15036	PS	H136GVM						

15044-15051 — Dennis Dominator DDA1016 — East Lancs — B45/31F — 1988

| 15044 | HL | F144BKH | 15047 | HL | F147BKH | 15049 | HL | F149BKH | 15051 | HL | F151BKH |
| 15046 | HL | F146BKH | 15048 | HL | F148BKH | | | | | | |

15077	GY	F77TFU	Dennis Dominator DDA1021	Alexander RH	B45/33F	1989
15079	GY	G79VFW	Dennis Dominator DDA1028	Alexander RH	B45/33F	1990
15080	GY	G80VFW	Dennis Dominator DDA1028	Alexander RH	B45/33F	1990
15081	GY	G81VFW	Dennis Dominator DDA1029	Alexander RH	B45/33F	1990
15084	GY	H484BEE	Dennis Dominator DDA1034	East Lancs	B45/33F	1991
15085	GY	H485BEE	Dennis Dominator DDA1034	East Lancs	B45/33F	1991
15092	GY	J92DJV	Dennis Dominator DDA1036	East Lancs	B45/33F	1992
15093	GY	J93DJV	Dennis Dominator DDA1036	East Lancs	B45/33F	1992
15094	GY	J94DJV	Dennis Dominator DDA1036	East Lancs	B45/33F	1992

15180-15199 — Dennis Dragon DDA1820 — Duple Metsec/AVA — B51/37F* — 1995-96 — Stagecoach Kenya, 1998-99
*15182/4/6-8/90-2/4/6/8/9 are BC55/37F

15180	PS	M680TDB	15185	PS	M685TDB	15190	PS	M690TDB	15195	PS	M695TDB
15181	PS	M681TDB	15186	PS	M686TDB	15191	PS	M691TDB	15196	PS	M696TDB
15182	PS	M682TDB	15187	PS	M687TDB	15192	PS	M692TDB	15197	PS	M379TJA
15183	PS	M683TDB	15188	PS	M688TDB	15193	PS	M693TDB	15198	PS	L392LNA
15184	PS	M684TDB	15189	PS	M689TDB	15194	PS	M694TDB	15199	PS	M699TDB

15201-15212 — Volvo Citybus B10M-50 — Northern Counties — BC43/33F — 1989

15201	CR	F301MYJ	15204	PM	F304MYJ	15207	HS	F307MYJ	15210	AL	F310MYJ
15202	PM	F302MYJ	15205	HS	F305MYJ	15208	HS	F308MYJ	15211	AL	F311MYJ
15203	PM	F303MYJ	15206	CR	F306MYJ	15209	HS	F309MYJ	15212	DE	F312MYJ

15246	AY	VCS376	Volvo Citybus B10M-50	Alexander RV	B47/37F	1985	A1 Service, 1995
15247	GW	E864RCS	Volvo Citybus B10M-50	Alexander RV	BC41/29F	1987	
15248	AL	E865RCS	Volvo Citybus B10M-50	Alexander RV	B45/35F	1987	
15249	GW	E866RCS	Volvo Citybus B10M-50	Alexander RV	BC45/33F	1987	
15250	AN	126ASV	Volvo Citybus B10M-50	Alexander RV	BC45/33F	1987	
15259	AN	128ASV	Volvo Citybus B10M-50	Alexander RV	BC45/35F	1986	
15260	AN	127ASV	Volvo Citybus B10M-50	Alexander RV	BC45/35F	1986	

The operation of Dennis Dominators is now confined to Grimsby, Hull and Manchester where the vehicles operate alongside the tri-axle version called the Dragon. Allocated to Hull, 15048, F148BKH, is one of six with East Lancs bodywork. *Bob Downham*

15269-15276

Volvo Citybus B10M-50 — Alexander RV — B47/37F — 1986

15269	AL	C807USG	15271	AL	C801USG	15273	GS	C803USG	15275	GW	C805USG
15270	WSw	C800USG	15272	GS	C802USG	15274	GS	C804USG	15276	AL	C806USG

15279-15299

Volvo Citybus B10M-50 — Alexander RV — B47/37F — 1985-86 — *15295/9 are BC45/35F

15279	WSu	B179FFS	15284	KK	B184FFS	15289	AL	C789USG	15295	AL	C795USG
15280	KK	B180FFS	15285	KK	B185FFS	15290	GS	C790USG	15296	WSu	C796USG
15281	KK	B181FFS	15286	ESw	B186FFS	15292	CJ	C792USG	15297	CJ	C797USG
15282	KK	B182FFS	15287	CJ	C787USG	15293	SA	C793USG	15299	GW	C799USG
15283	KK	B183FFS	15288	SA	C788USG						

15301-15310

Scania N113DRB — Alexander RH — B47/29F — 1990

15301	WA	H421BNL	15304	NEu	H424BNL	15307	WA	H427BNL	15309	WA	H429BNL
15302	WA	H422BNL	15305	WA	H425BNL	15308	WA	H428BNL	15310	WA	H430BNL
15303	WA	H423BNL	15306	WA	H426BNL						

15311	CA	F781KKP	Scania N113DRB	Alexander RH	B47/33F	1989
15312	CA	F782KKP	Scania N113DRB	Alexander RH	B47/33F	1989

15313-15317

Scania N113DRB — Northern Counties Palatine — B47/28F — 1991

15313	GP	H463GVM	15315	GP	H465GVM	15316	GP	H466GVM	15317	GP	H467GVM
15314	GP	H464GVM									

15322-15329

Scania N113DRB — Alexander RH — O47/31F* — 1991 — *15324/5/8/9 are B47/31F

15322	EX	J822HMC	15324	EX	J824HMC	15326	EX	J826HMC	15328	SWu	J828HMC
15323	EX	J823HMC	15325	EX	J825HMC	15327	SWu	J827HMC	15329	SWu	J829HMC

15330	TH	J230XKY	Scania N113DRB	Northern Counties Palatine	B47/33F	1991
15331	TH	J231XKY	Scania N113DRB	Northern Counties Palatine	B47/33F	1991

15332-15345

Scania N113DRB — Northern Counties Palatine — B41/27F — 1991

15332	ST	J132HMT	15336	HE	J136HMT	15340	HE	J140HMT	15343	ST	J143HMT
15333	ST	J133HMT	15337	ST	J137HMT	15341	HE	J141HMT	15344	ST	J144HMT
15334	CA	J134HMT	15338	TH	J138HMT	15342	ST	J142HMT	15345	HE	J145HMT
15335	ST	J135HMT	15339	TH	J139HMT						

Five Scania OmniDekka buses are operated by Stagecoach alongside some similarly liveried Dennis Tridents on the *Corby Star* network. Seen in service is the first of the batch, 15401, KX04RCV. *Mark Lyons*

| **15346-15371** | | | | | | | | | Scania N113DRB | | Northern Counties Palatine | B41/27F | 1991-92 |

15346	ST	K846LMK	**15353**	ST	K853LMK	**15360**	ST	K860LMK	**15366**	TH	K866LMK
15347	HE	K847LMK	**15354**	ST	K854LMK	**15361**	HE	K861LMK	**15367**	TH	K867LMK
15348	HE	K848LMK	**15355**	HE	K855LMK	**15362**	HE	K862LMK	**15368**	HE	K868LMK
15349	TH	K849LMK	**15356**	MAu	K856LMK	**15363**	HE	K863LMK	**15369**	TH	K869LMK
15350	TH	K850LMK	**15357**	TH	K857LMK	**15364**	TH	K864LMK	**15370**	MAu	K870LMK
15351	HE	K851LMK	**15358**	HE	K858LMK	**15365**	ST	K865LMK	**15371**	MAu	K871LMK
15352	ST	K852LMK	**15359**	ST	K859LMK						

| **15401-15405** | | | Scania N94UD 10.6m | East Lancs OmniDekka 4.4m | N47/32F | 2004 |

15401	CX	KX04RCV	**15403**	CX	KX04RCZ	**15404**	CX	KX04RDU	**15405**	CX	KX04RDV
15402	CX	KX04RCY						

15513	EMu	MBE613R	Leyland Fleetline FE30AGR	Roe	O45/29D	1976	
15731	CE	PHH149W	Bristol VRT/SL3/6LXB	Eastern Coach Works	B43/31F	1980	
15751	FOu	JWW251W	Bristol VRT/SL3/6LXB	Eastern Coach Works	B43/31F	1980	
15760	CRu	JOU160P	Bristol VRT/SL3/501 (6LXB)	Eastern Coach Works	B43/28F	1975	
15917	SYu	SAG517W	MCW Metrobus DR102/7	MCW	PO43/30F	1981	On loan during summer

16001	NS	P801GMU	Volvo Olympian YN2RV18Z4	Northern Counties Palatine	B49/31D	1996
16002	NS	P802GMU	Volvo Olympian YN2RV18Z4	Northern Counties Palatine	B49/31D	1996
16003	NS	P803GMU	Volvo Olympian YN2RV18Z4	Northern Counties Palatine	B49/31D	1996

16004-16026 Volvo Olympian YN2RV18Z4 Northern Counties Palatine B49/31F 1996

16004	NN	P804GMU	**16010**	CB	P810GMU	**16016**	SWu	P816GMU	**16022**	CB	P822GMU
16005	NN	P805GMU	**16011**	CB	P811GMU	**16017**	EH	P817GMU	**16023**	CB	P823GMU
16006	NN	P806GMU	**16012**	CB	P812GMU	**16018**	CB	P818GMU	**16024**	CB	P824GMU
16007	NN	P807GMU	**16013**	CB	P813GMU	**16019**	CB	P819GMU	**16025**	CB	P825GMU
16008	CB	P808GMU	**16014**	CB	P814GMU	**16020**	CB	P820GMU	**16026**	CB	P826GMU
16009	CB	P809GMU	**16015**	CB	P815GMU	**16021**	CB	P821GMU			

16044-16081 Volvo Olympian Alexander RL B51/26F* 1997 *seating varies
*16047/8/53/61/3/6/72/6/8/9/80 dual doored

16044	SN	P644SEV	**16054**	DE	R154VPU	**16064**	EX	R164VPU	**16073**	DE	R173VPU
16045	SA	P645SEV	**16055**	SN	R155VPU	**16065**	DE	R165VPU	**16074**	AS	R174VPU
16046	AL	P646SEV	**16056**	PE	R156VPU	**16066**	HL	R166VPU	**16075**	CJ	R175VPU
16047	HL	R747XAR	**16057**	SA	R157VPU	**16067**	AL	R167VPU	**16076**	LE	R176VPU
16048	HL	R148VPU	**16058**	EX	R158VPU	**16068**	AS	R168VPU	**16077**	CJ	R177VPU
16049	PE	R149VPU	**16059**	EX	R159VPU	**16069**	EX	R169VPU	**16078**	LE	R178VPU
16050	EX	R150VPU	**16060**	SA	R160VPU	**16070**	PE	R170VPU	**16079**	LE	R179VPU
16051	HL	R151VPU	**16061**	HL	R161VPU	**16071**	EX	R171VPU	**16080**	SZ	R180VPU
16052	EX	R152VPU	**16062**	EH	R162VPU	**16072**	LE	R172VPU	**16081**	SN	R181VPU
16053	HL	R153VPU	**16063**	HL	R163VPU						

16082-16100 Volvo Olympian Northern Counties Palatine B45/27F* 1997 *16085/7/8/90/3/6 B45/23D

16082	PE	R82XNO	**16087**	PS	R87XNO	**16092**	GS	R92XNO	**16097**	PE	R97XNO
16083	PE	R83XNO	**16088**	GY	R188XNO	**16093**	GY	R93XNO	**16098**	AL	R98XNO
16084	AL	R84XNO	**16089**	PE	R89XNO	**16094**	GY	R94XNO	**16099**	SN	R207XNO
16085	PS	R85XNO	**16090**	PS	R190XNO	**16095**	PE	R95XNO	**16100**	GS	R210XNO
16086	PE	R86XNO	**16091**	PE	R91XNO	**16096**	GY	R96XNO			

16101-16121 Volvo Olympian Northern Counties Palatine B45/31F* 1998 *seating varies

16101	AL	R101XNO	**16107**	DE	R107XNO	**16112**	AN	R112XNO	**16117**	AN	R117XNO
16102	PE	R102XNO	**16108**	DE	R108XNO	**16113**	PE	R113XNO	**16118**	AN	R118XNO
16103	PS	R103XNO	**16109**	PE	R109XNO	**16114**	CJ	R114XNO	**16119**	AN	R119XNO
16104	GS	R104XNO	**16110**	GR	S110SHJ	**16115**	AN	R115XNO	**16120**	AN	R120XNO
16105	GY	R105XNO	**16111**	AN	R311XNO	**16116**	AN	R116XNO	**16121**	AN	R121XNO
16106	PE	R206XNO									

16122-16148 Volvo Olympian Alexander RL B45/23D* 1998 *converting to B45/32F

16122	TB	R122EVX	**16129**	SZ	R129EVX	**16136**	HL	R136EVX	**16143**	HL	R143EVX
16123	TB	R123EVX	**16130**	PE	R130EVX	**16137**	EH	R137EVX	**16144**	AL	R144EVX
16124	PE	R124EVX	**16131**	HL	R131EVX	**16138**	CJ	R138EVX	**16145**	HL	R145EVX
16125	PE	R125EVX	**16132**	AL	R132EVX	**16139**	PE	R139EVX	**16146**	PE	R146EVX
16126	GR	R126EVX	**16133**	HL	R133EVX	**16140**	DE	R140EVX	**16147**	HL	R147EVX
16127	SZ	R127EVX	**16134**	HL	R134EVX	**16141**	AL	R141EVX	**16148**	HL	R148EVX
16128	SZ	R128EVX	**16135**	SN	R135EVX	**16142**	SZ	R142EVX			

16149-16178 Volvo Olympian Northern Counties Palatine B49/27D* 1998 *converting to B49/31F

16149	CN	R149HHK	**16157**	AL	R157HHK	**16165**	AL	R165HHK	**16172**	DE	R172HHK
16150	AL	R150HHK	**16158**	DE	R158HHK	**16166**	DE	R166HHK	**16173**	CJ	R173HHK
16151	CH	R151HHK	**16159**	DE	R159HHK	**16167**	PE	R167HHK	**16174**	PE	R174HHK
16152	DE	R152HHK	**16160**	GS	R160HHK	**16168**	HL	R168HHK	**16175**	PE	R175HHK
16153	AN	R153HHK	**16161**	CJ	R161HHK	**16169**	MD	R169HHK	**16176**	AL	R176HHK
16154	DE	R154HHK	**16162**	PE	R162HHK	**16170**	GS	R170HHK	**16177**	DE	R177HHK
16155	CJ	R155HHK	**16163**	DE	R163HHK	**16171**	GS	R171HHK	**16178**	GS	R178HHK
16156	DE	R156HHK	**16164**	EH	R164HHK						

16198	IS	L26JSA	Volvo Olympian YN2RV18Z4	Northern Counties Palatine	BC43/25F	1993
16199	FH	L27JSA	Volvo Olympian YN2RV18Z4	Northern Counties Palatine	BC43/25F	1993
16200	IS	L28JSA	Volvo Olympian YN2RV18Z4	Northern Counties Palatine	BC43/25F	1993
16201	IS	L101JSA	Volvo Olympian YN2RV18Z4	Northern Counties Palatine	BC43/25F	1993
16202	IS	L102JSA	Volvo Olympian YN2RV18Z4	Northern Counties Palatine	BC43/25F	1993

16203-16208 — Volvo Olympian — Alexander RL — B47/32F — 1998

16203	RY	R203DHB	16205	RY	R205DHB	16207	RY	R207DHB	16208	RY	R208DHB
16204	RY	R204DHB	16206	RY	R206DHB						

16209-16232 — Volvo Olympian — Alexander RL — BC45/32F* — 1997 — *16621/2 are B51/36F

16209	NN	83CBD	16216	BD	R566DRP	16223	NN	S753DRP	16228	NN	S758DRP
16210	BD	R560DRP	16217	BD	R567DRP	16224	NN	S754DRP	16229	NN	S759DRP
16212	BD	R562DRP	16218	BD	R568DRP	16225	NN	S755DRP	16230	NN	S760DRP
16213	BD	R563DRP	16221	NN	R701DNH	16226	NN	S756DRP	16231	NN	S761DRP
16214	BD	R564DRP	16222	NN	R702DNH	16227	NN	S757DRP	16232	NN	S762DRP
16215	BD	R565DRP									

16241-16250 — Volvo Olympian YN2RV18Z4 — Northern Counties Palatine — BC43/25F — 1993

16241	TH	L241SDY	16244	BD	L244SDY	16247	TH	L247SDY	16249	FH	L249SDY
16242	TH	L242SDY	16245	BD	L245SDY	16248	FH	L248SDY	16250	IS	L250SDY
16243	BD	L243SDY	16246	TH	L246SDY						

16260-16290 — Volvo Olympian — Alexander RL — B51/36F* — 1996-98 — *16260-3 are B51/32F *16288-90 are BC47/32F

16260	WI	P260WPN	16268	BE	P268VPN	16276	WI	P276VPN	16284	CA	P284VPN
16261	WI	P261WPN	16269	BE	P269VPN	16277	WI	P277VPN	16285	FO	P285VPN
16262	BE	P262WPN	16270	CA	S270CCD	16278	CR	P278VPN	16286	TH	P286VPN
16263	WI	P263WPN	16271	CA	S271CCD	16279	WI	P279VPN	16287	FO	P287VPN
16264	CA	P264VPN	16272	CA	S272CCD	16281	CR	P281VPN	16288	WI	P288VPN
16265	CA	P265VPN	16273	CA	S273CCD	16282	CR	P282VPN	16289	WI	P289VPN
16266	CA	P266VPN	16274	CA	S274CCD	16283	CA	P283VPN	16290	WI	P290VPN
16267	CA	P267VPN	16275	CA	S275CCD						

16291-16305 — Volvo Olympian — Alexander RL — B51/36F — 1998

16291	WI	R291HCD	16295	AR	R295HCD	16299	CA	R299HCD	16303	WI	S303CCD
16292	WI	R292HCD	16296	CA	R296HCD	16301	TH	R301HCD	16304	WI	S304CCD
16293	AR	R293HCD	16297	CA	R297HCD	16302	AT	S302CCD	16305	AT	S305CCD
16294	AR	R294HCD	16298	CA	R298HCD						

16306-16324 — Volvo Olympian — Alexander RL — BC43/36F — 1998

16306	PM	S306CCD	16311	WG	S311CCD	16316	HS	S316CCD	16320	AT	S320CCD
16307	PM	S307CCD	16312	WG	S312CCD	16317	HS	S317CCD	16322	PM	S322CCD
16308	WG	S308CCD	16313	WG	S313CCD	16318	HS	S318CCD	16323	PM	S323CCD
16309	WG	S309CCD	16314	WG	S314CCD	16319	BE	S319CCD	16324	PM	S324CCD
16310	WG	S310CCD	16315	HS	S315CCD						

16325-16340 — Volvo Olympian YN2RC16V3 — Alexander RL — B47/32F — 1996

16325	PR	N325NPN	16329	PR	N329NPN	16334	KL	N334NPN	16338	KL	N338NPN
16326	PR	N326NPN	16330	KL	N330NPN	16335	KL	N335NPN	16339	KL	N339NPN
16327	PR	N327NPN	16331	KL	N331NPN	16336	KL	N336NPN	16340	KL	N340NPN
16328	PR	N328NPN	16332	KL	N332NPN	16337	KL	N337NPN			

16341-16359 — Volvo Olympian YN2RC16V3 — Alexander RL — BC47/28F — 1996

16341	PM	N341MPN	16346	WG	N346MPN	16351	PR	N351MPN	16356	PM	N356MPN
16342	PM	N342MPN	16347	WG	N347MPN	16352	PR	N352MPN	16357	LS	N357MPN
16343	PR	N343MPN	16348	CR	N348MPN	16353	PR	N353MPN	16358	PR	N358MPN
16344	PM	N344MPN	16349	WG	N349MPN	16354	LS	N354MPN	16359	PR	N359MPN
16345	SEu	N345MPN	16350	WG	N350MPN	16355	PR	N355MPN			

16360-16380 — Volvo Olympian YN2RC16V3 — Alexander RL — B47/32F — 1995

16360	CA	N360LPN	16366	BE	N366LPN	16371	FO	N371LPN	16376	FO	N376LPN
16361	CA	N361LPN	16367	BE	N367LPN	16372	FO	N372LPN	16377	FO	N377LPN
16362	CA	N362LPN	16368	DO	N368LPN	16373	AT	N373LPN	16378	FO	N378LPN
16363	DO	N363LPN	16369	DO	N369LPN	16374	WI	N374LPN	16379	BE	N379LPN
16364	DO	N364LPN	16370	DO	N370LPN	16375	FO	N375LPN	16380	BE	N380LPN
16365	FO	N365LPN									

One of a large batch with Alexander bodywork initially used for South operations is 16313, S313CCD, seen in Cornfield Road, Eastbourne. *Mark Lyons*

16381-16399
Volvo Olympian YN2RC16V3   Alexander RL   BC47/28F   1995-96

16381	TH	N381LPN	**16386**	DO	N386LPN	**16391**	PR	N391LPN	**16396**	WI	N396LPN
16382	HS	N382LPN	**16387**	DO	N387LPN	**16392**	PR	N392LPN	**16397**	PR	N397LPN
16383	HS	N383LPN	**16388**	CA	N388LPN	**16393**	AR	N393LPN	**16398**	AR	N398LPN
16384	DO	N384LPN	**16389**	DO	N389LPN	**16394**	AR	N394LPN	**16399**	BE	N399LPN
16385	CA	N385LPN	**16390**	DO	N390LPN	**16395**	PM	N395LPN			

16401-16420
Volvo Olympian YN2RV18Z4   Northern Counties Palatine   B45/29F*   1995   *seating varies

16401	CJ	M301DGP	**16406**	AL	M306DGP	**16411**	GR	M311DGP	**16416**	AL	M316DGP
16402	CJ	M302DGP	**16407**	CJ	M307DGP	**16412**	GS	M312DGP	**16417**	GS	M317DGP
16403	GS	M303DGP	**16408**	CJ	M308DGP	**16413**	AL	M313DGP	**16418**	AL	M318DGP
16404	GS	M304DGP	**16409**	SA	M309DGP	**16414**	AL	M314DGP	**16419**	GS	M319DGP
16405	DE	M305DGP	**16410**	GS	M310DGP	**16415**	AL	M315DGP	**16420**	SA	M320DGP

16421-16430
Volvo Olympian YN2RV18Z4   Northern Counties Palatine   B45/26F*   1995   *16423/30 are B45/27F

16421	AL	N321HGK	**16424**	AL	N325HGK	**16427**	AL	N327HGK	**16429**	AL	N329HGK
16422	AL	N322HGK	**16425**	AL	N324HGK	**16428**	AL	N328HGK	**16430**	AL	N330HGK
16423	AL	N323HGK	**16426**	AL	N326HGK						

16431-16437
Volvo Olympian YN2RV18Z4   Northern Counties Palatine   B45/26F   1995

16431	WA	VLT255	**16433**	WA	WLT528	**16435**	WA	WLT908	**16437**	WA	685DYE
16432	WA	WLT512	**16434**	WA	WLT682	**16436**	WA	647DYE			

16438-16452
Volvo Olympian YN2RV18Z4   Northern Counties Palatine   B45/27F   1995

16438	AL	N338HGK	**16442**	GR	N342HGK	**16446**	CN	N346HGK	**16449**	SN	N349HGK
16439	CJ	N339HGK	**16443**	SN	N343HGK	**16447**	CN	N347HGK	**16450**	SA	N350HGK
16440	GS	N340HGK	**16444**	CN	N344HGK	**16448**	GR	N348HGK	**16452**	SN	N352HGK
16441	RY	N341HGK	**16445**	CN	N345HGK						

16453-16460
Volvo Olympian   Alexander RL   B51/35F   1996-97

16453	CH	P153KWJ	**16455**	CH	P151KWJ	**16457**	CH	P157KWJ	**16459**	CH	P159KAK
16454	CH	P154KWJ	**16456**	CH	P156KWJ	**16458**	CH	P158KWJ	**16460**	CH	P160KAK

16461-16469 Volvo Olympian Alexander RL B51/36F 1998

16461	WP	S161RET	16464	WP	S164RET	16466	WP	S166RET	16468	WP	S168RET
16462	WP	S162RET	16465	WP	S165RET	16467	WP	S167RET	16469	WP	S169RET
16463	WP	S163RET									

16471-16479 Volvo Olympian YN2RV18Z4 Northern Counties Palatine B47/29F 1993

16471	HL	K101JWJ	16474	HL	K104JWJ	16476	MD	K106JWJ	16478	MD	L108LHL
16472	HL	K102JWJ	16475	HL	K105JWJ	16477	MD	K107JWJ	16479	MD	L109LHL
16473	HL	K103JWJ									

16480-16494 Volvo Olympian YN2RV18Z4 Alexander RL B47/32F 1995

16480	MD	N130AET	16484	CH	N134AET	16488	CH	N138AET	16492	CH	N142AET
16481	MD	N131AET	16485	CH	N135AET	16489	CH	N139AET	16493	CH	N143AET
16482	MD	N132AET	16486	CH	N136AET	16490	CH	N140AET	16494	CH	N144AET
16483	CH	N133AET	16487	CH	N137AET	16491	CH	N141AET			

16495-16500 Volvo Olympian Alexander RL B51/36F 1996-97

16495	CH	P145KWJ	16497	CH	P152KWJ	16499	HL	P149KWJ	16500	CH	P150KWJ
16496	CH	P146KWJ	16498	HL	P148KWJ						

16501-16513 Volvo Olympian Alexander RL B51/36F 1997

16501	HE	R501UWL	16505	HE	R505UWL	16508	ST	R508UWL	16511	ST	R511UWL
16502	HE	R502UWL	16506	ST	R506UWL	16509	ST	R509UWL	16512	ST	R512UWL
16503	HE	R503UWL	16507	ST	R507UWL	16510	ST	R510UWL	16513	ST	R513UWL
16504	HE	R504UWL									

16514-16526 Volvo Olympian Alexander RL B51/36F 1998

16514	LE	R414XFC	16518	OX	R418XFC	16521	OX	R421XFC	16524	OX	R424XFC
16515	LE	R415XFC	16519	OX	R419XFC	16522	OX	R422XFC	16525	BB	R425XFC
16516	LE	R416XFC	16520	OX	R420XFC	16523	OX	R423XFC	16526	WY	R426XFC
16517	LE	R417XFC									

16527-16555 Volvo Olympian YN2RV18V3 Northern Counties Palatine B49/33F 1996

16527	BD	P527EFL	16537	BD	P537EFL	16541	CB	P541EFL	16544	CB	P544EFL
16528	BD	P528EFL	16538	BD	P538EFL	16542	CB	P542EFL	16545	CB	P545EFL
16534	CB	P534EFL	16539	BD	P539EFL	16543	CB	P543EFL	16555	BD	P526EFL

16580-16586 Volvo Olympian Alexander RL B47/27F 1998

16580	PE	R580JVA	16582	PE	R582JVA	16584	BD	R584JVA	16586	BD	R586JVA
16581	PE	R581JVA	16583	PE	R583JVA						

16587-16593 Volvo Olympian Alexander RL BC47/32F 1998

16587	PE	S587BCE	16589	PE	S589BCE	16591	PE	S591BCE	16593	PE	S593BCE
16588	PE	S588BCE	16590	PE	S590BCE	16592	PE	S592BCE			

16598	LE	N518XER	Volvo Olympian YN2RV18Z4	Northern Counties Palatine	BC45/31F	1995
16599	LE	N519XER	Volvo Olympian YN2RV18Z4	Northern Counties Palatine	BC45/31F	1995
16600	LE	N520XER	Volvo Olympian YN2RV18Z4	Northern Counties Palatine	BC45/31F	1995
16601	TQ	R901FDV	Volvo Olympian	Alexander RL	B45/27F	1997
16602	EX	R902JDV	Volvo Olympian	Alexander RL	B51/36F	1998
16603	EX	R903JDV	Volvo Olympian	Alexander RL	B51/36F	1998
16604	EX	R904JDV	Volvo Olympian	Alexander RL	B51/36F	1998
16610	IS	L100JLB	Volvo Olympian YN2RV18Z4	Northern Counties Palatine	BC43/25F	1993

16614-16620 Volvo Olympian Alexander RL B51/36F 1999

16614	LE	S914ANH	16616	LE	S916ANH	16618	LE	S918ANH	16620	LE	S920ANH
16615	LE	S915ANH	16617	LE	S917ANH	16619	LE	S919ANH			

16624-16635 Volvo Olympian YN2RV18Z4 Northern Counties Palatine B49/33F 1996

16624	AT	P224VCK	16627	AT	P227VCK	16630	AT	P230VCK	16633	AT	P233VCK
16625	AT	P225VCK	16628	AT	P228VCK	16631	AT	P231VCK	16634	CY	P234VCK
16626	AT	P226VCK	16629	AT	P229VCK	16632	AT	P232VCK	16635	CY	P235VCK

While the Volvo Olympian with Alexander bodywork was the standard double-deck, some vehicles were bodied by Northern Counties though generally when destined for the Group's provincial operations. One with Alexander bodywork from 1996 is 16637, P261VPN. Now allocated to Chorley, it was heading home when pictured in Blackburn. *Bob Downham*

16636-16645

Volvo Olympian YN2RV18Z4 — Alexander RL — B51/36F — 1996

16636	CY	P260VPN	16639	CY	P263VPN	16642	ME	P272VPN	16644	CEw	P274VPN
16637	CY	P261VPN	16640	ME	P270VPN	16643	LL	P273VPN	16645	PR	P275VPN
16638	CY	P262VPN	16641	ME	P271VPN						

16646-16668

Volvo Olympian — Alexander RL — B51/36F — 1997

16646	PR	R246NBV	16652	LL	R252NBV	16658	ME	R258NBV	16664	ME	R264NBV
16647	PR	R247NBV	16653	LL	R253NBV	16659	ME	R259NBV	16665	ME	R265NBV
16648	PR	R248NBV	16654	LL	R254NBV	16660	ME	R260NBV	16666	ME	R266NBV
16649	PR	R249NBV	16655	LL	R255NBV	16661	ME	R261NBV	16667	ME	R267NBV
16650	PR	R250NBV	16656	ME	R256NBV	16662	ME	R262NBV	16668	ME	R268NBV
16651	PR	R251NBV	16657	ME	R257NBV	16663	ME	R263NBV			

16669	PR	S903JHG	Volvo Olympian	Alexander RL	BC43/26F	1998
16670	PR	S904JHG	Volvo Olympian	Alexander RL	BC43/26F	1998

16671-16685

Volvo Olympian YN2RV18Z4 — Northern Counties Palatine — B47/29F — 1993

16671	BD	L671HNV	16675	BD	L675HNV	16679	NN	L679HNV	16683	NN	L683HNV
16672	BD	L672HNV	16676	BD	L676HNV	16680	NN	L680HNV	16684	NN	L684HNV
16673	BD	L673HNV	16677	BD	L677HNV	16681	NN	L681HNV	16685	NN	L685JBD
16674	BD	L674HNV	16678	BD	L678HNV	16682	NN	L682HNV			

16686-16692

Volvo Olympian YN2RV18Z4 — Alexander RL — B51/36F — 1996

16686	NN	P686JBD	16688	NN	P688JBD	16690	NN	P690JBD	16692	NN	P692JBD
16687	NN	P687JBD	16689	NN	P689JBD	16691	NN	P691JBD			

16693-16699

Volvo Olympian — Alexander RL — B51/36F — 1997

16693	NN	R693DNH	16695	NN	R695DNH	16697	NN	R697DNH	16699	NN	R699DNH
16694	NN	R694DNH	16696	NN	R696DNH	16698	NN	R698DNH			

16701-16740
Volvo Olympian YN2RV18Z4 — Alexander RL — B47/28F — 1995

16701	WA	N701LTN	16711	WA	N711LTN	16721	WA	N721LTN	16731	SC	N731LTN
16702	WA	N702LTN	16712	WA	N712LTN	16722	WA	N722LTN	16732	SS	N732LTN
16703	WA	N703LTN	16713	WA	N713LTN	16723	WA	N723LTN	16733	SS	N733LTN
16704	WA	N704LTN	16714	WA	N714LTN	16724	WA	N724LTN	16734	SS	N734LTN
16705	WA	N705LTN	16715	WA	N715LTN	16725	WA	N725LTN	16735	SS	N735LTN
16706	WA	N706LTN	16716	WA	N716LTN	16726	WA	N726LTN	16736	SS	N736LTN
16707	WA	N707LTN	16717	WA	N717LTN	16727	WA	N727LTN	16737	SS	N737LTN
16708	WA	N708LTN	16718	WA	N718LTN	16728	WA	N728LTN	16738	SS	N738LTN
16709	WA	N709LTN	16719	WA	N719LTN	16729	WA	N729LTN	16739	SS	N739LTN
16710	WA	N710LTN	16720	WA	N720LTN	16730	WA	N730LTN	16740	SS	N740LTN

16744-16782
Volvo Olympian — Alexander RL — B51/36F — 1998

16744	ST	R744DRJ	16755	HE	R755DRJ	16764	HE	S764SVU	16773	PS	S773RVU
16745	ST	R745DRJ	16756	HE	R756DRJ	16765	HE	R765DRJ	16774	PS	S774RVU
16746	ST	R746DRJ	16757	HE	R757DRJ	16766	HE	S766SVU	16775	PS	S775RVU
16747	ST	R747DRJ	16758	HE	R758DRJ	16767	PS	S767SVU	16776	PS	S776RVU
16748	ST	R748DRJ	16759	HE	R759DRJ	16768	PS	S768SVU	16778	PS	S778RVU
16749	ST	R749DRJ	16760	HE	R760DRJ	16769	PS	S769RVU	16779	PS	S779RVU
16751	ST	R751DRJ	16761	HE	R761DRJ	16770	PS	S770RVU	16780	PS	S780RVU
16752	ST	R752DRJ	16762	HE	R762DRJ	16771	PS	S771RVU	16781	PS	S781RVU
16753	ST	R753DRJ	16763	HE	R763DRJ	16772	PS	S772RVU	16782	PS	S782RVU
16754	HE	R754DRJ									

16786-16800
Volvo Olympian — Alexander RL — B51/36F — 1996

16786	PS	P716GND	16790	PS	P720GND	16794	PS	P724GND	16798	PS	P728GND
16787	PS	P717GND	16791	PS	P721GND	16795	PS	P725GND	16799	PS	P729GND
16788	PS	P718GND	16792	PS	P722GND	16796	PS	P726GND	16800	PS	P730GND
16789	PS	P719GND	16793	PS	P723GND	16797	PS	P727GND			

16817-16827
Volvo Olympian YN2RC16V3 — Northern Counties Palatine — B47/29F — 1995

16817	HL	M817KRH	16819	HL	M819KRH	16824	HL	M224SVN	16826	HL	M226SVN
16818	HL	M818KRH	16823	HL	M223SVN	16825	HL	M225SVN	16827	HL	M227SVN

16831-16840
Volvo Olympian — Alexander RL — B51/36F — 1998

16831	SC	R831OVN	16834	SC	R834OVN	16837	SC	R837OVN	16839	SC	R839OVN
16832	SC	R832OVN	16835	SC	R835OVN	16838	SC	R838OVN	16840	SC	R640OVN
16833	SC	R833OVN	16836	SC	R836OVN						

The Alexander RL-bodied Olympian was supplied in two lengths, the longer version being identified by a half bay inserted in the centre in similar fashion to the longer Routemasters. Manchester is the location of this view of 16757, R757DRJ. *Malcolm Flynn*

Several of the early Trident buses are now employed on *Park & Ride* duties in Cambridge. The majority carry a colour for their specific route, though 17053, T653KPU, seen here heading for Newmarket Road, has a cream and fawn scheme for use on any of the routes. *Mark Doggett*

16846-16866   Volvo Olympian YN2RC16V3   Alexander RL   B47/32F   1995

16846	CJ	M490ASW	16852	DS	N852VHH	16857	GS	N857VHH	16862	KK	N862VHH
16847	CJ	M491ASW	16853	DS	N853VHH	16858	GS	N858VHH	16863	KK	N863VHH
16848	DE	M492ASW	16854	DS	N854VHH	16859	CC	N859VHH	16864	KK	N864VHH
16849	DE	N849VHH	16855	GS	N855VHH	16860	GS	N860VHH	16865	KK	N865VHH
16850	GS	N850VHH	16856	GS	N856VHH	16861	CC	N861VHH	16866	KK	N866VHH
16851	GS	N851VHH									

17001-17098   Dennis Trident 10.5m   Alexander ALX400 4.2m   N51/22D*   1999   *many now N51/26F

17001	T	S801BWC	17026	HL	S826BWC	17050	CB	T650KPU	17075	LS	T675KPU
17002	EX	S802BWC	17027	HL	S827BWC	17051	CB	T651KPU	17076	CB	T676KPU
17003	EX	S803BWC	17028	HL	S828BWC	17052	CB	T652KPU	17077	LS	T677KPU
17004	EX	S804BWC	17029	HL	S829BWC	17053	CB	T653KPU	17078	CB	T678KPU
17005	EX	S805BWC	17030	HL	S830BWC	17054	CB	T654KPU	17079	CB	T679KPU
17006	EX	S806BWC	17031	HL	S831BWC	17055	CB	T655KPU	17080	BK	T680KPU
17007	CB	S807BWC	17032	HL	S832BWC	17056	CB	T656KPU	17081	U	T681KPU
17008	CB	S808BWC	17033	HL	S833BWC	17057	CB	T657KPU	17082	U	T682KPU
17009	CB	S809BWC	17034	HL	S834BWC	17058	CB	T658KPU	17083	U	T683KPU
17010	CB	S810BWC	17035	HL	S835BWC	17059	CB	T659KPU	17084	U	T684KPU
17011	CB	S811BWC	17036	CB	S836BWC	17060	T	T660KPU	17085	U	T685KPU
17012	ME	S812BWC	17037	CB	S837BWC	17061	T	T661KPU	17086	U	T686KPU
17013	ME	S813BWC	17038	CB	S838BWC	17062	U	T662KPU	17087	U	T687KPU
17014	ME	S814BWC	17039	BK	S839BWC	17063	BK	T663KPU	17088	U	T688KPU
17015	ME	S815BWC	17040	U	T640KPU	17064	BK	T664KPU	17089	U	T689KPU
17016	ME	S816BWC	17041	U	T641KPU	17065	BK	T665KPU	17090	U	T690KPU
17017	ME	S817BWC	17042	U	T642KPU	17066	LS	T699KVX	17091	U	T691KPU
17018	ME	S818BWC	17043	U	T643KPU	17067	AR	T667KPU	17092	U	T692KPU
17019	ME	S819BWC	17044	U	T644KPU	17068	AR	T668KPU	17093	U	T693KPU
17020	ME	S820BWC	17045	U	T645KPU	17069	LS	T669KPU	17094	U	T694KPU
17021	ME	S821BWC	17046	U	T646KPU	17070	AR	T670KPU	17095	U	T695KPU
17022	ME	S822BWC	17047	U	T647KPU	17071	LS	T671KPU	17096	U	T696KPU
17023	ME	S823BWC	17048	U	T648KPU	17072	LS	T672KPU	17097	U	T697KPU
17024	ME	S824BWC	17049	U	T649KPU	17073	LS	T673KPU	17098	U	T698KPU
17025	HL	S825BWC									

With only a few Olympians remaining in London, the Trident is now the standard bus for all Stagecoach double-deck services in the capital. Seen operating route 87, 17114, V114MEV, illustrates the latest colour scheme that omits the rear swept blue area, as it heads for Barking. *Laurie Rufus*

17099-17222   Dennis Trident 10.5m   Alexander ALX400 4.4m   N47/24D   1999-2000

17099	PD	VLT14	17130	PD	V130MEV	17161	PD	V161MEV	17192	NS	V192MEV
17100	PD	WLT491	17131	PD	V131MEV	17162	PD	V162MEV	17193	PD	V193MEV
17101	PD	WLT461	17132	NS	V132MEV	17163	PD	V163MEV	17194	NS	V194MEV
17102	PD	V102MEV	17133	PD	V133MEV	17164	PD	V164MEV	17195	PD	V195MEV
17103	PD	V103MEV	17134	PD	V134MEV	17165	U	V165MEV	17196	SD	V196MEV
17104	PD	V104MEV	17135	NS	V135MEV	17166	PD	V166MEV	17197	SD	V197MEV
17105	PD	V105MEV	17136	NS	V136MEV	17167	SD	V167MEV	17198	SD	V198MEV
17106	BK	V106MEV	17137	NS	V137MEV	17168	SD	V168MEV	17199	SD	V199MEV
17107	PD	V107MEV	17138	PD	V138MEV	17169	SD	V169MEV	17200	SD	V363OWC
17108	PD	V108MEV	17139	TL	V139MEV	17170	SD	V170MEV	17201	SD	V201MEV
17109	PD	V109MEV	17140	PD	V140MEV	17171	SD	V171MEV	17202	SD	V202MEV
17110	PD	V476KJN	17141	PD	V141MEV	17172	SD	V172MEV	17203	U	V203MEV
17111	SD	V477KJN	17142	PD	V142MEV	17173	SD	V173MEV	17204	U	V204MEV
17112	PD	V112MEV	17143	TL	V143MEV	17174	SD	V174MEV	17205	U	V205MEV
17113	PD	V113MEV	17144	NS	V144MEV	17175	SD	V175MEV	17206	U	V206MEV
17114	NS	V114MEV	17145	PD	V145MEV	17176	SD	V176MEV	17207	U	V207MEV
17115	PD	V115MEV	17146	NS	V146MEV	17177	SD	V177MEV	17208	U	V208MEV
17116	PD	V116MEV	17147	U	V147MEV	17178	SD	V178MEV	17209	U	V209MEV
17117	PD	V117MEV	17148	TL	V148MEV	17179	SD	V179MEV	17210	NS	V210MEV
17118	PD	V118MEV	17149	PD	V149MEV	17180	SD	W187CNO	17211	NS	V211MEV
17119	PD	V119MEV	17150	TL	V150MEV	17181	T	V181MEV	17212	NS	V212MEV
17120	PD	V120MEV	17151	TL	V151MEV	17182	T	V182MEV	17213	NS	V213MEV
17121	PD	V478KJN	17152	TL	V152MEV	17183	T	V183MEV	17214	PD	V214MEV
17122	PD	V122MEV	17153	TL	V153MEV	17184	T	V184MEV	17215	PD	V215MEV
17123	PD	V479KJN	17154	TL	V154MEV	17185	T	V185MEV	17216	PD	V216MEV
17124	NS	V124MEV	17155	TL	V155MEV	17186	T	V186MEV	17217	PD	V217MEV
17125	PD	V125MEV	17156	TL	V156MEV	17187	T	V362OWC	17218	PD	V218MEV
17126	PD	V126MEV	17157	TL	V157MEV	17188	T	V188MEV	17219	PD	V219MEV
17127	PD	V127MEV	17158	TL	V158MEV	17189	T	V189MEV	17220	PD	V220MEV
17128	PD	V128MEV	17159	PD	V159MEV	17190	T	V190MEV	17221	PD	V221MEV
17129	U	V129MEV	17160	TL	V160MEV	17191	T	V191MEV	17222	PD	V364OWC

17223-17260 — Dennis Trident 9.9m — Alexander ALX400 4.4m — N43/21D — 2000

17223	TL	X361NNO	17233	TL	X233NNO	17243	U	X243NNO	17252	U	X252NNO
17224	TL	X362NNO	17234	U	X234NNO	17244	SD	X369NNO	17253	U	X253NNO
17225	TL	X363NNO	17235	NS	X235NNO	17245	SD	X371NNO	17254	U	X254NNO
17226	TL	X364NNO	17236	NS	X236NNO	17246	SD	X246NNO	17255	U	X373NNO
17227	TL	X365NNO	17237	SD	X237NNO	17247	U	X247NNO	17256	U	X256NNO
17228	TL	X366NNO	17238	SD	X238NNO	17248	U	X248NNO	17257	U	X257NNO
17229	TL	X229NNO	17239	SD	X239NNO	17249	U	X249NNO	17258	U	X258NNO
17230	TB	X367NNO	17240	SD	X368NNO	17250	U	X372NNO	17259	U	X259NNO
17231	TL	X231NNO	17241	SD	X241NNO	17251	U	X251NNO	17260	U	WLT575
17232	TL	X232NNO	17242	SD	X242NNO						

17261-17358 — Dennis Trident 10.5m — Alexander ALX400 4.4m — N47/24D — 2000

17261	BK	X261NNO	17286	TB	X286NNO	17311	PD	X311NNO	17335	TB	X335NNO
17262	BK	X262NNO	17287	TB	X287NNO	17312	PD	X312NNO	17336	TB	X336NNO
17263	BK	X263NNO	17288	TB	X288NNO	17313	PD	X313NNO	17337	TB	X337NNO
17264	BK	X264NNO	17289	TB	X289NNO	17314	PD	X314NNO	17338	TB	X338NNO
17265	BK	X265NNO	17290	TB	X379NNO	17315	PD	X315NNO	17339	TB	X339NNO
17266	BK	X266NNO	17291	U	X291NNO	17316	PD	X385NNO	17340	TB	X395NNO
17267	BK	X267NNO	17292	NS	X292NNO	17317	TL	X317NNO	17341	TB	X341NNO
17268	NS	X268NNO	17293	NS	X293NNO	17318	TL	X386NNO	17342	TB	X342NNO
17269	BK	X269NNO	17294	NS	X294NNO	17319	TL	X319NNO	17343	TB	X343NNO
17270	BK	X376NNO	17295	NS	X295NNO	17320	TL	X387NNO	17344	TB	X344NNO
17271	BK	X271NNO	17296	NS	X296NNO	17321	TL	X388NNO	17345	TB	X396NNO
17272	BK	X272NNO	17297	NS	X297NNO	17322	TL	X322NNO	17346	TB	X346NNO
17273	BK	X273NNO	17298	NS	X298NNO	17323	TL	X389NNO	17347	TB	X347NNO
17274	BK	X274NNO	17299	NS	X299NNO	17324	TB	X324NNO	17348	TB	X348NNO
17275	BK	X377NNO	17300	NS	X381NNO	17325	TL	X391NNO	17349	TB	X349NNO
17276	PD	X276NNO	17301	NS	X301NNO	17326	TL	X326NNO	17350	TL	X397NNO
17277	PD	X277NNO	17302	PD	X302NNO	17327	TL	X327NNO	17351	TB	X351NNO
17278	PD	X278NNO	17303	PD	X303NNO	17328	TL	X392NNO	17352	TB	X352NNO
17279	TB	X279NNO	17304	PD	X304NNO	17329	TL	X329NNO	17353	TB	X353NNO
17280	TB	X378NNO	17305	PD	X382NNO	17330	TL	X393NNO	17354	TB	X354NNO
17281	TB	X281NNO	17306	PD	X383NNO	17331	TL	X331NNO	17355	TB	X398NNO
17282	TB	X282NNO	17307	PD	X307NNO	17332	TL	X332NNO	17356	TB	X356NNO
17283	TB	X283NNO	17308	PD	X308NNO	17333	TL	X394NNO	17357	TB	X357NNO
17284	TB	X284NNO	17309	PD	X309NNO	17334	TB	X334NNO	17358	TB	X358NNO
17285	TB	X285NNO	17310	PD	X384NNO						

17359-17435 — Dennis Trident 10.5m — Alexander ALX400 4.4m — N45/23D* — 2001 — *17402 is N45/27F

17359	BK	Y359NHK	17379	BK	Y379NHK	17398	SD	Y368NHK	17417	T	LX51FJE
17360	BK	Y508NHK	17380	BK	Y512NHK	17399	SD	LX51FHP	17418	T	LX51FJF
17361	BK	Y361NHK	17381	BK	Y381NHK	17400	SD	Y514NHK	17419	T	LX51FJJ
17362	BK	Y362NHK	17382	BK	Y382NHK	17401	SD	Y401NHK	17420	T	LX51FJK
17363	BK	Y363NHK	17383	BK	LX51FPF	17402	CA	Y103GHC	17421	T	LX51FJN
17364	BK	Y364NHK	17384	BK	Y384NHK	17403	SD	LX51FHS	17422	T	LX51FJO
17365	BK	Y365NHK	17385	BK	Y385NHK	17404	SD	Y404NHK	17423	T	LX51FJP
17366	BK	Y366NHK	17386	BK	Y386NHK	17405	SD	LX51FHT	17424	T	LX51FJV
17367	BK	Y367NHK	17387	BK	LX51FPC	17406	SD	Y517NHK	17425	T	LX51FJY
17368	BK	Y368NHK	17388	BK	Y388NHK	17407	SD	Y407NHK	17426	T	LX51FJZ
17369	BK	Y369NHK	17389	BK	Y389NHK	17408	SD	LX51FHU	17427	T	LX51FKA
17370	BK	Y509NHK	17390	BK	LX51FPD	17409	T	Y409NHK	17428	NS	LX51FKB
17371	BK	Y371NHK	17391	BK	Y391NHK	17410	T	LX51FHV	17429	NS	Y429NHK
17372	BK	Y372NHK	17392	BK	Y392NHK	17411	T	LX51FHW	17430	NS	LX51FKD
17373	BK	Y373NHK	17393	BK	Y393NHK	17412	T	LX51FHY	17431	NS	LX51FKE
17374	BK	Y374NHK	17394	BK	LX51FHN	17413	T	LX51FHZ	17432	NS	LX51FKF
17375	BK	Y511NHK	17395	SD	Y395NHK	17414	T	LX51FJA	17433	NS	LX51FKG
17376	BK	Y376NHK	17396	SD	LX51FHO	17415	T	LX51FJC	17434	NS	Y434NHK
17377	BK	Y377NHK	17397	SD	Y367NHK	17416	T	LX51FJD	17435	NS	LX51FKJ
17378	BK	Y378NHK									

17436-17534 — Dennis Trident 9.9m — Alexander ALX400 — N43/19D — 2001

17436	NS	Y436NHK	17461	NS	LX51FKW	17486	SD	LX51FME	17511	SD	LX51FNO
17437	NS	Y437NHK	17462	NS	Y462NHK	17487	U	LX51FMF	17512	SD	LX51FNP
17438	NS	Y438NHK	17463	NS	LX51FKZ	17488	U	LX51FMG	17513	SD	LX51FNR
17439	NS	LX51FKL	17464	NS	Y464NHK	17489	U	LX51FMJ	17514	SD	LX51FNS
17440	NS	Y522NHK	17465	NS	LX51FLB	17490	U	LX51FMK	17515	SD	LX51FNT
17441	NS	Y441NHK	17466	SD	LX51FLC	17491	U	LX51FML	17516	SD	LX51FNU
17442	NS	Y442NHK	17467	TL	LX51FLD	17492	U	LX51FMM	17517	SD	LX51FNV
17443	NS	Y443NHK	17468	TL	LX51FLE	17493	U	LX51FMO	17518	SD	LX51FNW
17444	NS	LX51FKO	17469	TL	LX51FLF	17494	U	LX51FMP	17519	SD	LX51FNY
17445	NS	Y445NHK	17470	TL	Y531NHK	17495	U	LX51FMU	17520	SD	LX51FNZ
17446	NS	Y446NHK	17471	TL	LX51FLG	17496	U	LX51FMV	17521	SD	LX51FOA
17447	NS	Y447NHK	17472	TL	LX51FLH	17497	U	LX51FMY	17522	SD	LX51FOC
17448	NS	Y448NHK	17473	TL	LX51FLJ	17498	U	LX51FMZ	17523	TL	LX51FOD
17449	NS	Y449NHK	17474	TL	LX51FLK	17499	U	LX51FNA	17524	TL	LX51FOF
17450	NS	Y524NHK	17475	TL	LX51FLL	17500	U	LX51FNC	17525	TL	LX51FOH
17451	NS	LX51FKR	17476	TL	LX51FLM	17501	U	LX51FND	17526	TL	LX51FOJ
17452	NS	Y452NHK	17477	TL	LX51FLN	17502	SD	LX51FNE	17527	TL	LX51FOK
17453	NS	Y453NHK	17478	TL	LX51FLP	17503	SD	LX51FNF	17528	TL	LX51FOM
17454	NS	Y454NHK	17479	TL	LX51FLR	17504	SD	LX51FNG	17529	TL	LX51FON
17455	NS	Y526NHK	17480	TL	LX51FLV	17505	SD	LX51FNH	17530	TL	LX51FOP
17456	NS	Y527NHK	17481	TL	LX51FLW	17506	SD	LX51FNJ	17531	TL	LX51FOT
17457	NS	LX51FKT	17482	TL	LX51FLZ	17507	SD	LX51FNK	17532	TL	LX51FOU
17458	NS	Y458NHK	17483	TL	LX51FMA	17508	SD	LX51FNL	17533	TL	LX51FOV
17459	NS	LX51FKU	17484	TL	LX51FMC	17509	SD	LX51FNM	17534	TL	LX51FPA
17460	NS	Y529NHK	17485	TL	LX51FMD	17510	SD	LX51FNN			

17535-17591 — Dennis Trident 9.9m — Alexander ALX400 — N43/21D — 2002

17535	U	LY02OAA	17550	BW	LY02OBB	17564	SD	LV52HDX	17578	TL	LV52HFL
17536	U	LY02OAB	17551	BW	LY02OBC	17565	SD	LV52HDY	17579	TL	LV52HFM
17537	BW	LY02OAC	17552	BW	LY02OBD	17566	SD	LV52HDZ	17580	TL	LV52HFN
17538	BW	LY02OAD	17553	BW	LY02OBE	17567	TL	LV52HEJ	17581	TL	LV52HFO
17539	BW	LY02OAE	17554	BW	LY02OBF	17568	TL	LV52HFU	17582	TL	LV52HFP
17540	BW	LY02OAG	17555	BW	LY02OBG	17569	TL	LV52HFA	17583	TL	LV52HFR
17541	BW	LY02OAN	17556	BW	LY02OBH	17570	TL	LV52HFB	17584	TL	LV52HFS
17542	BW	LY02OAO	17557	BW	LY02OBJ	17571	TL	LV52HFC	17585	TL	LV52HFT
17543	BW	LY02OAP	17558	BW	LY02OBK	17572	TL	LV52HFD	17586	TL	LV52HFU
17544	BW	LY02OAS	17559	BW	LY02OBL	17573	TL	LV52HFE	17587	TL	LV52HFW
17545	BW	LY02OAU	17560	BW	LY02OBM	17574	TL	LV52HFF	17588	TL	LV52HFX
17546	BW	LY02OAV	17561	TL	LV52USV	17575	TL	LV52HFH	17589	TL	LV52HFY
17547	BW	LY02OAW	17562	TL	LV52HDO	17576	TL	LV52HFJ	17590	TL	LV52HFZ
17548	BW	LY02OAX	17563	SD	LV52HDU	17577	TL	LV52HFK	17591	TL	LV52HGA
17549	BW	LY02OAZ									

17592-17611 — Dennis Trident 10.5m — Alexander ALX400 4.4m — N51/23D — 2002

17592	T	LV52HHA	17597	T	LV52HHF	17602	T	LV52HHM	17607	T	LV52HHS
17593	T	LV52HHB	17598	T	LV52HHG	17603	T	LV52HHN	17608	T	LV52HHT
17594	T	LV52HHC	17599	T	LV52HHJ	17604	T	LV52HHO	17609	T	LV52HHU
17595	T	LV52HHD	17600	T	LV52HHK	17605	T	LV52HHP	17610	T	LV52HHW
17596	T	LV52HHE	17601	T	LV52HHL	17606	T	LV52HHR	17611	T	LV52HHX

17612-17624 — Dennis Trident 10.5M — Alexander ALX400 4.4m — N51/28F — 1999

17612	HE	T612MNF	17616	ST	V616DJA	17619	ST	V619DJA	17622	ST	V622DJA
17613	HE	T613MNF	17617	PS	V617DJA	17620	ST	V620DJA	17623	ST	V623DJA
17614	PS	V614DJA	17618	PS	V618DJA	17621	ST	V621DJA	17624	ST	V624DJA
17615	PS	V615DJA									

17626-17647 — Dennis Trident 10.5M — Alexander ALX400 4.4m — N51/28F — 2000

17626	HE	W626RND	17632	HE	W632RND	17637	PS	W637RND	17643	HE	W643RND
17627	HE	W627RND	17633	HE	W633RND	17638	ST	W638RND	17644	HE	W644RND
17628	HE	W628RND	17634	HE	W634RND	17639	ST	W639RND	17645	HE	W645RND
17629	ST	W629RND	17635	ST	W635RND	17641	HE	W641RND	17646	HE	W646RND
17631	HE	W631RND	17636	ST	W636RND	17642	HE	W642RND	17647	HE	W647RND

To identify the shorter 9.9m version of the Trident an 's' suffix is displayed on this type of bus. Pictured in Sidcup while operating route 160, 17578, LV52HFL, illustrates the modification. Buses operating in Fife use similar additions to their numbers to show depot allocations. *Laurie Rufus*

17651-17672 | Dennis Trident 10.5m | Alexander ALX400 4.4m | N51/29F | 1999

17651	PS	V151DFT	17657	PS	V157DFT	17663	PS	V163DFT	17668	PS	V168DFT
17652	PS	V152DFT	17658	PS	V158DFT	17664	PS	V164DFT	17669	PS	V169DFT
17653	PS	V153DFT	17659	PS	V159DFT	17665	PS	V165DFT	17670	PS	V170DFT
17654	PS	V154DFT	17660	PS	V160DFT	17666	PS	V166DFT	17671	PS	V171DFT
17655	PS	V155DFT	17661	PS	V161DFT	17667	PS	V167DFT	17672	PS	V172DFT
17656	PS	V156DFT	17662	PS	V162DFT						

17673-17688 | Dennis Trident 10.5m | Alexander ALX400 | N51/28F | 1999

17673	GY	T373FUG	17677	GY	T377FUG	17681	GY	V381EWE	17685	GY	V385EWE
17674	GY	T374FUG	17678	GY	V378EWE	17682	GY	V382EWE	17686	GY	T370FUG
17675	GY	T375FUG	17679	GY	V379EWE	17683	GY	V383EWE	17687	GY	T371FUG
17676	GY	T376FUG	17680	GY	V380EWE	17684	GY	V384EWE	17688	GY	T372FUG

17689	CA	X601VDY	Dennis Trident 10.5m	Alexander ALX400	N47/27F	2000
17690	CA	X602VDY	Dennis Trident 10.5m	Alexander ALX400	N47/27F	2000

17691-17697 | Dennis Trident 10.5m | Plaxton President 4.1m | N49/29F | 2000

17691	CB	X701JVV	17693	CB	X703JVV	17695	CB	X705JVV	17697	CB	X707JVV
17692	CB	X702JVV	17694	CB	X704JVV	17696	CB	X706JVV			

The provincial delivery for 2002 again returned to the lower 4.2 metre height version of the ALX400 body. While the whole batch was initially used in Manchester, three have subsequently been transferred to Cheltenham where they operate in an orange and red livery for the University of Gloucester's *campus to campus* service. Showing *Skyline* lettering is 17701, ML02RWO. *Skyline* is a network of services to Manchester International airport that has special fares for staff commuting to the airport. *Mark Doggett*

17701-17730 — Dennis Trident 10.5m — Alexander ALX400 4.2m — N51/28F — 2002

17701	PS	ML02RWO	17709	PS	ML02KCV	17717	PS	MK02EFW	17724	HE	MK02EGF
17702	PS	ML02RWU	17710	PS	MK02EHC	17718	PS	MK02EFX	17725	HE	MK02EGJ
17703	PS	ML02KCO	17711	PS	MK02EHD	17719	PS	MK02EFY	17726	HE	MK02EGU
17704	PS	ML02KNO	17712	PS	ML02RWJ	17720	PS	MK02EFZ	17727	HE	MK02EGV
17705	PS	ML02RWV	17713	PS	ML02RWK	17721	PS	MK02EGC	17728	CT	MK02EGX
17706	PS	ML02KCU	17714	PS	ML02RWN	17722	CT	MK02EGD	17729	CT	MK02EGY
17707	PS	ML02RWW	17715	PS	MK02EFU	17723	HE	MK02EGE	17730	PS	MK02EGZ
17708	PS	ML02RWX	17716	PS	MK02EFV						

17731	SD	LV52HHY	Dennis Trident 10.5m	Alexander ALX400	N51/27D	2002
17732	SD	LV52HHZ	Dennis Trident 10.5m	Alexander ALX400	N51/27D	2002
17733	SD	LV52HJA	Dennis Trident 10.5m	Alexander ALX400	N51/27D	2002
17734	EX	SK52USN	Dennis Trident 10.5m	Alexander ALX400	N47/28F	2002
17735	EX	SK52USO	Dennis Trident 10.5m	Alexander ALX400	N47/28F	2002
17736	EX	SK52USP	Dennis Trident 10.5m	Alexander ALX400	N47/28F	2002
17737	MD	YM52UOU	Dennis Trident 10.5m	Alexander ALX400	N47/27F	2002
17738	MD	YM52UOV	Dennis Trident 10.5m	Alexander ALX400	N47/27F	2002
17739	MD	YM52UOW	Dennis Trident 10.5m	Alexander ALX400	N47/27F	2002

Going down the Strand is Trident 17785, LX03BVY, from a large batch delivered into London in 2003. It dates from the short period of TransBus' existence during which badging and registration of vehicles was rather inconsitent. *Gerry Mead*

17740-17854

TransBus Trident 10.5m TransBus ALX400 4.4m N51/27D 2003

17740	SD	LY52ZDX	17769	SD	LX03BVE	17798	T	LX03BWM	17827	T	LX03BYA
17741	SD	LY52ZDZ	17770	SD	LX03BVF	17799	T	LX03BWN	17828	T	LX03BYB
17742	SD	LY52ZFA	17771	SD	LX03BVG	17800	T	LX03BWP	17829	T	LX03BYC
17743	SD	LY52ZFB	17772	SD	LX03BVH	17801	T	LX03BWU	17830	T	LX03BYD
17744	SD	LY52ZFC	17773	SD	LX03BVJ	17802	T	LX03BWV	17831	T	LX03BYF
17745	SD	LY52ZFD	17774	SD	LX03BVK	17803	T	LX03BWW	17832	T	LX03BYG
17746	SD	LY52ZFE	17775	SD	LX03BVL	17804	T	LX03BWY	17833	T	LX03BYH
17747	SD	LY52ZFF	17776	SD	LX03BVM	17805	T	LX03BWZ	17834	U	LX03BYJ
17748	SD	LY52ZFG	17777	SD	LX03BVN	17806	T	LX03BXA	17835	U	LX03BYL
17749	SD	LY52ZFH	17778	SD	LX03BVP	17807	T	LX03BXB	17836	U	LX03BYM
17750	BW	LX03BTE	17779	T	LX03BVR	17808	T	LX03BXC	17837	U	LX03BYN
17751	BW	LX03BTF	17780	T	LX03BVS	17809	T	LX03BXD	17838	U	LX03BYP
17752	BW	LX03BTU	17781	T	LX03BVT	17810	T	LX03BXE	17839	U	LX03BYR
17753	BW	LX03BTV	17782	BW	LX03BVU	17811	T	LX03BXF	17840	U	LX03BYS
17754	BW	LX03BTY	17783	BW	LX03BVV	17812	T	LX03BXG	17841	U	LX03BYT
17755	BW	LX03BTZ	17784	BW	LX03BVW	17813	T	LX03BXH	17842	U	LX03BYU
17756	BW	LX03BUA	17785	BW	LX03BVY	17814	T	LX03BXJ	17843	U	LX03BYV
17757	BW	LX03BUE	17786	BW	LX03BVZ	17815	T	LX03BXK	17844	U	LX03BYW
17758	SD	LX03BUF	17787	BW	LX03BWA	17816	T	LX03BXL	17845	U	LX03BYY
17759	SD	LX03BUH	17788	T	LX03BWB	17817	T	LX03BXM	17846	U	LX03BYZ
17760	SD	LX03BUJ	17789	T	LX03BWC	17818	T	LX03BXN	17847	U	LX03BZA
17761	SD	LX03BUP	17790	T	LX03BWD	17819	T	LX03BXP	17848	U	LX03BZB
17762	SD	LX03BUU	17791	T	LX03BWE	17820	T	LX03BXR	17849	U	LX03BZC
17763	SD	LX03BUV	17792	T	LX03BWF	17821	T	LX03BXS	17850	U	LX03BZD
17764	SD	LX03BUW	17793	T	LX03BWG	17822	T	LX03BXU	17851	PD	LX03BZE
17765	SD	LX03BVA	17794	T	LX03BWH	17823	T	LX03BXV	17852	PD	LX03BZF
17766	SD	LX03BVB	17795	T	LX03BWJ	17824	T	LX03BXW	17853	PD	LX03BZG
17767	SD	LX03BVC	17796	T	LX03BWK	17825	T	LX03BXY	17854	BW	LX03BZH
17768	SD	LX03BVD	17797	T	LX03BWL	17826	T	LX03BXZ			

17855-17933 TransBus Trident 10.5m   TransBus ALX400 4.4m   N51/27D   2003

17855	BK	LX03NEU	17875	PD	LX03NFZ	17895	BK	LX03ORH	17915	BW	LX03OSL
17856	BK	LX03NEY	17876	PD	LX03NGE	17896	BK	LX03ORJ	17916	BW	LX03OSM
17857	BK	LX03NFA	17877	PD	LX03NGF	17897	BK	LX03ORK	17917	BW	LX03OSN
17858	BK	LX03NFC	17878	PD	LX03NGJ	17898	BK	LX03ORN	17918	BW	LX03OSP
17859	BK	LX03NFD	17879	BW	527CLT	17899	BK	LX03ORP	17919	BW	LX03OSR
17860	BK	LX03NFE	17880	BW	LX03NGU	17900	BK	LX03ORS	17920	BW	LX03OSU
17861	BK	LX03NFF	17881	BW	LX03NGV	17901	BK	LX03ORT	17921	BW	LX03OSV
17862	BK	LX03NFG	17882	BW	LX03NGY	17902	BK	LX03ORU	17922	BW	LX03OSW
17863	BK	LX03NFH	17883	BW	LX03NGZ	17903	U	LX03ORV	17923	BW	LX03OSY
17864	U	LX03NFJ	17884	BW	LX03NHA	17904	U	LX03ORW	17924	BW	LX03OSZ
17865	U	LX03NFK	17885	BW	LX03OPT	17905	PD	LX03ORY	17925	BW	LX03OTA
17866	PD	LX03NFL	17886	BW	LX03OPU	17906	PD	LX03ORZ	17926	BW	LX03OTB
17867	PD	LX03NFM	17887	BW	LX03OPV	17907	PD	LX03OSA	17927	BW	LX03OTC
17868	PD	LX03NFN	17888	BW	LX03OPW	17908	PD	LX03OSB	17928	BW	LX03OTD
17869	PD	LX03NFP	17889	U	LX03OPY	17909	BW	LX03OSC	17929	BW	LX03OTE
17870	PD	LX03NFR	17890	U	LX03OPZ	17910	BW	LX03OSD	17930	BW	LX03OTF
17871	PD	LX03NFT	17891	U	LX03ORA	17911	BW	LX03OSE	17931	BW	LX03OTG
17872	PD	LX03NFU	17892	BK	LX03ORC	17912	BW	LX03OSG	17932	BW	LX03OTH
17873	PD	LX03NFV	17893	BK	LX03ORF	17913	BW	LX03OSJ	17933	BW	LX03OTJ
17874	PD	LX03NFY	17894	BK	LX03ORG	17914	BW	LX03OSK			

17934-17975 TransBus Trident 10.5m   TransBus ALX400   N51/28D   2003

17934	PD	LX53JXU	17945	PD	LX53JYH	17956	PD	LX53JYW	17966	TB	LX53JZJ
17935	PD	LX53JXV	17946	PD	LX53JYJ	17957	PD	LX53JYY	17967	TB	LX53JZK
17936	PD	LX53JXW	17947	PD	LX53JYK	17958	PD	LX53JYZ	17968	TB	LX53JZL
17937	PD	LX53JXY	17948	PD	LX53JYL	17959	PD	LX53JZA	17969	TB	LX53JZM
17938	PD	LX53JYA	17949	PD	LX53JYN	17960	PD	LX53JZC	17970	TB	LX53JZN
17939	PD	LX53JYB	17950	PD	LX53JYO	17961	PD	LX53JZD	17971	TB	LX53JZO
17940	PD	LX53JYC	17951	PD	LX53JYP	17962	PD	LX53JZE	17972	TB	LX53JZP
17941	PD	LX53JYD	17952	PD	LX53JYR	17963	PD	LX53JZF	17973	TB	LX53JZR
17942	PD	LX53JYE	17953	PD	LX53JYT	17964	PD	LX53JZG	17974	TB	LX53JZT
17943	PD	LX53JYF	17954	PD	LX53JYU	17965	TB	LX53JZH	17975	TB	LX53JZU
17944	PD	LX53JYG	17955	PD	LX53JYV						

17976-17999 TransBus Trident 10.5m   TransBus ALX400   N43/21D   2004

17976	NS	LX53JZV	17982	NS	LX53KAU	17988	NS	LX53KBO	17994	NS	LX53KCC
17977	NS	LX53JZW	17983	NS	LX53KBE	17989	NS	LX53KBP	17995	NS	LX53KCE
17978	NS	LX53KAE	17984	NS	LX53KBF	17990	NS	LX53KBV	17996	NS	LX53KCF
17979	NS	LX53KAJ	17985	NS	LX53KBJ	17991	NS	LX53KBW	17997	NS	LX53KCG
17980	NS	LX53KAK	17986	NS	LX53KBK	17992	NS	LX53KBZ	17998	NS	LX53KCJ
17981	NS	LX53KAO	17987	NS	LX53KBN	17993	NS	LX53KCA	17999	NS	LX53KCK

18000-18020 TransBus Trident 10.5m   TransBus ALX400   N47/27F   2003

18000	KK	SF53BZG	18006	KK	SF53BYY	18011	AS	SF53BZD	18016	AS	SF53BYO
18001	KK	SF53BZH	18007	KK	SF53BYZ	18012	AS	SF53BZE	18017	AS	SF53BYP
18002	KK	SF53BZJ	18008	KK	SF53BZA	18013	AS	SF53BYL	18018	AS	SF53BYR
18003	KK	SF53BYV	18009	KK	SF53BZB	18014	AS	SF53BYM	18019	AS	SF53BYT
18004	KK	SF53BYW	18010	AS	SF53BZC	18015	AS	SF53BYN	18020	AS	SF53BYU
18005	KK	SF53BYZ									

18021-18060 TransBus Trident 10.5m   TransBus President   N47/27F   2003

18021	HE	MX53FLA	18031	HE	MX53FLL	18041	HE	MX53FMF	18051	OX	KX53VNB
18022	HE	MX53FLB	18032	HE	MX53FLM	18042	HE	MX53FMG	18052	OX	KX53VNC
18023	HE	MX53FLC	18033	HE	MX53FLN	18043	HE	MX53FMJ	18053	OX	KX53VND
18024	HE	MX53FLD	18034	HE	MX53FL	18044	HE	MX53FMK	18054	OX	KX53VNE
18025	HE	MX53FLE	18035	HE	MX53FLR	18045	HE	MX53FML	18055	OX	KX53VNF
18026	HE	MX53FLF	18036	HE	MX53FLV	18046	HE	MX53FMM	18056	OX	KX53VNG
18027	HE	MX53FLG	18037	HE	MX53FLZ	18047	HE	MX53FMP	18057	CB	AE53TZJ
18028	HE	MX53FLH	18038	HE	MX53FMA	18048	HE	MX53FMU	18058	CB	AE53TZK
18029	HE	MX53FLJ	18039	HE	MX53FMC	18049	HE	MX53FMV	18059	CB	AE53TZL
18030	HE	MX53FLK	18040	HE	MX53FME	18050	HE	MX53FMZ	18060	CB	AE53TZM

In 2003, forty of the Tridents were diverted to Wigan for bodying where TransBus assembled the President model. These were all intended for use in Manchester and Cambridge, where seven earlier low-height versions are allocated. A need for new buses for Brookes College in Oxford saw the diversion of six. These carry *brookesbus* names and a special livery as shown on 18054, KX53VNE. *Tony Wilson*

18061-18159   TransBus Trident 10.5m   TransBus ALX400 4.2m   N47/28F   2004

18061	TQ	WA04CPY	18086	CT	VX04GHK	18111	KG	KX04RVN	18136	WY	KN04XJL
18062	TQ	WA04CPZ	18087	CT	VX04GHN	18112	EX	WA04FNZ	18137	WY	KN04XJM
18063	TQ	WA04CRF	18088	CT	VX04GHU	18113	EX	WA04FOC	18138	CY	PX04DMZ
18064	TQ	WA04CRJ	18089	DE	VX04GHV	18114	EX	WA04FOD	18139	CY	PX04DND
18065	TQ	WA04CRK	18090	DE	VX04GHY	18115	EX	WA04FOF	18140	CY	PX04DNE
18066	TQ	WA04CRU	18091	DE	VX04GHZ	18116	EX	WA04FOH	18141	CY	PX04DNF
18067	TQ	WA04CRV	18092	AL	ST04DBV	18117	EX	WA04FOJ	18142	CY	PX04DNJ
18068	TQ	WA04CRX	18093	AL	ST04DBX	18118	EX	WA04FOK	18143	CY	PX04DNN
18069	TQ	WA04CRZ	18094	AL	ST04DBY	18119	EX	WA04FOM	18144	CY	PX04DNU
18070	TQ	WA04CSF	18095	AL	ST04DBZ	18120	WP	YN04KGA	18145	CY	PX04DNV
18071	TQ	WA04CSU	18096	AL	ST04DCE	18121	WP	YN04KGE	18146	CY	PX04DNY
18072	TQ	WA04CSV	18097	AL	ST04DCF	18122	WP	YN04KGF	18147	CY	PX04DOA
18073	TQ	WA04CSX	18098	AL	ST04DCU	18123	WP	YN04KGG	18148	CY	PX04DOH
18074	TQ	WA04CSY	18099	AL	ST04DCV	18124	WP	YN04KGJ	18149	CY	PX04DOJ
18075	TQ	WA04CSZ	18100	AL	ST04DCX	18125	CH	YN04KGK	18150	CY	PX04DOU
18076	PN	WA04CTE	18101	KG	KX04RDY	18126	CH	YN04KGP	18151	CY	PX04DPE
18077	PN	WA04CTF	18102	KG	KX04RDZ	18127	WY	KN04XJB	18152	CY	PX04DPF
18078	PN	WA04CTK	18103	KG	KX04REU	18128	WY	KN04XJC	18153	CY	PX04DPJ
18079	PN	WA04CTU	18104	KG	KX04RFE	18129	WY	KN04XJD	18154	CY	PX04DPN
18080	PN	WA04CTV	18105	KG	KX04RFF	18130	WY	KN04XJE	18155	CY	PX04DPU
18081	PN	WA04CTX	18106	KG	KX04RVF	18131	WY	KN04XJF	18156	CY	PX04DPV
18082	CT	VX04GHF	18107	KG	KX04RVJ	18132	WY	KN04XJG	18157	CY	PX54AWU
18083	CT	VX04GHG	18108	KG	KX04RVK	18133	WY	KN04XJH	18158	CY	PX54AWV
18084	CT	VX04GHH	18109	KG	KX04RVL	18134	WY	KN04XJJ	18159	CY	PX54AWW
18085	CT	VX04GHJ	18110	KG	KX04RVM	18135	WY	KN04XJK			

18160-18200   TransBus Trident 10.5m   TransBus ALX400 4.2m   N47/28F   2004-05

18160	CA	GX54DVA	18171	CA	GX54DVO	18181	OX	MX54LPE	18191	ST	MX54LPY
18161	CA	GX54DVB	18172	CA	GX54DVP	18182	ST	MX54LPF	18192	ST	MX54LPZ
18162	CA	GX54DVC	18173	CA	GX54DVR	18183	ST	MX54LPJ	18193	ST	MX54LRA
18163	CA	GX54DVF	18174	CA	GX54DVT	18184	ST	MX54LPK	18194	ST	MX54LRE
18164	CA	GX54DVG	18175	CA	GX54DVU	18185	ST	MX54LPL	18195	OXu	KN04ZXK
18165	CA	GX54DVH	18176	CA	GX54DVV	18186	ST	MX54LPN	18196	OXu	KN54ZXL
18166	CA	GX54DVJ	18177	OX	MX04XFV	18187	ST	MX54LPO	18197	OXu	KN54ZXM
18167	CA	GX54DVK	18178	OX	MX04XFW	18188	ST	MX54LPP	18198	OXu	KN54ZXO
18168	CA	GX54DVL	18179	OX	MX54LPA	18189	ST	MX54LPU	18199	OXu	KN54ZXP
18169	CA	GX54DVM	18180	OX	MX54LPC	18190	ST	MX54LPV	18200	CT	VN54NNK
18170	CA	GX54DVN									

Representing the 2004 delivery for London, 18228, LX04FXT, is seen at Hyde Park. A further batch is expected during March 2005 after which deliveries are intended for the provincial fleets. *Richard Godfrey*

18201-18265 TransBus Trident 10.5m TransBus ALX400 N51/28D 2004

18201	BW	LX04FWL	18218	BW	LX04FXF	18234	BW	LX04FYA	18250	T	LX04FYT
18202	BW	LX04FWM	18219	BW	LX04FXG	18235	BW	LX04FYB	18251	T	LX04FYU
18203	BW	LX04FWN	18220	BW	LX04FXH	18236	BW	LX04FYC	18252	T	LX04FYV
18204	BW	LX04FWP	18221	BW	LX04FXJ	18237	BW	LX04FYD	18253	T	LX04FYW
18205	BW	LX04FWR	18222	BW	LX04FXK	18238	BW	LX04FYE	18254	T	LX04FYY
18206	BW	LX04FWS	18223	BW	LX04FXL	18239	T	LX04FYF	18255	T	LX04FYZ
18207	BW	LX04FWT	18224	BW	LX04FXM	18240	T	LX04FYG	18256	T	LX04FZA
18208	BW	LX04FWU	18225	BW	LX04FXP	18241	T	LX04FYH	18257	U	LX04FZB
18209	BW	LX04FWV	18226	BW	LX04FXR	18242	T	LX04FYK	18258	U	LX04FZC
18210	BW	LX04FWW	18227	BW	LX04FXS	18243	T	LX04FYL	18259	U	LX04FZD
18211	BW	LX04FWY	18228	BW	LX04FXT	18244	T	LX04FYM	18260	U	LX04FZE
18212	BW	LX04FWZ	18229	BW	LX04FXU	18245	T	LX04FYN	18261	U	LX04FZF
18213	BW	LX04FXA	18230	BW	LX04FXV	18246	T	LX04FYP	18262	U	LX04FZG
18214	BW	LX04FXB	18231	BW	LX04FXW	18247	T	LX04FYR	18263	U	LX04FZH
18215	BW	LX04FXC	18232	BW	LX04FXY	18248	T	LX04FYS	18264	U	LX04FZJ
18216	BW	LX04FXD	18233	BW	LX04FXZ	18249	T	LX04FYT	18265	U	LX04FZK
18217	BW	LX04FXE									

18266-18277 Alexander-Dennis Trident 10.5m Alexander-Dennis ALX400 N51/28D 2005

18266	SD	LX05BVY	18269	SD	LX05BWB	18272	SD	LX05BWE	18275	SD	LX05BWH
18267	SD	LX05BVZ	18270	SD	LX05BWC	18273	SD	LX05BWF	18276	SD	LX05BWJ
18268	SD	LX05BWA	18271	SD	LX05BWD	18274	SD	LX05BWG	18277	SD	LX05BWK

Taking a break at North Woolwich is the last of the TransBus Tridents 18265, LX04FZK. Following a period of administration the TransBus operation was purchased by a group of Scottish businessmen in 2004 who have adopted the Alexander-Dennis name for their products. Until September 2004 buses continued to be built as TransBus with Alexander Dennis names being applied to both chassis and bodies built by the new company. *Laurie Rufus*

18301-18420

Alexander-Dennis Trident 10.5m Alexander-Dennis ALX400 N47/28F On order for provincial duties in 2005

18301	-	-	18331	-	-	18361	-	-	18391	-	-
18302	-	-	18332	-	-	18362	-	-	18392	-	-
18303	-	-	18333	-	-	18363	-	-	18393	-	-
18304	-	-	18334	-	-	18364	-	-	18394	-	-
18305	-	-	18335	-	-	18365	-	-	18395	-	-
18306	-	-	18336	-	-	18366	-	-	18396	-	-
18307	-	-	18337	-	-	18367	-	-	18397	-	-
18308	-	-	18338	-	-	18368	-	-	18398	-	-
18309	-	-	18339	-	-	18369	-	-	18399	-	-
18310	-	-	18340	-	-	18370	-	-	18400	-	-
18311	-	-	18341	-	-	18371	-	-	18401	-	-
18312	-	-	18342	-	-	18372	-	-	18402	-	-
18313	-	-	18343	-	-	18373	-	-	18403	-	-
18314	-	-	18344	-	-	18374	-	-	18404	-	-
18315	-	-	18345	-	-	18375	-	-	18405	-	-
18316	-	-	18346	-	-	18376	-	-	18406	-	-
18317	-	-	18347	-	-	18377	-	-	18407	-	-
18318	-	-	18348	-	-	18378	-	-	18408	-	-
18319	-	-	18349	-	-	18379	-	-	18409	-	-
18320	-	-	18350	-	-	18380	-	-	18410	-	-
18321	-	-	18351	-	-	18381	-	-	18411	-	-
18322	-	-	18352	-	-	18382	-	-	18412	-	-
18323	-	-	18353	-	-	18383	-	-	18413	-	-
18324	-	-	18354	-	-	18384	-	-	18414	-	-
18325	-	-	18355	-	-	18385	-	-	18415	-	-
18326	-	-	18356	-	-	18386	-	-	18416	-	-
18327	-	-	18357	-	-	18387	-	-	18417	-	-
18328	-	-	18358	-	-	18388	-	-	18418	-	-
18329	-	-	18359	-	-	18389	-	-	18419	-	-
18330	-	-	18360	-	-	18390	-	-	18420	-	-

Stagecoach operates several buses on special events or for promotional purposes. Two former Cambus Bristol FLF buses are retained and these carry full livery, as illustrated by 19952, JAH552D, seen in Peterborough. Early in 2005 one of the remaining Bristol VRs will join these ranks, though one VR at Carlisle continues in service. *Mark Doggett*

Special event vehicles - (initial owners shown and traditional vintage body codes used)

19909	CR	409DCD	Leyland Titan PD3/4	Northern Counties	FCO39/30F	1964	Southdown
19912	SUu	LCU112	Daimler CCG6 DD	Roe	H35/28R	1964	South Shields
19913	SEu	UF4813	Leyland Titan TD1	Brush	O27/24R	1929	Southdown
19935	ES	HGM335E	Bristol FLF6G	Eastern Coach Works	H44/34F	1967	Central SMT
19945	SEu	CD7045	Leyland N Special	Short (1928)	O27/24RO	1922	Southdown
19946	ADu	MFN946F	AEC Regent V 3D3RA	Park Royal	H40/32F	1967	East Kent
19952	KG	JAH552D	Bristol FLF6G	Eastern Coach Works	O38/32F	1966	Eastern Counties
19953	NN	JAH553D	Bristol FLF6G	Eastern Coach Works	L38/32F	1966	Eastern Counties
19959	WSu	UCS659	Albion Lowlander LR7	Alexander	H40/31F	1963	Western SMT
19982	WSu	RCS382	Leyland Titan PD3A/3	Alexander	L35/32RD	1961	Western SMT
19992	SW	LRV992	Leyland Titan PD2/12	Metro-Cammell	O33/26R	1956	Portsmouth

The 2005 Stagecoach Bus Handbook

While the principal body style for Stagecoach's Volvo B10M buses is the Alexander PS, orders were also placed with Northern Counties with their Paladin body. The few other body styles have mostly originated with the operations with which they were acquired. Seen in Oxford, 20004, R904XFC, features Paladin bodywork. These comprise six Alexander P-type, five East Lancs EL2000 and one each Duple 300 and Plaxton Derwent. *Richard Godfrey*

| 20001 | PTt | A14RBL | Volvo B10M-50 | | East Lancs (1995) | | BC53F | 1984 | | |

20004-20012

Volvo B10M-55 — Plaxton Paladin — B48F — 1998

20004	OX	R904XFC	20007	OX	R907XFC	20009	OX	R909XFC	20011	OX	R811XFC
20005	OX	R905XFC	20008	OX	R908XFC	20010	OX	R910XFC	20012	OX	R912XFC
20006	OX	R906XFC									

20101-20117

Volvo B10M-55 — Alexander PS — B49F — 1995

20101	SU	N201LTN	20106	SU	N206LTN	20110	AY	N210LTN	20114	AY	N214LTN
20102	SU	N202LTN	20107	DE	N207LTN	20111	PH	N211LTN	20115	SU	N215LTN
20103	SU	N203LTN	20108	AY	N208LTN	20112	AN	N212LTN	20116	SS	N216LTN
20104	SU	N204LTN	20109	CE	N209LTN	20113	PH	N213LTN	20117	SS	N217LTN
20105	SU	N205LTN									

20118-20135

Volvo B10M-55 — Alexander PS — B49F — 1996

20118	AN	P118XCN	20123	SS	P123XCN	20128	PR	P128XCN	20132	CY	P132XCN
20119	AY	P119XCN	20124	HP	P124XCN	20129	BA	P129XCN	20133	LL	P133XCN
20120	HP	P120XCN	20125	SS	P125XCN	20130	CY	P130XCN	20134	LL	P134XCN
20121	HP	P121XCN	20126	SS	P126XCN	20131	CY	P131XCN	20135	SS	P135XCN
20122	HP	P122XCN	20127	LL	P127XCN						

20141-20154

Volvo B10M-55 — Alexander PS — B49F — 1997-98

20141	AN	R641LSO	20145	DS	R645LSO	20149	SA	R649LSO	20152	DS	R652VSE
20142	AN	R642LSO	20146	DS	R646LSO	20150	AN	R650LSO	20153	AN	R653VSE
20143	AN	R643LSO	20147	GS	R647LSO	20151	AN	R651VSE	20154	AN	R654VSE
20144	AN	R644LSO	20148	GS	R648LSO						

To celebrate the centenary of Midland Red several buses in the area have received that operator's traditional colours. The Stagecoach example is 20202, M202LHP, Currently at Rugby and is seen here while at Showbus 2004. The vehicle features high-back seating and carries the then 'dual-purpose' livery, a class which disappeared in 1968 with the new Transport Act. *Richard Godfrey*

20171-20178   Volvo B10M-55   Alexander PS   B49F   1993

20171	PH	K571LTS	20173	PH	K573LTS	20175	PH	K575LTS	20177	PH	K577LTS
20172	PH	K572LTS	20174	PH	K574LTS	20176	PH	K576LTS	20178	PH	K578LTS

20189-20198   Volvo B10M-55   Alexander PS   BC48F   1994

20189	WI	M589OSO	20192	PH	M592OSO	20195	AN	M595OSO	20197	AN	M597OSO
20190	HS	M590OSO	20193	PH	M593OSO	20196	CJ	M596OSO	20198	SEu	M598OSO
20191	PH	M591OSO	20194	AN	M594OSO						

20201-20220   Volvo B10M-55   Alexander PS   BC48F*   1995   *20206-8 are B49F

20201	LE	M201LHP	20206	LE	N206TDU	20211	NU	N211TDU	20216	NU	N216TDU
20202	RU	M202LHP	20207	NU	N207TDU	20212	NU	N212TDU	20217	LE	P217HBD
20203	SMu	M203LHP	20208	NU	N208TDU	20213	NU	N213TDU	20218	LE	P218HBD
20204	SMu	M204LHP	20209	NU	M209LHP	20214	NU	N214TDU	20219	LE	P219HBD
20205	SMu	M205LHP	20210	NU	M210LHP	20215	NU	N215TDU	20220	LE	P220HBD

20221-20228   Volvo B10M-55   Alexander PS   B49F   1997-98

20221	RU	R221CRW	20224	RU	R224CRW	20226	NU	R226CRW	20228	OX	R228CRW
20223	RU	R223CRW	20225	RU	R225CRW	20227	NU	R227CRW			

20243-20252   Volvo B10M-55   Northern Counties Paladin   B48F   1995

20243	SC	M543SPY	20246	SC	M546SPY	20249	SC	M549SPY	20251	SC	M551SPY
20244	SC	M544SPY	20247	SC	M547SPY	20250	SC	M550SPY	20252	SC	M552SPY
20245	SC	M545SPY	20248	SC	M548SPY						

Over six hundred of Stagecoach's early standard bus, the Alexander PS-bodied Volvo, are currently in use, with a further 120 that carry the Paladin body. Pictured in Matlock in June 2004, 20418, H618ACK, is seen heading for Chesterfield. Unusually, this vehicle was not new to the fleet, having been acquired with the Burnley and Pendle company. *Bob Downham*

20253	SC	R653RPY	Volvo B10M-55	Northern Counties Paladin	B48F	1998
20254	SC	R654RPY	Volvo B10M-55	Northern Counties Paladin	B48F	1998
20255	SC	R655RPY	Volvo B10M-55	Northern Counties Paladin	B48F	1998
20256	HP	R556RPY	Volvo B10M-55	Plaxton Paladin	B48F	1998
20257	HP	R557RPY	Volvo B10M-55	Plaxton Paladin	B48F	1998
20258	HP	R558RPY	Volvo B10M-55	Plaxton Paladin	B48F	1998
20261	DA	N551VDC	Volvo B10M-55	Alexander PS	BC48F	1995
20262	SS	N552VDC	Volvo B10M-55	Alexander PS	BC48F	1995
20263	HP	N553VDC	Volvo B10M-55	Alexander PS	BC48F	1995
20264	HP	R554RPY	Volvo B10M-55	Plaxton Paladin	B48F	1998
20265	HP	R755RPY	Volvo B10M-55	Plaxton Paladin	B48F	1998

20267-20278

			Volvo B10M-55			Northern Counties Paladin		B48F	1995

20267	SC	M707KRH	20270	HP	M710KRH	20273	SS	M713KRH	20276	HL	M716KRH
20268	SC	M708KRH	20271	HP	M711KRH	20274	HL	M714KRH	20277	HL	M717KRH
20269	SC	M709KRH	20272	SC	M712KRH	20275	HL	M715KRH	20278	HL	M718KRH

20279-20286

Volvo B10M-55 — Northern Counties Paladin — B48F — 1998

20279	HL	R719RPY	20281	HL	R721RPY	20283	HL	R723RPY	20285	HL	R725RPY
20280	HL	R720RPY	20282	HL	R722RPY	20284	HL	R724RPY	20286	HL	R726RPY

20291-20300

Volvo B10M-55 — Northern Counties Paladin — B48F — 1995

20291	CE	M401SPY	20294	HP	M404SPY	20297	HP	M407SPY	20299	HP	M409SPY
20292	HP	M402SPY	20295	HP	M405SPY	20298	HP	M408SPY	20300	HP	M410SPY
20293	HP	M403SPY	20296	HP	M406SPY						

20301-20310 Volvo B10M-55 Alexander PS B49F 1994

20301	CJ	L301PSC	20304	SA	L304PSC	20307	SA	L307PSC	20309	GS	L309PSC
20302	SA	L302PSC	20305	SA	L305PSC	20308	DS	L308PSC	20310	SA	L310PSC
20303	SA	L303PSC	20306	SA	L306PSC						

20311	TH	M311YSC	Volvo B10M-55	Alexander PS	BC48F	1995
20312	CA	M312YSC	Volvo B10M-55	Alexander PS	BC48F	1995
20313	AR	M313YSC	Volvo B10M-55	Alexander PS	BC48F	1995

20314-20329 Volvo B10M-55 Alexander PS B49F* 1995-96 *20314/5 are BC48F

20314	SA	M314PKS	20318	GS	N318VMS	20322	SA	N322VMS	20326	DE	N326VMS
20315	SA	M315PKS	20319	GS	N319VMS	20323	GS	N323VMS	20327	GS	N327VMS
20316	CJ	N316VMS	20320	GS	N320VMS	20324	GS	N324VMS	20328	GS	N328VMS
20317	GS	N317VMS	20321	SA	N321VMS	20325	DE	N325VMS	20329	SA	N329VMS

20330-20342 Volvo B10M-55 Alexander PS B49F 1998

20330	DE	R330HFS	20334	GS	R334HFS	20337	DE	R337HFS	20340	CJ	R340HFS
20331	CJ	R331HFS	20335	GS	R335HFS	20338	DE	R338HFS	20341	GS	R341HFS
20332	GS	R332HFS	20336	GS	R336HFS	20339	DE	R339HFS	20342	AL	R342HFS

20347	EX	R807JDV	Volvo B10M-55	Alexander PS	B49F	1998

20350-20370 Volvo B10M-55 Alexander PS BC48F 1995

20350	AE	M750LAX	20356	MR	M756LAX	20361	MR	M761LAX	20366	MR	M766RAX
20351	AE	M751LAX	20357	MR	M757LAX	20362	MR	M762LAX	20367	MR	M767RAX
20352	AE	M752LAX	20358	AE	M758LAX	20363	MR	M763LAX	20368	MR	M768RAX
20353	AE	M753LAX	20359	MR	M759LAX	20364	WXu	M764LAX	20369	MR	M769RAX
20354	MR	M754LAX	20360	MR	M760LAX	20365	MR	M765RAX	20370	CN	M770RAX
20355	MR	M755LAX									

20385-20392 Volvo B10M-55 Alexander PS BC48F 1997-98

20385	BR	R785DHB	20388	BR	R788DHB	20390	BR	R790DHB	20392	CN	R792DHB
20387	BR	R787DHB	20389	BR	R789DHB	20391	BR	R791DHB			

20401-20406 Volvo B10M-55 Alexander P BC53F 1988

20401	LE	E61JFV	20403	CN	E63JFV	20405	CN	E65JFV	20406	PTt	E66JFV
20402	LE	E62JFV	20404	CN	E64JFV						

20407	CE	G67PFR	Volvo B10M-55	East Lancs EL2000	B51F	1990
20408	CE	G68PFR	Volvo B10M-55	East Lancs EL2000	B51F	1990

20411-20414 Volvo B10M-55 Alexander PS BC48F 1994

20411	CH	M411RRN	20412	WP	M412RRN	20413	WP	M413RRN	20414	WP	M414RRN

20417-20423 Volvo B10M-55 Alexander PS B51F 1991

20417	RU	H617ACK	20419	MD	H619ACK	20421	CN	H621ACK	20423	NU	H623ACK
20418	CH	H618ACK	20420	CN	H620ACK	20422	AY	H622ACK			

20424	CE	J24MCW	Volvo B10M-50	East Lancs EL2000	B45F	1992
20425	CE	J25MCW	Volvo B10M-50	East Lancs EL2000	B45F	1992
20430	PR	M230TBV	Volvo B10M-55	Alexander PS	BC48F	1995
20435	PR	M235TBV	Volvo B10M-55	Alexander PS	BC48F	1995
20436	ME	M236TBV	Volvo B10M-55	Alexander PS	BC48F	1995

20438-20447 Volvo B10M-55 Alexander PS BC48F 1994

20438	AR	L338KCK	20441	CH	L341KCK	20444	CH	L344KCK	20446	AT	L346KCK
20439	CH	L339KCK	20442	CH	L342KCK	20445	CA	L345KCK	20447	AT	L347KCK
20440	CH	L340KCK	20443	CH	L343KCK						

Currently allocated to Andover where it is one of six Volvo B10Ms based there, 20438, L338KCK is seen in Worthing while operating to Winchester. *Mark Lyons*

20451-20463

| | | | Volvo B10M-55 | | | Alexander PS | | | B48F | 1995 |

20451	ME	M451VCW	20455	PR	M455VCW	20458	KL	M458VCW	20461	AT	M461VCW
20452	ME	M452VCW	20456	KL	M456VCW	20459	KL	M459VCW	20462	AT	M462VCW
20454	PR	M454VCW	20457	KL	M457VCW	20460	WI	M460VCW	20463	ME	M463VCW

20473-20482

| | | | Volvo B10M-55 | | | Alexander PS | | | B49F | 1997 |

20473	PR	R473MCW	20476	PR	R476MCW	20479	EX	R479MCW	20481	EX	R481MCW
20474	PR	R474MCW	20477	BA	R477MCW	20480	TQ	R480MCW	20482	TQ	R482MCW
20475	PR	R475MCW	20478	BA	R478MCW						

20491-20499

| | | | Volvo B10M-55 | | | Alexander PS | | | BC48F | 1995 |

20491	WP	M601VHE	20494	WP	M604VHE	20496	CH	M606VHE	20498	MD	M608WET
20492	WP	M602VHE	20495	WP	M605VHE	20497	CH	M607VHE	20499	MD	M609WET
20493	WP	M603VHE									

20502	AY	R502KSA	Volvo B10M-55			Alexander PS			B49F	1997
20503	AY	R503KSA	Volvo B10M-55			Alexander PS			B49F	1997
20504	SR	R504KSA	Volvo B10M-55			Alexander PS			B49F	1997

20505-20512

| | | | Volvo B10M-55 | | | Alexander PS | | | BC48F | 1995 |

20505	AY	M488ASW	20507	KK	M871ASW	20510	AS	M481ASW	20512	DS	M468ASW
20506	KK	M869ASW	20509	KK	M469ASW	20511	AS	M483ASW			

20513	AY	R513KSA	Volvo B10M-55			Alexander PS			B49F	1997
20514	AY	R514KSA	Volvo B10M-55			Alexander PS			B49F	1997
20515	AS	R515KSA	Volvo B10M-55			Alexander PS			B49F	1997

20516-20526

| | | | Volvo B10M-55 | | | Alexander PS | | | B49F | 1998 |

20516	CE	R516VSE	20518	AY	R518VSE	20521	SR	R521VSE	20524	AA	R524VSE
20517	AY	R517VSE	20519	SR	R519VSE	20522	SR	R522VSE	20526	AA	R526VSE

Two of the five East Lancs-bodied B10M buses now carry Magic Bus livery. Pictured in Ayr in August 2004, 20424, J24MCW was transferred to Carlisle in January 2005 as a replacement for one of the flood-damaged buses. *Bob Downham*

20530-20560

Volvo B10M-55   Alexander PS   B49F   1997

20530	CC	P530ESA	20538	AA	P538ESA	20546	ME	P546ESA	20553	SS	P553ESA
20531	CC	P531ESA	20539	AA	P539ESA	20547	ME	P547ESA	20554	SC	P554ESA
20532	AS	P532ESA	20540	ME	P540ESA	20548	AY	P548ESA	20556	AS	P556ESA
20533	CC	P533ESA	20541	LE	P541ESA	20549	AY	P549ESA	20557	SMu	P557ESA
20534	CC	P534ESA	20542	OX	P542ESA	20550	HP	P550ESA	20558	LE	P558ESA
20535	CC	P535ESA	20543	OX	P543ESA	20551	SS	P551ESA	20559	LE	P559ESA
20536	AS	P536ESA	20544	ME	P544ESA	20552	SS	P552ESA	20560	LE	P560ESA
20537	AA	P537ESA	20545	ME	P545ESA						

20565-20594

Volvo B10M-55   Alexander PS   BC48F   1995

20565	AY	M480ASW	20573	CC	M473ASW	20581	AY	M484ASW	20588	KK	M788PRS
20566	AY	M486ASW	20574	CC	M474ASW	20582	AY	M872ASW	20589	KK	M789PRS
20567	AY	M487ASW	20575	CC	M475ASW	20583	DS	M466ASW	20590	KK	M790PRS
20568	AS	M489ASW	20576	CC	M476ASW	20584	AY	M784PRS	20591	CC	M791PRS
20569	AS	M482ASW	20577	CC	M477ASW	20585	SR	M785PRS	20592	CE	M792PRS
20570	CC	M470ASW	20578	CC	M478ASW	20586	KK	M786PRS	20593	AY	M793PRS
20571	DS	M471ASW	20579	KK	M479ASW	20587	AY	M787PRS	20594	AY	M467ASW
20572	CC	M472ASW	20580	AY	M870ASW						

20595	AA	R595LSO	Volvo B10M-55	Alexander PS	B49F	1997
20596	AA	R596LSO	Volvo B10M-55	Alexander PS	B49F	1997
20597	BQ	WLT774	Volvo B10M-56	Duple 300	B53F	1988	A1 Service, 1995
20599	BQ	WLT439	Volvo B10M-55	Plaxton Derwent II	B55F	1990	A1 Service, 1995

20601-20605

Volvo B10M-55   Northern Counties Paladin   BC49F   1994

20601	CR	L601VCD	20603	CR	L603VCD	20604	CR	L424TJK	20605	CR	L425TJK
20602	CR	L602VCD									

Basingstoke-based 20668, M668ECD, is a Northen Counties- bodied Paladin. In 1998 Northern Counties entered Plaxton owenership but production continued with no significant changes until the model was dropped with last of the type assembled in Scarborough. *Mark Lyons*

20606-20645   Volvo B10M-55   Alexander PS   BC48F   1994-95

20606	AT	L426TJK	20616	EX	L616TDY	20626	LS	L626TDY	20636	DO	M636BCD
20607	WI	L427TJK	20617	AR	L617TDY	20627	LS	L627TDY	20637	DO	M637BCD
20608	CE	L608TDY	20618	AT	L618TDY	20628	WI	L628TDY	20638	DO	M638BCD
20609	TH	L609TDY	20619	CA	L619TDY	20629	CR	L629TDY	20639	DO	M639BCD
20610	PM	M610APN	20620	HS	L620TDY	20630	EX	L630TDY	20640	DO	N640LPN
20611	PM	M611APN	20621	EX	L621TDY	20631	AR	L631TDY	20641	HS	N641LPN
20612	HS	M612APN	20622	FO	L622TDY	20632	WI	L632TDY	20642	TH	N642LPN
20613	FO	M613APN	20623	CR	L623TDY	20633	DO	L633TDY	20643	LS	N643LPN
20614	HS	M614APN	20624	FO	L624TDY	20634	WI	L634TDY	20644	CA	N644LPN
20615	AR	M615APN	20625	FO	L625TDY	20635	AT	L635TDY	20645	AD	N645LPN

20646	HS	R646HCD	Volvo B10M-55	Plaxton Paladin	B48F	1998
20647	HS	R647HCD	Volvo B10M-55	Plaxton Paladin	B48F	1998
20648	CR	R648HCD	Volvo B10M-55	Plaxton Paladin	B48F	1998
20649	SEu	R649HCD	Volvo B10M-55	Plaxton Paladin	B48F	1998
20650	HS	M650BCD	Volvo B10M-55	Alexander PS	BC48F	1995
20651	EX	M651BCD	Volvo B10M-55	Alexander PS	BC48F	1995
20652	LS	M652BCD	Volvo B10M-55	Alexander PS	BC48F	1995
20653	HE	R653HCD	Volvo B10M-55	Plaxton Paladin	B48F	1998
20654	HS	R654HCD	Volvo B10M-55	Plaxton Paladin	B48F	1998
20659	AD	K789DAO	Volvo B10M-55	Alexander PS	BC48F	1993
20660	CA	K790DAO	Volvo B10M-55	Alexander PS	BC48F	1993
20661	CH	K791DAO	Volvo B10M-55	Alexander PS	BC48F	1993

20662-20670   Volvo B10M-55   Northern Counties Paladin   BC47F   1995

20662	CR	M662ECD	20664	CR	M664ECD	20667	CR	M667ECD	20669	BE	M669ECD
20663	CR	M663ECD	20665	WI	M665ECD	20668	BE	M668ECD	20670	BE	M670ECD

20674-20680   Volvo B10M-55   Plaxton Paladin   B48F   1998

20674	HE	R674HCD	20676	HS	R676HCD	20678	HS	R678HCD	20680	HS	R680HCD
20675	HS	R675HCD	20677	HE	R677HCD	20679	HS	R679HCD			

20681-20689 — Volvo B10M-55 — Alexander PS — BC48F — 1995

20681	SN	N401LDF	20684	SN	N404LDF	20686	SN	N406LDF	20688	SN	N408LDF
20682	SN	N402LDF	20685	SN	N405LDF	20687	SN	N407LDF	20689	SN	N409LDF
20683	SN	N403LDF									

20694-20698 — Volvo B10M-55 — Alexander PS — BC48F — 1995

20694	OX	P319EFL	20696	HP	P316EFL	20697	MR	P317EFL	20698	BR	P318EFL
20695	HP	P315EFL									

20699-20788 — Volvo B10M-55 — Alexander PS — B49F* — 1992-93 — *20772-788 are BC48F

20699	KL	K699ERM	20721	LL	K721DAO	20744	CH	K744DAO	20767	LL	K767DAO
20700	LL	K700DAO	20722	SS	K722DAO	20745	CEw	K745DAO	20768	LL	K768DAO
20701	LL	K701DAO	20723	SS	K723DAO	20746	CE	K746DAO	20769	LL	K769DAO
20702	LL	K702DAO	20724	SS	K724DAO	20748	BA	K748DAO	20770	LL	K770DAO
20703	SS	K703DAO	20725	BA	K725DAO	20749	BA	K749DAO	20771	LL	K771DAO
20704	LE	K704ERM	20726	SS	K726DAO	20750	KL	K750DAO	20772	CEw	K772DAO
20705	KL	K705DAO	20727	CE	K727DAO	20751	LL	K751DAO	20773	CEw	K773DAO
20706	MR	K706DAO	20728	CEw	K728DAO	20752	LL	K752DAO	20774	KL	K774DAO
20707	BR	K707DAO	20729	SS	K729DAO	20753	LL	K753DAO	20775	KL	K775DAO
20708	MR	K708DAO	20730	SS	K730DAO	20754	BA	K754DAO	20776	KL	K776DAO
20709	BR	K709DAO	20731	CE	K731DAO	20755	BA	K755DAO	20777	LL	K777DAO
20710	NWu	K710DAO	20732	CEw	K732DAO	20756	BA	K756DAO	20778	BA	K778DAO
20711	KL	K711DAO	20733	PR	K733DAO	20757	BA	K757DAO	20779	LL	K779DAO
20712	NWu	K712DAO	20734	BA	K734DAO	20758	BA	K758DAO	20780	BA	K780DAO
20713	LL	K713DAO	20735	KL	K735DAO	20759	BA	K759DAO	20781	CEw	K781DAO
20714	SS	K714DAO	20736	CEw	K736DAO	20760	BA	K760DAO	20783	DS	K783DAO
20715	CE	K715DAO	20737	PR	K737DAO	20761	BA	K761DAO	20784	CE	K784DAO
20716	SS	K716DAO	20738	PR	K738DAO	20762	BA	K762DAO	20785	HL	K785DAO
20717	CEw	K717DAO	20739	CEw	K739DAO	20763	LL	K763DAO	20786	BA	K786DAO
20718	CE	K718DAO	20741	CE	K741DAO	20764	LL	K764DAO	20787	BA	K787DAO
20719	CEw	K719DAO	20742	CEw	K742DAO	20765	LL	K765DAO	20788	CEw	K788DAO
20720	CH	K720DAO	20743	PR	K743DAO	20766	CEw	K766DAO			

20789	CE	N789VRM	Volvo B10M-55	Alexander PS	BC48F	1995
20790	CE	N790VRM	Volvo B10M-55	Alexander PS	BC48F	1995
20793	ME	R793URM	Volvo B10M-55	Alexander PS	B51F	1998
20794	ME	R794URM	Volvo B10M-55	Alexander PS	B51F	1998
20795	ME	R795URM	Volvo B10M-55	Alexander PS	B51F	1998

20801-20868 — Volvo B10M-55 — Alexander PS — B49F — 1996

20801	TQ	N801DNE	20818	GR	N818DNE	20835	WG	P835FVU	20852	ST	P852GND
20802	TQ	N802DNE	20819	GR	P819GNC	20836	WG	P836GND	20853	ST	P853GND
20803	LE	N803DNE	20820	OX	P820GNC	20837	SC	P837GND	20854	ST	P854GND
20804	LE	N804DNE	20821	LE	P821FVU	20838	CE	P838GND	20855	ST	P855GND
20805	OX	N805DNE	20822	OX	P822FVU	20839	HP	P839GND	20856	ST	P856GND
20806	MR	N806DNE	20823	LE	P823FVU	20840	SS	P840GND	20857	ST	P857GND
20807	MR	N807DNE	20824	MR	P824FVU	20841	HP	P841GND	20858	ST	P858GND
20808	LE	N808DNE	20825	MR	P825FVU	20842	SS	P842GND	20859	ST	P859GND
20809	RU	N809DNE	20826	MR	P826FVU	20843	HP	P843GND	20860	PS	P860GND
20810	MR	N810DNE	20827	GR	P827FVU	20844	SC	P844GND	20861	PS	P861GND
20811	MR	N811DNE	20828	GR	P828FVU	20845	ST	P845GND	20862	PS	P862GND
20812	OX	N812DNE	20829	CE	P829FVU	20846	ST	P846GND	20863	PS	P863GND
20813	RU	N813DNE	20830	WG	P830FVU	20847	ST	P847GND	20864	PS	P864GND
20814	LE	N814DNE	20831	LS	P831FVU	20848	ST	P848GND	20865	PS	P865GND
20815	MR	N815DNE	20832	WG	P832FVU	20849	ST	P849GND	20866	PS	P866GND
20816	RU	N816DNE	20833	LS	P833FVU	20850	ST	P850GND	20867	CE	P867GND
20817	GR	N817DNE	20834	LS	P834FVU	20851	ST	P851GND	20868	PS	P868GND

20869-20894 — Volvo B10M-55 — Northern Counties Paladin — B48F* — 1997 — *20869-74/83-5/90/1 are BC47F

20869	CN	P869MNE	20876	ST	P876MNE	20882	ST	P882MNE	20889	CW	P889MNE
20870	CW	P870MNE	20877	ST	P877MNE	20883	PT	P883MNE	20890	PT	P890MNE
20871	PT	P871MNE	20878	ST	P878MNE	20884	PT	P884MNE	20891	PT	P891MNE
20872	PT	P872MNE	20879	CE	P879MNE	20885	PT	P885MNE	20892	PT	P892MNE
20873	PT	P873MNE	20880	ST	P880MNE	20886	CW	P886MNE	20893	ST	P893MNE
20874	CW	P874MNE	20881	CE	P881MNE	20887	CW	P887MNE	20894	CE	P894MNE
20875	CE	P875MNE									

Stockport-based 20996, R996XVM, is a notable Paladin, numerically being the last built. Assembled initially by Northern Counties, the late arrivals of the 120 of this type currently in the fleet were constructed after Henlys (the then owners of Plaxtons) acquired the Northern Counties Wigan facility. Shortly after the 1998 batch was delivered production at Wigan turned wholly double-deck. *Mark Doggett*

20895-20984 Volvo B10M-55 Alexander PS B49F 1997-98

20895	HE	R895XVM	20919	HE	R919XVM	20941	HE	R941XVM	20963	GP	R963XVM
20896	CE	R896XVM	20920	HE	R920XVM	20942	HE	R942XVM	20964	GP	R964XVM
20897	PS	R897XVM	20921	HE	R921XVM	20943	CE	R943XVM	20965	HE	R965XVM
20898	PS	R898XVM	20922	HE	R922XVM	20944	CE	R944XVM	20966	HE	R966XVM
20899	PS	R899XVM	20923	HE	R923XVM	20945	PS	R945XVM	20967	HE	R967XVM
20901	HE	R901XVM	20924	CE	R924XVM	20946	PS	R946XVM	20968	HE	R968XVM
20902	HE	R902XVM	20925	HE	R925XVM	20947	PS	R947XVM	20969	HE	R969XVM
20903	HE	R903XVM	20926	HE	R926XVM	20948	PS	R948XVM	20970	HE	R970XVM
20904	CE	R904XVM	20927	HE	R927XVM	20949	PS	R949XVM	20971	HE	R971XVM
20905	GP	R905XVM	20928	HE	R928XVM	20950	HE	R950XVM	20972	HE	R972XVM
20906	GP	R906XVM	20929	HE	R929XVM	20951	HE	R951XVM	20973	HE	R973XVM
20907	GP	R907XVM	20930	HE	R930XVM	20952	HE	R952XVM	20974	HE	R974XVM
20908	GP	R908XVM	20931	HE	R932XVM	20953	HE	R953XVM	20975	HE	R975XVM
20909	GP	R909XVM	20932	HE	R933XVM	20954	HE	R954XVM	20976	HE	R976XVM
20910	GP	R910XVM	20933	HE	R934XVM	20955	HE	R955XVM	20977	CE	R977XVM
20912	HE	R912XVM	20934	HE	R935XVM	20956	HE	R956XVM	20978	HE	R978XVM
20913	HE	R913XVM	20935	HE	R936XVM	20957	HE	R957XVM	20979	CE	R979XVM
20914	HE	R914XVM	20936	HE	R936XVM	20958	PS	R958XVM	20980	HE	R980XVM
20915	HE	R915XVM	20937	HE	R937XVM	20959	CE	R959XVM	20981	HE	R981XVM
20916	HE	R916XVM	20938	GP	R938XVM	20960	CE	R960XVM	20982	HE	R982XVM
20917	HE	R917XVM	20939	HE	R939XVM	20961	GP	R961XVM	20983	HE	R983XVM
20918	GP	R918XVM	20940	HE	R940XVM	20962	GP	R962XVM	20984	HE	R984XVM

20985-20996 Volvo B10M-55 Plaxton Paladin B48F 1998

20985	HE	R985XVM	20988	HE	R988XVM	20991	ST	R991XVM	20994	CE	R994XVM
20986	HE	R986XVM	20989	ST	R989XVM	20992	ST	R992XVM	20995	ST	R995XVM
20987	HE	R987XVM	20990	GP	R990XVM	20993	ST	R993XVM	20996	ST	R996XVM

The 21xxx series is allocated to rear-engined Volvo B10B buses, all but one of which operate in the north-east. All the Plaxton Verde-bodied examples are allocated to Stockton with 21034, L34HHN, shown here. In January 2005 following the floods, one of the pair of Alexander Striders was transferred to Carlisle. *Phillip Stephenson*

21001	CE	M901DRG	Volvo B10B			Alexander Strider		B51F	1994		
21002	SS	M902DRG	Volvo B10B			Alexander Strider		B51F	1994		

21031-21042 — Volvo B10B — Plaxton Verde — B52F — 1994

21031	SC	L31HHN	21034	SC	L34HHN	21037	SC	L37HHN	21040	SC	M40PVN
21032	SC	L32HHN	21035	SC	L35HHN	21038	SC	M38PVN	21041	SC	M41PVN
21033	SC	L33HHN	21036	SC	L36HHN	21039	SC	M39PVN	21042	SC	M42PVN

21051	AS	M151FGB	Volvo B10B		Wright Endurance	B51F	1994	A1 Service, 1995

21101-21105 — Volvo B10BLE — Northern Counties Prestige — N43F — 1997

21101	WA	P601JBU	21103	WA	P603JBU	21104	WA	P604JBU	21105	WA	P605JBU
21102	WA	P602JBU								

21136-21158 — Volvo B10BLE — Alexander ALX300 — N44F — 1997-98

21136	WA	R236KRG	21142	WA	R242KRG	21148	WA	R248KRG	21154	WA	R254KRG
21137	WA	R237KRG	21143	WA	R243KRG	21149	WA	R249KRG	21155	WA	R255KRG
21138	WA	R238KRG	21144	WA	R244KRG	21150	WA	R250KRG	21156	WA	R256KRG
21139	WA	R239KRG	21145	WA	R245KRG	21151	WA	R251KRG	21157	WA	R257KRG
21140	WA	R240KRG	21146	WA	R246KRG	21152	WA	R252KRG	21158	WA	R258KRG
21141	WA	R241KRG	21147	WA	R247KRG	21153	WA	R253KRG			

22004-22009 — MAN 18.220 — Alexander ALX300 — N42F — 2000-01

22004	CA	X604VDY	22006	CA	X606VDY	22008	CA	X948VAP	22009	CA	GX51PUJ
22005	CA	X605VDY	22007	CA	X607VDY						

The current full-length bus for Stagecoach is the MAN 18.220 fitted with the ALX300 body. Since 2002 all ALX300s have been built for Stagecoach alone with a further fifty expected during 2005. Allocated to Newcastle's Walkergate depot is 23012, NK03XJB, which is seen during the summer of 2004. *Richard Godfrey*

22011-22060   MAN 18.220   Alexander ALX300   N42F   2003

22011	WA	NK03XJA	22024	WA	NK03XJT	22037	SY	NK53KFA	22049	SY	NK53KFT
22012	WA	NK03XJB	22025	WA	NK03XJU	22038	SY	NK53KFC	22050	SY	NK53KFU
22013	WA	NK03XJC	22026	WA	NK03XJV	22039	SY	NK53KFD	22051	SY	NK53KFV
22014	WA	NK03XJD	22027	SY	NK03XJW	22040	SY	NK53KFE	22052	OX	KX53VNH
22015	WA	NK03XJE	22028	SY	NK03XJX	22041	SY	NK53KFF	22053	OX	KX53VNJ
22016	WA	NK03XJF	22029	SY	NK03XJY	22042	SY	NK53KFG	22054	OX	KX53VNK
22017	WA	NK03XJG	22030	SY	NK03XJZ	22043	SY	NK53KFJ	22055	HE	MX53FNA
22018	WA	NK03XJH	22031	SY	NK03XKA	22044	SY	NK53KFL	22056	HE	MX53FNB
22019	WA	NK03XJJ	22032	SY	NK03XKB	22045	SY	NK53KFN	22057	OX	KV53FAA
22020	WA	NK03XJL	22033	SY	NK03XKB	22046	SY	NK53KFO	22058	CB	KV53FAF
22021	WA	NK03XJM	22034	SY	NK53KDZ	22047	SY	NK53KFP	22059	CB	KV53FAJ
22022	WA	NK03XJN	22035	SY	NK53KEJ	22048	SY	NK53KFR	22060	CB	KV53FAK
22023	WA	NK03XJP	22036	SY	NK53KEU						

22061-22100   MAN 18.220   Alexander ALX300   N42F   2004

22061	SC	NK54BFE	22071	SY	NK54BFX	22081	SU	NK54BGZ	22091	PS	MX54LRY
22062	SC	NK54BFF	22072	SU	NK54BFY	22082	SU	NK54BHA	22092	PS	MX54LRZ
22063	SC	NK54BFJ	22073	SU	NK54BFZ	22083	PS	MX54LRF	22093	PS	MX54LSC
22064	SC	NK54BFL	22074	SU	NK54BGE	22084	PS	MX54LRJ	22094	PS	MX54LSD
22065	SC	NK54BFM	22075	SU	NK54BGF	22085	PS	MX54LRK	22095	PS	MX54LES
22066	SC	NK54BFN	22076	SU	NK54BGO	22086	PS	MX54LRL	22096	PS	MX54XLB
22067	SY	NK54BFO	22077	SU	NK54BGU	22087	PS	MX54LRN	22097	PS	MX54XLC
22068	SY	NK54BFP	22078	SU	NK54BGV	22088	PS	MX54LRO	22098	PS	MX54XLD
22069	SY	NK54BFU	22079	SU	NK54BGX	22089	PS	MX54LRU	22099	PS	MX54XLE
22070	SY	NK54BFV	22080	SU	NK54BGY	22090	PS	MX54LRV	22100	PS	MX54XLF

22101-22159 — MAN 18.220 — Alexander ALX300 — N42F — 1998

22101	ST	S101TRJ	22116	ST	S116TRJ	22131	ST	S131TRJ	22145	ST	S145TRJ
22102	ST	S102TRJ	22117	ST	S117TRJ	22132	ST	S132TRJ	22146	HE	S146TRJ
22103	ST	S103TRJ	22118	ST	S118TRJ	22133	ST	S133TRJ	22147	ST	S147TRJ
22104	ST	S104TRJ	22119	ST	S119TRJ	22134	HE	S134TRJ	22148	HE	S148TRJ
22105	ST	S105TRJ	22120	ST	S120TRJ	22135	HE	S135TRJ	22149	HE	S149TRJ
22106	ST	S106TRJ	22121	ST	S121TRJ	22136	HE	S136TRJ	22150	ST	S150TRJ
22107	HE	S107TRJ	22122	ST	S122TRJ	22137	HE	S137TRJ	22151	ST	S151TRJ
22108	HE	S108TRJ	22124	ST	S124TRJ	22138	HE	S138TRJ	22152	ST	S152TRJ
22109	AN	S109TRJ	22125	ST	S125TRJ	22139	HE	S139TRJ	22153	HE	S153TRJ
22110	AN	S110TRJ	22126	ST	S126TRJ	22140	HE	S140TRJ	22154	HE	S154TRJ
22112	AN	S112TRJ	22127	ST	S127TRJ	22141	ST	S141TRJ	22156	PS	S156TRJ
22113	PS	S113TRJ	22128	ST	S128TRJ	22142	ST	S142TRJ	22157	PS	S157TRJ
22114	ST	S114TRJ	22129	ST	S129TRJ	22143	ST	S143TRJ	22158	PS	S158TRJ
22115	ST	S115TRJ	22130	ST	S130TRJ	22144	ST	S144TRJ	22159	PS	S159TRJ

22160-22215 — MAN 18.220 — Alexander ALX300 — N42F — 1999

22160	PS	T160MVM	22178	PS	T178MVM	22191	AD	NDZ3021	22204	WA	T204TND
22161	PS	T161MVM	22179	PS	T179MVM	22192	AD	NDZ3022	22205	OX	T205TND
22162	PS	T162MVM	22180	ST	T180MVM	22193	WA	T193MVM	22206	WA	T206TND
22163	PS	T163MVM	22181	ST	T181MVM	22194	AD	NDZ3023	22207	OX	T207TND
22164	PS	T164MVM	22182	ST	T182MVM	22195	WA	T195MVM	22208	WA	T208TND
22165	PS	T165MVM	22183	ST	T183MVM	22196	WA	T196MVM	22209	OX	T209TND
22166	HE	T166MVM	22184	ST	T184MVM	22197	SY	T197MVM	22210	WA	T210TND
22167	HE	T167MVM	22185	HE	T185MVM	22198	SY	T198TND	22211	WA	T211TND
22168	HE	T168MVM	22186	HE	T186MVM	22199	SY	T199TND	22212	PS	T212TND
22169	ST	T169MVM	22187	HE	T187MVM	22201	SY	T201TND	22213	PS	T213TND
22172	WA	T172MVM	22188	ST	T188MVM	22202	WA	T202TND	22214	SY	T214TND
22173	ST	T173MVM	22189	ST	T189MVM	22203	OX	T203TND	22215	SY	T215TND
22174	WA	T174MVM	22190	SY	T190MVM						

22216-22246 — MAN 18.220 — Alexander ALX300 — N42F — 2000

22216	ST	X216BNE	22226	ST	X226BNE	22233	ST	X233BNE	22239	ST	X239BNE
22217	ST	X217BNE	22227	ST	X227BNE	22234	ST	X234BNE	22241	ST	X241ATD
22218	ST	X218BNE	22228	ST	X228BNE	22235	PS	X235BNE	22242	ST	X242ATD
22219	ST	X219BNE	22229	ST	X229BNE	22236	PS	X236BNE	22243	ST	X243ATD
22221	ST	X221BNE	22231	ST	X231BNE	22237	PS	X237BNE	22244	ST	X244ATD
22223	ST	X223BNE	22232	ST	X232BNE	22238	PS	X238BNE	22246	ST	X246ATD
22224	ST	X224BNE									

22252-22268 — MAN 18.220 — Alexander ALX300 — N47F — 1999

22252	CJ	V252ESX	22257	CJ	V257ESX	22261	CJ	V261ESX	22265	CJ	V265ESX
22253	CJ	V253ESX	22258	CJ	V258ESX	22262	CJ	V262ESX	22266	GS	V266ESX
22254	CJ	V254ESX	22259	CJ	V259ESX	22263	CJ	V263ESX	22267	GS	V267ESX
22255	CJ	V255ESX	22260	CJ	V260ESX	22264	CJ	V264ESX	22268	GS	V268ESX
22256	CJ	V256ESX									

22269-22279 — MAN 18.220 — Alexander ALX300 — N47F — 2000-01

22269	CJ	X269MTS	22273	CJ	X273MTS	22276	DE	X276MTS	22278	CB	SP51AMK
22271	CJ	X271MTS	22274	CJ	X274MTS	22277	PH	X277MTS	22279	OX	SP51AMO
22272	CJ	X272MTS									

22301-22340 — MAN 18.220 — Alexander ALX300 — N42F — 2001

22301	CB	AE51RXW	22311	CB	AE51RYH	22321	CB	AE51RYX	22331	CB	AE51RZK
22302	CB	AE51RXX	22312	CB	AE51RYK	22322	CB	AE51RYY	22332	CB	AE51RZL
22303	CB	AE51RXY	22313	CB	AE51RYN	22323	CB	AE51RYZ	22333	CB	AE51RZM
22304	CB	AE51RXZ	22314	CB	AE51RYO	22324	CB	AE51RZA	22334	CB	AE51RZN
22305	CB	AE51RYA	22315	CB	AE51RYP	22325	CB	AE51RZB	22335	CB	AE51RZO
22306	CB	AE51RYB	22316	CB	AE51RYR	22326	CB	AE51RZC	22336	CB	AE51RZP
22307	CB	AE51RYC	22317	CB	AE51RYT	22327	CB	AE51RZF	22337	CB	AE51RZR
22308	CB	AE51RYD	22318	CB	AE51RYU	22328	CB	AE51RZG	22338	CB	AE51RZS
22309	CB	AE51RYF	22319	CB	AE51RYV	22329	CB	AE51RZH	22339	CB	AE51RZT
22310	CB	AE51RYG	22320	CB	AE51RYW	22330	CB	AE51RZJ	22340	CB	AE51RZU

Twenty-three MAN buses are allocated to the Fife operation with 22266, V266ESX, seen with route branding for the X1 that links Leslie with Kirkcaldy. It is seen passing through Glenrothes in June 2004. *Bob Downham*

22341-22390

22341-22390			MAN 18.220			Alexander ALX300			N42F	On order for 2005		
22341	-	-	22354	-	-	22367	-	-	22379	-	-
22342	-	-	22355	-	-	22368	-	-	22380	-	-
22343	-	-	22356	-	-	22369	-	-	22381	-	-
22344	-	-	22357	-	-	22370	-	-	22382	-	-
22345	-	-	22358	-	-	22371	-	-	22383	-	-
22346	-	-	22359	-	-	22372	-	-	22384	-	-
22347	-	-	22360	-	-	22373	-	-	22385	-	-
22348	-	-	22361	-	-	22374	-	-	22386	-	-
22349	-	-	22362	-	-	22375	-	-	22387	-	-
22350	-	-	22363	-	-	22376	-	-	22388	-	-
22351	-	-	22364	-	-	22377	-	-	22389	-	-
22352	-	-	22365	-	-	22378	-	-	22390	-	-
22353	-	-	22366	-	-						

22451-22495

MAN 18.220   Alexander ALX300   N45F   1999

22451	SC	S451OFT	22463	SY	T463BNL	22474	SY	T474BNL	22485	SY	T485BNL
22452	SC	S452OFT	22464	SY	T464BNL	22475	SY	T475BNL	22486	SU	T486BNL
22453	SY	S453OFT	22465	SY	T465BNL	22476	SY	T476BNL	22487	SU	T487BNL
22454	SC	S454OFT	22466	SY	T466BNL	22477	SY	T477BNL	22488	SU	T488BNL
22455	SC	S455OFT	22467	SY	T467BNL	22478	SY	T478BNL	22489	SU	T489BNL
22456	SC	S456OFT	22468	SY	T468BNL	22479	SY	T479BNL	22490	SY	T490BNL
22457	CB	S457OFT	22469	SY	T469BNL	22480	SY	T480BNL	22491	SU	T491BNL
22458	CB	S458OFT	22470	SY	T470BNL	22481	SY	T481BNL	22492	SY	T492BNL
22459	CB	S459OFT	22471	SY	T471BNL	22482	SY	T482BNL	22493	SY	T493BNL
22460	CB	S460OFT	22472	SY	T472BNL	22483	SY	T483BNL	22494	SY	T494BNL
22461	CB	T461BNL	22473	SY	T473BNL	22484	SY	T484BNL	22495	SU	T495BNL
22462	SY	T462BNL									

22601-22606   MAN 18.220   Alexander ALX300   N42F   1999

| 22601 | KK | V601GCS | 22603 | KK | V603GCS | 22605 | KK | V605GCS | 22606 | KK | V606GCS |
| 22602 | KK | V602GCS | 22604 | KK | V604GCS | | | | | | |

22656-22665   MAN 18.220   Alexander ALX300   N42F   1999

22656	SC	T656OEF	22659	SC	T659OEF	22662	SC	T662OEF	22664	SU	T664OEF
22657	SC	T657OEF	22660	SC	T660OEF	22663	SC	T663OEF	22665	SC	T665OEF
22658	SC	T658OEF	22661	SC	T661OEF						

22666-22675   MAN 18.220   Alexander ALX300   N42F   1999

22666	WA	V166DEF	22669	SC	V669DDC	22672	SU	V672DDC	22674	SC	V674DDC
22667	SC	V667DDC	22670	SC	V670DDC	22673	SU	V673DDC	22675	SU	V675DDC
22668	SC	V668DDC	22671	SC	V671DDC						

22701-22713   MAN 18.220   Alexander ALX300   N42F   1999

22701	AN	V701DSA	22705	AN	V705DSA	22708	AN	V708DSA	22711	AN	V711DSA
22702	AN	V702DSA	22706	AN	V706DSA	22709	AN	V709DSA	22712	PH	V712DSA
22703	AN	V703DSA	22707	AN	V707DSA	22710	AN	V710DSA	22713	PH	V713DSA
22704	AN	V704DSA									

22714-22722   MAN 18.220   Alexander ALX300   N42F   2000

| 22714 | PH | X714NSE | 22716 | PH | X716NSE | 22718 | PH | X718NSE | 22721 | ME | X721NSO |
| 22715 | PH | X715NSE | 22717 | PH | X717NSE | 22719 | PH | X719NSE | 22722 | PH | X722NSO |

22727-22736   MAN 18.220   Alexander ALX300   N42F   1999

22727	SU	T727OEF	22730	SU	T730OEF	22733	SU	T733OEF	22735	SU	T735OEF
22728	SU	T728OEF	22731	SU	T731OEF	22734	SU	T734OEF	22736	SU	T736OEF
22729	SU	T729OEF	22732	SU	T732OEF						

22801-22812   MAN 18.220   Alexander ALX300   N42F*   1999-2000 *22805 is NC42F

22801	CEw	V801DFV	22804	CE	V804DFV	22807	CEw	V807DFV	22811	CEw	V811DFV
22802	CEw	V802DFV	22805	CEw	X805SRM	22808	CEw	V808DFV	22812	CEw	V812DFV
22803	CEw	V803DFV	22806	CEw	V806DFV	22809	CEw	V809DFV			

22813-22827   MAN 18.220   Alexander ALX300   N42F*   1999-2000 *22813/4 are NC42F

22813	CE	X813SRM	22817	ME	X817SRM	22822	ME	X822SRM	22825	ME	X825SRM
22814	CEw	X814SRM	22818	ME	X818SRM	22823	ME	X823SRM	22826	ME	X826SRM
22815	ME	X815SRM	22819	CEw	X819SRM	22824	ME	X824SRM	22827	ME	X827SRM
22816	ME	X816SRM	22821	ME	X821SRM						

22913-22941   MAN 18.220   Alexander ALX300   N42F   1998

22913	OX	S913CFC	22921	OX	S921CFC	22928	OX	S928CFC	22935	OX	S935CFC
22914	OX	S914CFC	22922	OX	S922CFC	22929	OX	S929CFC	22936	OX	S936CFC
22915	OX	S915CFC	22923	OX	S923CFC	22930	OX	S930CFC	22937	OX	S937CFC
22916	OX	S916CFC	22924	OX	S924CFC	22931	OX	S931CFC	22938	OX	S938CFC
22917	OX	S917CFC	22925	OX	S925CFC	22932	OX	S932CFC	22940	OX	S940CFC
22918	OX	S918CFC	22926	OX	S926CFC	22933	OX	S933CFC	22941	OX	S941CFC
22919	OX	S919CFC	22927	OX	S927CFC	22934	OX	S934CFC			
22920	OX	S920CFC									

22942-22948   MAN 18.220   Alexander ALX300   N42F   2001

| 22942 | OX | OU51WLK | 22944 | OX | OU51WLN | 22946 | OX | OU51KAG | 22948 | OX | OU51KAO |
| 22943 | OX | OU51WLL | 22945 | OX | OU51KAE | 22947 | OX | OU51KAK | | | |

The arrival of the 2004 batch of articulated buses for London duties brought the number with Stagecoach to seventy-seven. Their arrival also brought the type onto Oxford Street where 23050, LX04KZZ, is seen heading for Ilford. *Colin Lloyd*

23001-23035

Mercedes-Benz Citaro O530 G   Mercedes-Benz   AN49D   2003

23001	PD	LV52VFW	23010	PD	LX03HCJ	23019	PD	LX03HDC	23028	PD	LX03HDN
23002	PD	LV52VFX	23011	PD	LX03HCK	23020	PD	LX03HDD	23029	PD	LX03HDU
23003	PD	LV52VFY	23012	PD	LX03HCL	23021	PD	LX03HDE	23030	PD	LX03HDV
23004	PD	LV52VFZ	23013	PD	LX03HCN	23022	PD	LX03HDF	23031	PD	LX03HDY
23005	PD	LV52VGA	23014	PD	LX03HCP	23023	PD	LX03HDG	23032	PD	LX03HDZ
23006	PD	LX03HCE	23015	PD	LX03HCU	23024	PD	LX03HDH	23033	PD	LX03HEJ
23007	PD	LX03HCF	23016	PD	LX03HCV	23025	PD	LX03HDJ	23034	PD	LX03HEU
23008	PD	LX03HCG	23017	PD	LX03HCY	23026	PD	LX03HDK	23035	PD	LX03HEV
23009	PD	LX03HCH	23018	PD	LX03HCZ	23027	PD	LX03HDL			

23036-23077

Mercedes-Benz Citaro O530 G   Mercedes-Benz   AN49D   2004

23036	WD	LX04KZG	23047	WD	LX04KZV	23058	WD	LX04LBN	23068	WD	LX04LCG
23037	WD	LX04KZJ	23048	WD	LX04KZW	23059	WD	LX04LBP	23069	WD	LX04LCJ
23038	WD	LX04KZK	23049	WD	LX04KZY	23060	WD	LX04LBU	23070	WD	LX04LCK
23039	WD	LX04KZL	23050	WD	LX04KZZ	23061	WD	LX04LBV	23071	WD	LX04LCM
23040	WD	LX04KZM	23051	WD	LX04LBA	23062	WD	LX04LBY	23072	WD	LX04LCN
23041	WD	LX04KZN	23052	WD	LX04LBE	23063	WD	LX04LBZ	23073	WD	LX04LCP
23042	WD	LX04KZP	23053	WD	LX04LBF	23064	WD	LX04LCA	23074	WD	LX04LCT
23043	WD	LX04KZR	23054	WD	LX04LBG	23065	WD	LX04LCC	23075	WD	LX04LCU
23044	WD	LX04KZS	23055	WD	LX04LBJ	23066	WD	LX04LCE	23076	WD	LX04LCV
23045	WD	LX04KZT	23056	WD	LX04LBK	23067	WD	LX04LCF	23077	WD	LX04LCW
23046	WD	LX04KZU	23057	WD	LX04LBL						

23950	PT	N550MTG	Mercedes-Benz O405	Optare Prisma	B49F	1995	Rhondda, 1997
23951	PT	N551MTG	Mercedes-Benz O405	Optare Prisma	B49F	1995	Rhondda, 1997

The Optare Delta buses are all allocated to training duties and, while most remain in London, three have now migrated to depots outside the capital. Pictured in a livery promoting the Learn and Earn slogan, 26023, J723CYG, illustrates the type as it passes Marble Arch. *Colin Lloyd*

25475	KK	OIW7025	Leyland National 11351A/3R			B48F	1979	British Airways, 1993	
25476	WSu	UIB3076	Leyland National 11351A/3R			B48F	1979	British Airways, 1993	

25704	MEt	SHH124M	Leyland Leopard PSU3/3R	Alexander AY	TV	1974			
25710	DOt	TEC310W	Leyland Leopard PSU3F/4R	Plaxton Supreme IV Express	TV	1981			
25728	AAu	WLT546	Leyland Leopard PSU3F/4R	Plaxton Supreme IV Express	Staff	1981			
25739	ESt	GSU839T	Leyland Leopard PSU3E/2R	Alexander AYS	TV	1979	Graham, Perth, 1997		
25753	BAt	EGB53T	Leyland Leopard PSU3E/3R	Alexander AY	TV	1978			
25759	MEt	GSU859T	Leyland Leopard PSU3E/2R	Alexander AYS	TV	1979	Graham, Perth, 1997		
25769	SR	GCS69V	Leyland Leopard PSU3E/4R	Alexander AY	B53F	1980			
25771	SR	TSJ71S	Leyland Leopard PSU3E/4R	Alexander AY	B53F	1977			
25797	SR	BSJ917T	Leyland Leopard PSU3E/4R	Alexander AY	B53F	1979			
25800	KL	B900WRN	Leyland Tiger TRCTL11/1R	Duple Dominant	B49F	1984			

25825-25833

Leyland Tiger TRCTL11/2RH   Alexander P   B52F   1985

25825	PMt	B625DWF	25830	EMw	B630DWF	25832	HLt	B632DWF	25833	HSt	B633DWF
25829	HLt	B629DWF	25831	EMw	B631DWF						

26001	NSt	J401LKO	DAF SB220LC550	Optare Delta	TV	1991	
26002	Ut	J402LKO	DAF SB220LC550	Optare Delta	TV	1991	
26003	TBt	J403LKO	DAF SB220LC550	Optare Delta	TV	1991	
26010	PDt	G684KNW	DAF SB220LC550	Optare Delta	TV	1989	

26011-26035

DAF SB220LC550   Optare Delta   TV   1992-93

26011	TBt	J711CYG	26018	TBt	J718CYG	26024	TBt	J724CYG	26030	DEt	K630HWX
26012	BKt	J712CYG	26019	GRt	J719CYG	26025	BKt	J725CYG	26031	BKt	K631HWX
26013	TLt	J713DAP	26020	Ut	J720CYG	26026	TBt	J726CYG	26032	BKt	K632HWX
26014	TLt	J714CYG	26021	Ut	J721CYG	26027	BKt	J727CYG	26033	BKt	K633HWX
26015	TLt	J715DAP	26022	CJt	J722CYG	26028	TQt	J728CYG	26034	PDt	K634HWX
26016	TLt	J716CYG	26023	Ut	J723CYG	26029	Ut	J729CYG	26035	TLt	K635HWX
26017	FOt	J717CYG									

The 2005 Stagecoach Bus Handbook

Following a period with Southern operations, the former London Lances migrated to Carlisle following refurbishment. Unfortunately, they were all in the depot when the River Eden and Caldew overflowed where they enter the Salway Firth on 8th January 2005 and are now withdrawn. A full list of the vehicles involved is included under the Carlisle depot heading on page 122. In sunnier times, 27211, L211YAG, is seen on Carlisle route 76, once operated by Routemasters. *Bob Downham*

27034	WWw	EJV34Y	Dennis Falcon H	Wadham Stringer Vanguard	B42F	1983	
27035	ME	F135SPX	Dennis Javelin 11m	Duple 300	B63F	1989	
27036	ME	F136SPX	Dennis Javelin 11m	Duple 300	B63F	1989	
27037	ME	F137SPX	Dennis Javelin 11m	Duple 300	B63F	1989	

27201-27212

Dennis Lance 11m · Plaxton Verde · B46F · 1994

27201	CEw	L201YAG	27204	CEw	L204YAG	27207	CEw	L207YAG	27210	CEw	L210YAG
27202	CEw	L202YAG	27205	CEw	L205YAG	27208	CEw	L208YAG	27211	CEw	L211YAG
27203	CEw	L203YAG	27206	CEw	L206YAG	27209	CEw	L209YAG	27212	CEw	L942RJN

27301	GY	M201DRG	Dennis Lance 11m	Plaxton Verde	B49F	1994
27302	GY	M202DRG	Dennis Lance 11m	Plaxton Verde	B49F	1994
27303	GY	M203DRG	Dennis Lance 11m	Plaxton Verde	B49F	1994
27304	GY	M204DRG	Dennis Lance 11m	Optare Sigma	B47F	1994

27404-27408

Dennis Lance SLF · Berkhof 2000 · N40F · 1994

27404	WG	414DCD	27406	WG	M406OKM	27407	WG	417DCD	27408	WG	418DCD
27405	WG	415DCD						

27501	PS	RV52OGL	TransBus Enviro 300 12.5m	TransBus	N48F	2002

27502-27505

TransBus Enviro 300 12.5m · TransBus · N48F · 2004

27502	RU	SN04EFS	27503	RU	SN04EFT	27504	RU	SN04EFU	27505	RU	SN04EFV

27506-27510

TransBus Enviro 300 12.5m · TransBus · N48F · On order for 2005

27506	-	-	27508	-	-	27509	-	-	27510	-	-
27507	-	-						

27701-27709

Dennis Lance 11m · East Lancs EL2000 · B45F · 1993

27701	GY	K701NDO	27704	GY	K704NDO	27706	GY	L706HFU	27708	GY	L708HFU
27702	GY	K702NDO	27705	GY	L705HFU	27707	GY	L707HFU	27709	GY	L709HFU
27703	GY	K703NDO						

27901	CEw	N901PFC	Dennis Lance 11m	Plaxton Verde	B49F	1996
27902	CEw	N902PFC	Dennis Lance 11m	Plaxton Verde	B49F	1996
27903	CEw	N903PFC	Dennis Lance 11m	Plaxton Verde	B49F	1996

Sixteen Scania buses are the only full-length single-deck buses remaining with Stagecoach London. They are expected to be replaced during 2005, only just over ten years since they pioneered the 'low-entrance, low-floor' revolution in the capital. Seen in Wanstead, 28620, RDZ6120, heads for North Woolwich.
Richard Godfrey

28615-28630		Scania N113CRL		Wright Pathfinder 320		N37D	1994	
28615	U	RDZ6115	28619	WDt	RDZ6119	28623	U	RDZ6123	28627	U	RDZ6127
28616	WDt	RDZ6116	28620	U	RDZ6120	28624	WDt	RDZ6124	28628	U	RDZ6128
28617	U	RDZ6117	28621	U	RDZ6121	28625	U	RDZ6125	28629	WDt	RDZ6129
28618	WDt	RDZ6118	28622	U	RDZ6122	28626	U	RDZ6126	28630	U	RDZ6130

28704-28706		Scania N112CRB		East Lancs European		B50F	1988
28704	EXt	F704BAT	28705	EX	F705BAT	28706	EX	F706CAG

28901-28919		Scania N113CRB		Alexander PS		B51F*	1989	*seating varies
28901	SY	F901JRG	28907	NEu	F907JRG	28912	WA	F912JRG	28916	SY	F916JRG
28902	SY	F902JRG	28908	SY	F908JRG	28913	EX	F913JRG	28917	SY	F917JRG
28903	SC	F903JRG	28910	KKt	F910JRG	28914	NEu	F914JRG	28918	SY	F918JRG
28905	SY	F905JRG	28911	SC	F911JRG	28915	CE	F915JRG	28919	EX	F919JRG
28906	SY	F906JRG									

28921-28927		Scania N113CRB		Alexander PS		B51F*	1989-90	*28926 is B49F
28921	SY	G921TCU	28924	WSu	G924TCU	28926	WA	G926TCU	28927	WA	G113SKX
28923	SY	G923TCU	28925	SY	G925TCU						

28928-28937		Scania N113CRB		Alexander PS		B51F	1991	
28928	WSu	H428EFT	28931	WA	H431EFT	28934	SY	H434EFT	28936	SY	H436EFT
28929	WA	H429EFT	28932	CE	H432EFT	28935	SY	H435EFT	28937	CE	H437EFT
28930	SY	H430EFT	28933	CE	H433EFT						

The 2004 edition of this Handbook illustrated Enviro 300 80001 then on evaluation in Manchester. That vehicle has now been renumbered 27501 to start a class series for the type, and has been joined by four further Enviro 300 buses operated for Warwickshire. These latter buses are painted in *County Links* colours with 27504, SN04EFU, pictured leaving Leamington Spa. A further five Enviro buses are on order for 2005. *Mark Lyons*

28938	SY	G108CEH	Scania N113CRB	Alexander PS	B49F	1990	
28951	DS	M951DRG	Scania L113CRL	Northern Counties Paladin	N49F	1994	
28952	DS	M952DRG	Scania L113CRL	Northern Counties Paladin	NC49F	1994	
28953	DS	M953DRG	Scania L113CRL	Alexander Strider	N51F	1994	
28954	DS	M954DRG	Scania L113CRL	Alexander Strider	N51F	1994	
28955	DS	M100AAB	Scania L113CRL	Alexander Strider	N51F	1994	AA Buses, Ayr, 1997

29101-29122

| | | | Leyland Lynx LX112L10ZR1S | Leyland Lynx | B49F | 1988-89 |

| 29101 | CBt | F101HVK | 29107 | SCt | F107HVK | 29111 | CBt | F111HVK | 29116 | GRt | F116HVK |
| 29105 | CTt | F105HVK | 29108 | OXt | F108HVK | 29115 | CBt | F115HVK | 29122 | SCt | F122HVK |

| 29127 | OXt | H127ACU | Leyland Lynx LX2R11C15Z4S | Leyland Lynx | BC47F | 1990 |
| 29541 | SSt | F251JRM | Leyland Lynx LX112L10ZR1 | Leyland Lynx | B51F | 1989 |

29601-29610

| | | | Leyland Lynx LX112L10ZR1R | Leyland Lynx | B49F | 1989 |

| 29601 | SUt | F601UVN | 29608 | PEt | F608UVN | 29609 | CBt | F609UVN | 29610 | SCt | F610UVN |
| 29607 | PEt | F607UVN | | | | | | | | | |

29611-29620

| | | | Leyland Lynx LX2R11C15Z4R | Leyland Lynx | B49F | 1989 |

| 29611 | NEu | G611CEF | 29613 | SNt | G613CEF | 29615 | OXt | G615CEF | 29617 | LEt | G617CEF |
| 29612 | SNt | G612CEF | 29614 | SZ | G614CEF | 29616 | SUt | G616CEF | 29620 | NEu | G620CEF |

| 29621 | DA | J901UKV | Leyland Lynx LX2R11V18Z4S | Leyland Lynx 2 | B49F | 1991 |

29622-29630

| | | | Leyland Lynx LX2R11V18Z4S | Leyland Lynx 2 | B49F | 1992 |

| 29622 | DA | K622YVN | 29626 | NEu | K626YVN | 29628 | NEu | K628YVN | 29630 | DA | K630YVN |
| 29624 | NEu | K624YVN | 29627 | DA | K627YVN | 29629 | DA | K629YVN | | | |

| 29801 | GP | MX53VHO | Irisbus Scolabus 150E04 | Vehixel | B67F | 2003 |
| 29802 | GP | MX53VHP | Irisbus Scolabus 150E04 | Vehixel | B67F | 2003 |

30141	PM	N421PWV	Volvo B6-9.9m	Plaxton Pointer	BC35F	1997	Citybus, Hong Kong, 2000
30142	PM	N422PWV	Volvo B6-9.9m	Plaxton Pointer	BC35F	1997	Citybus, Hong Kong, 2000
30241	CY	L241CCK	Volvo B6-9.9m	Alexander Dash	BC40F	1993	
30267	FH	L267CCK	Volvo B6-9.9m	Alexander Dash	BC40F	1993	
30268	FH	L268CCK	Volvo B6-9.9m	Alexander Dash	BC40F	1993	

30270-30274   Volvo B6-9.9m   Alexander Dash   B40F   1993

30270	KL	L270LHH	30272	CEw	L272LHH	30273	CEw	L273LHH	30274	CEw	L274LHH
30271	CEw	L271LHH

30270	KL	L270LHH	30272	CEw	L272LHH	30273	CEw	L273LHH	30274	CEw	L274LHH
30271	CEw	L271LHH									

30275-30283   Volvo B6-9.9m   Alexander Dash   B40F   1994

30275	KL	L275JAO	30277	ME	L277JAO	30281	CE	L281JAO	30283	LL	L283JAO
30276	KL	L276JAO	30278	LL	L278JAO	30282	KL	L282JAO			

30301-30310   Volvo B6-9.9m   Alexander Dash   B40F   1994

30301	LL	M741PRS	30305	LL	M745PRS	30307	CY	M847PRS	30309	KL	M749PRS
30303	CY	M743PRS	30306	LL	M746PRS	30308	PR	M748PRS	30310	CEw	M750PRS
30304	PR	M744PRS									

30312-30340   Volvo B6-9.9m   Alexander Dash   BC40F   1994

30312	KK	M772BCS	30322	KK	M722BCS	30325	AS	M725BCS	30337	CE	M737BSJ
30313	WS	M773BCS	30332	AS	M732BSJ	30326	AS	M726BCS	30338	CE	M738BSJ
30318	DS	M718BCS	30323	CE	M723BCS	30334	CEw	M734BSJ	30339	KK	M739BSJ
30320	WS	M720BCS	30324	KK	M724BCS	30335	CE	M735BSJ	30340	KK	M740BSJ

30342	CE	N416KPS	Volvo B6-9.9m	Wright Crusader	B39F	1995	Docherty, irvine, 2004

30426-30431   Volvo B6-9.9m   Alexander Dash   B40F   1993

30426	CJ	L426MVV	30428	CJ	L428MVV	30430	CJ	L424MVV	30431	CJ	L425MVV
30427	CF	L427MVV	30429	CJ	L423MVV						

30454-30461   Volvo B6-9.9m   Alexander Dash   B40F   1994

30454	KL	M454VHE	30456	KL	M456VHE	30458	ME	M458VHE	30461	BA	M461VHE
30455	KL	M455VHE	30457	ME	M457VHE	30460	NWu	M460VHE			

30651-30659   Volvo B6-9.9m   Alexander Dash   B40F   1993-94

30651	CE	L651HKS	30653	CE	L653HKS	30656	DE	L656HKS	30658	DE	L658HKS
30652	CJ	L652HKS	30655	DE	L655HKS	30657	DE	L657HKS	30659	DE	L659HKS

30665-30669   Volvo B6-9.9m   Alexander Dash   BC40F   1993

30665	PR	L665MSF	30668	CE	L668MSF

30670-30681   Volvo B6-9.9m   Alexander Dash   B40F   1993

30670	DE	M670SSX	30673	CJ	M673SSX	30675	AS	M675SSX	30680	FH	M680SSX
30671	DE	M671SSX	30674	KK	M674SSX	30679	FH	M679SSX	30681	FH	M681SSX
30672	DE	M672SSX									

30702-30712   Volvo B6-9.9m   Alexander Dash   B40F   1994

30705	WXu	L705FWO	30709	GR	L709FWO	30711	GR	L711FWO	30712	GR	L712FWO
30706	WXu	L706FWO									

30723	CT	M73HHB	Volvo B6-9m	Plaxton Pointer	B35F	1994
30724	NWu	M74HHB	Volvo B6-9m	Plaxton Pointer	B35F	1994
30726	CE	M76HHB	Volvo B6-9m	Plaxton Pointer	B35F	1994
30800	AN	M510FWV	Volvo B6-9.9m	Alexander Dash	BC35F	1994
30801	AN	M511FWV	Volvo B6-9.9m	Alexander Dash	BC35F	1994
30802	AN	M512FWV	Volvo B6-9.9m	Alexander Dash	BC35F	1994
30803	AN	M553FWV	Volvo B6-9.9m	Alexander Dash	BC31F	1994
30831	WWu	L831CDG	Volvo B6-9.9m	Alexander Dash	B40F	1994
30832	GR	L832CDG	Volvo B6-9.9m	Alexander Dash	B40F	1994
30846	BA	M753PRS	Volvo B6-9.9m	Alexander Dash	B40F	1994

Many of the early Volvo B6 buses left Stagecoach during 2004, with under 200 now remaining. The low-floor B6BLE continues their operational role and 31331, P331JND, is seen in Banbury on local service B8. Until late 2004, all the B6BLEs carried ALX200 bodywork, but with the acquisition of Docherty's services two with Wrightbus Crusader bodywork entered service. *Laurie Rufus*

31043-31052

			Volvo B6BLE			Alexander ALX200		N34F		1997		Citybus, Hong Kong, 2000-01
31043	PM	R133NPN	31046	PM	R196NPN	31049	PM	R119NPN	31051	PM	R71NPN	
31044	PM	R144NPN	31047	PM	R177NPN	31050	PM	R270NPN	31052	PM	R132NPN	
31045	PM	R95NPN	31048	PM	R178NPN							

31319	BB	P321EFL	Volvo B6BLE			Alexander ALX200		N35F	1997	
31320	BB	P320EFL	Volvo B6BLE			Alexander ALX200		N35F	1997	

31321-31357

			Volvo B6BLE			Alexander ALX200		N36F		1997	
31321	RU	P321JND	31327	NU	P327JND	31333	LE	P677NOJ	31353	BB	P353JND
31322	RU	P322JND	31328	NU	P328JND	31334	NU	P344JND	31354	NU	P354JND
31323	RU	P323JND	31329	NU	P329JND	31350	NU	P350JND	31355	NU	P355JND
31324	RU	P324JND	31330	RU	P330JND	31351	NU	P351JND	31356	NU	P356JND
31325	RU	P325JND	31331	BB	P331JND	31352	NU	P352JND	31357	NU	P357JND
31326	RU	P326JND	31332	NU	P332JND						

31361-31386

			Volvo B6BLE			Alexander ALX200		NC36F		1997	
31361	BB	P361DSA	31368	AY	P368DSA	31375	KK	P375DSA	31381	KK	P381DSA
31362	BB	P362DSA	31369	KK	P369DSA	31376	KK	P376DSA	31382	KK	P382DSA
31363	NU	P363DSA	31370	KK	P370DSA	31377	KK	P377DSA	31383	KK	P383DSA
31364	NU	P364DSA	31371	KK	P371DSA	31378	AY	P378DSA	31384	KK	P384DSA
31365	BB	P365DSA	31372	KK	P372DSA	31379	AY	P379DSA	31385	KK	P385DSA
31366	AY	P366DSA	31373	KK	P373DSA	31380	AY	P380DSA	31386	KK	P386DSA
31367	AY	P367DSA	31374	KK	P374DSA						

31387	AY	T601TSD	Volvo B6BLE		Wrightbus Crusader 2	N37F	2001	Docherty, Irvine, 2004
31388	AY	T602TSD	Volvo B6BLE		Wrightbus Crusader 2	N37F	2001	Docherty, Irvine, 2004

31491-31499

			Volvo B6BLE			Alexander ALX200		N36F		1996	
31491	AN	P491BRS	31494	PH	P494BRS	31496	PH	P496BRS	31498	PH	P498BRS
31492	AN	P492BRS	31495	PH	P495BRS	31497	PH	P497BRS	31499	PH	P499BRS
31493	AN	P493BRS									

Services acquired from the A1 Service consortium and Dodds buses operate with new buses in local liveries. Seen in Irvine, 31376, P376DSA, illustrates the Dodds scheme as it heads for Bourtreehill. *Bob Downham*

31701-31714   Volvo B6BLE   Alexander ALX200   N35F   1997

31701	EX	P701BTA	31705	EX	P706BTA	31709	EX	P709BTA	31712	EX	P712BTA
31702	EX	P702BTA	31706	EX	P707BTA	31710	EX	P710BTA	31713	EX	P713BTA
31703	SWu	P703BTA	31707	EX	P708BTA	31711	EX	P711BTA	31714	EX	P714BTA
31704	EX	P704BTA	31708	EX	P708BTA					

31852	BB	P852SMR	Volvo B6BLE	Alexander ALX200	N35F	1997
31853	BB	P853SMR	Volvo B6BLE	Alexander ALX200	N35F	1997
31854	BB	P854SMR	Volvo B6BLE	Alexander ALX200	N35F	1997

32001-32008   Dennis Dart 9.8m   Alexander Dash   BC40F   1996

32001	NU	P101HNH	32003	NU	P103HNH	32005	DS	P105HNH	32007	NU	P451KRP
32002	NU	P102HNH	32004	NU	P104HNH	32006	NU	P450KRP	32008	NU	P452KRP

32014-32022   Dennis Dart 9.8m   Plaxton Pointer   B33D   1994

32014	TQ	L714JUD	32017	TQ	L717JUD	32019	TQ	L719JUD	32021	TQ	L721JUD
32015	TQ	L715JUD	32018	TQ	L718JUD	32020	TQ	L720JUD	32022	PN	L722JUD
32016	TQ	L716JUD								

32041	BE	M61VJO	Dennis Dart 9.8m	Plaxton Pointer	B40F	1995
32047	BE	N47EJO	Dennis Dart 9.8m	Plaxton Pointer	B40F	1995
32048	CS	N48EJO	Dennis Dart 9.8m	Plaxton Pointer	B40F	1995

32051-32064   Dennis Dart 9.8m   Plaxton Pointer   B40F   1996

32051	CL	N51KBW	32054	DS	N54KBW	32058	DS	N58KBW	32063	AY	N63KBW
32052	PT	N52KBW	32056	EH	N56KBW	32061	DS	N61KBW	32064	EH	N64KBW
32053	PT	N53KBW	32057	AY	N57KBW	32062	AY	N62KBW			

32065-32099 — Dennis Dart 9.8SDL3054 — Plaxton Pointer — B37D — 1995

32065	BE	M65VJO	32075	AT	M75VJO	32084	EH	M84WBW	32092	BE	M92WBW
32066	CH	M59VJO	32076	BE	M76VJO	32085	CT	M85WBW	32093	AT	M93WBW
32067	HL	M67VJO	32077	WG	M63VJO	32086	CT	M86WBW	32094	BE	M94WBW
32068	HL	M68VJO	32078	AE	M78VJO	32087	HL	M87WBW	32095	LS	M95WBW
32069	HL	M69VJO	32079	EH	M79VJO	32088	BE	M101WBW	32096	WG	M96WBW
32070	AT	M62VJO	32080	HL	M64VJO	32089	HL	M89WBW	32097	LS	M97WBW
32071	HL	M71VJO	32081	HL	M81WBW	32090	AT	M102WBW	32098	BE	M98WBW
32073	HL	M73VJO	32082	HL	M82WBW	32091	LS	M91WBW	32099	EH	M103WBW
32074	BE	M74VJO	32083	HL	M83WBW						

32101-32106 — Dennis Dart 9.8SDL3017 — Alexander Dash — B40F — 1993

32101	BQ	K101XHG	32103	BQ	K103XHG	32105	FH	K105XHG	32106	SA	K106XHG
32102	FH	K102XHG	32104	AN	K104XHG						

32111-32148 — Dennis Dart 9SDL3024 — Plaxton Pointer — B34F — 1993

32111	GY	K211SRH	32120	DS	K120SRH	32128	SS	K128SRH	32138	SR	L138VRH
32112	SS	K112SRH	32121	SS	K121SRH	32129	SS	K129SRH	32139	EX	L139VRH
32113	CH	K113SRH	32122	AL	K122SRH	32130	GR	K130SRH	32140	EX	L140VRH
32114	CH	K114SRH	32123	HL	K123SRH	32132	SZ	K132SRH	32141	EX	L141VRH
32115	CH	K115SRH	32124	CE	K124SRH	32133	SS	K133SRH	32145	AY	L145VRH
32116	CH	K116SRH	32125	SS	K125SRH	32134	SS	K134SRH	32147	CH	K109SRH
32117	SS	K117SRH	32126	CT	K126SRH	32137	AY	L137VRH	32148	CH	K110SRH
32118	HL	K118SRH	32127	SS	K127SRH						

32163	EH	R63UFC	Dennis Dart 10m	Plaxton Pointer	B40F	1997
32164	EH	R64UFC	Dennis Dart 10m	Plaxton Pointer	B40F	1997
32165	EH	R65UFC	Dennis Dart 10m	Plaxton Pointer	B40F	1997

32201-32205 — Dennis Dart 9.8SDL3017 — Alexander Dash — B40F — 1992

32201	SA	K601ESH	32203	AL	K603ESH	32204	SA	K604ESH	32205	AL	K605ESH
32202	AL	K602ESH									

32206-32213 — Dennis Dart 9.8m — Alexander Dash — B40F — 1996

32206	DE	P606CMS	32208	CJ	P608CMS	32210	AL	P610CMS	32212	AL	P612CMS
32207	CJ	P607CMS	32209	CJ	P609CMS	32211	GS	P611CMS	32213	DE	P613CMS

32221-32223 — Dennis Dart 9SDL3016 — Wright Handy-bus — B35F — 1993

32221	TH	K921OWV	32222	TH	K922OWV	32223	TH	K923OWV

Carrying Plaxton Pointer bodywork, Dart 32097, M97WBW, is based at the historic town of Lewes but is seen here in Brighton.
Richard Godfrey

Dart 32382, L208PSB, is an unusual bus operating in Scotland. It was seen in Dumfries when heading for Lockerbie. Acquired from Arran Coaches, the bus has a Marshall body onto which a Pointer-style front has subsequently been fitted during refurbishment. *Bob Downham*

32234-32257

Dennis Dart 8.5SDL3015 Wright Handybus B29F 1993

32234	CT	NDZ3134	32241	SZ	K986CBO	32251	EX	NDZ3151	32253	EX	NDZ3153
32236	CT	NDZ3136	32242	WXu	K987CBO	32252	EX	NDZ3152	32257	CT	NDZ3157

32260	EX	JDZ2360	Dennis Dart 8.5SDL3003	Wright Handybus	B28F	1991	
32262	EX	JDZ2362	Dennis Dart 8.5SDL3003	Wright Handybus	B28F	1991	
09999	EX	JDZ2371	Dennis Dart 8.5SDL3003	Wright Handybus	B28F	1991	re-instated from 32271

32301-32327

Dennis Dart 9.8SDL3054 Alexander Dash B36F 1995

32301	DA	N301AMC	32308	DE	N308AMC	32315	WI	N315AMC	32322	WI	N322AMC
32302	WA	N302AMC	32309	WI	N309AMC	32316	AT	N316AMC	32323	WI	N323AMC
32303	DA	N303AMC	32310	WI	N310AMC	32317	SN	N317AMC	32324	WI	N324AMC
32304	DE	N304AMC	32311	FO	N311AMC	32318	WWu	N318AMC	32325	WI	N325AMC
32305	DA	N305AMC	32312	WI	N312AMC	32319	SN	N319AMC	32326	WI	N326AMC
32306	DE	N306AMC	32313	SN	N313AMC	32320	GR	N320AMC	32327	LS	N327AMC
32307	DE	N307AMC	32314	WI	PSU787	32321	BE	N321AMC			

32342	ESw	H162NON	Dennis Dart 8.5SDL3003	Carlyle Dartline	B28F	1991	Allisons, Dunfermline, 2000
32344	SA	H154MOB	Dennis Dart 8.5SDL3003	Carlyle Dartline	B28F	1990	Allisons, Dunfermline, 2000
32346	ESw	H146MOB	Dennis Dart 8.5SDL3003	Carlyle Dartline	B28F	1990	Allisons, Dunfermline, 2000
32347	ESw	H71MOB	Dennis Dart 8.5SDL3003	Carlyle Dartline	B28F	1990	Allisons, Dunfermline, 2000
32349	AL	G49TGW	Dennis Dart 8.5SDL3003	Carlyle Dartline	B28F	1990	

32351-32368

Dennis Dart 9.8m Plaxton Pointer B37D 1997

32351	CS	R701YWC	32356	CS	R706YWC	32361	CS	R711YWC	32365	CS	R715YWC
32352	CS	R702YWC	32357	CS	R707YWC	32362	CS	R712YWC	32366	CS	R716YWC
32353	CS	R703YWC	32358	CS	R708YWC	32363	CS	R713YWC	32367	CS	R717YWC
32354	CS	R704YWC	32359	CS	R709YWC	32364	CS	R714YWC	32368	CS	R718YWC
32355	CS	R705YWC	32360	CS	R710YWC						

Winchester's 32314, PSU787, carries the colours of respected operator King Alfred Motor Services which operated in the area from 1920 to 1973. While many will have seen the bus at transport festivities, it is seen here on normal duties in Stockbridge. *Mark Lyons*

32380	SR	M949EGE	Dennis Dart 9.8SDL3054	Plaxton Pointer	B40F	1994	AA Buses, Ayr, 1997
32381	DS	M950EGE	Dennis Dart 9.8SDL3054	Plaxton Pointer	B40F	1994	AA Buses, Ayr, 1997
32382	DS	L208PSB	Dennis Dart 9SDL3031	Marshall C36	B39F	1994	Arran Coaches, 1994

32390-32398   Dennis Dart 9.8m   Alexander Dash   B40F*   1996-97   *32395-8 are BC40F

32390	DS	P390LPS	32393	DS	P393LPS	32395	DS	P395BRS	32397	AY	P397BRS
32391	DS	P391LPS	32394	DS	P394LPS	32396	AY	P396BRS	32398	DS	P398BRS
32392	DS	P392LPS

32410-32427   Dennis Dart 9.8SDL3054   Plaxton Pointer   B40F   1996

32410	EX	N410MBW	32415	CH	N415MBW	32420	GY	N420MBW	32424	WP	N424MBW
32411	EX	N411MBW	32416	CH	N416MBW	32421	CH	N421MBW	32425	MD	N425MBW
32412	AT	N412MBW	32417	CH	N417MBW	32422	MD	N422MBW	32426	GY	N426MBW
32413	AT	N413MBW	32418	CH	N418MBW	32423	MD	N423MBW	32427	MD	N427MBW
32414	AT	N414MBW	32419	GY	N419MBW

32429-32450   Dennis Dart 9.8SDL3060   Plaxton Pointer   BC39F   1995   Citybus, Hong Kong, 1999

32429	PM	403DCD	32434	EH	N734XDV	32439	EX	N739XDV	32446	EX	N998RCD
32430	PM	404DCD	32435	EH	N735XDV	32440	EX	N740XDV	32447	PM	407DCD
32431	EX	N731XDV	32436	EH	N736XDV	32442	EX	N742XDV	32448	PM	400DCD
32432	EX	N732XDV	32437	EH	N737XDV	32443	EX	N743XDV	32449	PM	401DCD
32433	TQ	N733XDV	32438	EH	N738XDV	32444	EX	N744XDV	32450	PM	402DCD

32451-32467   Dennis Dart 9.8m   Alexander Dash   B40F*   1996   *32451-5 are BC40F

32451	BE	XYK976	32456	LS	N456PAP	32460	BE	N460PAP	32464	HS	N464PAP
32452	PM	NFX667	32457	HS	N457PAP	32461	BE	N461PAP	32465	HS	N465PAP
32453	WI	YLJ332	32458	CA	N458PAP	32462	BE	N462PAP	32466	HS	N466PAP
32454	WI	XSU682	32459	BE	N459PAP	32463	BE	N463PAP	32467	FO	N467PAP
32455	PM	WVT618

32501-32552

Dennis Dart 9.8SDL3017 — Alexander Dash — B40F* — 1992 — *32501-33 are B41F

32501	WG	J501GCD	**32513**	AR	J513GCD	**32526**	AR	J526GCD	**32541**	CR	J541GCD
32502	WG	J502GCD	**32515**	AT	J515GCD	**32529**	AT	J529GCD	**32542**	BD	J542GCD
32503	WG	J503GCD	**32517**	AT	J517GCD	**32530**	AR	J530GCD	**32546**	CR	J546GCD
32508	WG	J508GCD	**32518**	CR	J518GCD	**32532**	CR	J532GCD	**32547**	WG	J547GCD
32509	SEu	J509GCD	**32519**	AT	J519GCD	**32536**	AT	J536GCD	**32548**	SEu	J548GCD
32510	WG	J510GCD	**32522**	AT	J522GCD	**32537**	CR	J537GCD	**32550**	BD	J550GCD
32511	CR	J511GCD	**32524**	CR	J524GCD	**32538**	SEw	J538GCD	**32552**	CR	J552GCD

32553-32580

Dennis Dart 9.8SDL3017 — Alexander Dash — B40F — 1992

32553	CR	K553NHC	**32561**	WG	K561NHC	**32567**	SEu	K567NHC	**32577**	AT	K577NHC
32554	SEu	K554NHC	**32562**	CR	K562NHC	**32568**	SY	K568NHC	**32578**	AT	K578NHC
32555	CR	K655NHC	**32563**	DA	K563NHC	**32569**	SY	K569NHC	**32579**	DA	K579NHC
32556	CR	K556NHC	**32564**	DA	K564NHC	**32575**	BD	K575NHC	**32580**	CR	K580NHC
32560	WG	K660NHC	**32565**	AT	K565NHC						

32582	BD	J702YRM	Dennis Dart 9.8SDL3017	Alexander Dash	B41F	1992
32585	AT	K585ODY	Dennis Dart 9.8SDL3017	Alexander Dash	B40F	1992
32599	EX	N599DWY	Dennis Dart 9.8SDL3054	Plaxton Pointer	B40F	1995	East Devon, Aylesbeare, 1997

32601-32640

Dennis Dart 9.8SDL3054 — Alexander Dash — B40F — 1995-96

32601	FO	N601KGF	**32611**	AE	N611LGC	**32621**	SU	P621PGP	**32631**	SU	P631PGP
32602	HS	N602KGF	**32612**	CL	N612LGC	**32622**	SU	P622PGP	**32632**	SU	P632PGP
32603	HS	N603KGF	**32613**	WY	N613LGC	**32623**	SU	P623PGP	**32633**	SU	P633PGP
32604	CE	N604KGF	**32614**	DA	N614LGC	**32624**	SS	P624PGP	**32634**	SU	P634PGP
32605	CE	N605KGF	**32615**	DA	P615PGP	**32625**	WY	P625PGP	**32636**	TQ	P636PGP
32606	AD	N606KGF	**32616**	DA	P616PGP	**32626**	WY	P626PGP	**32637**	SU	P637PGP
32607	AD	N607KGF	**32617**	DA	P617PGP	**32627**	WY	P627PGP	**32638**	SU	P638PGP
32608	FO	N608KGF	**32618**	TQ	P618PGP	**32628**	WY	P628PGP	**32639**	TQ	P639PGP
32609	CL	N609KGF	**32619**	TQ	P619PGP	**32629**	WY	P629PGP	**32640**	TQ	P640PGP
32610	AE	N610KGF	**32620**	SU	P620PGP	**32630**	WY	P630PGP			

32650	WA	N350YFL	Dennis Dart 9.8m	Alexander Dash	B40F	1996
32651	SS	N351YFL	Dennis Dart 9.8m	Alexander Dash	B40F	1996
32652	SS	N352YFL	Dennis Dart 9.8m	Alexander Dash	B40F	1996

32655-32661

Dennis Dart 9.8m — Alexander Dash — B40F — 1996

32655	DA	P455EEF	**32657**	WA	P457EEF	**32659**	DA	P459EEF	**32661**	DA	P461EEF
32656	DA	P456EEF	**32658**	DA	P458EEF	**32660**	DA	P460EEF			

32701	SY	J701KCU	Dennis Dart 9.8SDL3017	Plaxton Pointer	B40F	1992
32702	DA	J702KCU	Dennis Dart 9.8SDL3017	Plaxton Pointer	B40F	1992

32703-32743

Dennis Dart 9.8m — Alexander Dash — B40F — 1992-93

32703	SU	K703PCN	**32713**	MD	K713PCN	**32725**	SY	K725PNL	**32735**	SU	L735VNL
32704	CE	K704PCN	**32714**	WA	K714PCN	**32726**	SU	K726PNL	**32736**	SU	L736VNL
32705	CE	K705PCN	**32715**	CE	K715PCN	**32727**	SY	K727PNL	**32737**	SU	L737VNL
32706	CE	K706PCN	**32717**	SC	K717PCN	**32728**	SY	K728PNL	**32738**	SU	L738VNL
			32718	CE	K718PCN	**32729**	DA	K729PNL	**32739**	SU	L739VNL
			32720	SU	K720PCN	**32730**	SU	L730VNL	**32740**	DA	L740VNL
32709	DA	K709PCN	**32721**	WA	K721PCN	**32731**	SU	L731VNL	**32741**	DA	L741VNL
32710	SU	K710PCN	**32722**	SU	K722PCN	**32732**	SU	L732VNL	**32742**	DA	L742VNL
32711	DA	K711PCN	**32723**	SY	K723PNL	**32733**	SU	L733VNL	**32743**	DA	L743VNL
32712	DA	K712PCN	**32724**	SY	K724PNL	**32734**	SU	L734VNL			

32744-32759

Dennis Dart 9.8SDL3035 — Plaxton Pointer — B40F — 1993

32744	SY	L744VNL	**32748**	SC	L748VNL	**32751**	SS	L751VNL	**32757**	CB	L757VNL
32745	WA	L745VNL	**32749**	SS	L749VNL	**32752**	SY	L752VNL	**32758**	CB	L758VNL
32746	SS	L746VNL	**32750**	SU	L750VNL	**32753**	WA	L753VNL	**32759**	DA	L759VNL

32760-32765

Dennis Dart 9.8SDL3040 — Alexander Dash — B40F — 1994

32760	SU	L760ARG	**32762**	SU	L762ARG	**32764**	SU	L764ARG	**32765**	SU	L765ARG
32761	SU	L761ARG	**32763**	SU	L763ARG						

32766-32771   Dennis Dart 9.8SDL3040   Plaxton Pointer   B40F   1994

| 32766 | SS | M766DRG | 32768 | WA | M768DRG | 32770 | DA | M770DRG | 32771 | BD | M771DRG |
| 32767 | SS | M767DRG | 32769 | SS | M769DRG | | | | | | |

32772-32785   Dennis Dart 9.8m   Alexander Dash   B40F   1996

32772	BD	N772RVK	32776	SS	N776RVK	32780	SU	P780WCN	32783	SS	P783WCN
32773	SU	N773RVK	32777	SU	N778RVK	32781	SU	P781WCN	32784	SS	P784WCN
32774	SS	N774RVK	32778	SU	N779RVK	32782	SU	P782WCN	32785	SS	P785WCN
32775	SS	N775RVK	32779	SU	N780RVK						

32786-32793   Dennis Dart 9.8m   Alexander Dash   B40F   1996-97

| 32786 | SU | P786WVK | 32788 | SU | P788WVK | 32790 | SU | P790WVK | 32792 | SS | P792WVK |
| 32787 | SU | P787WVK | 32789 | SU | P789WVK | 32791 | SS | P791WVK | 32793 | SS | P793WVK |

| 32794 | SS | M387KVR | Dennis Dart 9.8SDL3054 | Northern Counties Paladin | B40F | 1995 | Redby, Sunderland, 2001 |
| 32795 | SS | M597SSB | Dennis Dart 9.8SDL3031 | Plaxton Pointer | B31F | 1995 | Redby, Sunderland, 2002 |

32801-32812   Dennis Dart 9.8SDL3017   Alexander Dash   B41F   1992

32801	IS	J501FPS	32804	AN	J504FPS	32807	CH	J507FPS	32810	IS	J510FPS
32802	AN	J502FPS	32805	PH	J505FPS	32808	IS	J508FPS	32811	IS	J511FPS
32803	BQ	J503FPS	32806	CH	J506FPS	32809	IS	J509FPS	32812	IS	J512FPS

32818	MD	P418KWF	Dennis Dart 9.8m	Alexander Dash	B41F	1996	
32819	MD	P419KWF	Dennis Dart 9.8m	Alexander Dash	B41F	1996	
32820	MD	P420KWF	Dennis Dart 9.8m	Alexander Dash	B41F	1996	
32901	SZ	P901SMR	Dennis Dart 9.8m	Alexander Dash	B40F	1997	
32902	SZ	P902SMR	Dennis Dart 9.8m	Alexander Dash	B40F	1997	
32903	SZ	P903SMR	Dennis Dart 9.8m	Alexander Dash	B40F	1997	
32936	SZ	M85DEW	Dennis Dart 9.8SDL3054	Marshall C37	B40F	1994	Glossopdale, Dukinfield, 1999
32937	SZ	M86DEW	Dennis Dart 9.8SDL3054	Marshall C37	B40F	1994	Glossopdale, Dukinfield, 1999
32960	CL	L414SFL	Dennis Dart 9.8SDL3054	Marshall C37	BC37F	1994	
32962	CT	N62MTG	Dennis Dart 9.8SDL3054	Plaxton Pointer	B40F	1995	
32963	CT	N63MTG	Dennis Dart 9.8SDL3054	Plaxton Pointer	B40F	1995	
32964	PT	M64HHB	Dennis Dart 9.8SDL3054	Wright Handybus	B39F	1995	
32965	PT	M65HHB	Dennis Dart 9.8SDL3054	Wright Handybus	B39F	1995	
32966	AE	M562JTG	Dennis Dart 9.8SDL3040	Plaxton Pointer	B43F	1994	
32967	MR	M67HHB	Dennis Dart 9.8SDL3054	Wright Handybus	B39F	1995	
32968	CL	M68HHB	Dennis Dart 9SDL3031	Marshall C36	B34F	1994	
32969	WXu	M69HHB	Dennis Dart 9SDL3031	Marshall C36	B34F	1994	
32970	GR	M625KKG	Dennis Dart 9.8SDL3040	Plaxton Pointer	B43F	1994	
32983	CL	L83CWO	Dennis Dart 9SDL3034	Plaxton Pointer	B35F	1993	
32984	AE	L84CWO	Dennis Dart 9SDL3034	Plaxton Pointer	B35F	1993	

Plaxton Pointer 32984, L84CWO, is seen heading for Blaencwm. The south Wales allocation includes several unusual vehicles whose heritage can be traced to acquired independents.
Phillip Stephenson

32985	AE	L85CWO	Dennis Dart 9SDL3034	Plaxton Pointer	B35F	1993	
32986	CE	L86CWO	Dennis Dart 9SDL3024	Wright Handybus	B35F	1993	
32988	AE	L270EHB	Dennis Dart 9.8SDL3035	Plaxton Pointer	B43F	1994	
32989	CE	L89CWO	Dennis Dart 9SDL3024	Wright Handybus	B35F	1993	
32990	CL	K402EDT	Dennis Dart 9SDL3016	Northern Counties Paladin	B35F	1992	
32991	SWu	K91BNY	Dennis Dart 9SDL3011	Plaxton Pointer	B35F	1993	
32992	AE	K92BNY	Dennis Dart 9SDL3011	Plaxton Pointer	B35F	1993	
32993	SWu	K93BNY	Dennis Dart 9SDL3011	Plaxton Pointer	B35F	1993	
32994	AS	K94AAX	Dennis Dart 9SDL3011	Wright Handybus	B35F	1993	
32995	WXu	K95AAX	Dennis Dart 9SDL3011	Wright Handybus	B35F	1993	
32996	CL	K96AAX	Dennis Dart 9SDL3016	Plaxton Pointer	B35F	1992	
32997	MR	K97XNY	Dennis Dart 9SDL3011	Plaxton Pointer(1995)	B35F	1992	
32998	WXu	K98XNY	Dennis Dart 9.8SDL3017	Wright Handybus	B39F	1992	
32999	AE	J454JRH	Dennis Dart 9.8SDL3017	Plaxton Pointer	B40F	1991	

33001-33019   Dennis Dart SLF 322   Alexander ALX200   N37F   1997-98

33001	HL	R701DNJ	33006	WG	R706DNJ	33011	WG	R711DNJ	33016	BE	R816HCD
33002	WG	R702DNJ	33007	HS	R707DNJ	33012	WG	XSU612	33017	BE	R817HCD
33003	WG	R703DNJ	33008	WG	R708DNJ	33013	WG	R813HCD	33018	AD	R818HCD
33004	WG	R704DNJ	33009	HS	R709DNJ	33014	BE	R814HCD	33019	AD	R819HCD
33005	HS	405DCD	33010	HS	R710DNJ	33015	BE	R815HCD			

33020	AT	T593CGT	Dennis Dart SLF 10.7m	Plaxton Pointer 2	N39F	1999
33021	AD	R821HCD	Dennis Dart SLF 322	Alexander ALX200	N37F	1998
33022	AD	R822HCD	Dennis Dart SLF 322	Alexander ALX200	N37F	1998
33023	HS	R823HCD	Dennis Dart SLF 322	Alexander ALX200	N37F	1998
33024	AD	R824HCD	Dennis Dart SLF 322	Alexander ALX200	N37F	1998
33025	WI	NDZ3019	Dennis Dart SLF 10.7m	Plaxton Pointer 2	N37F	2000
33026	WI	W426NFG	Dennis Dart SLF 10.7m	Plaxton Pointer 2	N37F	2000
33027	WI	NDZ3017	Dennis Dart SLF 10.7m	Plaxton Pointer 2	N37F	2000
33028	WI	NDZ3018	Dennis Dart SLF 10.7m	Plaxton Pointer 2	N37F	2000

33029-33040   Dennis Dart SLF 10.7m   Plaxton Pointer 2   N37F   1997   Citybus, Hong Kong, 2000

33029	AT	P299AYJ	33032	AT	P302AYJ	33035	BE	P435AYJ	33038	BE	P458AYJ
33030	BE	P330AYJ	33033	AT	P343AYJ	33036	BE	P426AYJ	33039	BE	P479AYJ
33031	AT	P301AYJ	33034	BE	P434AYJ	33037	BE	P457AYJ	33040	BE	P466AYJ

33053-33072   Dennis Dart SLF 11.3m   Plaxton Pointer SPD   N41F   2000

33053	PM	X953VAP	33059	PM	X959VAP	33064	PM	X964VAP	33068	PM	X968VAP
33054	PM	X954VAP	33061	PM	X961VAP	33065	PM	X965VAP	33069	PM	X969VAP
33056	PM	X956VAP	33062	PM	X962VAP	33066	PM	X966VAP	33071	PM	X971VAP
33057	PM	X957VAP	33063	PM	X963VAP	33067	PM	X967VAP	33072	PM	X972VAP
33058	PM	X958VAP									

Pictured in Hull, 33107, R107KRG, was heading for the Boothferry Estate. The low-floor Dart carries an ALX200 body, a model that ceased production in preference to the Pointer which was then produced alongside it at Falkirk.
Phillip Stephenson

76

33073	DS	V973DRM	Dennis Dart SLF 8.5m		Plaxton Pointer MPD	N29F	2000	White Star, Lockerbie, 2003
33074	DS	V974DRM	Dennis Dart SLF 8.5m		Plaxton Pointer MPD	N29F	2000	White Star, Lockerbie, 2003
33075	DS	V975DRM	Dennis Dart SLF 8.5m		Plaxton Pointer MPD	N29F	2000	White Star, Lockerbie, 2003
33076	CEw	V972DRM	Dennis Dart SLF 8.5m		Plaxton Pointer MPD	N29F	2000	White Star, Lockerbie, 2003
33077	DS	X523SHH	Dennis Dart SLF 8.5m		Alexander ALX200	N29F	2000	White Star, Lockerbie, 2003
33078	DS	PY02KTO	Dennis Dart SLF		Plaxton Pointer 2	N37F	2002	White Star, Lockerbie, 2003
33079	DS	PY02KTP	Dennis Dart SLF		Plaxton Pointer 2	N37F	2002	White Star, Lockerbie, 2003
33080	FO	P998AFV	Dennis Dart SLF		East Lancs Spryte	N36F	1996	Town & Around, 2003
33088	DS	T35VCS	Dennis Dart SLF 8.5m		Plaxton Pointer MPD	N29F	1999	
33089	DS	T36VCS	Dennis Dart SLF 8.5m		Plaxton Pointer MPD	N29F	1999	

33101-33128

		Dennis Dart SLF		Alexander ALX200	N37F	1997-98

33101	SC	R101KRG	33109	HL	R109KRG	33117	HL	R117KRG	33123	SU	R123KRG
33102	HP	R102KRG	33110	HL	R110KRG	33118	SU	R118KRG	33124	SU	R124KRG
33103	HL	R103KRG	33112	HL	R112KRG	33119	AT	R119KRG	33125	SU	R125KRG
33104	HL	R104KRG	33113	HL	R113KRG	33120	SU	R120KRG	33126	SU	R126KRG
33105	EMu	R105KRG	33114	HL	R114KRG	33121	SU	R121KRG	33127	SU	R127KRG
33107	HL	R107KRG	33115	HL	R115KRG	33122	SU	R122KRG	33128	SU	R128KRG
33108	HL	R108KRG	33116	HL	R116KRG						

33158	EX	P758FOD	Dennis Dart SLF 10.7m		Plaxton Pointer	N37F	1997	Citybus, Hong Kong, 2000
33159	EX	P762FOD	Dennis Dart SLF 10.7m		Plaxton Pointer	N37F	1997	Citybus, Hong Kong, 2000
33160	EX	P760FOD	Dennis Dart SLF 10.7m		Plaxton Pointer	N37F	1997	Citybus, Hong Kong, 2000
33200	EX	W102PMS	Dennis Dart SLF		Alexander ALX200	N28F	1999	
33201	EH	WA51OSE	Dennis Dart SLF		Alexander ALX200	N28F	2001	
33202	EH	WA51OSF	Dennis Dart SLF		Alexander ALX200	N28F	2001	
33322	PE	P322EFL	Dennis Dart SLF 10.7m		Plaxton Pointer	N39F	1997	
33323	PE	P323EFL	Dennis Dart SLF 10.7m		Plaxton Pointer	N39F	1997	
33324	PE	P324EFL	Dennis Dart SLF 10.7m		Plaxton Pointer	N39F	1997	

33351-33361

		Dennis Dart SLF 10m		Alexander ALX200	N29D	1997-99

33351	SY	P801NJN	33354	SY	P804NJN	33357	HS	P807NJN	33360	HS	S410TNO
33352	SY	P802NJN	33355	SY	P805NJN	33358	HS	P208XNO	33361	HS	S411TNO
33353	SY	P803NJN	33356	SY	P806NJN	33359	HS	P209XNO			

33393	CB	R353LER	Dennis Dart SLF		Alexander ALX200	N39F	1997	
33394	PE	R354LER	Dennis Dart SLF		Alexander ALX200	N39F	1997	
33395	PE	R355LER	Dennis Dart SLF		Alexander ALX200	N39F	1997	
33396	CB	R356LER	Dennis Dart SLF		Alexander ALX200	N39F	1997	
33397	PE	P564APM	Dennis Dart SLF		Plaxton Pointer	N39F	1996	Plaxton demonstrator, 1997
33398	PE	R365JVA	Dennis Dart SLF		Alexander ALX200	N39F	1997	
33399	CB	R366JVA	Dennis Dart SLF		Alexander ALX200	N39F	1997	
33401	CH	T801OHL	Dennis Dart SLF		Plaxton Pointer 2	NC38F	1999	
33402	CH	T802OHL	Dennis Dart SLF		Plaxton Pointer 2	NC38F	1999	
33403	CH	T803OHL	Dennis Dart SLF		Plaxton Pointer 2	NC38F	1999	
33404	HL	S401SDT	Dennis Dart SLF		Alexander ALX200	N37F	1998	
33405	HL	S402SDT	Dennis Dart SLF		Alexander ALX200	N37F	1998	

Lettered for route 2 in Ashford, 33019, R819HCD illustrates the low-floor motif used on several easy-access services. *Dave Heath*

| 33406 | HL | S403SDT | Dennis Dart SLF | | | Alexander ALX200 | N37F | 1998 |
| 33407 | PM | T905XCD | Dennis Dart SLF | | | Plaxton Pointer SPD | N36F | 1999 |

33414-33419

			Dennis Dart SLF			Alexander ALX200	N37F	1997-98
33414	IS	R614GFS	33416	DE	S616CSC	33418	DE	S618CSC	33419	DE	S619CSC
33415	DE	S615CSC	33417	DE	S617CSC

33428-33439

			Dennis Dart SLF			Alexander ALX200	N37F	2001
33428	PH	X428NSE	33431	PH	X431NSE	33434	PH	X434NSE	33437	IS	X437NSE
33429	PH	X429NSE	33432	PH	X432NSE	33435	PH	X435NSE	33438	IS	X438NSE
33430	PH	X441NSE	33433	PH	X433NSE	33436	PH	X436NSE	33439	IS	X439NSE

33443-33447

			Dennis Dart SLF			Alexander ALX200	N38F	2001
33443	AY	X613JCS	33445	AY	X615JCS	33446	AY	X616JCS	33447	AY	X617JCS
33444	AY	X614JCS

33453-33464

			Dennis Dart SLF			Alexander ALX200	N37F	1998-9
33453	BD	S453CVV	33456	NN	S456CVV	33459	NN	S459CVV	33462	CB	V462TVV
33454	BD	S454CVV	33457	NN	S457CVV	33460	NN	S460CVV	33463	CB	V463TVV
33455	NN	S455CVV	33458	NN	S458CVV	33461	CB	S461CVV	33464	CB	V464TVV

33469-33479

			Dennis Dart SLF			Alexander ALX200	N37F	1998
33469	AN	T469GPS	33472	IS	S472JSE	33475	IS	S475JSE	33478	AN	S478JSE
33470	AN	T470GPS	33473	IS	S473JSE	33476	IS	S476JSE	33479	AN	S479JSE
33471	IS	T471GPS	33474	IS	S474JSE	33477	AN	S477JSE

33482-33492

			Dennis Dart SLF			Alexander ALX200	N37F	1997
33482	HP	R462SEF	33485	HP	R465SEF	33488	HP	R468SEF	33491	SC	R471MVN
33483	HP	R463SEF	33486	HP	R466SEF	33489	SC	R469MVN	33492	SC	R472MVN
33484	HP	R464SEF	33487	HP	R467SEF	33490	SC	R470MVN

33501-33513

			Dennis Dart SLF 11.3m			Plaxton Pointer SPD	N41F	2000
33501	SN	W501VDD	33505	SN	W805VDD	33508	GR	W508VDD	33511	GR	X511ADF
33502	SN	X502ADF	33506	CT	X506ADF	33509	GR	W509VDD	33512	GR	X512ADF
33503	CT	X503ADF	33507	GR	X507ADF	33510	CT	X510ADF	33513	GR	X513ADF
33504	SN	W504VDD

33554	BR	P54XBO	Dennis Dart SLF			Wright Crusader	N43F	1997
33556	BR	P56XBO	Dennis Dart SLF			Marshall Capital C39	N43F	1997
33557	BR	P57XBO	Dennis Dart SLF			Marshall Capital C39	N43F	1997
33558	BR	P58XBO	Dennis Dart SLF			Marshall Capital C39	N43F	1997
33559	CL	P59VTG	Dennis Dart 9.8m			Marshall C37	B40F	1997
33561	CL	P61VTG	Dennis Dart 9.8m			Marshall C37	B40F	1997

33601-33627

			Dennis Dart SLF			Alexander ALX200	N37F	1998
33601	GR	R601SWO	33609	CL	R609SWO	33616	CL	R616SWO	33622	PT	S622TDW
33602	GR	R602SWO	33610	CL	R610SWO	33617	CL	R617SWO	33623	PT	S623TDW
33603	GR	R603SWO	33611	CL	R611SWO	33618	CL	R618SWO	33624	PT	S624TDW
33604	PE	R604SWO	33612	CL	R612SWO	33619	CL	R619SWO	33625	PT	S625TDW
33606	PT	R606SWO	33613	CL	R613SWO	33620	CL	R620SWO	33626	PT	S626TDW
33607	PT	R607SWO	33614	CL	R614SWO	33621	PT	R621SWO	33627	PT	S627TDW
33608	PT	R608SWO	33615	CL	R615SWO

33650-33655

			Dennis Dart SLF			Alexander ALX200	N37F	1998
33650	OX	R150CRW	33652	OX	R152CRW	33654	OX	R154CRW	33655	OX	R155CRW
33651	OX	R151CRW	33653	OX	R153CRW

| 33751 | EX | R751BDV | Dennis Dart SLF | | | Alexander ALX200 | N37F | 1997 |

33760-33771

			Dennis Dart SLF			Alexander ALX200	N37F	1997
33760	CH	R460LSO	33763	OX	R463LSO	33766	CH	R466LSO	33769	HL	R469LSO
33761	CH	R461LSO	33764	CH	R464LSO	33767	CH	R467LSO	33770	HL	R470LSO
33762	CH	R462LSO	33765	CH	R465LSO	33768	CH	R468LSO	33771	HL	R471LSO

The last model from Marshalls, before the low-floor Capital product became standard, was the C37, seen here on Dennis Dart 33559, P59VTG. It is allocated to Caerphilly where a recent *Kick Start* scheme has seen the arrival of sixteen new vehicles launched by Stagecoach Chairman, Brian Souter. *Phillip Stephenson*

33772	DS	T402UCS	Dennis Dart SLF		Alexander ALX200	N37F	1999	
33773	DS	T403UCS	Dennis Dart SLF		Alexander ALX200	N37F	1999	
33774	TQ	T404UCS	Dennis Dart SLF		Alexander ALX200	N37F	1999	

33775-33780

Dennis Dart SLF 11.3m — Plaxton Pointer SPD — N41F — 2000

33775	AY	X739JCS	33777	AY	X742JCS	33779	AY	X744JCS	33780	AY	X59RCS
33776	AY	X741JCS	33778	AY	X743JCS						

33781	EX	T575KGB	Dennis Dart SLF	Marshall Capital	N43F	1999	Dart Buses, 2001
33782	EX	T131MGB	Dennis Dart SLF	Marshall Capital	N43F	1999	Dart Buses, 2001
33783	EX	T132MGB	Dennis Dart SLF	Marshall Capital	N43F	1999	Dart Buses, 2001

33801-33829

Dennis Dart SLF 10.1m — Alexander ALX200 — B37F — 1998

33801	EH	R801YUD	33809	SZ	R809YUD	33816	NN	R816YUD	33823	EX	R823YUD
33802	CB	R802YUD	33810	SZ	R810YUD	33817	NN	R817YUD	33824	EX	R824YUD
33803	EX	R803YUD	33811	SZ	R811YUD	33818	NN	R818YUD	33825	SC	R825YUD
33804	EX	R804YUD	33812	SZ	R812YUD	33819	NN	R819YUD	33826	SC	R826YUD
33805	EX	R805YUD	33813	NN	R813YUD	33820	NN	R720YUD	33827	SU	R827YUD
33806	PE	R706YUD	33814	NN	R814YUD	33821	OX	R821YUD	33828	SC	R828YUD
33807	EX	R807YUD	33815	NN	R815YUD	33822	OX	R822YUD	33829	NEu	R829YUD
33808	SN	R808YUD									

33831-33837

Dennis Dart SLF 11.3m — Plaxton Pointer SPD — N41F — 2001

33831	MD	X831AKW	33833	MD	X833AKW	33835	MD	X835AKW	33837	MD	X837AKW
33832	MD	X832AKW	33834	MD	X834AKW	33836	MD	X836AKW			

33828-33841

Dennis Dart SLF — Plaxton Pointer 2 — N37F — 2001

33838	CH	X838HHE	33839	CH	X839HHE	33840	CH	X840HHE	33841	CH	X841HHE

33847	MD	X827AKW	Dennis Dart SLF 11.3m	Plaxton Pointer SPD	N41F	2001
33848	MD	X828AKW	Dennis Dart SLF 11.3m	Plaxton Pointer SPD	N41F	2001
33849	MD	X829AKW	Dennis Dart SLF 11.3m	Plaxton Pointer SPD	N41F	2001

Stagecoach operates just six Mini Pointer Darts and all are allocated to Dumfries. Replicated for posterity in a Creative Masters model bus set, 33089, T36VCS, is seen heading out of the town on route 236 to Thornhill in August 2004. *Bob Downham*

33904-33914   Dennis Dart SLF 10m   Alexander ALX200   N36F   1996-97

33904	SN	P904SMR	33907	SN	P907SMR	33910	SN	P910SMR	33913	SN	P913SMR
33905	SN	P905SMR	33908	SN	P908SMR	33911	SN	P911SMR	33914	SN	P914SMR
33906	SN	P906SMR	33909	SN	P909SMR	33912	SN	P912SMR			

33915-33918   Dennis Dart SLF   Alexander ALX200   N37F   1997

33915	GR	R915GMW	33916	GR	R916GMW	33917	GR	R917GMW	33918	SN	R918GMW

33924-33930   Dennis Dart SLF   Alexander ALX200   N37F   1998

33924	SN	S924PDD	33926	GR	S926PDD	33928	GR	S928PDD	33930	CT	S930PDD
33925	SN	S925PDD	33927	GR	S927PDD	33929	GR	S929PDD			

33938-33962   Dennis Dart SLF   Alexander ALX200   N37F   1999

33938	CT	V938DFH	33945	GR	V945DFH	33951	GR	V951DDG	33957	CT	V957DDG
33939	CT	V939DFH	33946	GR	V946DFH	33952	GR	V952DDG	33958	CT	V958DDG
33940	CT	V940DFH	33947	RY	V947DFH	33953	CT	V953DDG	33959	GR	V959DDG
33941	CT	V941DFH	33948	CT	V948DDG	33954	CT	V954DDG	33960	CT	V960DDG
33942	SN	V942DFH	33949	GR	V949DDG	33955	CT	V955DDG	33961	CT	V961DFH
33943	SN	V943DFH	33950	GR	V950DDG	33956	CT	V956DDG	33962	CT	V962DFH
33944	GR	V944DFH									

33966-33977   Dennis Dart SLF   Alexander ALX200   N37F   2001

33966	GR	X966AFH	33969	SN	X969AFH	33972	CT	X972AFH	33975	CT	X975AFH
33967	SN	X967AFH	33970	SN	X978AFH	33973	CT	X973AFH	33976	CT	X976AFH
33968	SN	X968AFH	33971	SN	X971AFH	33974	CT	X974AFH	33977	CT	X977AFH

33978	RY	VX51NXR	Dennis Dart SLF	Alexander ALX200	N38F	2001
33979	RY	VX51NXS	Dennis Dart SLF	Alexander ALX200	N38F	2001
33980	RY	VX51NXT	Dennis Dart SLF	Alexander ALX200	N38F	2001

Caught at an unfortunate moment, the destination display of 34025, R125VPU failed to advise that the bus is about to head for Ayr. It is seen in Irvine and is one of several that have undergone refurbishment on transfer from London. *Bob Downham*

34001-34009 — Dennis Dart SLF 10m — Alexander ALX200 — N36F — 1996

34001	WP	P21HMF	**34004**	WP	P24HMF	**34006**	WP	P26HMF	**34008** WP P28HMF
34002	WP	P31HMF	**34005**	WP	P25HMF	**34007**	WP	P27HMF	**34009** WP P29HMF
34003	WP	P23HMF							

34010-34020 — Dennis Dart SLF 10m — Alexander ALX200 — N36F — 1997

34010	AT	P610SEV	**34013**	AT	413DCD	**34016**	AT	R116VPU	**34019** BE R119VPU
34011	AT	411DCD	**34014**	AT	NDZ3020	**34017**	AT	R117VPU	**34020** AT 420DCD
34012	BE	412DCD	**34015**	BE	421DCD	**34018**	BE	408DCD	

34021-34029 — Dennis Dart SLF 10m — Alexander ALX200 — N33F — 1997

34021	AY	R121VPU	**34024**	AY	R124VPU	**34026**	AY	R126VPU	**34028** FH R128VPU
34022	AN	R122VPU	**34025**	AY	R125VPU	**34027**	AY	R127VPU	**34029** FH R129VPU
34023	FH	R123VPU							

34030-34041 — Dennis Dart SLF 10m — Alexander ALX200 — N29F — 1998

34030	BE	R930FOO	**34033**	BE	R933FOO	**34036**	FH	R936FOO	**34039** AN R939FOO
34031	HS	R931FOO	**34034**	BE	R934FOO	**34037**	PT	R937FOO	**34040** BQ R940FOO
34032	BE	R932FOO	**34035**	HS	R935FOO	**34038**	PT	R938FOO	**34041** PT R941FOO

34042-34058 — Dennis Dart SLF 9.4m — Alexander ALX200 — N29F — 1998

34042	MR	R942FOO	**34047**	CS	R947FOO	**34051**	CN	R451FVX	**34055** CN R455FVX
34043	CN	R943FOO	**34048**	CS	R948FOO	**34052**	CN	R452FVX	**34056** CN R456FVX
34044	CN	R944FOO	**34049**	CN	R949FOO	**34053**	CS	R453FVX	**34057** CS R457FVX
34045	CN	R945FOO	**34050**	CS	R950FOO	**34054**	CS	R454FVX	**34058** CN R458FVX
34046	CN	R946FOO							

34059-34078 — Dennis Dart SLF 10m — Alexander ALX200 — N33F — 1998

34059	BE	S459BWC	**34064**	HS	XIL1284	**34069**	BQ	S469BWC	**34074** HS S474BWC
34060	BE	S460BWC	**34065**	HS	XIL1560	**34070**	BQ	S470BWC	**34075** HS XIL1575
34061	BQ	S461BWC	**34066**	HS	XIL1296	**34071**	HS	S471BWC	**34076** FH S476BWC
34062	BQ	S462BWC	**34067**	BE	S467BWC	**34072**	BE	S472BWC	**34077** TQ S477BWC
34063	AY	S463BWC	**34068**	BE	S468BWC	**34073**	BE	S473BWC	**34078** HS XIL1568

Seen in Effra Road, Brixton, once to home to London Transport ticket machine works, Dart 34201, W201DNO, illustrates the nearside layout of the dual-doored 10.1metre version. The bus is in the latest London scheme that uses a simple blue skirt on the red livery. *Mark Lyons*

34079-34088

Dennis Dart SLF 9.4m   Alexander ALX200   N29F   1999

34079	CS	S479BWC	34082	DE	S482BWC	34085	SA	S485BWC	34087	SA	S487BWC
34080	CS	S480BWC	34083	CE	S483BWC	34086	SA	S486BWC	34088	CE	S488BWC
34081	CS	S481BWC	34084	DE	S484BWC						

34089-34095

Dennis Dart SLF 10m   Alexander ALX200   N33F*   1999   *34089 is N29F, 34090 is N31F

34089	HS	S489BWC	34091	HS	S491BWC	34093	HS	S493BWC	34095	TQ	S495BWC
34090	HS	S490BWC	34092	BE	S492BWC	34094	HS	S494BWC			

34096-34106

Dennis Dart SLF 9.4m   Alexander ALX200   N29F*   1999

34096	CN	S496BWC	34099	CE	S499BWC	34102	LNu	S102WHK	34105	CN	S105WHK
34097	TB	S497BWC	34100	CN	S210WHK	34103	CE	S103WHK	34106	CN	S106WHK
34098	LNu	S498BWC	34101	CE	S101WHK	34104	DE	S104WHK			

34107	BE	V107MVX	Dennis Dart SLF 10.1m	Plaxton Pointer 2	N33F	1999
34108	BE	V108MVX	Dennis Dart SLF 10.1m	Plaxton Pointer 2	N33F	1999
34109	BE	V109MVX	Dennis Dart SLF 10.1m	Plaxton Pointer 2	N33F	1999
34110	BE	V110MVX	Dennis Dart SLF 10.1m	Plaxton Pointer 2	N33F	1999

34111-34138

Dennis Dart SLF 10.1m   Plaxton Pointer 2   N31D   1999

34111	LNu	V173MVX	34118	TL	V118MVX	34125	CN	V125MVX	34132	CN	V132MVX
34112	LNu	V112MVX	34119	BK	V119MVX	34126	CN	V126MVX	34133	CL	V133MVX
34113	LNu	V113MVX	34120	BK	V120MVX	34127	CN	V127MVX	34134	PT	V134MVX
34114	TL	V114MVX	34121	BK	V174MVX	34128	CN	V128MVX	34135	PT	V135MVX
34115	EX	V115MVX	34122	BK	V122MVX	34129	CN	V129MVX	34136	CN	V136MVX
34116	TL	V116MVX	34123	BK	V123MVX	34130	CN	V130MVX	34137	CN	V137MVX
34117	TL	V117MVX	34124	PT	V124MVX	34131	CN	V131MVX	34138	CN	V138MVX

Part of the vehicle intake for the local Hastings partnership, 34089, S489BWC, seats only twenty-nine with additional room for mobility impaired passengers. It is seen on route 20 in the town. *Richard Godfrey*

34139-34172 Dennis Dart SLF 9.3m Plaxton Pointer 2 N27D 1999-2000

34139	CE	V139MVX	34148	PD	V148MVX	34157	SD	V157MVX	34165	SD	V165MVX
34140	CE	V140MVX	34149	PD	V149MVX	34158	U	V158MVX	34166	SD	V166MVX
34141	TB	V141MVX	34150	PD	V150MVX	34159	SD	V159MVX	34167	SD	V167MVX
34142	SD	V142MVX	34151	SD	V151MVX	34160	U	V160MVX	34168	SD	V168MVX
34143	SD	V143MVX	34152	TB	V152MVX	34161	SD	V161MVX	34169	SD	V169MVX
34144	SD	V144MVX	34153	SD	V153MVX	34162	SD	V162MVX	34170	SD	V170MVX
34145	SD	V145MVX	34154	SD	V154MVX	34163	SD	V163MVX	34171	SD	V171MVX
34146	SD	V146MVX	34155	SD	V155MVX	34164	SD	V164MVX	34172	SD	V172MVX
34147	PD	V147MVX	34156	SD	V156MVX						

34173-34203 Dennis Dart SLF 10.1m Plaxton Pointer 2 N31D 2000

34173	TL	W173DNO	34181	U	W181DNO	34189	SD	W189DNO	34197	SD	W197DNO
34174	U	W174DNO	34182	SD	W182DNO	34190	U	W231DNO	34198	U	W198DNO
34175	U	W224DNO	34183	SD	W183DNO	34191	SD	W191DNO	34199	BK	W199DNO
34176	U	W176DNO	34184	SD	W184DNO	34192	SD	W192DNO	34200	TL	W233DNO
34177	TL	W177DNO	34185	SD	W185DNO	34193	SD	W193DNO	34201	TL	W201DNO
34178	U	W178DNO	34186	SD	W186DNO	34194	SD	W194DNO	34202	BK	W202DNO
34179	U	W226DNO	34187	SD	W187DNO	34195	SD	W195DNO	34203	TL	W203DNO
34180	TL	W227DNO	34188	SD	W188DNO	34196	SD	W196DNO			

34204-34211 Dennis Dart SLF 9.3m Plaxton Pointer 2 N27D 2000

34204	TB	W204DNO	34206	TB	W229DNO	34208	SD	W208DNO	34210	SD	W232DNO
34205	TB	W228DNO	34207	SD	W207DNO	34209	SD	W209DNO	34211	SD	W211DNO

34212-34223 Dennis Dart SLF 9.3m Plaxton Pointer 2 N30F 2000

34212	SD	W212DNO	34215	PD	W215DNO	34218	TB	W218DNO	34221	TB	W221DNO
34213	TB	W213DNO	34216	PD	W216DNO	34219	TB	W219DNO	34222	TB	W236DNO
34214	SD	W214DNO	34217	TB	W234DNO	34220	TB	W235DNO	34223	TB	W223DNO

Only a few of the 9-metre version of the ALX200 were made before production the model ceased. Pictured at the Queen Elizabeth Hospital in Woolwich is 34248, Y248FJN. *Laurie Rufus*

34224-34236

Dennis Dart SLF 11.3m — Plaxton Pointer SPD — N37D — 2001

34224	TB	X224WNO	34228	TB	X228WNO	34231	TB	X231WNO	34234	TB	X234WNO
34225	TB	X237WNO	34229	TB	X229WNO	34232	TB	X232WNO	34235	TB	X235WNO
34226	TB	X226WNO	34230	TB	X238WNO	34233	TB	X233WNO	34236	TB	X236WNO
34227	TB	X227WNO									

34237-34253

Dennis Dart SLF 9m — Alexander ALX200 — N28F — 2001

34237	TL	Y237FJN	34242	TL	Y242FJN	34246	TL	Y246FJN	34250	TL	Y349FJN
34238	TL	Y238FJN	34243	TL	Y243FJN	34247	TL	Y247FJN	34251	TL	Y251FJN
34239	TL	Y239FJN	34244	TL	Y244FJN	34248	PD	Y248FJN	34252	TL	Y252FJN
34240	PD	Y347FJN	34245	PD	Y348FJN	34249	TL	Y249FJN	34253	TL	Y253FJN
34241	TL	Y241FJN									

34254-34272

Dennis Dart SLF 10.1m — Alexander ALX200 — N30D — 2001

34254	BK	Y254FJN	34259	BK	Y259FJN	34264	BK	Y264FJN	34269	BK	Y269FJN
34255	BK	Y351FJN	34260	BK	Y352FJN	34265	BK	Y265FJN	34270	BK	Y353FJN
34256	BK	Y256FJN	34261	BK	Y261FJN	34266	BK	Y266FJN	34271	BK	Y271FJN
34257	BK	Y257FJN	34262	BK	Y262FJN	34267	BK	Y267FJN	34272	BK	Y272FJN
34258	BK	Y258FJN	34263	BK	Y263FJN	34268	BK	Y268FJN			

34273-34327

Dennis Dart SLF 10.1m — Alexander ALX200 — N30D — 2001

34273	BK	Y273FJN	34287	BK	Y287FJN	34301	BK	Y301FJN	34315	TL	LX51FGU
34274	BK	Y274FJN	34288	BK	Y671JSG	34302	BK	Y302FJN	34316	TL	LX51FGZ
34275	BK	Y354FJN	34289	BK	Y289FJN	34303	TL	LX51FGA	34317	TL	LX51FHG
34276	BK	Y276FJN	34290	BK	LX51FFW	34304	TL	LX51FGF	34318	TL	LX51FHB
34277	BK	Y277FJN	34291	BK	Y291FJN	34305	TL	LX51FGE	34319	TL	LX51FHA
34278	BK	LX51FPE	34292	BK	Y292FJN	34306	TL	LX51FGD	34320	TL	LX51FHC
34279	BK	Y279FJN	34293	BK	Y293FJN	34307	TL	LX51FGG	34321	TL	LX51FHD
34280	BK	Y356FJN	34294	BK	Y294FJN	34308	TL	LX51FGM	34322	TL	LX51FHE
34281	BK	Y281FJN	34295	BK	Y295FJN	34309	TL	LX51FGK	34323	TL	LX51FHF
34282	BK	Y282FJN	34296	BK	Y296FJN	34310	TL	LX51FGV	34324	TL	LX51FHK
34283	BK	Y283FJN	34297	BK	Y297FJN	34311	TL	LX51FGJ	34325	TL	LX51FHL
34284	BK	Y284FJN	34298	BK	Y298FJN	34312	TL	LX51FGN	34326	TL	LX51FHH
34285	BK	Y285FJN	34299	BK	Y299FJN	34313	TL	LX51FGO	34327	TL	LX51FHJ
34286	BK	Y286FJN	34300	BK	LX51FPJ	34314	TL	LX51FGP			

From 2002, TransBus started to use its own name for the products, thus displacing familar names such as Alexander, Dennis and Plaxton. The vehicles were produced at Larbert in central Scotland and sent as kits to Scarborough, Falkirk, Belfast and Wigan for assembly. Shown in London colours, 34349, LV52HKA, is devoid of badges. *Laurie Rufus*

34328-34346

			Dennis Dart SLF 10.8m			Alexander ALX200			N33D	2001

34328	SD	Y371FJN	34333	SD	Y373FJN	34338	SD	Y338FJN	34343	SD	Y343FJN
34329	SD	Y329FJN	34334	SD	Y334FJN	34339	SD	Y339FJN	34344	SD	Y344FJN
34330	SD	Y372FJN	34335	SD	Y335FJN	34340	SD	Y374FJN	34345	SD	Y376FJN
34331	SD	Y331FJN	34336	SD	Y336FJN	34341	SD	LX51FFO	34346	SD	Y346FJN
34332	SD	Y332FJN	34337	SD	Y337FJN	34342	SD	Y342FJN			

34347-34365

			Dennis Dart SLF 10.8m			TransBus Pointer			N30D	2002

34347	BK	LV52HJY	34352	BK	LV52HKD	34357	TB	LV52HKJ	34362	TB	LV52HKO
34348	BK	LV52HJZ	34353	BK	LV52HKE	34358	TB	LV52HKK	34363	TB	LV52HKP
34349	BK	LV52HKA	34354	TB	LV52HKF	34359	TB	LV52HKL	34364	TB	LV52HKT
34350	BK	LV52HKB	34355	TB	LV52HKG	34360	TB	LV52HKM	34365	TB	LV52HKU
34351	BK	LV52HKC	34356	TB	LV52HKH	34361	TB	LV52HKN			

34366-34376

			Dennis Dart SLF 8.8m			TransBus Pointer			N28F	2003

34366	PD	LV52HGC	34369	PD	LV52HGF	34372	PD	LV52HGK	34375	PD	LV52HGN
34367	PD	LV52HGD	34370	PD	LV52HGG	34373	PD	LV52HGL	34376	PD	LV52HGO
34368	PD	LV52HGE	34371	PD	LV52HGJ	34374	PD	LV52HGM			

34377-34386

			TransBus Dart 9.3m			TransBus Pointer			N30F	2003

34377	PD	LX03BZJ	34380	PD	LX03BZM	34383	PD	LX03BZR	34385	PD	LX03BZT
34378	PD	LX03BZK	34381	PD	LX03BZN	34384	PD	LX03BZS	34386	PD	LX03BZU
34379	PD	LX03BZL	34382	PD	LX03BZP						

34387-34397

			TransBus Dart 10.1m			TransBus Pointer			N30D	2003

34387	TL	LX03BZV	34390	TL	LX03CAA	34393	TL	LX03CAV	34396	TL	LX03CBV
34388	TL	LX03BZW	34391	TL	LX03CAE	34394	TL	LX03CBF	34397	TL	LX03CBY
34389	TL	LX03BZY	34392	TL	LX03CAU	34395	TL	LX03CBU			

34398	RU	KN04XCT	Dennis Dart SLF 8.8m	TransBus Mini Pointer	N29F	2004
34399	EH	WA03WWZ	Dennis Dart SLF 8.8m	Caetano Nimbus	B28F	2003

Large batches of Darts have been taken into stock to displace earlier midi-buses and also many of the time-expired minibuses. Cardiff is the location for this view of 34510, CN53HWX, which carries lettering for route 122. *Mark Lyons*

34401-34500

TransBus Dart 10.1m   TransBus Pointer   N38F   2003-04

34401	SC	NK53KFW	34426	BD	KV53EZC	34451	PM	GX53MWV	34476	CEw	PX53DKA
34402	RY	VA53LCV	34427	BD	KV53EZD	34452	PM	GX53MWW	34477	CEw	PX53DKD
34403	RY	VA53LCW	34428	BD	KV53EZE	34453	PM	GX53MWY	34478	CEw	PX53DKE
34404	CT	VA53LCY	34429	BD	KV53EZF	34454	PM	GX53MWZ	34479	CEw	PX53DKF
34405	CT	VA53LCZ	34430	BD	KV53EZG	34455	MD	YN53ZSG	34480	CEw	PX53DKJ
34406	WI	GX53MVU	34431	BD	KV53EZH	34456	MD	YN53ZSJ	34481	CEw	PX53DKK
34407	WI	GX53MVV	34432	BD	KV53EZJ	34457	MD	YN53ZRT	34482	IS	SV53DDJ
34408	WI	GX53MVW	34433	BD	KV53EZK	34458	MD	YN53ZRU	34483	IS	SV53DDK
34409	WI	GX53MVY	34434	BD	KV53EZL	34459	MD	YN53ZRV	34484	IS	SV53DDL
34410	WI	GX53MVZ	34435	BD	KV53EZM	34460	MD	YN53ZRX	34485	IS	SV53DDM
34411	WI	GX53MWA	34436	BD	KV53EZN	34461	MD	YN53ZRY	34486	IS	SV53DDO
34412	WI	GX53MWC	34437	BD	KV53EZO	34462	MD	YN53ZRZ	34487	IS	SV53DDU
34413	WI	GX53MWD	34438	BD	KV53EZP	34463	MD	YN53ZSD	34488	IS	SV53DDX
34414	WI	GX53MWE	34439	BD	KV53EZR	34464	MD	YN53ZSE	34489	IS	SV53DDY
34415	WI	GX53MWF	34440	BD	KV53EZT	34465	MD	YN53ZSF	34490	IS	SV53DDZ
34416	WI	GX53MWG	34441	BD	KV53EZU	34466	OX	KV53NHA	34491	NU	KV53NHH
34417	WI	GX53MWJ	34442	BD	KV53EZW	34467	OX	KV53NHB	34492	NU	KV53NHJ
34418	WI	GX53MWK	34443	BD	KV53EZY	34468	OX	KV53NHC	34493	NU	KV53NHK
34419	BD	KV53EYU	34444	BD	KV53EZZ	34469	OX	KV53NHD	34494	NU	KV53NHL
34420	BD	KV53EYW	34445	PM	GX53MWL	34470	OX	KV53NHE	34495	NU	KV53NHM
34421	BD	KV53EYX	34446	PM	GX53MWM	34471	OX	KV53NHF	34496	NU	KV53NHN
34422	BD	KV53EYY	34447	PM	GX53MWN	34472	OX	KV53NHG	34497	NU	KV53NHO
34423	BD	KV53EYZ	34448	PM	GX53MWO	34473	CEw	PX53DJV	34498	NU	KV53NHP
34424	BD	KV53EZA	34449	PM	GX53MWP	34474	CEw	PX53DJY	34499	NU	KX53VNL
34425	BD	KV53EZB	34450	PM	GX53MWU	34475	CEw	PX53DJZ	34500	PT	CN53HWZ

The 2005 Stagecoach Bus Handbook

The latest batch of Darts for London duties consists of ten 10.1 metre examples allocated to Plumstead. Representing the type is 34552, LX53LGG, which is seen on route 386 in Woolwich. *Laurie Rufus*

34501-34550

TransBus Dart 10.1m   TransBus Pointer   N38F   2004

34501	PT	CN53HXA	34514	WG	GX04EXH	34527	PM	GX04EXZ
34502	PT	CN53HXB	34515	WG	GX04EXJ	34528	PM	GX04EYA
34503	PT	CN53HXC	34516	WG	GX04EXK	34529	PM	GX04EYB
34504	PT	CN53HWO	34517	WG	GX04EXL	34530	PE	GX04EYC
34505	PT	CN53HWP	34518	WG	GX04EXM	34531	PM	GX04EYD
34506	PT	CN53HWR	34519	WG	GX04EXN	34532	PE	GX04EYF
34507	PT	CN53HWU	34520	WG	GX04EXP	34533	PE	GX04EYG
34508	PT	CN53HWV	34521	WG	GX04EXR	34534	PE	GX04EYH
34509	PT	CN53HWW	34522	WG	GX04EXS	34535	PE	GX04EYJ
34510	PT	CN53HWX	34523	PM	GX04EXT	34536	PE	GX04EYK
34511	PT	CN53HWY	34524	WG	GX04EXU	34537	PE	GX04EYL
34512	PT	CN53UZG	34525	WG	GX04EXV	34538	PE	GX04EYM
34513	PT	CN04JDK	34526	PE	GX04EXW			

34539	PE	GX04EYP			
34540	PE	GX04EYR			
34541	PE	GX04EYS			
34542	PE	GX04EYT			
34543	PE	GX04EYU			
34544	PE	GX04EYV			
34545	PE	GX04EYW			
34546	PE	GX04EYY			
34547	PE	GX04EYZ			
34548	PE	GX04EZA			
34549	PE	GX04EZB			
34550	HP	NK04KZT			

34551-34560

TransBus Dart 10.1m   TransBus Pointer   N31D   2003

34551	PD	LX53LGF	34554	PD	LX53LGK	34557	PD	LX53LGO
34552	PD	LX53LGG	34555	PD	LX53LGL	34558	PD	LX53LGU
34553	PD	LX53LGJ	34556	PD	LX53LGN			

34559	PD	LX53LGV
34560	PD	LX53LGW

34561-34620

TransBus Dart 10.1m   TransBus Pointer   N38F   2004

34561	HP	NK04KZU	34576	CH	YN04YYA	34591	NN	KX04GZL
34562	HP	NK04KZV	34577	CH	YN04YYB	34592	NN	KX04GZM
34563	HP	NK04KZW	34578	CH	YN04YYC	34593	NN	KX04GZN
34564	HP	NK04KZX	34579	CEw	PX04DRZ	34594	NN	KX04GZR
34565	HP	NK04KZY	34580	CEw	PX04DSE	34595	NN	KX04GZS
34566	HP	NK04KZZ	34581	CH	YN04YYD	34596	KK	SF04VSV
34567	HP	NK04LBA	34582	CH	YN04YXR	34597	KK	SF04VSX
34568	HP	NK04LBB	34583	CH	YN04YXS	34598	KK	SF04VSY
34569	HP	NK04LBE	34584	CH	YN04YXT	34599	KK	SF04VSZ
34570	HL	YN04YKU	34585	NN	KX04RUW	34600	KK	SF04VTA
34571	HL	YN04YKV	34586	NN	KX04RUY	34601	KK	SF04VTC
34572	HL	YN04YKW	34587	NN	KX04RVA	34602	KK	SF04VTD
34573	HL	YN04YKX	34588	NN	KX04RVC	34603	KK	SF04VTE
34574	CH	YN04YKY	34589	NN	KX04RVE	34604	KK	SF04VTG
34575	CH	YN04YKZ	34590	NN	KX04RVP	34605	SS	NK04NPF

34606	SS	NK04NPJ
34607	SS	NK04NPN
34608	SS	NK04NPP
34609	SS	NK04NPU
34610	SS	NK04NPV
34611	SS	NK04NPX
34612	SS	NK04NPY
34613	SS	NK04NPZ
34614	SS	NK04NRE
34615	SS	NK04NRF
34616	PR	PX04HTT
34617	PR	PX04HTU
34618	PR	PX04HTX
34619	PR	PX04HTY
34620	PR	PX04HTZ

The second delivery of Darts in 2004 was predominantly allocated to south Wales and southern England. Seen at the opposite end of Britain however is 34601, SF04VTC, which is based at Kilmarnock where the type can be found on town services. *Bob Downham*

34621-34680   Alexander-Dennis Dart 10.1m   Alexander-Dennis Pointer   N38F   2004

34621	BR	CN04VJV	34636	AT	GX54DWF	34651	TH	GX54DXB	34666	CL	CN54EDK
34622	BR	CN04VJX	34637	AT	GX54DWG	34652	TH	GX54DXC	34667	CL	CN54EDL
34623	BR	CN04VJY	34638	AT	GX54DWJ	34653	TH	GX54DXD	34668	CL	CN54EDO
34624	BR	CN04VJZ	34639	AT	GX54DWK	34654	TH	GX54DXE	34669	CL	CN54EDP
34625	NU	KX54HJK	34640	AT	GX54DWL	34655	TH	GX54DXF	34670	CL	CN54EDR
34626	NU	KX54DPA	34641	LS	GX54DWM	34656	TH	GX54DXG	34671	CL	CN54EDU
34627	NU	KX54DPB	34642	LS	GX54DWN	34657	TH	GX54DXH	34672	CL	CN54EDV
34628	NU	KX54DPC	34643	LS	GX54DWO	34658	TH	GX54DXJ	34673	CL	CN54ECT
34629	AT	GX54DVW	34644	LS	GX54DWP	34659	TH	GX54FVU	34674	CL	CN54ECV
34630	AT	GX54DVY	34645	TH	GX54DWU	34660	TH	GX54FVV	34675	CL	CN54ECW
34631	AT	GX54DVZ	34646	TH	GX54DWV	34661	TH	GX54FVW	34676	CL	CN54ECX
34632	AT	GX54DWA	34647	TH	GX54DWW	34662	TH	GX54FVY	34677	CL	CN54ECY
34633	AT	GX54DWC	34648	TH	GX54DWY	34663	CL	CN54EDC	34678	CL	CN54ECZ
34634	AT	GX54DWD	34649	TH	GX54DWZ	34664	CL	CN54EDF	34679	CY	PX54EJO
34635	AT	GX54DWE	34650	TH	GX54DXA	34665	CL	CN54EDJ	34680	CY	PX54EJU

As we go to press, fleet numbers have been allocated for the 2005 supply of Darts. All 120 are destined for provincial depots with a spread covering much of Britain. In 2004 nine of the type were allocated to Carlisle for the 67/68 services for which they are lettered, though these have now been taken out of service following nearly two metres of water flooding at the depot. 34475, PX53DJZ was pictured in the city during 2004.
Phillip Stephenson

34671-34790

			Alexander-Dennis Dart 10.1m			Alexander-Dennis Pointer			N38F	2005 delivery plan	
34671	-	-	34701	-	-	34731	-	-		34761	-
34672	-	-	34702	-	-	34732	-	-		34762	-
34673	-	-	34703	-	-	34733	-	-		34763	-
34674	-	-	34704	-	-	34734	-	-		34764	-
34675	-	-	34705	-	-	34735	-	-		34765	-
34676	-	-	34706	-	-	34736	-	-		34766	-
34677	-	-	34707	-	-	34737	-	-		34767	-
34678	-	-	34708	-	-	34738	-	-		34768	-
34679	-	-	34709	-	-	34739	-	-		34769	-
34680	-	-	34710	-	-	34740	-	-		34770	-
34681	-	-	34711	-	-	34741	-	-		34771	-
34682	-	-	34712	-	-	34742	-	-		34772	-
34683	-	-	34713	-	-	34743	-	-		34773	-
34684	-	-	34714	-	-	34744	-	-		34774	-
34685	-	-	34715	-	-	34745	-	-		34775	-
34686	-	-	34716	-	-	34746	-	-		34776	-
34687	-	-	34717	-	-	34747	-	-		34777	-
34688	-	-	34718	-	-	34748	-	-		34778	-
34689	-	-	34719	-	-	34749	-	-		34779	-
34690	-	-	34720	-	-	34750	-	-		34780	-
34691	-	-	34721	-	-	34751	-	-		34781	-
34692	-	-	34722	-	-	34752	-	-		34782	-
34693	-	-	34723	-	-	34753	-	-		34783	-
34694	-	-	34724	-	-	34754	-	-		34784	-
34695	-	-	34725	-	-	34755	-	-		34785	-
34696	-	-	34726	-	-	34756	-	-		34786	-
34697	-	-	34727	-	-	34757	-	-		34787	-
34698	-	-	34728	-	-	34758	-	-		34788	-
34699	-	-	34729	-	-	34759	-	-		34789	-
34700	-	-	34730	-	-	34760	-	-		34790	-

35000-35515 Optare Excel L1150 — Optare — N40F — 2001-02

35000	CH	YN51VHH	35004	CH	YN51VHM	35008	WP	YN51VHT	35012	WP	YN51VHX
35001	CH	YN51VHJ	35005	CH	YN51VHN	35009	WP	YN51VHU	35013	WP	YN51VHY
35002	CH	YN51VHK	35006	CH	YN51VHP	35010	WP	YN51VHV	35014	WP	YN51VHZ
35003	CH	YN51VHL	35007	WP	YN51VHR	35011	WP	YN51VHW	35015	WP	YN51VJA

35016	AY	N207LCK	Optare Excel L1170	Optare	N36F	1996	Docherty, Irvine, 2004
35017	CC	N208LCK	Optare Excel L1170	Optare	N36F	1996	Docherty, Irvine, 2004

Special event vehicles - (initial owners shown)

39925	ES	DGS625	Leyland Tiger PS1/1	McLennan	C39F	1951	McLennan, Spittalfield
39957	NWu	VY957	Leyland Lion PLSC3	Ribble 1984 replica	B32R	1929	Ribble
39995	NWu	CK3825	Leyland Lion PLSC1	Ribble 1982 replica	B31F	1927	Ribble

40001-40015 Mercedes-Benz 709D — Alexander Sprint — B23F — 1995

40001	CE	N201UHH	40005	BA	N205UHH	40009	CY	N209UHH	40013	LL	N213UHH
40002	CEw	N202UHH	40006	LL	N206UHH	40010	CY	N210UHH	40014	LL	N214UHH
40003	CEw	N203UHH	40007	CY	N207UHH	40011	LL	N211UHH	40015	LL	N215UHH
40004	BA	N204UHH	40008	CY	N208UHH	40012	LL	N212UHH			

40016-40033 Mercedes-Benz 709D — Alexander Sprint — B23F — 1996

40016	BA	N116YHH	40021	BA	N121YHH	40025	LL	N125YHH	40029	LL	N129YRM
40017	BA	N117YHH	40022	BA	N122YHH	40026	BA	N126YRM	40030	LL	N130YRM
40018	BA	N118YHH	40023	BA	N123YHH	40027	LL	N127YRM	40031	LL	N131YRM
40019	BA	N119YHH	40024	CY	N124YHH	40028	LL	N128YRM	40033	LL	N133YRM
40020	BA	N120YHH									

40034-40040 Mercedes-Benz 709D — Alexander Sprint — B25F — 1993

40036	BJ	K873GHH	40038	BJ	K875GHH	40039	NWw	K876GHH	40040	NWw	K877GHH

40041-40052 Mercedes-Benz 709D — Alexander Sprint — B25F — 1996

40041	BQ	P341ASO	40044	GS	P344ASO	40047	AN	P347ASO	40050	AN	P350ASO
40042	BQ	P342ASO	40045	IS	P345ASO	40048	ESw	P348ASO	40051	IS	P351ASO
40043	BQ	P343ASO	40046	PH	P346ASO	40049	GS	P349ASO	40052	IS	P352ASO

40053-40069 Mercedes-Benz 709D — Alexander Sprint — B25F — 1995

40053	CC	M653FYS	40058	KK	M658FYS	40062	AY	M662FYS	40066	KK	M651FYS
40054	AY	M654FYS	40059	AS	M659FYS	40063	AS	M663FYS	40067	KK	M667FYS
40055	AA	M655FYS	40060	CC	M660FYS	40064	CC	M664FYS	40068	AS	M668FYS
40056	AA	M656FYS	40061	AS	M661FYS	40065	CC	M665FYS	40069	CC	M652FYS
40057	AY	M657FYS									

40070-40080 Mercedes-Benz 709D — Alexander Sprint — B25F — 1994

40070	DE	M770TFS	40073	ESw	M773TFS	40076	SA	M776TFS	40079	BQ	M779TFS
40071	DE	M771TFS	40074	GS	M774TFS	40078	ESw	M778TFS	40080	GS	M780TFS
40072	ESw	M772TFS	40075	ESw	M775TFS						

40081	KL	K878GHH	Mercedes-Benz 709D	Alexander Sprint	B25F	1993

40087-40093 Mercedes-Benz 709D — Alexander Sprint — B25F — 1993

40087	ESw	K487FFS	40090	ESw	K490FFS	40091	ALt	K491FFS	40092	NEw	K492FFS
40089	AN	K489FFS									

40095	GS	N95ALS	Mercedes-Benz 709D	Alexander Sprint	B25F	1996
40096	GS	N96ALS	Mercedes-Benz 709D	Alexander Sprint	B25F	1996
40097	GS	N97ALS	Mercedes-Benz 709D	Alexander Sprint	B25F	1996
40098	AS	M648FYS	Mercedes-Benz 709D	Alexander Sprint	B25F	1995
40099	CC	M649FYS	Mercedes-Benz 709D	Alexander Sprint	B25F	1995
40100	KK	M650FYS	Mercedes-Benz 709D	Alexander Sprint	B25F	1995
40101	AA	L301JSA	Mercedes-Benz 709D	Alexander Sprint	BC25F	1993
40102	FH	L302JSA	Mercedes-Benz 709D	Alexander Sprint	BC25F	1993
40103	ESw	L303JSA	Mercedes-Benz 709D	Alexander Sprint	BC25F	1993

While the Mercedes-Benz 709 with Alexander Sprint bodywork still dominates the mini class, many have been sold during 2004, and others are retained as reserves. Carrying *Magic Mini* colours in Scotland is 40066, M651FYS, which was allocated to Kilmarnock when photographed. *Phillip Stephenson*

40108-40130

			Mercedes-Benz 709D			Alexander Sprint			B23F	1994		
40108	OX	L308YDU	40117	SEu	L317YDU	40123	CR	L323YDU	40130	SEu	L330YKV
40110	OX	L310YDU	40120	SEu	L320YDU	40125	ESu	L325YDU			

40134-40146

			Mercedes-Benz 709D			Alexander Sprint			B23F	1995		
40134	BJ	M334LHP	40138	BJ	M338LHP	40141	BJ	M341LHP	40144	WXu	M344LHP
40135	ESu	M335LHP	40139	NN	M339LHP	40142	LE	M342LHP	40145	CN	M345LHP
40136	BJ	M336LHP	40140	BD	M340LHP	40143	LE	M343LHP	40146	SMw	M346KWK
40137	NN	M337LHP									

40147-40172

			Mercedes-Benz 709D			Alexander Sprint			B25F	1996		
40147	NU	N347AVV	40154	ESw	N354AVV	40161	FH	N361AVV	40167	BQ	N367AVV
40148	NU	N348AVV	40155	RU	N355AVV	40162	OX	N362AVV	40168	BQ	N368AVV
40149	NU	N349AVV	40156	RU	N356AVV	40163	LE	N363AVV	40169	BQ	N369AVV
40150	SMw	N350AVV	40157	ESw	N357AVV	40164	CR	N364AVV	40170	FH	N370AVV
			40158	RU	N358AVV	40165	FH	N365AVV	40171	AN	N371AVV
40152	NU	N352AVV	40159	RU	N359AVV	40166	BQ	N366AVV	40172	OX	N372AVV
40153	RU	N353AVV	40160	RU	N360AVV						

40192-40203

			Mercedes-Benz 709D			Alexander Sprint			BC25F	1990		
40192	CE	G192PAO	40195	ESu	G195PAO	40198	ESw	G198PAO	40203	ESw	G203PAO
40194	ESu	G194PAO	40197	ESu	G197PAO						

40205	WXu	F392DHL	Mercedes-Benz 709D		Reeve Burgess Beaver		Publicity	1989

Typical of the Alexander Sprint model is Mercedes-Benz 709 40958, N958NAP, currently allocated to Folkestone. It was pictured during 2004 en route for Aycliff. *Phillip Stephenson*

40226-40250

		Mercedes-Benz 709D		Marshall C19			B21D	1995		
40226	SWu M226UTM				40239	SWu M239UTM		40245	SWu M245UTM
40227	SWu M227UTM	40234	SWu M234UTM		40240	SWu M240UTM		40246	SWu M246UTM
40228	SWu M228UTM				40241	SWu M241UTM			
40229	SWu M229UTM	40236	SWu M236UTM		40242	SWu M242UTM		40248	SWu M248UTM
40230	SWu M230UTM	40237	SWu M237UTM		40243	SWu M243UTM		40249	SWu M249UTM
40232	SWu M232UTM				40244	SWu M244UTM		40250	SWu M250UTM

40277	WSu G277TSL	Mercedes-Benz 709D		Alexander Sprint			B23F	1990

40301-40329

		Mercedes-Benz 709D		Alexander Sprint			B23F	1996		
40301	NN	N301XRP	40308	KG	N308XRP	40315	KG	N315XRP	40322	BD	N322XRP
40302	BD	N302XRP	40309	KG	N309XRP	40316	KG	N316XRP	40323	BD	N323XRP
40303	BD	N303XRP	40310	KG	N310XRP	40317	BD	N317XRP	40324	BD	N324XRP
40304	BD	N304XRP	40311	KG	N311XRP	40318	BD	N318XRP	40327	BA	N327XRP
40305	NN	N305XRP	40312	KG	N312XRP	40319	BD	N319XRP	40328	LL	N328XRP
40306	KG	N306XRP	40313	KG	N313XRP	40320	BD	N320XRP	40329	CEw	N329XRP
40307	KG	N307XRP	40314	KG	N314XRP	40321	BD	N321XRP			

40332-40349

		Mercedes-Benz 709D		Alexander Sprint			B25F	1994		
40332	BD	M332DRP	40338	NN	M338DRP	40342	KG	M342DRP	40346	KG	M346DRP
40334	BD	M334DRP	40339	NN	M339DRP	40343	KG	M343DRP	40347	KG	M347DRP
40335	BD	M335DRP	40340	KG	M340DRP	40344	KG	M344DRP	40348	KG	M348DRP
40336	BD	M336DRP	40341	KG	M341DRP	40345	KG	M345DRP	40349	KG	M349DRP
40337	BD	M337DRP									

40350-40383

		Mercedes-Benz 709D		Alexander Sprint			B25F*	1992-93	*40351-66 are B21F	
40350	EAw	K350ANV	40362	AN	L362JBD	40374	EAu	L374JBD	40379	EAu	L379JBD
40351	EAw	K351ANV	40365	ESw	L365JBD	40375	EAu	L375JBD	40380	EAu	L380JBD
40353	ESw	K353ANV	40366	EAw	L366JBD	40376	EAu	L376JBD	40381	NN	L381NBD
40356	EAw	K356ANV	40371	KG	L371JBD	40377	EAu	L377JBD	40382	EAu	L382NBD
40359	EAu	K359ANV	40373	EAw	L373JBD	40378	EAu	L378JBD	40383	BD	L383NBD

Pictured in Banbury in August 2004 was Optare Solo 40162, N382AVV. With a further fifty of this type due during 2005, further withdrawals of the Mercedes minibuses are expected. *Laurie Rufus*

40394-40402

		Mercedes-Benz 709D			Alexander Sprint			B25F	1996		
40394	LL	N194LFV	40396	CE	N196LFV	40398	KL	N198LFV	40401	CE	N201LFV
40395	CE	N195LFV	40397	PR	N197LFV	40399	CY	N199LFV	40402	CEw	N202LFV

40412-40428

		Mercedes-Benz 709D			Alexander Sprint			B25F	1993		
40417	CEu	K117XHG	40419	BQ	L119DRN	40424	CE	K124XHG	40427	NWu	L127DRN

40429-40435

		Mercedes-Benz 709D			Alexander Sprint			B25F	1996		
40429	GP	N879AVV	40431	GP	N881AVV	40433	GP	N883AVV	40435	BA	N885AVV
40430	GP	N880AVV	40432	GP	N882AVV	40434	GP	N884AVV			

40441-40455

		Mercedes-Benz 709D			Alexander Sprint			B25F	1996		
40441	NWu	N461VOD	40443	NWu	N463VOD	40446	CEw	N456VOD	40452	CE	N452VOD
40442	CY	N462VOD	40445	LL	N465VOD	40447	NWu	N457VOD	40455	PR	N455VOD

40461-40501

		Mercedes-Benz 709D			Alexander Sprint			B23F	1996		
40461	WA	N461RVK	40471	SY	N471RVK	40481	SY	N481RVK	40492	WA	N492RVK
40462	NEw	N462RVK	40472	SY	N472RVK	40482	NEu	N482RVK	40493	SY	N493RVK
40463	WA	N463RVK	40473	SY	N473RVK	40483	SY	N483RVK	40494	SY	N494RVK
40464	WA	N464RVK	40474	SY	N474RVK	40484	SY	N484RVK	40495	WA	N495RVK
40465	WA	N465RVK	40475	SY	N475RVK	40485	WA	N485RVK	40496	AL	N496RVK
40466	SY	N466RVK	40476	SY	N476RVK	40486	SY	N486RVK	40497	SY	N497RVK
40467	WA	N467RVK	40477	SY	N477RVK	40487	SY	N487RVK	40498	SY	N498RVK
40468	SA	N468RVK	40478	SY	N478RVK	40488	AL	N488RVK	40499	SY	N499RVK
40469	SY	N469RVK	40479	SY	N479RVK	40489	NEu	N489RVK	40501	WA	N501RVK
40470	SY	N470RVK	40480	SY	N480RVK	40491	WA	N491RVK			

40506-40520 — Mercedes-Benz 709D — Alexander Sprint — B23F — 1996

40506	PN	N506BJA	40510	PN	N510BJA	40514	TQ	N514BJA	40518 TQ N518BJA
40507	PN	N507BJA	40511	PN	N511BJA	40515	TQ	N515BJA	40519 CE N519BJA
40508	PN	N508BJA	40512	PN	N512BJA	40516	TQ	N516BJA	40520 NWw N520BJA
40509	PN	N509BJA	40513	PN	N513BJA	40517	TQ	N517BJA	

40525	DS	J217XKY	Mercedes-Benz 709D	Alexander Sprint	B25F	1993
40530	KK	N446TOS	Mercedes-Benz 709D	Alexander Sprint	B29F	1996	Shuttle Buses, Kilwinning,

40534-40560 — Mercedes-Benz 709D — Alexander Sprint — B25F — 1994

40534	IS	L334FWO	40541	BR	L341FWO	40548	AN	M348JBO	40554	TQ	M354JBO
40535	FH	L335FWO	40542	CE	L342FWO	40549	PN	M349JBO	40555	CN	M355JBO
40536	ESu	L336FWO	40543	CN	L343FWO	40550	TQ	M350JBO	40556	MR	M356JBO
40537	CN	L337FWO	40544	WXu	M344JBO	40551	PN	M351JBO	40557	WXu	M357JBO
40538	FH	L338FWO	40545	PN	M345JBO	40552	MR	M352JBO	40558	FH	M358JBO
40539	WXu	L339FWO	40547	CN	M347JBO	40553	TQ	M353JBO	40560	PN	M360JBO
40540	AN	L340FWO									

40561-40571 — Mercedes-Benz 709D — Alexander Sprint — B25F — 1995

40562	MR	M362LAX	40565	MR	M365LAX	40568	BR	M368LAX	40570	BR	M370LAX
40563	MR	M363LAX	40566	CN	M366LAX	40569	CN	M369LAX	40571	BR	M371LAX
40564	MR	M364LAX	40567	WXu	M367LAX						

40572-40584 — Mercedes-Benz 709D — Alexander Sprint — B25F — 1996

40572	CN	N372PNY	40576	WWu	N376PNY	40579	CN	N379PNY	40582	CN	N382PNY
40573	CN	N373PNY	40577	CN	N377PNY	40580	CN	N380PNY	40583	CN	N383PNY
40574	CN	N374PNY	40578	CN	N378PNY	40581	CN	N381PNY	40584	CN	N384PNY
40575	CN	N375PNY									

40585-40591 — Mercedes-Benz 709D — Alexander Sprint — BC25F — 1993-94

40585	ESw	L315JSA	40587	ESu	M317RSO	40589	BQ	M319RSO	40591	AL	M321RSO
40586	GS	L316JSA	40588	GS	M318RSO	40590	BQ	M320RSO			

40593	ESw	K320YKG	Mercedes-Benz 709D	Wright NimBus	B25F	1992	
40594	ESw	K321YKG	Mercedes-Benz 709D	Wright NimBus	B25F	1992	
40595	PY	M92JHB	Mercedes-Benz 709D	Wadham Stringer	B29F	1995	Phil Anslow, Pontypool, 2004

40601-40665 — Mercedes-Benz 709D — Alexander Sprint — B25F — 1996

40601	KK	N601VSS	40618	CN	N618VSS	40634	KK	N634VSS	40650	CEw	N650VSS
40602	AY	N602VSS	40619	CEw	N619VSS	40635	KK	N635VSS	40651	KL	N651VSS
			40620	SY	N620VSS	40636	BQ	N636VSS	40652	BA	N652VSS
40604	AY	N604VSS	40621	KK	N621VSS	40637	BQ	N637VSS	40653	OX	N653VSS
40605	AY	N605VSS	40622	SR	N622VSS	40638	CN	N638VSS	40654	WY	N654VSS
40606	AY	N606VSS				40639	AY	N639VSS	40655	CR	N655VSS
40607	AY	N607VSS	40624	AS	N624VSS	40640	BQ	N640VSS	40656	CR	N656VSS
40608	AY	N608VSS	40625	AS	N625VSS	40641	KL	N641VSS	40657	WY	N657VSS
40609	KK	N609VSS	40626	AS	N626VSS	40642	SA	N642VSS	40658	WY	N658VSS
40610	AY	N610VSS	40627	AS	N627VSS	40643	CN	N643VSS	40659	WY	N659VSS
40611	AS	N611VSS	40628	KK	N628VSS	40644	WXu	N644VSS	40660	GP	N660VSS
40612	SR	N612VSS				40645	NWu	N645VSS	40661	CR	N661VSS
40613	KL	N613VSS	40630	AA	N630VSS	40646	BA	N646VSS	40662	BE	N662VSS
40614	NWu	N614VSS	40631	AA	N631VSS	40647	CE	N647VSS	40663	GP	N663VSS
40615	KL	N615VSS	40632	AS	N632VSS	40648	CE	N648VSS	40664	GP	N664VSS
40616	CE	N616VSS	40633	AA	N633VSS	40649	LL	N649VSS	40665	GP	N665VSS
40617	KL	N617VSS									

40670	AY	G570PRM	Mercedes-Benz 709D	Alexander Sprint	BC25F	1990
40671	AY	G571PRM	Mercedes-Benz 709D	Alexander Sprint	BC25F	1990
40678	SLt	G578PRM	Mercedes-Benz 709D	Alexander Sprint	BC25F	1990

40689-40703 — Mercedes-Benz 709D — Alexander Sprint — B25F — 1994

40689	ESw	L689CDD	40697	SWu	M697EDD	40699	TQu	M699EDD	40702	TQu	M702EDD
40692	SWu	L692CDD	40698	TQu	M698EDD	40701	PN	M701EDD	40703	SWu	M703EDD
40696	SWu	L696CDD									

There are two roof variants of the Alexander Sprint. Here the destination is retained within the roofline while most of those supplied to Stagecoach have a bustle in which the destination equipment is incorporated. 40671, G571PRM, is seen in Ayr. *Bob Downham*

40704-40717

			Mercedes-Benz 709D			Alexander Sprint		B25F*		1995		*40704 is BC25F
40704	TQ	M704JDG	40708	CN	M708JDG	40712	BR	M712FMR	40715	BR	M715FMR
40705	TQ	M705JDG	40709	CN	M709JDG	40713	WXu	M713FMR	40716	EH	N716KAM
40706	TQ	M706JDG	40710	CN	M710JDG	40714	CN	M714FMR	40717	EH	N717KAM
40707	TQ	M707JDG	40711	EX	M711FMR						

40718-40735

			Mercedes-Benz 709D			Alexander Sprint		B25F*		1996		*40731-5 are BC25F
40718	EH	N718RDD	40723	MR	N723RDD	40728	SEu	N728RDD	40732	TQ	N732RDD
40719	EH	N719RDD	40724	WXw	N724RDD	40729	LS	N729RDD	40733	AR	N733RDD
40720	WXw	N720RDD	40725	WWu	N725RDD	40730	AR	N730RDD	40734	EH	N734RDD
40721	WXw	N721RDD	40726	AR	N726RDD	40731	AR	N731RDD	40735	WWu	N735RDD
40722	WXw	N722RDD	40727	WWu	N727RDD						

40736	EMu	L736LWA	Mercedes-Benz 709D	Alexander Sprint	B25F	1993
40739	CH	L739LWA	Mercedes-Benz 709D	Alexander Sprint	B25F	1993
40742	EMw	L742LWA	Mercedes-Benz 709D	Alexander Sprint	B25F	1993

40752-40761

			Mercedes-Benz 709D			Alexander Sprint		B23F		1995
40752	CH	N752CKU	40756	CH	N756CKU	40758	CH	N758CKU	40760	CH	N760CKU
40754	EMw	N754CKU	40757	CH	N757CKU	40759	CH	N759CKU	40761	WP	N761CKU
40755	CH	N755CKU									

40762-40776

			Mercedes-Benz 709D			Alexander Sprint		B25F		1996
40762	CH	N762EWG	40767	CH	N767EWG	40771	GY	N771EWG	40774	EMu	N774EWG
40763	WP	N763EWG	40769	WP	N769EWG	40772	CH	N772EWG	40775	CH	N775EWG
40764	CH	N764EWG	40770	WP	N770EWG	40773	CH	N773EWG	40776	EMu	N776EWG
40765	CH	N765EWG									

40777-40781 Mercedes-Benz 709D Alexander Sprint B25F 1993

40777	EMu	L731LWA	**40779**	EMu	L733LWA	**40780**	EMw	L734LWA	**40781** WP L735LWA
40778	EMw	L732LWA							

40791-40800 Mercedes-Benz 709D Alexander Sprint B23F 1996

40791	NEu	N341KKH	**40794**	AL	N344KKH	**40797**	WP	N347KKH	**40799** WP N349KKH
40792	WA	N342KKH	**40795**	SA	N345KKH	**40798**	WP	N348KKH	**40800** WP N350KKH
40793	AL	N343KKH	**40796**	NEu	N346KKH				

40801-40804 Mercedes-Benz 709D Alexander Sprint B23F 1996

40801	EMu	P351NKH	**40802**	GY	P352NKH	**40803**	GY	P353NKH	**40804** WP P354NKH

40810	ESu	K610UFR	Mercedes-Benz 709D	Alexander Sprint	B25F	1993
40822	NWu	K622UFR	Mercedes-Benz 709D	Alexander Sprint	B25F	1993
40823	CEw	K623UFR	Mercedes-Benz 709D	Alexander Sprint	B25F	1993
40834	CEw	L634BFV	Mercedes-Benz 709D	Alexander Sprint	B25F	1993

40882-40904 Mercedes-Benz 709D Alexander Sprint B23F* 1993-95 *seating varies

40882	BA	L882SDY	**40891**	CR	N191LPN	**40896**	WI	N196LPN	**40901** AR N201LPN
40883	NWu	L883SDY	**40892**	AT	N192LPN	**40897**	CR	N197LPN	**40902** AR N202LPN
40885	NWu	L885SDY	**40893**	CR	N193LPN	**40898**	AD	N198LPN	**40903** CR N203LPN
40886	NWu	L886SDY	**40894**	PMu	N194LPN	**40899**	WI	N199LPN	**40904** CR N204LPN
40889	SEw	M889ECD	**40895**	CR	N195LPN				

40905-40982 Mercedes-Benz 709D Alexander Sprint B25F* 1996 *40905-23 are B23F

40905	AT	N905NAP	**40925**	SEw	N925NAP	**40945**	CR	N945NAP	**40964**	DO	N964NAP
40906	AT	N906NAP	**40926**	TH	N926NAP	**40946**	SEw	N946NAP	**40965**	SEw	N965NAP
40907	AT	N907NAP	**40927**	TH	N927NAP	**40947**	CA	N947NAP	**40966**	TH	N966NAP
40908	AT	N908NAP	**40928**	TH	N928NAP	**40948**	AD	N948NAP	**40967**	DO	N967NAP
40909	AT	N909NAP	**40929**	TH	N929NAP	**40949**	AD	N949NAP	**40968**	DO	N968NAP
40910	AT	N910NAP	**40930**	TH	N930NAP	**40950**	AD	N950NAP	**40969**	BE	N969NAP
40911	AT	N911NAP	**40931**	TH	N931NAP	**40951**	AD	N951NAP	**40970**	DO	N970NAP
40912	AT	N912NAP	**40932**	TH	N932NAP	**40952**	AD	N952NAP	**40971**	LS	N971NAP
40913	AT	N913NAP	**40933**	CA	N933NAP	**40953**	DO	N953NAP	**40972**	SEw	N972NAP
40914	AT	N914NAP	**40934**	CA	N934NAP	**40954**	DO	N954NAP	**40973**	SEw	N973NAP
40915	AR	N915NAP	**40935**	AT	N935NAP	**40955**	DO	N955NAP	**40974**	SEw	N974NAP
40916	AR	N916NAP	**40936**	AT	N936NAP	**40956**	SEw	N956NAP	**40975**	SEu	N975NAP
40917	CR	N917NAP	**40937**	AT	N937NAP	**40957**	DO	N957NAP	**40976**	SEw	N976NAP
40918	CR	N918NAP	**40938**	SEu	N938NAP	**40958**	FO	N958NAP	**40977**	CA	N977NAP
			40939	SEu	N939NAP	**40959**	DO	N959NAP	**40978**	TQ	N978NAP
40920	AR	N920NAP	**40940**	AT	N940NAP	**40960**	DO	N960NAP	**40979**	TQ	N979NAP
40921	AR	N921NAP	**40941**	CA	N941NAP	**40961**	SEw	N961NAP	**40980**	TQ	N980NAP
40922	AR	N922NAP	**40942**	CA	N942NAP	**40962**	DO	N962NAP	**40981**	TQ	N981NAP
40923	AR	N923NAP	**40943**	CA	N943NAP	**40963**	DO	N963NAP	**40982**	TQ	N982NAP
40924	AR	N924NAP	**40944**	SEw	N944NAP						

40985	KK	M395KVR	Mercedes-Benz 709D	Alexander Sprint	B27F	1995	AA Buses, Ayr, 1997
40986	KK	M396KVR	Mercedes-Benz 709D	Alexander Sprint	B27F	1995	AA Buses, Ayr, 1997
40987	KK	M397KVR	Mercedes-Benz 709D	Alexander Sprint	B27F	1995	AA Buses, Ayr, 1997
41150	PT	M866LNY	Mercedes-Benz 711D	Plaxton Beaver	B27F	1995	

41152-41159 Mercedes-Benz 711D UVG CitiStar B27F 1995 Rhondda, 1997

41152	SZ	N152MTG	**41154**	PT	N154MTG	**41156**	WXu	N156MTG	**41159** GR N159MTG
41153	WWu	N153MTG	**41155**	CL	N155MTG	**41158**	GR	N158MTG	

41161	WWu	P161TDW	Mercedes-Benz 709D	Plaxton Beaver	B27F	1996	Rhondda, 1997
41162	PT	P162TDW	Mercedes-Benz 709D	Plaxton Beaver	B27F	1996	Rhondda, 1997

41163-41171 Mercedes-Benz 711D Plaxton Beaver B27F 1996 Rhondda, 1997

41163	PT	P163TNY	**41166**	PT	P166TNY	**41168**	PT	P168TNY	**41170** PT P170TNY
41164	PT	P164TNY	**41167**	GR	P167TNY	**41169**	PT	P169TNY	**41171** GR P171TNY
41165	PT	P165TNY							

41304	PH	J304UKG	Mercedes-Benz 811D	Wright NimBus	B33F	1992	
41315	AN	K315YKG	Mercedes-Benz 811D	Wright NimBus	B33F	1992	
41330	WWu	L330CHB	Mercedes-Benz 811D	Marshall C16	B33F	1993	

Though initially used in Stockport, Wales now operates more of the more-powerful Mercedes-Benz 811 model than other areas. Seen at Cardiff, is 41427, N427WVR. *Phillip Stephenson*

41401-41430 Mercedes-Benz 811D Alexander Sprint B31F 1995-96

41401	AE	N401WVR	41409	MR	N409WVR	41417	CN	N417WVR	41424	PY	N424WVR
41402	MR	N402WVR	41410	MR	N410WVR	41418	PT	N418WVR	41425	CN	N425WVR
41403	AE	N403WVR	41411	PT	N411WVR	41419	PT	N419WVR	41426	PT	N426WVR
41404	PT	N404WVR	41412	CN	N412WVR	41420	CN	N420WVR	41427	PT	N427WVR
41405	CN	N405WVR	41413	CN	N413WVR	41421	AE	N421WVR	41428	PT	N428WVR
41406	MR	N406WVR	41414	CN	N414WVR	41422	PT	N422WVR	41429	WXu	N429WVR
41407	MR	N407WVR	41415	CN	N415WVR	41423	CN	N423WVR	41430	CN	N430WVR
41408	CN	N408WVR	41416	PT	N416WVR						

41505-41517 Mercedes-Benz 811D Wright NimBus BC31F* 1991 *41505/6/13/7 are B31F

41505	RU	H405MRW	41507	AN	J407PRW	41511	AN	J411PRW	41513	PH	J413PRW
41506	SMw	H406MRW	41509	PH	J409PRW	41512	BQ	J412PRW	41517	PH	J417PRW

41520	AN	K420ARW	Mercedes-Benz 811D	Wright NimBus	B31F	1993

41714-41719 Mercedes-Benz 811D Alexander Sprint B31F 1992

41714	CH	J214AET	41716	CH	J216AET	41717	CH	J217AET	41719	CH	J219AET
41715	CH	J215AET							

41801	BQ	K801OMW	Mercedes-Benz 811D	Wright NimBus	B22FL	1993
41802	BJ	K802OMW	Mercedes-Benz 811D	Wright NimBus	B22FL	1993
41803	SZ	L803XDG	Mercedes-Benz 811D	Marshall C16	B33F	1993
41804	WWu	L804XDG	Mercedes-Benz 811D	Marshall C16	B33F	1993
41805	SZ	L805XDG	Mercedes-Benz 811D	Marshall C16	B33F	1993
41806	WWu	L806XDG	Mercedes-Benz 811D	Marshall C16	B33F	1993
41983	KGt	H838GLD	Mercedes-Benz 609D	North West Coach Sales	TV	1990
41998	BDt	D560RCK	Mercedes-Benz L608D	Reeve Burgess	TV	1988
42000	PR	R36LSO	Mercedes-Benz Vario O810	Plaxton Beaver 2	B27F	1997

The Stockport operation has recently seen the arrival of more short Darts to replace Mercedes-Benz Vario buses which are being prepared for transfer elsewhere. Pictured entering Stockport bus station is 42542, P542PNE. *Mark Doggett*

42001-42018 — Mercedes-Benz Vario 0810 — Plaxton Beaver 2 — B29F — 1997

42001	HE	R501YWC	42006	CS	R506YWC	42011	CS	R511YWC	42015	HE	R515YWC
42002	CS	R502YWC	42007	CS	R507YWC	42012	HE	R512YWC	42016	CS	R516YWC
42003	CS	R503YWC	42008	CS	R508YWC	42013	CS	R513YWC	42017	CS	R517YWC
42004	CS	R504YWC	42009	HE	R509YWC	42014	CS	R514YWC	42018	CS	R518YWC
42005	HE	R505YWC	42010	CS	R510YWC						

42019	WSu	V772GCS	Mercedes-Benz Vario 0814	Plaxton Beaver 2	B31F	1999	Docherty, Irvine, 2004
42020	CC	V773GCS	Mercedes-Benz Vario 0814	Plaxton Beaver 2	B31F	1999	Docherty, Irvine, 2004
42021	WSu	V774GCS	Mercedes-Benz Vario 0814	Plaxton Beaver 2	B31F	1999	Docherty, Irvine, 2004
42022	CC	SN03FHK	Mercedes-Benz Vario 0814	TransBus Beaver 2	B31F	2003	Docherty, Irvine, 2004
42023	CC	SN03FHL	Mercedes-Benz Vario 0814	TransBus Beaver 2	B31F	2003	Docherty, Irvine, 2004
42024	CC	SN03FHM	Mercedes-Benz Vario 0814	TransBus Beaver 2	B31F	2003	Docherty, Irvine, 2004
42025	PY	S638MGA	Mercedes-Benz Vario 0814	Marshall	B31F	1998	Phil Anslow, 2004
42026	PY	T667RET	Mercedes-Benz Vario 0814	Crest	B31F	1998	Phil Anslow, 2004
42027	PY	W851TBC	Mercedes-Benz Vario 0814	Plaxton Beaver 2	B29F	2000	Phil Anslow, 2004
42028	PY	W852TBC	Mercedes-Benz Vario 0814	Plaxton Beaver 2	B29F	2000	Phil Anslow, 2004

42090-42096 — Mercedes-Benz Vario 0814 — Alexander ALX100 — B29F — 1998

42090	PR	S190RAO	42092	PR	S192RAO	42094	PR	S194RAO	42096	PR	S196RAO
42091	PR	S191RAO	42093	PR	S193RAO	42095	PR	S195RAO			

42101-42118 — Mercedes-Benz Vario 0814 — Alexander ALX100 — B29F — 1998

42101	TQ	R101NTA	42105	TQ	R105NTA	42110	EX	R110NTA	42115	EX	R115NTA
42102	TQ	R102NTA	42107	TQ	R107NTA	42112	EX	R112NTA	42116	EX	R116NTA
42103	TQ	R103NTA	42108	EX	R108NTA	42113	EX	R113NTA	42117	EX	S117JFJ
42104	TQ	R104NTA	42109	EX	R109NTA	42114	EX	R114NTA	42118	EX	S118JFJ

42355-42358 — Mercedes-Benz Vario 0814 — Alexander ALX100 — B29F — 1998

42355	HL	S355KEF	42356	HL	S356KEF	42357	HL	S357KEF	42358	HL	S358KEF

Two of the Plaxton Beaver-bodied Vario buses acquired with the Phil Anslow business in 2000 are now in Banbury. One of these, 42588, T588SKG, is seen on local service. *Laurie Rufus*

42371-42383

| | | | Mercedes-Benz Vario 0814 | | Alexander ALX100 | | B29F | 1998 |

42371	OX	S371DFC	42375	WY	S375DFC	42378	WY	S378DFC	42381	WY	S381DFC
42372	OX	S372DFC	42376	OX	S376DFC	42379	WY	S379DFC	42382	WY	S382DFC
42373	WY	S373DFC	42377	WY	S377DFC	42380	WY	S380DFC	42383	OX	S383DFC
42374	WY	S374DFC									

42530-42566

| | | | Mercedes-Benz Vario 0814 | | Plaxton Beaver 2 | | B27F | 1997 |

42530	MAu	P530PNE	42539	MAu	P539PNE	42548	GP	P548PNE	42557	GY	P557PNE
42531	ME	P531PNE	42540	MAu	P540PNE	42549	ME	P549PNE	42558	GP	P558PNE
42532	GY	P532PNE	42541	MAu	P541PNE	42550	ME	P550PNE	42559	MAu	P559PNE
42533	ME	P533PNE	42542	MAu	P542PNE	42551	CS	P551PNE	42562	ME	P562PNE
42534	ME	P534PNE	42543	MAu	P543PNE	42552	CS	P552PNE	42563	GP	P563PNE
42535	ME	P535PNE	42544	MAu	P544PNE	42553	ME	P553PNE	42564	GP	P564PNE
42536	GP	P536PNE	42545	CS	P545PNE	42554	GP	P554PNE	42565	ME	P565PNE
42537	MAu	P537PNE	42546	CS	P546PNE	42556	CS	P556PNE	42566	ME	P566PNE
42538	ME	P538PNE	42547	MAu	P547PNE						

42567	CS	R276CBU	Mercedes-Benz Vario 0814	Plaxton Beaver 2	B31F	1998	Glossopdale, Dukinfield, 1999
42568	CS	R277CBU	Mercedes-Benz Vario 0814	Plaxton Beaver 2	B31F	1998	Glossopdale, Dukinfield, 1999
42569	CS	R446YNF	Mercedes-Benz Vario 0814	Plaxton Beaver 2	B31F	1997	Glossopdale, Dukinfield, 1999
42570	CS	R447YNF	Mercedes-Benz Vario 0814	Plaxton Beaver 2	B31F	1997	Glossopdale, Dukinfield, 1999
42571	CS	R899AVM	Mercedes-Benz Vario 0814	Plaxton Beaver 2	B27F	1997	Glossopdale, Dukinfield, 1999
42572	CS	R898AVM	Mercedes-Benz Vario 0814	Plaxton Beaver 2	B27F	1997	Glossopdale, Dukinfield, 1999
42573	CS	R901AVM	Mercedes-Benz Vario 0814	Plaxton Beaver 2	B27F	1997	Glossopdale, Dukinfield, 1999

42576-42590

| | | | Mercedes-Benz Vario 0814 | | Plaxton Beaver 2 | | B31F | 1999 | Phil Anslow, Pontypool, 2000 |

42576	CH	T56JKG	42582	CH	T582SKG	42585	EMu	T585SKG	42588	BB	T588SKG
42577	MD	T57JKG	42583	MD	T583SKG	42586	BB	T586SKG	42589	CH	T589SKG
42578	CH	T58JKG	42584	MD	T584SKG	42587	CH	T587SKG	42590	EMu	T590SKG
42579	CH	T38PTG									

42624	BB	R624LTX	Mercedes-Benz Vario O814	UVG CitiStar		B29F	1997	
42670	PR	R670LFV	Mercedes-Benz Vario O814	Plaxton Beaver 2		B27F	1997	
42672	PR	R672LFV	Mercedes-Benz Vario O814	Plaxton Beaver 2		B27F	1997	
46271	WXu	P969UKG	Iveco TurboDaily 59.12	UVG Citi Star		TV	1996	Phil Anslow, Pontypool, 2000
46272	BRt	P970UKG	Iveco TurboDaily 59.12	UVG Citi Star		TV	1996	Phil Anslow, Pontypool, 2000
46273	CN	R971UKG	Iveco TurboDaily 59.12	UVG Citi Star		B29F	1996	Phil Anslow, Pontypool, 2000
46319	SWu	M639HDV	Iveco TurboDaily 59.12	WS Wessex II		B21D	1994	
46321	SWu	M624HDV	Iveco TurboDaily 59.12	WS Wessex II		B21D	1994	
46378	SWu	N182CMJ	Iveco TurboDaily 59.12	Alexander AM		B29F	1996	
46379	SWu	N183CMJ	Iveco TurboDaily 59.12	Alexander AM		B29F	1996	
46381	SWu	N190GFR	Iveco TurboDaily 59.12	Mellor		B27F	1996	
46382	SWu	N463HRN	Iveco TurboDaily 59.12	Mellor		B27F	1996	
46398	SWu	N188GFR	Iveco TurboDaily 59.12	Mellor		B27F	1996	
46399	SWu	N464HRN	Iveco TurboDaily 59.12	Mellor		B27F	1996	

46602-46612			Iveco Daily 49.10	Mellor		B17F	1997	46612 is a mobile control 46602/3/4/8/9 are ancillary

46602	CEw	R602KDD	46607	SZu	R607KDD	46611	THu	R611KDD	46614	CRu	R614KDD
46603	PRu	R603KDD	46608	SWu	R608KDD	46612	WIu	R612KDD	46615	ADu	R615KDD
46604	SWu	R604KDD	46609	TQu	R609KDD	46613	ATu	R613KDD	46616	HSu	R616KDD
46606	SNu	R606KDD	46610	CTu	R610KDD						

47001-47015			Optare Solo M850		Optare		N26F	2001	

47001	LE	KX51CRU	47005	LE	KX51CSO	47009	LE	KX51CSZ	47013	LE	KX51CTO
47002	LE	KX51CRV	47006	LE	KX51CSU	47010	LE	KX51CTE	47014	LE	KX51CTU
47003	LE	KX51CRZ	47007	LE	KX51CSV	47011	LE	KX51CTF	47015	LE	KX51CYV
47004	LE	KX51CSF	47008	LE	KX51CSY	47012	LE	KX51CTK			

47016-47024			Optare Solo M850		Optare		N27F	2001	

47016	PR	PO51WLF	47019	PR	PO51WLJ	47021	PR	PO51WLL	47023	PR	PO51WLP
47017	PR	PO51WLG	47020	PR	PO51WLK	47022	PR	PO51WLN	47024	PR	PO51WLR
47018	PR	PO51WLH									

47025	WA	YL02FKY	Optare Solo M850	Optare		N27F	2002	Operated for Countryside Com
47026	NU	YG52DHM	Optare Solo M850	Optare		N27F	2002	Operated for Warwickshire CC
47027	NU	YG52DFY	Optare Solo M850	Optare		N27F	2002	Operated for Warwickshire CC
47028	NU	YG52DFZ	Optare Solo M850	Optare		N27F	2002	Operated for Warwickshire CC

47029-47039			Optare Solo M920		Optare		N33F	2003	

47029	CX	KX03KYS	47032	CX	KX03KYV	47035	CX	KX03KYZ	47038	CX	KX03KZC
47030	CX	KX03KYT	47033	CX	KX03KYW	47036	CX	KX03KZA	47039	CX	KX03KZD
47031	CX	KX03KYU	47034	CX	KX03KYY	47037	CX	KX03KZB			

Services on the Fylde coast were early recipients of the Optare Solo. 47022, PO51WLN, is seen lettered for route F4, at Cleveleys. Early in 2005 this route is to be renumbered 84.
Richard Godfrey

47040	AR	YR02YRD	Optare Solo M850	Optare		N23F	2002	
47041	AY	SF03ZXU	Optare Solo M850	Optare		N23F	2003	
47042	CX	KX04RBV	Optare Solo M920	Optare		N33F	2004	
47043	CX	KX04RBY	Optare Solo M920	Optare		N33F	2004	
47044	CX	KX04RBZ	Optare Solo M920	Optare		N33F	2004	
47045	CX	KX04RCF	Optare Solo M920	Optare		N33F	2004	
47046	CX	KX04RCU	Optare Solo M920	Optare		N33F	2004	
47047	BE	YK04KVU	Optare Solo M850	Optare		N29F	2004	
47048	BE	YK04KVV	Optare Solo M850	Optare		N29F	2004	
47049	BE	YK04KVW	Optare Solo M850	Optare		N29F	2004	
47050	CX	KP04HVR	Optare Solo M920	Optare		N33F	2004	

47051-47080 Optare Solo M850 Optare N27F 2004

47051	PH	SV04DVK	47059	PR	PX04DMF	47067	DS	SF04SKN	47074	NU	KN04XKH
47052	PH	SV04DVL	47060	PR	PX04DMU	47068	DS	SF04VFS	47075	NU	KN04XKJ
47053	PH	SV04DVM	47061	PR	PX04DMV	47069	NU	KN04XKC	47076	NU	KN04XKK
47054	PH	SV04DVN	47062	PR	PX04DMY	47070	NU	KN04XKD	47077	NU	KN04XKL
47055	PR	PX04DLV	47063	DS	SF04SKD	47071	NU	KN04XKE	47078	BQ	SV04HLM
47056	PR	PX04DLY	47064	DS	SF04SKE	47072	NU	KN04XKF	47079	BQ	SV04HLN
47057	PR	PX04DLZ	47065	DS	SF04SKJ	47073	NU	KN04XKG	47080	BQ	SV04HLP
47058	PR	PX04DME	47066	DS	SF04SKK						

47081-47110 Optare Solo M850SL Optare N25F 2004

47081	EX	WA04TWU	47089	EX	WA04TXD	47097	EX	WA04TXM	47104	EX	WA04TXV
47082	EX	WA04TWV	47090	EX	WA04TXE	47098	EX	WA04TXN	47105	EX	WA04TXW
47083	EX	WA04TWW	47091	EX	WA04TXF	47099	EX	WA04TXP	47106	EX	WA04TXX
47084	EX	WA04TWX	47092	EX	WA04TXG	47100	EX	WA04TXR	47107	EX	WA04TXY
47085	EX	WA04TWY	47093	EX	WA04TXH	47101	EX	WA04TXS	47108	EX	WA04TXZ
47086	EX	WA04TWZ	47094	EX	WA04TXJ	47102	EX	WA04TXT	47109	EX	WA04TYB
47087	EX	WA04TXB	47095	EX	WA04TXK	47103	EX	WA04TXU	47110	EX	WA04TYC
47088	EX	WA04TXC	47096	EX	WA04TXL						

47111-47150 Optare Solo M850 Optare N27F 2004

47111	BQ	SV54BVM	47121	SZ	VX54LMJ	47131	BA	PX54EPL	47141	BA	PX54EOZ
47112	FO	GX54DXK	47122	SZ	VX54LMK	47132	BA	PX54EPN	47142	BA	PX54EPA
47113	FO	GX54DXL	47123	NN	KN54XYP	47133	BA	PX54EPO	47143	BA	PX54EPC
47114	FO	GX54DXM	47124	NN	KN54XYR	47134	BA	PX54EPP	47144	BA	PX54EPD
47115	FO	GX54DXO	47125	NN	KN54XYT	47135	BA	PX54EPU	47145	BA	PX54EPE
47116	FO	GX54DXP	47126	NN	KN54XYU	47136	BA	PX54EPV	47146	BA	PX54EPF
47117	FO	GX54DXR	47127	NN	KN54XYV	47137	BA	PX54EPY	47147	BA	PX54EPJ
47118	FO	GX54DXT	47128	NN	KN54XYY	47138	BA	PX54EPZ	47148	PR	PX54EXM
47119	FO	GX54DXU	47129	NN	KN54XYZ	47139	BA	PX54ERJ	47149	PR	PX54EXN
47120	FO	GX54DXV	47130	BA	PX54EPK	47140	BA	PX54EOY	47150	KK	SF54RJU

While the main supply of Optare Solo buses has been the shorter M850 model, those operating at Corby are the longer M920. Seen in *CorbyStar* colours is 47042, **KX04RBV**.
Bob Downham

Five Optare Solo on loan to Devon were being returned to the rental fleet at the end of 2004. A further fifty Solo buses are planned for delivery during 2005. Pictured in Nuneaton is Warwickshire-liveried 47026, YG52DHM.
Mark Doggett

47151	TQw	MX04VLN	Optare Solo M850	Optare	N29F	2004	on loan 2004
47152	TQw	MX04VLP	Optare Solo M850	Optare	N29F	2004	on loan 2004
47153	TQw	MX04VLR	Optare Solo M850	Optare	N29F	2004	on loan 2004
47154	TQw	MX04VLS	Optare Solo M850	Optare	N29F	2004	on loan 2004
47155	TQw	MX04VLT	Optare Solo M850	Optare	N29F	2004	on loan 2004

47161-47210		Optare Solo M850	Optare	N27F	2005 delivery

47161	-	**47174**	-	**47187**	-	**47199**	-
47162	-	**47175**	-	**47188**	-	**47200**	-
47163	-	**47176**	-	**47189**	-	**47201**	-
47164	-	**47177**	-	**47190**	-	**47202**	-
47165	-	**47178**	-	**47191**	-	**47203**	-
47166	-	**47179**	-	**47192**	-	**47204**	-
47167	-	**47180**	-	**47193**	-	**47205**	-
47168	-	**47181**	-	**47194**	-	**47206**	-
47169	-	**47182**	-	**47195**	-	**47207**	-
47170	-	**47183**	-	**47196**	-	**47208**	-
47171	-	**47184**	-	**47197**	-	**47209**	-
47172	-	**47185**	-	**47198**	-	**47210**	-
47173	-	**47186**	-				

The 2005 Stagecoach Bus Handbook

A number of the low-floor Optare Alero minibuses are operated on specific contract routes. One of three allocated to Andover is 47801, YR02YRY, which was pictured heading for Upton. *Phillip Stephenson*

47801-47807			Optare Alero			Optare		N13F	2002-03	Seating varies
47801	AR	YR02YRY	47803	SY	YU02GRK	47805	AR	UN03UXY	47807	AN	SV54BYN
47802	AR	YR02YTA	47804	SY	YU02GRX					

47900	CB	GAZ4381	Optare MetroRider MR17 (CNG)	Optare	B29F	1999	
47901	CBu	GAZ4382	Optare MetroRider MR17 (CNG)	Optare	B29F	1999	
47972	CBw	K972HUB	Optare MetroRider MR17	Optare	B29F	1993	
47975	CB	M975WWR	Optare MetroRider MR17	Optare	B29F	1995	
47976	PE	M976WWR	Optare MetroRider MR17	Optare	B29F	1995	
47977	PE	M977WWR	Optare MetroRider MR17	Optare	B29F	1995	
47978	PE	M978WWR	Optare MetroRider MR17	Optare	B29F	1995	
47979	CB	M959VWY	Optare MetroRider MR17	Optare	B29F	1995	
47988	PE	M808WWR	Optare MetroRider MR17	Optare	B29F	1995	
47989	PE	M809WWR	Optare MetroRider MR17	Optare	B29F	1995	
47990	CB	M810WWR	Optare MetroRider MR17	Optare	B29F	1995	

48007	SYt	B916JVK	Dodge Commando G13	Wadham Stringer Vanguard	TV	1984	MoD, 1997 (31KF09)
48022	WAt	D157HHN	Dodge Commando G13	Wadham Stringer Vanguard	TV	1986	MoD, 1998 (80KF95)
48029	CEt	D375DCK	Dodge Commando G13	Wadham Stringer Vanguard	TV	1986	MoD. 1999 ( )
48047	SYt	D918KPT	Dodge Commando G13	Wadham Stringer Vanguard	TV	1986	MoD, 1997 (80KF58)
48065	SYt	E875GRG	Dodge Commando G13	Wadham Stringer Vanguard	TV	1988	MoD, 2001( )
48078	WAt	G675XTN	Dodge Commando G13	Wadham Stringer Vanguard	TV	1990	USAF, 2000 (90B2063)
48080	EXt	G806YTA	Dodge Commando G13	Wadham Stringer Vanguard	TV	1989	USAF, 1999 (90B2051)
48083	WWw	HIL6075	Dodge Commando G13	Wadham Stringer Vanguard	TV	1989	USAF, 2000 (90B2068)

The arrival of twenty-five Neoplan Skyliners in 2004 has allowed many of the Jonckheere Monaco coaches to enter service on Scottish Megabus services. As Megabus expands, a further batch of Skyliners is entering service as we go to press. Carrying the blue livery scheme these vehicles are to be used on the longer services. Skyliner 50106, KP04GJU, is seen in London. *Mark Lyons*

50034-50066

MAN 24.350 — Jonckheere Monaco — C53/15FT — 1999-2000

50034	AY	T34DFC	50041	GW	T41BBW	50048	AN	T48BBW	50055	AN	T617DWL
50035	GW	T35DFC	50042	AN	T42BBW	50049	AY	T49BBW	50056	AY	T56BBW
50036	GW	T36DFC	50043	GW	T43BBW	50050	AY	T616DWL	50057	AY	T57BBW
50037	AY	T37BBW	50044	AY	T615DWL	50051	AY	T51BBW	50058	AN	T58BBW
50038	AY	T38BBW	50045	GW	T45BBW	50052	GW	T52BBW	50059	GW	T59BBW
50039	GW	T39BBW	50046	AN	T46BBW	50053	GW	T53BBW	50060	AY	T618DWL
50040	SMu	T614DWL	50047	AN	T47BBW	50054	GW	T54BBW	50066	GW	W66BBW

50101-50125

Neoplan Skyliner N122/3 — Neoplan — C63/18FT — 2004

50101	OX	KP04GJE	50108	OX	KP04GJX	50114	OX	KP04GKE	50120	OX	KP04GKN
50102	OX	KP04GJF	50109	OX	KP04GJY	50115	OX	KP04GKF	50121	OX	T40UBE
50103	OX	KP04GJG	50110	OX	KP04GJZ	50116	OX	KP04GKG	50122	OX	T44UBE
50104	OX	KP04GJJ	50111	OX	KP04GKA	50117	OX	KP04GKJ	50123	OX	T50UBE
50105	OX	KP04GJK	50112	OX	KP04GKC	50118	OX	KP04GKK	50124	OX	T55UBE
50106	OX	KP04GJU	50113	OX	KP04GKD	50119	OX	KP04GKL	50125	OX	T60UBE
50107	OX	KP04GJV									

50126-50150

Neoplan Skyliner N122/3 — Neoplan — C65/24FT — 2005

50126	ES	SV54ELC	50133	WX	CN05APV	50139	LNu	-	50145	NEu	-
50127	ES	SV54ELH	50134	WX	CN05APX	50140	LNu	-	50146	NEu	-
50128	ES	SV54ELJ	50135	WX	CN05APY	50141	SMu	-	50147	MAu	MX05BWL
50129	ES	SV54ELO	50136	LNu	-	50142	SMu	-	50148	MAu	MX05BWM
50130	ES	SV54ELU	50137	LNu	-	50143	NEu	-	50149	MAu	MX05BWO
50131	ES	SV54ELW	50138	LNu	-	50144	NEu	-	50150	u	-
50132	ES	SV54ELX									

Stagecoach original articulated Jonckheere Mistral-bodied Volvo B10M 51061, YSV730, now carries Megabus livery for the Scotland to London route. It is currently based with Bluebird in Aberdeen, and is seen in Glasgow while heading south. *Billy Nicol*

51061	AN	YSV730	Volvo B10MA-55	Jonckheere Mistral 35	AC72F	1996	
51062	AN	VCS391	Volvo B10MA-55	Jonckheere Mistral 35	AC72F	1996	
51063	CC	P563MSX	Volvo B10MA-55	Plaxton Première Interurban	AC71F	1996	
51064	CC	P564MSX	Volvo B10MA-55	Plaxton Première Interurban	AC71F	1996	
51070	AN	WLT720	Volvo B10MA-55	Plaxton Première Interurban	AC71F	1996	
51071	CC	UIB3543	Volvo B10MA-55	Plaxton Première Interurban	AC71F	1996	
51073	CC	495FFJ	Volvo B10MA-55	Plaxton Première Interurban	AC71F	1996	
51076	CC	MSU466	Volvo B10MA-55	Plaxton Première Interurban	AC71F	1996	
51092	AS	T640KCS	Volvo B10MA-55	Jonckheere Modulo	AC72F	1999	
51093	AS	T641KCS	Volvo B10MA-55	Jonckheere Modulo	AC72F	1999	
51094	AS	T642KCS	Volvo B10MA-55	Jonckheere Modulo	AC72F	1999	
51095	AS	T95JHN	Volvo B10MA-55	Jonckheere Modulo	AC72F	1999	
51096	AY	T96JHN	Volvo B10MA-55	Jonckheere Modulo	AC72F	1999	
51097	AY	T97JHN	Volvo B10MA-55	Jonckheere Modulo	AC72F	1999	
51098	CC	WLT978	Volvo B10MA-55	Plaxton Première Interurban	AC71F	1996	
51099	CC	WLT809	Volvo B10MA-55	Plaxton Première Interurban	AC71F	1996	
52001	KL	OIW5804	Volvo B10M-61	Van Hool Alizée H	C53F	1983	Arriva (Heysham Travel), 2000
52002	CAt	VKB708	Volvo B10M-61	Van Hool Alizée H	C53F	1985	Arriva (Heysham Travel), 2000
52004	ESw	C330DND	Volvo B10M-61	Van Hool Alizée H	TV	1986	Hardie's Coaches, 1994
52005	GY	PSU443	Volvo B10M-61	Van Hool Alizée H	C53F	1986	Shearings, 1991
52006	ISt	D548MVR	Volvo B10M-61	Van Hool Alizée H	TV	1987	Shearings, 1991
52007	CHt	PSU764	Volvo B10M-61	Van Hool Alizée H	TV	1987	Shearings, 1991
52008	GY	PS2743	Volvo B10M-61	Van Hool Alizée H	C53F	1987	Shearings, 1991
52011	BQt	D553MVR	Volvo B10M-61	Van Hool Alizée H	TV	1987	Shearings, 1991
52014	GSt	E644UNE	Volvo B10M-61	Van Hool Alizée H	TV	1988	
52015	PY	M134SKY	Volvo B10M-62	Van Hool Alizée H	C51FT	1995	Phil Anslow, 2004
52016	PY	M135SKY	Volvo B10M-62	Van Hool Alizée H	C51FT	1995	Phil Anslow, 2004
52019	PY	TJI4123	Volvo B10M-62	Jonckheere Deauville 45	C51FT	1993	Phil Anslow, 2004

52020-52024

			Volvo B10M-62	Jonckheere Deauville 45	C49FT	1994	
52020	RUt	498FYB	**52022**	NS	WLT890	**52023**	NS	630DYE	**52024**	BDt	L159LBW
52021	CXt	L156LBW					

Stagecoach is now replacing its Dodge trainers with older Volvo coaches, a task which has included the acquisition of similar vehicles from outside the fleet. Seen in its dedicated training livery while working in Chesterfield is 52007, PSU764. *Tony Wilson*

52025	PY	M321KRY	Volvo B10M-62			Jonckheere Deauville 45	C53F	1995	Phil Anslow, 2004	

52026-52030 Volvo B10M-62 — Berkhof Excellence 1000LD C51FT 1995

52026	SR	M103XBW	**52027**	CE	NSU133	**52029**	PH	LSK545	**52030**	CE	GSU341

52031-52038 Volvo B10M-62 — Berkhof Excellence 1000LD C51FT 1996

52031	NUt	WSU293	**52033**	KGt	N43MJO	**52036**	BDt	N46MJO	**52038**	IS	N48MJO
52032	NNt	N42MJO	**52035**	BDt	N45MJO	**52037**	BBt	4012VC			

52051	GY	IIL1321	Volvo B10M-61	Plaxton Paramount 3200 III	C51FT	1987
52056	PRt	YDG616	Volvo B10M-61	Plaxton Paramount 3500 III	TV	1987
52057	KL	JPU817	Volvo B10M-61	Plaxton Paramount 3500 III	C53F	1987
52058	CJt	283URB	Volvo B10M-60	Plaxton Paramount 3500 III	TV	1987
52059	CNt	HSV196	Volvo B10M-61	Plaxton Paramount 3500 III	TV	1988

52061-52065 Volvo B10M-61 — Plaxton Paramount 3200 III TV 1988

52061	LLt	E131ORP	**52063**	PRt	E133ORP	**52064**	CEt	E134ORP	**52065**	CEw	E135ORP
52062	BAt	E132ORP									

52069	KKt	WLT415	Volvo B10M-60	Plaxton Paramount 3500 III	TV	1989
52071	EXt	HSV195	Volvo B10M-61	Plaxton Paramount 3500 III	TV	1988
52072	CYt	C105DWR	Volvo B10M-61	Plaxton Paramount 3500 II	TV	1988
52073	BJ	G344FFX	Volvo B10M-60	Plaxton Expressliner	C53F	1990
52075	CEw	G386PNV	Volvo B10M-60	Plaxton Expressliner	TV	1990
52076	KKt	G387PNV	Volvo B10M-60	Plaxton Expressliner	TV	1990
52077	THt	G520LWU	Volvo B10M-60	Plaxton Paramount 3500 III	TV	1990
52078	GYt	G525LWU	Volvo B10M-60	Plaxton Paramount 3500 III	TV	1990
52079	CHt	WLT874	Volvo B10M-60	Plaxton Paramount 3500 III	TV	1990
52081	CRt	G530LWU	Volvo B10M-60	Plaxton Paramount 3500 III	TV	1990
52082	ESu	G531LWU	Volvo B10M-60	Plaxton Paramount 3500 III	TV	1990
52084	CHt	MIL4693	Volvo B10M-60	Plaxton Paramount 3500 III	TV	1990

52085	LSt	A14SOE	Volvo B10M-60	Plaxton Expressliner	TV	1990	Stephensons, Rochford, 2003
52086	KKt	H149CVU	Volvo B10M-60	Plaxton Expressliner	TV	1990	
52087	PH	H150CVU	Volvo B10M-60	Plaxton Expressliner	TV	1990	
52088	KKt	H406JAV	Volvo B10M-60	Plaxton Paramount 3500 III	TV	1991	
52089	Wlt	A16SOE	Volvo B10M-60	Plaxton Paramount 3500 III	TV	1990	Stephensons, Rochford, 2004
52090	MRt	H402DEG	Volvo B10M-61	Plaxton Paramount 3500 III	TV	1987	
52091	WPt	H181EGU	Volvo B10M-60	Plaxton Paramount 3500 III	TV	1991	Wallace Arnold, 1995
52092	WPt	H182EGU	Volvo B10M-60	Plaxton Paramount 3500 III	TV	1991	Wallace Arnold, 1995
52094	ASt	H640VWR	Volvo B10M-61	Plaxton Paramount 3500 III	TV	1992	Stephensons, Rochford, 2004
52095	GY	J456FSR	Volvo B10M-60	Plaxton Paramount 3500 III	C51F	1991	
52096	ATt	UWP105	Volvo B10M-61	Plaxton Paramount 3500 III	TV	1991	
52099	LL	PCK335	Volvo B10M-60	Plaxton Expressliner	C46FT	1991	
52103	BJt	MSU463	Volvo B10M-60	Plaxton Première 350	TV	1992	Parks of Hamilton, 1993
52104	ESu	866NHT	Volvo B10M-62	Plaxton Première 350	C51FT	1995	Parks of Hamilton, 1993
52106	ATt	J702CWT	Volvo B10M-60	Plaxton Première 350	TV	1992	Wallace Arnold, 1994
52108	BDt	ACZ7490	Volvo B10M-60	Plaxton Première 350	TV	1992	Wallace Arnold, 1994
52109	NNt	ACZ7491	Volvo B10M-60	Plaxton Première 350	TV	1992	Wallace Arnold, 1994
52115	HEt	J909NKP	Volvo B10M-60	Plaxton Expressliner	TV	1992	
52116	ESu	K758FYG	Volvo B10M-60	Plaxton Première 350	C50FT	1992	
52117	AN	K759FYG	Volvo B10M-60	Plaxton Première 350	C50FT	1992	
52118	BJ	TSU641	Volvo B10M-60	Plaxton Première 350	C50FT	1992	
52119	AN	TSU642	Volvo B10M-60	Plaxton Première 350	C50FT	1992	

52120-52124

			Volvo B10M-60		Plaxton Première Interurban	BC51F	1993	
52120	BD	K150DNV	52121	BD	K151DNV	52123	BD	K153DNV	52124	BD	K154DNV

52130	BQ	HSK760	Volvo B10M-60	Plaxton Expressliner 2	C49FT	1993	
52136	BQ	K566GSA	Volvo B10M-60	Plaxton Première Interurban	BC51F	1993	
52137	GW	K567GSA	Volvo B10M-60	Plaxton Première Interurban	BC51F	1993	

52141-52147

			Volvo B10M-60		Plaxton Première Interurban	BC53F	1993	
52141	GW	K571DFS	52144	GW	K574DFS	52146	CH	K576DFS	52147	CH	K577DFS
52143	GY	K573DFS	52145	MD	K575DFS						

52152	PY	L51CNY	Volvo B10M-60	Plaxton Première 320	C53F	1993	Phil Anslow, 2004
52153	PY	NIL8646	Volvo B10M-60	Plaxton Première 320	C53F	1992	Phil Anslow, 2004
52154	PY	NIL8656	Volvo B10M-60	Plaxton Première 320	C53F	1992	Phil Anslow, 2004

52155-52162

			Volvo B10M-60		Plaxton Première Interurban	BC51F	1993	
52155	NN	L155JNH	52157	GRt	L157JNH	52159	WGt	L159JNH	52161	NN	L161JNH
52156	NN	L156JNH	52158	SNt	L158JNH	52160	NN	L160JNH	52162	NN	L162JNH

52172	CB	L582JSA	Volvo B10M-60	Plaxton Première Interurban	BC51F	1993	
52173	CJ	WLT415	Volvo B10M-60	Plaxton Première Interurban	BC51F	1993	

52178-52190

			Volvo B10M-60		Plaxton Première Interurban	BC51F	1993	
52178	AA	L578HSG	52181	PT	L581HSG	52185	DE	L585HSG	52189	CB	L589JSA
52179	CB	L579HSG	52182	CN	L582HSG	52186	BR	L586HSG	52190	CB	L590JSA
52180	BR	L580HSG	52184	DE	L584HSG	52187	DE	L587HSG			

52194	HLt	NUF276	Volvo B10M-62	Plaxton Expressliner 2	TV	1993	
52195	CH	LJY145	Volvo B10M-62	Plaxton Expressliner 2	C46FT	1994	
52196	LL	VRR447	Volvo B10M-62	Plaxton Expressliner 2	C46FT	1994	
52197	BEt	L127NAO	Volvo B10M-62	Plaxton Expressliner 2	TV	1994	

52207-52213

			Volvo B10M-62		Plaxton Première Interurban	BC51F	1993	
52207	CH	L637LDT	52209	CH	L639LDT	52211	CH	L641LDT	52213	MD	L643LDT
52208	GW	L638LDT	52210	CH	L640LDT	52212	MD	L642LDT			

Megabus.com, Stagecoach's web-based low-cost inter-city bus and coach service, now covers thirty cities across the UK. By the end of 2004, the service had carried around 1.5million passengers. Showing off its Megabus livery at Victoria is 52298, N448XVA, which was initially used new on National Express duties.
Richard Godfrey

52214-52220   Volvo B10M-62   Plaxton Première 350   C53F*   1995   *52220 convertible to C49FT

| 52214 | PH | M404BFG | 52216 | SR | M406BFG | 52218 | SWu | CSU978 | 52220 | PT | M410BFG |
| 52215 | AE | M405BFG | 52217 | NS | SYC852 | 52219 | NS | CSU992 | | | |

| 52221 | PY | M35LHP | Volvo B10M-62 | | | Plaxton Première 350 | | C49FT | 1995 | | Phil Anslow, 2004 |

52227-52244   Volvo B10M-62   Plaxton Première Interurban   BC51F   1994

52227	BQ	HSV194	52232	AN	CSU920	52237	FH	M537RSO	52241	IS	M541RSO
52228	IS	TSV778	52233	FH	CSU921	52238	IS	M538RSO	52242	AN	M542RSO
52229	AN	TSV779	52234	iS	CSU922	52239	AN	M539RSO	52243	AN	M543RSO
52230	FH	TSV780	52235	BQ	CSU923	52240	AN	M540RSO	52244	IS	145CLT
52231	FH	TSV781	52236	BQ	M536RSO						

52245-52259   Volvo B10M-62   Plaxton Première Interurban   BC51F   1994

52245	DE	M945TSX	52250	GS	M950TSX	52254	KY	M954TSX	52257	MD	M943TSX
52246	DE	M946TSX	52251	GS	M951TSX	52255	GS	M955TSX	52258	GS	M944TSX
52248	GS	M948TSX	52252	AL	M952TSX	52256	AL	M956TSX	52259	GY	M942TSX
52249	AL	M949TSX	52253	GS	M953TSX						

52260-52266   Volvo B10M-62   Plaxton Première Interurban   BC51F   1994

| 52260 | GS | M160CCD | 52262 | AA | M162CCD | 52264 | KK | M164CCD | 52266 | PR | M166CCD |
| 52261 | CC | M161CCD | 52263 | AS | M163CCD | 52265 | GR | M165CCD | | | |

52267	AN	PSU788	Volvo B10M-62	Plaxton Expressliner 2	C46FT	1994
52268	LL	RBZ5459	Volvo B10M-62	Plaxton Expressliner 2	C46FT	1994
52269	BQ	M808JTY	Volvo B10M-62	Plaxton Expressliner 2	C44FT	1995

52271-52278   Volvo B10M-62   Plaxton Expressliner 2   C49FT   1994-95

| 52271 | AN | M911WJK | 52273 | BR | M913WJK | 52275 | BR | M915WJK | 52277 | BR | M917WJK |
| 52272 | AN | 147YFM | 52274 | WXu | M914WJK | 52276 | BR | M916WJK | 52278 | BR | M918WJK |

Pictured in Oxford while setting out on a journey back to Northampton, 52162, L162JNH, carries the Plaxton Interurban version of the Première. This model was designed in conjunction with Stagecoach and is employed on the longer services where a higher level of comfort is required. *Mark Lyons*

| 52279 | SR | N871MSU | Volvo B10M-62 | Plaxton Première 320 | C55F | 1996 | Rowe & Tudhope, 2005 |
| 52281 | MR | N91RVK | Volvo B10M-62 | Plaxton Expressliner 2 | C44FT | 1996 | |

52282-52294 — Volvo B10M-62 — Plaxton Première Interurban — BC51F — 1996

52282	DS	N142XSA	52285	AS	N145XSA	52289	BQ	N149XSA	52292	IS	N152XSA
52283	DS	N143XSA	52287	AS	N247XSA	52290	BQ	N150XSA	52293	BQ	N153XSA
52284	KK	N144XSA	52288	AN	N148XSA	52291	IS	N151XSA	52294	BQ	N154XSA

52295-52301 — Volvo B10M-62 — Plaxton Expressliner 2 — C49FT — 1995

| 52295 | SR | N445XVA | 52297 | SR | N447XVA | 52299 | MR | N449XVA | 52301 | BD | N451XVA |
| 52296 | SR | N446XVA | 52298 | T | N448XVA | 52300 | CN | N450XVA | | | |

52306-52310 — Volvo B10M-62 — Plaxton Expressliner 2 — C44FT — 1995

| 52306 | AN | DSV743 | 52308 | ESu | N618USS | 52309 | AN | FSU739 | 52310 | AN | 703DYE |
| 52307 | CJ | WLT447 | | | | | | | | | |

52312	BQ	N582XSA	Volvo B10M-62	Plaxton Première Interurban	BC51F	1996
52313	BQ	N583XSA	Volvo B10M-62	Plaxton Première Interurban	BC51F	1996
52314	BQ	N584XSA	Volvo B10M-62	Plaxton Première Interurban	BC51F	1996

52328-52332 — Volvo B10M-62 — Plaxton Expressliner 2 — C46FT — 1995

| 52328 | AY | N128VAO | 52330 | BD | 6253VC | 52331 | BD | 9258VC | 52332 | BD | 9737VC |
| 52329 | BD | 3063VC | | | | | | | | | |

52341-52346 — Volvo B10M-62 — Plaxton Première Interurban — BC51F — 1996

| 52341 | EX | P801XTA | 52343 | EX | P803XTA | 52345 | EX | P805XTA | 52346 | EX | P806XTA |
| 52342 | EX | P802XTA | 52344 | EX | P804XTA | | | | | | |

52348-52360 — Volvo B10M-62 — Plaxton Première Interurban — BC51F — 1996

52348	AS	P148ASA	52352	DE	P152ASA	52355	SR	P255ASA	52358	CC	P158ASA
52349	AS	P149ASA	52353	DE	P153ASA	52356	DE	P156ASA	52359	KK	13CLT
52350	KK	P150ASA	52354	AL	P154ASA	52357	GY	P157ASA	52360	KK	P160ASA
52351	GY	P151ASA									

52361-52367 — Volvo B10M-62 — Plaxton Première Interurban — BC51F — 1996

52361	AL	P568MSX	52365	AL	P565MSX	52366	GS	P566MSX	52367	GS	P567MSX
52362	AL	P569MSX									

52368-52373 — Volvo B10M-62 — Plaxton Première Interurban — BC51F — 1996

52368	NN	P168KBD	52370	NN	P170KBD	52372	BD	P172KBD	52373	BD	P173KBD
52369	NN	P169KBD	52371	BD	P171KBD						

52378-52381 — Volvo B10M-62 — Plaxton Première Interurban — BC51F — 1996

52378	HL	P178PRH	52379	HL	P179PRH	52380	GS	P180PRH	52381	GY	P181PRH

52382	BD	P622ESO	Volvo B10M-62	Plaxton Expressliner 2	C44FT	1997	
52385	AL	BSK744	Volvo B10M-62	Plaxton Expressliner 2	C44FT	1997	
52386	CJ	P626NSE	Volvo B10M-62	Plaxton Expressliner 2	C44FT	1997	
52387	BD	P627ESO	Volvo B10M-62	Plaxton Expressliner 2	C44FT	1997	
52392	AL	P92URG	Volvo B10M-62	Plaxton Expressliner 2	C44FT	1996	
52396	GR	P281XYS	Volvo B10M-62	Plaxton Première 350	C57F	1997	Crawford, Neilston, 1998

52397-52400 — Volvo B10M-62 — Plaxton Première Interurban — BC51F — 1997

52397	CW	P107FRS	52398	CB	P108FRS	52399	CW	P109FRS	52400	GR	P110FRS

52401-52404 — Volvo B10M-62 — Plaxton Première Interurban — BC51F — 1996

52401	CN	P771TTG	52402	CN	P772TTG	52403	CN	P773TTG	52404	CN	P774TTG

52405-52414 — Volvo B10M-62 — Plaxton Première Interurban — BC51F — 1997

52405	PR	P977UBV	52408	PR	P108DCW	52410	PR	P110DCW	52413	PR	P113DCW
52406	BR	P978UBV	52409	PR	P109DCW	52412	PR	P112DCW	52414	PR	P114DCW
52407	CC	P979UBV									

52415-52424 — Volvo B10M-62 — Plaxton Première Interurban — BC51F — 1997

52415	CB	R115OPS	52418	AS	R118OPS	52421	AS	R121OPS	52423	DE	R113OPS
52416	AS	R116OPS	52419	KK	R119OPS	52422	DE	R112OPS	52424	AL	R114OPS
52417	BR	R117OPS	52420	AL	R120OPS						

52425	KK	R103LSO	Volvo B10M-62	Plaxton Première Interurban	BC51F	1997	
52426	AS	R104LSO	Volvo B10M-62	Plaxton Première Interurban	BC51F	1997	
52427	DS	R105LSO	Volvo B10M-62	Plaxton Première Interurban	BC51F	1997	

52434-52439 — Volvo B10M-62 — Plaxton Expressliner 2 — C46FT — 1997

52434	BD	R34AKV	52436	EAu	R36AKV	52438	BD	R38AKV	52439	EAu	R39AKV
52435	EAu	R35AKV	52437	EAu	R37AKV						

52440-52443 — Volvo B10M-62 — Plaxton Première Interurban — BC51F — 1997

52440	GS	R539GSF	52441	AL	R541GSF	52442	GS	R542GSF	52443	GS	R543GSF

52444-52447 — Volvo B10M-62 — Plaxton Expressliner 2 — C46FT — 1997

52444	BD	R454FCE	52445	BD	R455FCE	52446	PE	R456FCE	52447	BD	R453FCE

52450-52454 — Volvo B10M-62 — Plaxton Expressliner 2 — C49FT — 1997

52450	EAu	R550JDF	52452	BD	R552JDF	52453	EAu	R553JDF	52454	CEw	R554JDF
52451	EAu	R551JDF									

52456-52458 — Volvo B10M-62 — Plaxton Première Interurban — BC51F — 1997

52456	KK	R636RSE	52458	AL	R638RSE	52459	AL	TSU639	52460	DE	R640RSE
52457	AL	R637RSE									

From 1998 the Jonckheere Mistral was chosen for coach work while the Jonckheere Modulo was employed on interurban duties. One of the latter, 52627, S797KRM, is based at Lillyhall depot and liveried for *The Cumbrian Connection*. It is seen at Rheged near Penrith in July 2004. *Tony Wilson*

52462-52465 — Volvo B10M-62 — Plaxton Première Interurban BC51F 1997

52462	AL	R82SEF	52463	BQ	R83SEF	52464	GW	R84SEF	52465	GW	R85SEF

52474-52486 — Volvo B10M-62 — Plaxton Première Interurban BC51F 1996-97

52474	PM	R174DNH	52478	CR	R178DNH	52481	CR	R181DNH	52484	BD	R184DNH
52475	CR	R175DNH	52479	CR	R179DNH	52482	BD	R182DNH	52485	BD	R185DNH
52476	PM	R176DNH	52480	PM	R180DNH	52483	BD	R183DNH	52486	BD	R186DNH
52477	CR	R177DNH									

52490	PR	R120VFR	Volvo B10M-62	Jonckheere Mistral 50	C46FT	1998
52491	CEw	R791PAO	Volvo B10M-62	Plaxton Première Interurban	BC51F	1997
52492	CEw	R792PAO	Volvo B10M-62	Plaxton Première Interurban	BC51F	1997
52493	BD	R663TKU	Volvo B10M-62	Plaxton Expressliner 2	C44FT	1997
52494	BD	R664TKU	Volvo B10M-62	Plaxton Expressliner 2	C44FT	1997

52495-52504 — Volvo B10M-62 — Plaxton Première Interurban BC51F 1997

52495	BR	R775CDW	52499	BR	R779CDW	52501	BR	R781CDW	52503	BR	R783CDW
52496	BR	R776CDW	52500	BR	R780CDW	52502	BR	R782CDW	52504	BR	R784CDW
52498	BR	R778CDW									

52510	SR	S860VAT	Volvo B10M-62	Plaxton Première 320	C51F	1998	Plaxton demonstrator, 2002
52601	MD	S173SVK	Volvo B10M-62	Jonckheere Mistral 50	C44FT	1998	
52602	MD	S174SVK	Volvo B10M-62	Jonckheere Mistral 50	C44FT	1998	
52603	RU	S133KRM	Volvo B10M-62	Jonckheere Mistral 50	C44FT	1998	
52604	RU	S134KRM	Volvo B10M-62	Jonckheere Mistral 50	C44FT	1998	

52605-52612 — Volvo B10M-62 — Jonckheere Modulo BC51F 1998

52605	BQ	S655JSE	52607	BQ	S657JSE	52609	BQ	S659JSE	52611	BQ	S661JSE
52606	BQ	S656JSE	52608	BQ	S658JSE	52610	BQ	S660JSE	52612	BQ	S662JSE

Further coaches were added in 2002 and 2003 for National Express work. These were Volvo B12s with Plaxton Paragon bodywork. Illustrating the type is 53005, GU52WTC. Changes to National Express duties have seen several transfers between depots recently. The order for an additonal batch in 2004, listed in the last edition was changed to the Volvo B7R model detailed opposite. These carry Interurban bodies and all this model are employed in the north of Scotland. *Dave Heath*

52613	PR	S269KHG	Volvo B10M-62		Jonckheere Modulo	BC51F	1998		
52614	PR	S270KHG	Volvo B10M-62		Jonckheere Modulo	BC51F	1998		
52615	PR	S905JHG	Volvo B10M-62		Jonckheere Mistral 50	C46FT	1998		
52616	PR	S906JHG	Volvo B10M-62		Jonckheere Mistral 50	C46FT	1998		

52617-52620			Volvo B10M-62		Jonckheere Mistral 50	C49FT	1988		
52617	PE	S457BCE	**52618**	PE	S458BCE	**52619**	PE	S459BCE	**52620**	PE	S460BCE

52621	DO	S901CCD	Volvo B10M-62		Jonckheere Mistral 50	C49FT	1998	
52622	PR	S902CCD	Volvo B10M-62		Jonckheere Mistral 50	C49FT	1998	
52623	PR	S903CCD	Volvo B10M-62		Jonckheere Mistral 50	C49FT	1998	

52626-52633			Volvo B10M-62		Jonckheere Modulo	BC51F	1998		
52626	LL	S796KRM	**52628**	LL	S798KRM	**52630**	MD	S670SDT	**52632**	CH	S672RWJ
52627	LL	S797KRM	**52629**	LL	S799KRM	**52631**	MD	S671SDT	**52633**	CH	S673RWJ

52635	MD	S665SDT	Volvo B10M-62		Jonckheere Mistral 50	C44FT	1998	
52638	BQ	S808BTT	Volvo B10M-62		Jonckheere Modulo	BC51F	1998	

52641-52649			Volvo B10M-62		Jonckheere Mistral 50	C44FT	1999		
52641	RU	T661OBD	**52643**	RU	T663OBD	**52645**	RU	KSU462	**52648**	RU	T668XTV
52642	RU	T662OBD	**52644**	MD	KSU461	**52647**	RU	T667XTV	**52649**	RU	T669XTV

52654-52659			Volvo B10M-62		Jonckheere Mistral 50	C49FT	1999		
52654	TH	V904DPN	**52656**	TH	V906DPN	**52658**	DO	V908DDY	**52659**	TH	V909DDY
52655	TH	V905DPN	**52657**	DO	V907DDY					

52666	AN	X676NSE	Volvo B10M-62		Jonckheere Mistral 50	C44FT	2001	
52667	AN	X677NSE	Volvo B10M-62		Jonckheere Mistral 50	C44FT	2001	
52668	AN	X678NSE	Volvo B10M-62		Jonckheere Mistral 50	C44FT	2001	
52669	AN	X679NSE	Volvo B10M-62		Jonckheere Mistral 50	C44FT	2001	

53001-53010 — Volvo B12M — Plaxton Paragon Expressliner — C46FT — 2002

53001	DO	GU52WSX	53004	DO	GU52WTA	53007	DO	GU52WTE	53009	DO	GU52WTG
53002	DO	GU52WSY	53005	DO	GU52WTC	53008	DO	GU52WTF	53010	DO	GU52WTJ
53003	DO	GU52WSZ	53006	DO	GU52WTD						

53011-53022 — Volvo B12M — Plaxton Paragon Expressliner — C46FT — 2003

53011	RU	YN03WNA	53014	LL	VU03VVY	53017	PR	VU03VVW	53020	LL	PX03KCV
53012	LL	VU03VVW	53015	PR	VU03VVZ	53018	PR	PX03KCN	53021	LL	PX03KCY
53013	LL	VU03VVX	53016	PR	VU03VWA	53019	PR	PX03KCU	53022	RU	YV03TZN

53201-53220 — Volvo B7R — Plaxton Profile Interurban — BC51F — 2004

53201	FH	SV54BYO	53206	FH	SV54BYW	53211	FH	SV54EKT	53216	FH	SV54EKZ
53202	FH	SV54BYP	53207	FH	SV54BYY	53212	FH	SV54EKU	53217	FH	SV54EMF
53203	FH	SV54BYR	53208	FH	SV54BYZ	53213	FH	SV54EKW	53218	IS	SV54EMJ
53204	FH	SV54BYT	53209	FH	SV54EKP	53214	FH	SV54EKX	53219	IS	SV54EMK
53205	FH	SV54BYU	53210	FH	SV54EKR	53215	FH	SV54EKY	53220	IS	SV54ENC

59001	SZt	OWO37X	Leyland Tiger TRCTL11/3R	Plaxton Supreme V	TV	1982	Ebley Coaches, Stroud, 2003
59002	PY	TJI4124	Leyland Tiger TRCTL11/3R	Plaxton Supreme V	C55F	1989	Phil Anslow, 2004
59014	PMt	C495LJV	Leyland Tiger TRCTL11/3RZ	Duple Caribbean 2	TV	1986	
59060	MDt	B53DWJ	Leyland Tiger TRCTL11/2RH	Alexander TE	TV	1985	
59087	MDt	PYE841Y	Leyland Tiger TRCTL11/3R	Duple Laser	TV	1983	
59101	PY	M180XHW	Dennis Javelin 11m	Wadham Stringer Vanguard III	B70F	1994	Phil Anslow, 2004
59102	PY	M182XHW	Dennis Javelin 11m	Wadham Stringer Vanguard III	B70F	1994	Phil Anslow, 2004
59601	PY	S174BLG	Mercedes-Benz Sprinter 412	Onyx	C16F	1998	Phil Anslow, 2004
59701	PY	UJI 4184	Volvo B6R	Jonckheere Deauville 35	C35F	1995	Phil Anslow, 2004
59801	PY	NIL 8647	Volvo B9M	Plaxton Paramount 3200 III	C35F	1989	Phil Anslow, 2004

Special event vehicle - (initial owners shown and traditional vintage body codes used)

59922	ESu	BMS222	Leyland Royal Tiger PSU1/15	Alexander	C41C	1952	Alexander
59931	ESu	FES831W	Volvo B58-61	Duple Dominant IV	BC50F	1981	Gloagtrotter, Perth
59939	ESu	HDV639E	Bristol MW6G	Eastern Coach Works	C39F	1967	Western National
59943	ESu	GRS343E	Albion Viking VK43AL	Alexander Y	C40F	1967	Alexander Northern
59950	WSu	YSD350L	Leyland Leopard PSU3/3R	Alexander AY	B41F	1973	Western SMT

60001-60013 — Mercedes-Benz Vito 110 CDi — Mercedes-Benz Traveliner — M8 — 2003

60001	PM	SW03OYA	60005	DE	SW03OYE	60008	DE	SW03OYJ	60011	DE	SW03OYM
60002	PM	SW03OYB	60006	DE	SW03OYF	60009	DE	SW03OYK	60012	DE	SW03OYN
60003	PM	SW03OYC	60007	DE	SW03OYG	60010	DE	SW03OYL	60013	DE	SW03OYP
60004	DE	SW03OYD									

80003	SYu	B58WUL	MCW Metrobus DR101/17	MCW	043/28D	1984	On loan during summer
80009	WA	VX04MZG	MAN 14.220	Designline	N30D	2004	Development vehicle.

Development vehicle 80009 (VX04MZG) is battery powered and constructed by New Zealand bodybuilder Designline. The vehicle has been shown to local authorities and further examples are expected to be bought into use in due course. The type has been used successfully by Stagecoach in New Zealand.
Dave Heath

Vehicle allocations

East Scotland (ES)

Aberdeen (Hillview Road) - Bluebird (AN)

Outstations - Alford; Ballater; Braemar; Fyvie; Inverurie; Stonehaven and Strathdon.

Leyland Titan	10858	10921	10922	11116	11122			
Leyland Olympian	14338	14957	14959	14962	14963			
Volvo Olympian	16111	16112	16115	16116	16117	16118	16119	16120
	16121	16153						
Volvo B10M bus	20112	20118	20141	20142	20143	20144	20150	20151
	20153	20154	20194	20195	20197			
MAN/ALX300	22109	22110	22112	22701	22702	22703	22704	22705
	22706	22707	22708	22709	22710	22711		
Volvo B6	30800	30801	30802	30803				
Volvo B6BLE	31491	31492	31493					
Dart	32104	32802	32804					
Dart SLF	33469	33470	33477	33478	33479	34022	34039	
Mercedes-Benz	40047	40050	40089	40171	40362	40540	40548	41315
	41507	41511	41520					
Optare Alero	47087							
Volvo B10M Interurban	52117	52119	52229	52232	52239	52240	52242	52243
	52271	52272	52288	52306	52309			
Ancillary	32110	40366	52104					

Aberhill (Methilhaven Road, Methil) - Fife (AL)

Leyland Olympian	14701	14702	14703	14704	14705	14720		
Volvo Citybus DD	15210	15211	15248	15269	15271	15276	15289	15295
Volvo Olympian	16046	16067	16084	16098	16101	16132	16141	16144
	16150	16157	16165	16176	16406	16413	16414	16415
	16416	16418	16421	16422	16423	16424	16425	16426
	16427	16428	16429	16430	16438			
Trident	18092	18093	18094	18095	18096	18097		
Volvo B10M bus	20342							
Dart	32122	32202	32203	32205	32210	32212	32349	
Mercedes-Benz	40488	40496	40591	40793	40794			
Volvo B10M coach	52385	52392						
VolvoB10M interurban	52249	52252	52254	52256	52354	52361	52362	52420
	52424	52441	52457	52458	52459	52462		
Ancillary	40091							

Buchan (Grange Road, Balmoor, Peterhead) - Bluebird (FH)

Outstations - Fraserburgh and Mintlaw

Leyland Titan	10571	10586	10591	10593		
Leyland Olympian	14410	14418	14455	14497	14964	
Volvo Olympian	16199	16248	16249			
Volvo B6	30267	30268	30679	30680	30681	
Dart	32102	32105				
Dart SLF	34023	34028	34029	34036	34076	
Mercedes-Benz	40161	40165	40170	40535	40538	40558
Volvo B10M interurban	52230	52231				
Volvo B7R	53201	53202	53203	53204	53205	53206
	53207	53208	53209	53210	53211	53212
	53213	53214	53215	53216	53217	
Shuttlebus	40102					

Banchory (Dykehead Garage, Blackhall) - J W Coaches (BJ)

Mercedes-Benz	40036	40038	40134	40136	40138	40141	41802
Volvo B10M	52103	52118	52073				

Cowdenbeath (Broad Street) - Fife (CJ)

Leyland Olympian	14707	14718	14719	14721	14722	14723	14725	
Volvo Citybus DD	15287	15292	15297					
Volvo Olympian	16075	16077	16114	16138	16155	16161	16173	16401
	16402	16407	16408	16439	16846	16847		
Volvo B10M bus	20196	20301	20316	20331	20340			
MAN/ALX300	22252	22253	22254	22255	22256	22257	22258	22259
	22260	22261	22262	22263	22264	22265	22269	22271
	22272	22273	22274					
Volvo B6	30426	20428	30429	30430	30431	30652	30673	
Dart	32207	32208	32209					
Volvo B10M coach	52386							
Volvo B10M interurban	52173							
Ancilliary	26022	52058						

Dunfermline (St Leonard's Street) - Fife (DE)

Leyland Olympian	14724							
Volvo Citybus	15212							
Volvo Olympian	16054	16065	16073	16107	16108	16140	16152	16154
	16156	16158	16159	16163	16166	16172	16177	16405
	16848	16849						
Trident	18098	18099	18100					
Volvo B10M bus	20107	20325	20326	20330	20337	20338	20339	
MAN ALX300	22276							
Volvo B6	30655	30656	30657	30658	30659	30670	30671	30672
Dart	32206	32213	32304	32306	32307	32308		
Dart SLF	33415	33416	33417	33418	33419	34082	34084	34104
Mercedes-Benz	40070	40071						
Volvo B10M Interurban	52184	52185	52187	52245	52246	52352	52353	52356
	52422	52423	52460					
Vito Taxi Bus	60004	60005	60006	60007	60008	60009	60010	60011
	60012	60013						
Ancilliary	26030							

Glenrothes (Flemington Road) - Fife (GS)

Volvo Citybus DD	15272	15273	15274	15290				
Volvo Olympian	16092	16100	16104	16160	16170	16171	16178	16403
	16404	16410	16412	16417	16419	16440	16850	16851
	16855	16856	16857	16858	16860			
Volvo B10M bus	20147	20148	20309	20317	20318	20319	20320	20323
	20324	20327	20328	20332	20334	20335	20336	20341
MAN/ALX300	22266	22267	22268					
Dart	32211							
Mercedes-Benz	40044	40049	40074	40080	40095	40096	40097	40586
	40588							
Volvo B10M Interurban	52248	52250	52251	52253	52255	52258	52260	52366
	52367	52380	52440	52442	52443			
Ancilliary	52014							

Inverness (Burnett Road) - Inverness (IS)

Outstation - Tain

Leyland Olympian	14490	14491	14492					
Volvo Olympian	16198	16200	16201	16202	16250	16610		
Dart	32801	32808	32809	32810	32811	32812		
Dart SLF	33414	33437	33438	33439	33471	33472	33473	33474
	33475	33476	34482	34483	34484	34485	34486	
	34487	34488	34489	34490				
Mercedes-Benz	40045	40051	40052	40534				
Volvo B10M interurban	52038	52228	52234	52238	52241	52244	52291	52292
Volvo B7R	53218	53219	53220					

Ancilliary   52006

Megabus (Perth/Inverness/Aberdeen):

Leyland Olympian	13602	13603	13653	14239	14240	
Volvo Olympian	15250	15259	15260			
MAN	50042	50046	50047	50048	50055	50058
Volvo B10M artic	51061	51062	51070			
Volvo B10M coach	52267	52310	52666	52667	52668	52669

Moray (Pinefield Depot, East Road, Elgin) - Bluebird (BQ)

Outstation - Macduff

Leyland Titan	10555	10560	10562	10577	10587	10601	10615	10626
	10751							
Volvo B10M bus	20597	20599						
Dart	32101	32803						
Dart SLF	34040	34061	34062	34069	34070			
Mercedes-Benz	40041	40042	40043	40079	40157	40166	40167	40168
	40169	40419	40589	40590	40636	40637	40640	41512
	41801							
Optare Solo	47078	47079	47080	47111				
Volvo B10M interurban	52130	52136	52227	52235	52236	52269	52289	52290
	52293	52294	52312	52313	52314	52463	52605	52606
	52607	52608	52609	52610	52611	52612	52638	

Ancilliary   52011

Perth (Ruthvenfield Road, Inveralmond) - Perth (PH)

Outstations - Crieff and Spittalfield

Leyland Titan (open-top)	11106	11114						
Leyland Olympian	14408	14409	14452	14457	14458	14467	14468	14469
	14471	14486	14487	14488	14496	14499	14706	
Volvo B10M bus	20111	20113	20171	20172	20173	20174	20175	20176
	20177	20178	20191	20192	20193			
MAN/ALX300	22277	22712	22713	22714	22715	22716	22717	22718
	22719	22722						
Volvo B6LE	31494	31495	31496	31497	31498	31499		
Dart	32805							
Dart SLF	33428	34329	33430	33431	33432	33433	33434	33435
	33436							
Mercedes-Benz	40046	41304	41509	41517				
Optare Solo	47051	47052	47053	47054				
Volvo B10M coach	52029	52214						

Ancilliary   52087

St Andrews (City Road) - Fife (SA)

Open-top	11093							
Citybus	15288	15293						
Volvo Olympian	16045	16057	16060	16409	16420	16450		
Volvo B10M bus	20149	20302	20303	20304	20305	20306	20307	20310 .
	20314	20315	20321	20322	20329			
Dart	32106	32201	32204	32344				
Dart SLF	34085	34086	34087					
Mercedes-Benz	40468	40642	40795					

East Scotland unallocated/reserve/disposal - (ES)

Titan	10566	10574	10622	10802	10819	10820	10996	11084
	11119							
Leyland Olympian	13603	14314	14444	14448	14456	14964		
Volvo B6	30427							
Dart	32342	32346	32347					
MAN ALX300	22709							
Mercedes-Benz	40072	40073	40075	40076	40078	40087	40090	40103
	40135	40194	40195	40197	40198	40203	40353	40365
	40536	40585	40587	40593	40594	40689	40810	
Volvo B10M coach	52004	52240	52244	52104				

Ancilliary	52739

West Scotland - (WS)

Ardrossan (Harbour Road) - Western, A1 Service (AS)

Leyland Titan	10462	10473						
Leyland Olympian	14392	14415	14485	14498				
Volvo Olympian	16068	16074						
Trident	18010	18011	18012	18013	18014	18015	18016	18017
	18018	18019	18020					
Volvo B10M bus	20510	20511	20532	20536	20556	20568	20569	
Volvo B10B	21051							
Volvo B6	30325	30326	30332	30675				
Mercedes-Benz	40059	40061	40063	40068	40098	40611	40624	40625
	40626	40627	40632					
Volvo B10M artic	51092	51093	51094	51095				
Volvo B10M coach	52263	52285	52287	52348	52349	52416	52418	52421
	52426							

Arran (Brodick) - Western (AA)

Volvo B10M bus	20524	20526	20537	20538	20539	20595	20596
Mercedes-Benz	40055	40056	40101	40630	40631	40633	
Volvo B10M coach	52178	52262	52328				

Ayr (Waggon Road) - Western, A1 Service, AA Buses (AY)

Leyland Titan	10005	10029	10209	10252	10999	11076	11083	11092
Leyland Olympian	14412							
Volvo Citybus	15246							
Volvo B10M bus	20108	20110	20114	20119	20422	20502	20503	20505
	20513	20514	20517	20518	20548	20549	20565	20566
	20567	20580	20581	20582	20584	20587	20593	20594
Volvo B6LE	31366	31367	31368	31378	31379	31380	31387	31388
Dart	32057	32062	32063	32137	32145	32396	32397	
Dart SLF	33443	33444	33445	33446	33447	33775	33776	33777
	33778	33779	33780	34021	34024	34025	34026	34027
	34063							

Excel	35016							
Mercedes-Benz	40054	40057	40062	40602	40604	40605	40606	40607
	40608	40610	40638	40639	40670	40671		
MAN - Jonckheere	50034	50037	50038	50044	50049	50050	50051	50056
	50057	50060						
Volvo B10M artic	51096	51097						

Cumnock (Ayr Road) - Western (CC)

Titan	10469	10874	10976	11032				
Leyland Olympian	14411							
Volvo Olympian	16859	16861						
Volvo B10M bus	20530	20531	20533	20534	20535	20570	20572	20573
	20574	20575	20576	20577	20578	20591		
Excel	35017							
Mercedes-Benz	40053	40060	40064	40065	40069	40099	42020	42022
	42023	42024						
Volvo B10M artic	51063	51064	51071	51073	51076	51098	51099	
Volvo B10M coach	52261	52358	52407					

Dumfries (Eastfield Road) - Western (DS)

Outstation - Kirkcudbright, Lockerbie

Titan	10246							
Volvo Olympian	16852	16853	16854					
Volvo B10M bus	20145	20146	20152	20308	20512	20571	20583	20783
Scania L113	28951	28952	28953	28954	28955			
Volvo B6	30318							
Dart	32005	32054	32058	32061	32120	32381	32382	32390
	32391	32392	32393	32394	32395	32398		
Dart SLF	33073	33074	33075	33077	33078	33079	33088	33089
	33772	33773						
Mercedes-Benz	40525							
Optare Solo	47063	47064	47065	47066	47067	47068		
Volvo B10M coach	52282	52283	52427					

Glasgow (Blochairn Road) - Glasgow (GW)

Leyland Olympian	14337	14462	14521	14522	14601	14602	14603	14608
	14612	14616	14619	14623	14625	14626	14627	14628
	14629	14638	14641	14642	14647	14650	14653	14654
	14656	14657	14659	14662	14663			
Volvo Citybus	15247	15249	15275	15299				
MAN - Jonckheere	50035	50036	50039	50041	50043	50045	50052	50053
	50054	50059	50066					
Volvo B10M coach	52137	52141	52144	52208	53464	52465		

Kilmarnock (Mackinlay Place) - Western (KK)

Outstation - Rothesay

Titan	10208	10585	10843	10950	11045			
Leyland Olympian	14454							
Volvo Citybus	15280	15281	15282	15283	15284	15285		
Volvo Olympian	16862	16863	16864	16865	16866			
Trident	18000	18001	18002	18003	18004	18005	18006	18007
	18008	18009						
Volvo B10 bus	20506	20507	20509	20579	20586	20588	20589	20590
MAN/ALX300	22601	22602	22603	22604	22605	22606		
National	25475							
Volvo B6	30312	30322	30324	30339	30340	30674		
Volvo B6LE	31369	31370	31371	31372	31373	31374	31375	31376
	31377	31381	31382	31383	31384	31385	31386	
Dart SLF	34596	34597	34598	34599	34600	34601	34602	34603
	34604							

Mercedes-Benz	40058	40066	40067	40100	40530	40601	40609	40621
	40628	40634	40635	40985	40986	40987		
Optare Solo	47150							
Volvo B10M coach	52264	52284	52350	52359	52360	52419	52425	52456
Ancilliary	28910	52069	52076	52086	52088			

Stranraer (Lewis Street) - Western (SR)

Outstation - Whithorn

Titan	10410	10762			
Volvo B10M bus	20504	20519	20521	20522	20585
Leopard	25769	25771	25797		
Dart	32138	32380			
Mercedes-Benz	40612	40622			
Volvo B10M coach	52026	52216	52279	52295	52296	52297	52355

West Scotland unallocated/stored - (WS)

Titan	10236	10700	10866
Titan open-top	11083	11092	
Routemaster	12060	12444	12550
Leyland Olympian	14622	14640	
Volvo Citybus	15279	15296	
Special event	19959	19982	
Volvo B10M	20109	20515	20591
Leyland National	25476		
Leopard	25728	59900	
Scania	28924	28928	
Mercedes-Benz	40277	42019	42021
MetroRider	47932		
Volvo B10M coach	52308		

North East (NE)

Newcastle (Shields Road, Walkergate) - (WA)

Leyland Olympian	13605	13630	13631	13633	13646	13652	14668	14669
	14676							
Scania DD	15301	15302	15303	15305	15306	15307	15308	15309
	15310							
Volvo Olympian	16431	16432	16433	16434	16435	16436	16437	16701
	16702	16703	16704	16705	16706	16707	16708	16709
	16710	16711	16712	16713	16714	16715	16716	16717
	16718	16719	16720	16721	16722	16723	16724	16725
	16726	16727	16728	16729	16730			
Volvo B10BLE	21101	21102	21103	21104	21105	21136	21137	21138
	21139	21140	21141	21142	21143	21144	21145	21146
	21147	21148	21149	21150	21151	21152	21153	21154
	21155	21156	21157	21158				
MAN/ALX300	22011	22012	22013	22014	22015	22016	22017	22018
	22019	22020	22021	22022	22023	22024	22025	22026
	22172	22174	22193	22195	22196	22202	22204	22206
	22208	22210	22211	22666				
Scania SD	28912	28926	28927	28929	28931			
Dart	32302	32650	32657	32714	32721	32745	32753	32768
Mercedes-Benz	40461	40463	40464	40465	40467	40485	40492	40495
	40501	40792						
Optare Alero	47025							
Ancillary vehicles	40491	48022	48078	52194				

Darlington (Faverdale) - Darlington (DA)

Leyland Olympian	14184	14186	14605	14611	14614	14645	14646	
Volvo B10M bus	20261							
Lynx	29621	29622	29627	29629	29630			
Dart	32301	32303	32305	32563	32564	32579	32615	32616
	32617	32655	32656	32658	32659	32660	32661	32702
	32709	32711	32712	32729	32740	32741	32742	32759
	32770							

Hartlepool (Brenda Road) - Hartlepool (HP)

Leyland Olympian	14191	14194	14639	14648	14651			
Volvo B10M bus	20120	20121	20122	20124	20256	20257	20258	20263
	20264	20265	20270	20271	20291	20292	20293	20294
	20295	20296	20297	20298	20299	20300	20550	20695
	20696	20839	20841	20843				
Dart SLF	33102	33482	33483	33484	33485	33486	33487	33488
	34550	34561	34562	34563	34564	34565	34566	34567
	34568	34569						

Slatyford (Slatyford Lane) - Newcastle (SY)

Metrobus OT	15917	80003						
MAN ALX300	22027	22028	22029	22030	22031	22032	22033	22034
	22035	22036	22037	22038	22039	22040	22041	22042
	22043	22044	22045	22046	22047	22048	22049	22050
	22051	22067	22068	22069	22070	22071	22190	22197
	22198	22199	22201	22214	22215	22453	22462	22463
	22464	22465	22466	22467	22468	22469	22470	22471
	22472	22473	22474	22475	22476	22477	22478	22479
	22480	22481	22482	22483	22484	22485	22492	22493
Scania SD	28901	28902	28905	28906	28908	28916	28917	28918
	28921	28923	28925	28930	28934	28935	28936	28938
Dart	32568	32569	32701	32723	32724	32725	32727	32728
	32744	32752						
Mercedes-Benz	40466	40469	40470	40471	40472	40473	40474	40475
	40476	40477	40478	40479	40480	40481	40483	40484
	40486	40487	40493	40494	40497	40498	40499	40620
	49501							
Alero	47803	47804						
Ancillary	40678	48007	48047	48065				

South Shields (Dean Road) - South Shields (SS)

Volvo Olympian	16732	16733	16734	16735	16736	16737	16738	16739
	16740							
Volvo B10M bus	20116	20117	20123	20125	20126	20135	20262	20273
	20551	20552	20553	20703	20714	20716	20722	20723
	20724	20726	20729	20730	20840	20842		
Volvo B10B	21002							
Dart	32112	32117	32121	32125	32127	32128	32129	32133
	32134	32624	32651	32652	32743	32746	32749	32751
	32766	32767	32769	32774	32775	32776	32783	32784
	32785	32791	32792	32793	32794	32795		
Dart SLF	34605	34606	34607	34608	34609	34610	34611	34612
	34613	34614	34615					
Ancillary	29541							

Stockton-on-Tees (Church Road) - Teesside (SC)

Leyland Olympian	14180	14181	14182	14185	14189	14192	14615	14617
	14618	14633	14636	14655	14658	14661	14670	14671
	14675							
Volvo Olympian	16731	16831	16832	16833	16834	16835	16836	16837
	16838	16839	16840					
Volvo B10M	20101	20102	20103	20104	20105	20106	20115	20243
	20244	20245	20246	20247	20248	20249	20250	20251
	20252	20253	20254	20255	20267	20268	20269	20272
	20554	20837	20844					
Volvo B10B	21031	21032	21033	21034	21035	21036	21037	21038
	21039	21040	21041	21042				
MAN ALX300	22061	22062	22063	22064	22065	22066	22451	22452
	22454	22455	22456	22656	22657	22658	22659	22660
	22661	22662	22663	22665	22667	22668	22669	22670
	22671	22674						
Dart	32717	32748						
Dart SLF	33101	33489	33490	33491	33492	33825	33826	33828
	34401							
Ancillary	29107	29122	29610					

Sunderland (North Bridge Street) - Sunderland (SU)

Leyland Olympian	14672	14673	14674					
MAN/ALX3000	22072	22073	22074	22075	22076	22077	22078	22079
	22080	22081	22082	22486	22487	22488	22489	22490
	22491	22494	22495	22664	22672	22673	22675	22727
	22728	22729	22730	22731	22732	22733	22734	22735
	22736							
Dart	32620	32621	32622	32623	32631	32632	32633	32634
	32637	32638	32703	32710	32720	32722	32726	32730
	32731	32732	32733	32734	32735	32736	32737	32738
	32739	32750	32760	32761	32762	32763	32764	32765
	32773	32777	32778	32779	32780	32781	32782	32786
	32787	32788	32789	32790				
Dart SLF	33118	33120	33121	33122	33123	33124	33125	33126
	33127	33128	33827					
Ancillary	29601	29616						

North East unallocated/stored - (NE)

Leyland Olympian	13022	14183	14198	14613	14667		
Scania DD	15304						
Scania SD	28903	28907	28911	28914			
Lynx	29611	29620	29624	29628			
Dart SLF	33829						
Mercedes-Benz	40092	40283	40482	40462	40489	40791	40796

North West - (NW)

Barrow (Walney Road) - Cumbria (BA)

Outstations - Coniston; Millom; Ulverston; Askam and Haverthwaite

Leyland Olympian	14187	14188	14193	14244	14245	14246	14247	14249
	14250	14256	14266	14267				
Volvo B10M bus	20129	20477	20478	20725	20748	20749	20754	20755
	20756	20757	20758	20759	20760	20761	20762	20778
	20780	20786	20787					
Volvo B6	30461	30846						
Mercedes-Benz	40004	40005	40016	40017	40018	40019	40020	40021
	40022	40023	40026	40327	40435	40646	40652	40882
Optare Solo	47130	47131	47132	47133	47134	47135	47136	47137
	47138	47139	47140	47141	47142	47143	47144	47145
	47146	47147						
Anciliary	25753	52062						

Carlisle (Willowholme Ind Est) - in Cumbria (CE)

Outstation - Penrith

Leyland Titan	10728							
Leyland Olympian	13022	13297	14232	14268				
Bristol VR	15731							
Volvo B10M	20291	20407	20408	20424	20425	20516	20592	20608
	20715	20718	20727	20731	20741	20746	20784	20838
	20867	20875	20879	20881	20894	20896	20904	20924
	20943	20944	20959	20960	20977	20979	20994	
Volvo B10B	21001							
MAN/ALX400	22804	22813						
Scania SD	28915	28932	28933	28937				
Volvo B6	30281	30323	30335	30337	30338	30342	30427	30651
	30653	30668	30726					
Dart	32124	32604	32605	32704	32705	32706	32715	32718
	32986	32989						
Dart SLF	34083	34088	34099	34101	34103	34139	34140	
Mercedes-Benz	40001	40192	40395	40396	40401	40424	40452	40519
	40616	40647	40648					
Volvo B10M coach	52027	52030						
Ancillary	25753	52064						

The following vehicles were damaged by flooding while in the Carlisle depot on 9th January 2005. As we go to press all had been removed from the fleet and are unlikely to see further use.

Titan Open top	10512							
Routemaster	12429	12451	12470	12488	12495	12592	12748	
Leyland Olympian	14229	14230	14231	14251				
Volvo Olympian	16644							
Volvo B10M bus	20717	20719	20728	20732	20736	20739	20742	20745
	20766	20772	20773	20781	20788			
MAN/ALX300	22801	22802	22803	22805	22806	22807	22808	22809
	22811	22812	22814	22819				
Lance	27201	27202	27203	27204	27205	27206	27207	27208
	27209	27210	27211	27212	27901	27902	27093	
Volvo B6	30271	30272	30273	30274	30310	30334		
Dart SLF	33076	34473	34474	34475	34476	34477	34478	34479
	34480	34481	34579	34580				
Mercedes-Benz	40002	40003	40329	40402	40446	40619	40650	40823
Volvo B10M coach	52454	52491	52492					
Ancillary	40834	46602	52065	52075				

Chorley (Eaves Lane) - in Lancashire (CY)

Leyland Olympian	14196	14197	14254				
Volvo Olympian	16636	16637	16638	16639			
Trident	18138	18139	18140	18141	18142	18143	18144	18145
	18146	18147	18148	18149	18150	18151	18152	18153
	18154	18155	18156	18157	18158	18159		
Volvo B10M bus	20130	20131	20132				
Volvo B6	30241	30303	30307				
Dart SLF	34679	34680					
Mercedes-Benz	40007	40008	40009	40010	40024	40399	40442
Ancillary vehicle	48029	52072					

Kendal (Station Road) - in Cumbria (KL)

Outstations - Ambleside; Appleby; Grange and Kirkby Stephen

Titan - Summer	10254	10281	11081	11091	11100	11110	
Leyland Olympian	14248	14252	14253				
Volvo Olympian	16330	16331	16332	16334	16335	16336	16337	16338
	16339	16340					
Volvo B10M bus	20456	20457	20458	20459	20699	20705	20710	20711
	20712	20735	20750	20774	20775	20776		
Tiger	25800						
Volvo B6	30270	30275	30276	30282	30309	30454	30455	30456
MB 709 - Summer	40081						
Mercedes-Benz	40613	40615	40617	40641	40651		
Volvo B10M coach	52057						
Ancillary	52001						

Lancaster (White Lund Estate, Morecambe) - in Lancaster (ME)

Outstations - Garstang and Ingleton

Titan	10056	10285	10311	10334	10340	10684	10686	10699
	10729	10738	10855				
Leyland Olympian	14201	14202	14204	14205	14206	14207	14208	14209
	14210	14235	14259				
Volvo Olympian	16641	16642	16656	16657	16658	16659	16660	16661
	16662	16663	16664	16665	16666	16667	16668	
Trident	17012	17013	17014	17015	17016	17017	17018	17019
	17020	17021	17022	17023	17024		
Volvo B10M bus	20436	20451	20452	20463	20540	20544	20545	20546
	20547	20793	20794	20795			
MAN/ALX300	22721	22815	22816	22817	22818	22821	22822	22823
	22824	22825	22826	22827			
Javelin bus	27035	27036	27037				
Volvo B6	30277	30457	30458				
Mercedes-Benz	42531	42533	42534	42535	42538	42549	42550	42553
	42562	42565	42566				
Ancillary	25704	25759					

Preston (Selbourne Street) - in Lancashire (PR)

Outstation: Fleetwood

Leyland Olympian	13296	14195	14199	14243	14260	14261	14265	
Volvo Olympian	16325	16326	16327	16328	16329	16343	16351	16352
	16353	16354	16355	16358	16359	16391	16392	16397
	16645	16646	16647	16648	16649	16650	16669	16670
Volvo B10M bus	20128	20430	20435	20454	20455	20473	20474	20475
	20476	20733	20734	20737	20738	20743	20789	20790
Volvo B6	30304	30308	30665					
Dart SLF	34616	34617	34618	34619	34620			
Mercedes-Benz	40397	40398	40455	42000	42091	42092	42093	42094
	42095	42096	42670	42672				
Solo	47016	47017	47018	47019	47020	47021	47022	47023
	47024	47055	47056	47057	47058	47059	47060	47061
	47062	47148	47149					
Volvo B10M coach	52266	52405	52408	52409	52410	52412	52413	52414
	52490	52613	52614	52615	52616	52622	52623	
Volvo B12M	53015	53016	53017	53018	53019			
Ancillary	46603	52056	52063					

West Cumbria (Blackwood Road, Lillyhall) - in Cumbria (LL)

Leyland Olympian	14203	14233	14234	14255	14257	14258		
Volvo Olympian	16643	16651	16652	16653	16654	16655		
Volvo B10M bus	20127	20133	20134	20700	20701	20702	20713	20721
	20751	20752	20753	20763	20764	20765	20767	20768
	20769	20770	20771	20777	20779			
Volvo B6	30278	30283	30301	30305	30306			
Mercedes-Benz	40006	40011	40012	40013	40014	40015	40025	40027
	40028	40029	40030	40031	40033	40328	40394	40445
	40649							
Volvo B10M coach	52099	52196	52268	52626	52627	52628	52629	
Volvo B12M	53012	53013	53014	53020	53021			
Ancillary	52061							

North West unallocated/stored - (NW)

Leyland Titan	10179							
Routemaster	12493	12624	12641	12642	12657	12671	12709	12749
Volvo B10M bus	20710	20712						
Volvo B6	30460	30724						
Mercedes-Benz	40039	40040	40427	40441	40443	40447	40520	40614
	40645	40822	40883	40885	40886			
Special event buses	39957	39995						

Manchester (MA)

Glossop (York Street) - (GP)

Scania	15313	15314	15315	15316	15317			
Volvo B10M bus	20905	20906	20907	20908	20909	20910	20918	20938
	20961	20962	20963	20964	20990			
Iveco schoolbus	29801	29802						
Mercedes-Benz	40429	40430	40431	40432	40433	40434	40660	40663
	40664	40665	42536	42548	42554	42558	42563	42564

Manchester (Hyde Road) - (HE)

Outstation: Chadderton

Leyland Olympian	13210	13212	13221	13224	13226	13255	13277	13282
	13283	13289	13291	13295	13298	13300	13301	13304
	13502	13503	13504	13505	13507	13508	13509	13510
	13511	13512	13513	13514	13517	13518	13519	14262
Scania DD	15336	15340	15341	15345	15347	15348	15351	15355
	15358	15361	15362	15363	15368			
Volvo Olympian	16501	16502	16503	16504	16505	16754	16755	16756
	16757	16758	16759	16760	16761	16762	16763	16764
	16765	16766						
Trident	17612	17613	17626	17627	17628	17631	17632	17633
	17641	17642	17643	17644	17645	17646	17647	17723
	17724	17725	17726	17727	18021	18022	18023	18024
	18025	18026	18027	18028	18029	18030	18031	18032
	18033	18034	18035	18036	18037	18038	18039	18040
	18041	18042	18043	18044	18045	18046	18047	18048
	18049	18050						
Volvo B10M bus	20653	20674	20677	20895	20901	20902	20903	20912
	20913	20914	20915	20916	20917	20919	20920	20921
	20922	20923	20925	20926	20927	20928	20929	20930
	20931	20932	20933	20934	20935	20936	20937	20939
	20940	20941	20942	20950	20951	20952	20953	20954
	20955	20956	20957	20965	20966	20967	20968	20969
	20970	20971	20972	20973	20974	20975	20976	20978
	20980	20981	20982	20983	20984	20985	20986	20987
	20988							
MAN/ALX300	22055	22056	22107	22108	22134	22135	22136	22137
	22138	22139	22140	22146	22148	22149	22153	22154
	22166	22167	22168	22185	22186	22187		
Mercedes-Benz	42001	42005	42009	42012	42015			
Ancillary	13027	13028	13207	13236	13260	13272	13285	13294
	15023	52115						

Manchester (Princess Road) - (PS)

Leyland Olympian	13208	13215	13234					
Olympian Tri-axle	13616	13623	13629	13643	13654			
Dominator	15031	15032	15033	15034	15035	15036	15037	15038
	15039	15040						
Dragon	15180	15181	15182	15183	15184	15185	15186	15187
	15188	15189	15190	15191	15192	15193	15194	15195
	15196	15197	15198	15199				
Volvo Olympian	16085	16087	16090	16103	16767	16768	16769	16770
	16771	16772	16773	16774	16775	16776	16778	16779
	16780	16781	16782	16786	16787	16788	16789	16790
	16791	16792	16793	16794	16795	16796	16797	16798
	16799	16800						

Trident	17614	17615	17617	17618	17637	17638	17639	17651
	17652	17653	17654	17655	17656	17657	17658	17659
	17660	17661	17662	17663	17664	17665	17666	17667
	17668	17669	17670	17671	17672	17701	17702	17703
	17704	17705	17706	17707	17708	17709	17710	17711
	17712	17713	17714	17715	17716	17717	17718	17719
	17720	17721	17730					
Volvo B10M bus	20860	20861	20862	20863	20864	20865	20866	20868
	20897	20898	20899	20945	20946	20947	20948	20949
	20958							
MAN/ALX300	22083	22084	22085	22086	22087	22088	22089	22090
	22091	22092	22093	22094	22095	22096	22097	22098
	22099	22100	22113	22156	22157	22158	22159	22160
	22161	22162	22163	22164	22165	22178	22179	22212
	22213	22235	22236	22237	22238			
Enviro 300	27501							

Stockport (Daw Bank) - (ST)

Scania DD	15332	15333	15335	15337	15342	15343	15344	15346
	15352	15353	15354	15359	15360	15365		
Volvo Olympian	16506	16507	16508	16509	16510	16511	16512	16513
	16744	16745	16746	16747	16748	16749	16750	16751
	16752	16753						
Trident	17616	17619	17620	17621	17622	17623	17624	17629
	17634	17635	17636	18182	18183	18184	18185	18186
	18187	18188	18189	18190	18191	18192	18193	18194
Volvo B10M bus	20845	20846	20847	20848	20849	20850	20851	20852
	20853	20854	20855	20856	20857	20858	20859	20876
	20877	20878	20880	20882	20893	20989	20991	20992
	20993	20995	20996					
MAN/ALX300	22101	22102	22103	22104	22105	22106	22114	22115
	22116	22117	22118	22119	22120	22121	22122	22124
	22125	22126	22127	22128	22129	22130	22131	22132
	22133	22141	22142	22143	22144	22145	22147	22150
	22151	22152	22169	22173	22180	22181	22182	22183
	22184	22188	22189	22216	22217	22218	22219	22221
	22223	22224	22226	22227	22228	22229	22231	22232
	22233	22234	22239	22241	22242	22243	22244	22246

Stockport (Charles Street) - (CS)

Dart	32048	32351	32352	32353	32354	32355	32356	32357
	32358	32359	32360	32361	32362	32363	32364	32365
	32366	32367	32368					
Dart SLF	34047	34048	34050	34053	34054	34057	34079	34080
	34081							
Mercedes-Benz	42002	42003	42004	42006	42007	42008	42010	42011
	42013	42014	42016	42017	42018	42545	42546	42551
	42552	42556	42567	42568	42569	42570	42571	42572
	42573							

Manchester reserve/stored/awaiting disposal - (MA)

Leyland Olympian	13121	13122	13165	13166	13170	13173	13174	13176
	13178	13181	13185	13191	13193	13195	13198	13205
	13214	13506	13515	13516				
Dominator	15011							
Scania DD	15356	15370	15371					
Mercedes-Benz	42530	42537	42539	42540	42541	42542	42543	42544
	42547	42559						
On loan to Oxford	18177	18178	18179	18180	18181			

East Midlands - (EM)

Chesterfield (Stonegravels, Sheffield Road) - in Chesterfield (CH)

Leyland Olympian	13632							
Volvo Olympian	16151	16453	16454	16455	16456	16457	16458	16459
	16460	16483	16484	16485	16486	16487	16488	16489
	16490	16491	16492	16493	16494	16495	16496	16497
	16500							
Trident	18125	18126						
Volvo B10M bus	20411	20418	20439	20440	20441	20442	20443	20444
	20496	20497	20661	20720	20744			
Dart	32066	32113	32114	32115	32116	32147	32148	32415
	32416	32417	32418	32421	32806	32807		
Dart SLF	33401	33402	33403	33760	33761	33762	33764	33765
	33766	33767	33768	33838	33839	33840	33841	34574
	34575	34576	34577	34578	34581	34582	34583	34584
Optare Excel	35000	35001	35002	35003	35004	35005	35006	
Mercedes-Benz	40739	40752	40755	40756	40757	40758	40759	40760
	40762	40764	40765	40767	40772	40773	40775	41714
	41715	41716	41717	41719	42576	42578	42579	42582
	42587	42589						
Volvo B10M coach	52146	52147	52195	52207	52209	52210	52211	52632
	52633							
Ancillary	52007	52079	52084					

Grimsby (Victoria Street) - Grimsby Cleethorpes (GY)

Dominator	15077	15079	15080	15081	15084	15085	15092	15093
	15094							
Fleetline OT - Summer	15513							
Volvo Olympian	16088	16093	16094	16096	16105			
Trident	17673	17674	17675	17676	17677	17678	17679	17680
	17681	17682	17683	17684	17685	17686	17687	17688
Lance	27301	27302	27303	27304	27701	27702	27703	27704
	27705	27706	27707	27708	27709			
Dart	32111	32419	32420	32426				
Mercedes-Benz	40771	40802	40803	42532	42557			
Volvo B10M coach	52005	52008	52051	52095				
Volvo B10M Interurban	52143	52259	52351	52357	52381			
Ancillary	52078							

Kingston-upon-Hull (Foster Street, Stoneferry) - in Hull (HL)

Leyland Olympian	14341	14359	14360	14361	14362	14363	14621	14630
	14632	14634	14635	14643	14644	14649	14664	14665
	14901	14908	14909	14912	14918	14922	14924	14925
Dominator	15044	15046	15047	15048	15049	15051		
Volvo Olympian	16047	16048	16051	16053	16061	16063	16066	16131
	16133	16134	16136	16143	16145	16147	16148	16168
	16471	16472	16473	16474	16475	16498	16499	16817
	16818	16819	16823	16824	16825	16826	16827	
Trident	17025	17026	17027	17028	17029	17030	17031	17032
	17033	17034	17035					
Volvo B10M Bus	20274	20275	20276	20277	20278	20279	20280	20281
	20282	20283	20284	20285	20286	20785		
Dart	32067	32068	32069	32071	32073	32080	32081	32082
	32083	32087	32089	32118	32123			
Dart SLF	33001	33103	33104	33107	33108	33109	33110	33112
	33113	33114	33115	33116	33117	33404	33405	33406
	33769	33770	33771	34570	34571	34572	34573	
Mercedes-Benz	42355	42356	42357	42358				
Volvo B10M coach	52378	52379						
Ancillary	25829	25832						

Mansfield (Sutton Road) - in Mansfield (MD)

Leyland Olympian	14319	14324	14335	14339	14340	14342	14343	14344
	14345	14346	14347	14348	14349	14350	14351	14352
	14353	14354	14355	14356	14357	14358		
Volvo Olympian	16169	16476	16477	16478	16479	16480	16481	16482
Tridents	17737	17738	17739					
Volvo B10M bus	20419	20498	20499					
Dart	32422	32423	32425	32427	32713	32818	32819	32820
Dart SLF	33831	33832	33833	33834	33835	33836	33837	33847
	33848	33849	34455	34456	34457	34458	34459	34460
	34461	34462	34463	34464	34465			
Mercedes-Benz	42577	42583	42584					
Volvo B10M Coach	52601	52602	52635	52644				
Volvo B10M Interurban	52145	52212	52213	52257	52630	52631		
Ancillary	59060	59087						

Worksop (Hardy Street) - in Bassetlaw (WP)

Volvo Olympian	16461	16462	16463	16464	16465	16466	16467	16468
	16469							
Trident	18120	18121	18122	18123	18124			
Volvo B10M bus	20412	20413	20414	20491	20492	20493	20494	20495
Dart	32424							
Dart SLF	34001	34002	34003	34004	34005	34006	34007	34008
	34009							
Optare Excel	35007	35008	35009	35010	35011	35012	35013	35014
	35015							
Mercedes-Benz	40761	40763	40769	40770	40781	40797	40798	40799
	40800	40804						
Ancillary	52091	52092						

East Midlands unallocated/stored (EM)

Leyland Olympian	14303							
Tiger	25830	25831						
Dart	33105							
Mercedes-Benz	40736	40742	40754	40774	40776	40777	40778	40779
	40780	40801	42585	42590				

East (EA)

Bedford (St Johns) - (BD)

Outstations - Biggleswade; Huntingdon; Northampton and Rushden

Leyland Olympian	14000	14020	14021	14022	14023	14024	14030	14032
	14034	14035	14036	14038	14040	14042	14476	14477
	14479	14483	14484	14510	14511	14512	14708	14709
	14710	14713						
Volvo Olympian	16210	16212	16213	16214	16215	16216	16217	16218
	16243	16244	16245	16527	16528	16537	16538	16539
	16555	16584	16586	16671	16672	16673	16674	16675
	16676	16677	16678					
Dart	32542	32550	32575	32582	32771	32772		
Dart SLF	33453	33454	34419	34420	34421	34422	34423	34424
	34425	34426	34427	34428	34429	34430	34431	34432
	34433	34434	34435	34436	34437	34438	34439	34440
	34441	34442	34443	34444				
Mercedes-Benz	40140	40302	40303	40304	40317	40318	40319	40320
	40321	40322	40323	40324	40332	40334	40335	40336
	40337	40383						
Volvo B10M coach	52120	52121	52123	52124	52301	52329	52330	52331
	52332	52371	52372	52373	52382	52387	52434	52438
	52444	52445	52447	52452	52482	52483	52484	52485
	52486	52493	52494					
Ancillary	41998	52024	52035	52036	52108			

Cambridge (Cowley Road) - in Cambridge (CB)

Outstations: Ely; Haverhill; King's Lynn; Littleport; Longstowe; Newmarket; Royston and St Ives.

Leyland Olympian	14506	14507	14508	14509	14513	14514	14523	14524
	14525							
Volvo Olympian	16008	16009	16010	16011	16012	16013	16014	16015
	16018	16019	16020	16021	16022	16023	16024	16025
	16026	16534	16541	16542	16543	16544	16545	
Trident	17007	17008	17009	17010	17011	17036	17037	17038
	17050	17051	17052	17053	17054	17055	17056	17057
	17058	17059	17076	17078	17079	17691	17692	17693
	17694	17695	17696	17697	18057	18058	18059	18060
MAN/ALX300	22058	22059	22060	22278	22301	22302	22303	22304
	22305	22306	22307	22308	22309	22310	22311	22312
	22313	22314	22315	22316	22317	22318	22319	22320
	22321	22322	22323	22324	22325	22326	22327	22328
	22329	22330	22331	22332	22333	22334	22335	22336
	22337	22338	22339	22340	22457	22458	22459	22460
	22461							
Dart	32757	32758						
Dart SLF	33393	33396	33399	33461	33462	33463	33464	33802
MetroRider	47900	47975	47979	47980				
Volvo B10M coach	52172	52179	52189	52190	52398	52415		
Ancillary	29101	29111	29115	29609	29626	40352		

Corby (Station Road) - (CX)

Leyland Olympian	13026	14179	14472	14520	14631	14935	14937	
Scania OmniDekka	15401	15402	15403	15404	15405			
Optare Solo	47029	47030	47031	47032	47033	47034	47035	47036
	47037	47038	47039	47042	47043	47044	47045	47046
	47050							
Ancillary	52021							

Kettering (Northampton Road) - (KG)

Outstations - Chown's Mill; Desborough; Thrapston and Wellingborough

Olympian	14025	14026	14027	14028	14029	14033	14043	14045
	14046	14054	14055	14056	14057	14058	14059	14060
	14061	14062	14063	14064	14067	14068	14069	14070
	14482	14947						
Tridents	18101	18102	18103	18104	18105	18106	18107	18108
	18109	18110	18111					
Mercedes-Benz	40306	40307	40308	40309	40310	40311	40312	40313
	40314	40315	40316	40340	40341	40342	40343	40344
	40345	40346	40347	40348	40349			

Special event vehicle	19952		
Ancillary	40371	41983	52033

Northampton (Rothersthorpe Avenue) - (NN)

Outstations - Chown's Mill; Daventry;and Milton Keynes

Leyland Olympian	14005	14047	14048	14049	14493	14494	14495	
Volvo Olympian	16004	16005	16006	16007	16209	16221	16222	16223
	16224	16225	16226	16227	16228	16229	16230	16231
	16232	16679	16680	16681	16682	16683	16684	16685
	16686	16687	16688	16689	16690	16691	16692	16693
	16694	16695	16696	16697	16698	16699		
Dart SLF	33455	33456	33457	33458	33459	33460	33813	33814
	33815	33816	33817	33818	33819	33820	34585	34586
	34587	34588	34589	34590	34591	34592	34593	34594
	34595							
Mercedes-Benz	40137	40139	40301	40305	40338	40339	40381	
Optare Solo	47123	47124	47125	47126	47127	47128	47129	
Volvo B10M coach	52155	52156	52160	52161	52162	52368	52369	52370

Special event vehicle	19953	
Ancillary	52032	52109

Peterborough (Lincoln Road) - in Peterborough - (PE)

Outstations: Holbeach Drove; Lincoln; March; Market Deeping and Oundle.

Volvo Olympian	16049	16056	16070	16082	16083	16086	16089	16091
	16095	16097	16102	16106	16109	16113	16124	16125
	16130	16139	16146	16162	16167	16174	16175	16580
	16581	16582	16583	16587	16588	16589	16590	16591
	16592	16593						
Dart SLF	33322	33323	33324	33394	33395	33397	33398	33604
	33806	34526	34530	34532	34533	34534	34535	34536
	34537	34538	34539	34540	34541	34542	34543	34544
	34545	34546	34547	34548	34549			
MetroRider	47976	47977	47978	47988	47989			
Volvo B10M coach	52446	52617	52618	52619	52620			

Ancillary	29607	29608

East unallocated/stored - (EA)

Mercedes-Benz	40350	40351	40356	40359	40373	40374	40375	40376
	40377	40378	40379	40380	40382			
MetroRider	47901	47972						
Volvo B10M	52435	52436	52437	52439	52450	52451	52453	

Oxfordshire and Warwickshire - (SM)

Banbury (Canal Street) - in Oxfordshire (BB)

Volvo Olympian	16525							
Volvo B6LE	31319	31320	31331	31353	31361	31362	31365	31852
	31853	31854						
Mercedes-Benz	42586	42588	42624					

Ancillary   52037

Leamington (Station Approach) - in Warwickshire (LE)

Leyland Olympian	13614	13615	13625	14369	14373	14375	14377	14378
	14515	14516	14517					
Volvo Olympian	16072	16076	16078	16079	16514	16515	16516	16517
	16598	16599	16600	16614	16615	16616	16617	16618
	16619	16620						
Volvo B10M bus	20201	20206	20217	20218	20219	20220	20401	20402
	20541	20558	20559	20560	20704	20803	20804	20808
	20814	20821	20823					
Volvo B6BLE	31333							
Mercedes-Benz	40142	40143	40163					
Optare Solo	47001	47002	47003	47004	47005	47006	47007	47008
	47009	47010	47011	47012	47013	47014	47015	

Ancillary   29617

Nuneaton (Newtown Road) - in Warwickshire (NU)

Leyland Olympian	13626	14382	14386					
Volvo B10M bus	20207	20208	20209	20210	20211	20212	20213	20214
	20215	20216	20226	20227	20423			
Volvo B6LE	31327	31328	31329	31332	31334	31350	31351	31352
	31354	31355	31356	31357	31363	31364		
Dart	32001	32002	32003	32004	32006	32007	32008	
Dart SLF	34491	34492	34493	34494	34495	34496	34497	34498
	34499	34625	34626	34627	34628			
Mercedes-Benz	40147	40148	40149	40152				
Solo	47026	47027	47028	47069	47070	47071	47072	47073
	47074	47075	47076	47077				

Ancillary   52031

Oxford (Horspath Road, Cowley) - in Oxford (OX)

Outstations: Bicester, Chipping Norton and Harwell.

Volvo Olympian	16518	16519	16520	16521	16522	16523	16524	
Trident	18051	18052	18053	18054	18055	18056	18177	18178
	18179	18180	18181	18195	18196	18197	18198	18199
Volvo B10M bus	20004	20005	20006	20007	20008	20009	20010	20011
	20012	20228	20542	20543	20694	20704	20805	20812
	20820	20822						
MAN/ALX300	22052	22053	22054	22057	22203	22205	22207	22209
	22279	22913	22914	22915	22916	22917	22918	22919
	22920	22921	22922	22923	22924	22925	22926	22927
	22928	22929	22930	22931	22932	22933	22934	22935
	22936	22937	22938	22940	22941	22942	22943	22944
	22945	22946	22947	22948				
Dart SLF	33650	33651	33652	33653	33654	33655	33763	34466
	34467	34468	34469	34470	34471	34472		
Mercedes-Benz	40108	40110	41062	40172	40653	42371	42372	42376
	42383							
MAN DD coach	50101	50102	50103	50104	50105	50106	50107	50108
	50109	50110	50111	50112	50113	50114	50115	50116
	50117	50118	50119	50120	50121	50122	50123	50124
	50125							
Ancillary	29108	29127	29615					

Rugby (Railway Terrace) - in Warwickshire (RU)

Leyland Olympian	14371	14374	14381	14387	14932	14942	14943	14944
Volvo B10M bus	20202	20221	20223	20224	20225	20417	20809	20813
	20816							
Enviro 300	27502	27503	27504	27505				
Volvo B6LE	31321	31322	31323	31324	31325	31326	31330	
Dart SLF	34398							
Mercedes-Benz	40153	40154	40155	40156	40158	40159	40160	41505
Volvo B10M coach	52603	52604	52641	52642	52643	52645	52647	52648
	52649							
Volvo B12B	53011	53022						
Ancillary	52020							

Witney (Corn Street) - in Oxfordshire (WY)

Volvo Olympian	16526							
Trident	18127	18128	18129	18130	18131	18132	18133	18134
	18135	18136	18137					
Dart	32613	32614	32625	32626	32627	32628	32629	32630
Mercedes-Benz	40657	40658	40659	42373	42374	42375	42377	42378
	42379	42380	42381	42382				

Oxfordshire and Warwickshire unallocated/stored - (SM)

Leyland Olympian	14936		
B10M bus	20203	20204	20205

West (WW)

Cheltenham (Lansdown Ind Est, Gloucester Road) - in Cheltenham (CT)

Leyland Olympian	13645	13648						
Trident	17722	17728	17729	18082	18083	18084	18085	18086
	18087	18088	18089	18090	18091	18200		
Volvo B6	30723							
Dart	32126	32234	32236	32257				
Dart SLF	33503	33506	33510	33930	33938	33939	33940	33941
	33953	33954	33955	33956	33957	33958	33961	33962
	33972	33973	33974	33975	33976	33977	34404	34405
Ancillary	29105	46610						

Gloucester (London Road) - in Gloucester (GR)

Leyland Olympian	14273	14289	14291	14292	14294	14500	14501	14502
	14958							
Volvo Olympian	16110	16126	16411	16442	16448			
Volvo B10M bus	20817	20818	20819	20827	20828			
Volvo B6	30709	30711	30712	30832				
Dart	32130	32320	32970					
Dart SLF	33507	33508	33509	33511	33512	33513	33601	33602
	33603	33915	33916	33917	33926	33927	33928	33929
	33944	33945	33946	33948	33949	33950	33951	33952
	33959	33960	33966					
Mercedes-Benz	41158	41159	41167	41171				
Volvo B10M coach	52265	52396	52400					
Ancillary	26109	29116	52157					

Ross-on-Wye (Platform 62, Business Park) - in Wye and Dean - (RY)

Volvo Olympian	16203	16204	16205	16206	16207	16208	16441
Dart SLF	33947	33978	33979	33980	34402	34403	

Stroud (London Road) - in the Cotswolds - (SZ)

Leyland Olympian	14282	14286	14288	14293	14610		
Volvo Olympian	16080	16127	16128	16129	16142		
Lynx	29614						
Dart	32132	32241	32901	32902	32903	32936	32937
Dart SLF	33809	33810	33811	33812			
Mercedes-Benz	41803	41805	41152				
Solo	47121	47122					
Ancillary	46607	59001					

Swindon (Eastcott Street) - in Swindon (SN)

Outstations - Chippenham and Cirencester

Leyland Olympian	14263	14264	14271	14272	14283	14287	14609	14624
Volvo Olympian	16044	16055	16081	16099	16135	16443	16449	16452
Volvo B10M bus	20681	20682	20683	20684	20685	20686	20687	20688
	20689							
Dart	32313	32317	32319					
Dart SLF	33501	33502	33504	33505	33808	33904	33905	33906
	33907	33908	33909	33910	33911	33912	33913	33914
	33918	33924	33925	33942	33943	33967	33968	33969
	33970	33971						
Ancillary	29613	46606	52158					

Unallocated (West) - (WW)

Olympian	14367				
Falcon	27034				
Volvo B6	30667	30709	30723	30831	30845
Dart	32318				
Mercedes-Benz	40725	40727	40729	40731	40735	41153	41161	41308
	41804	41330	41806		
Dodge	48046	48059	48068	48083	

Wales (WX)

Aberdare (Cwmbach New Road, Cwmbach) - Red & White (AE)

Volvo B10M bus	20350	20351	20352	20353	20358			
Dart	32078	32610	32611	32984	32985	32988	32992	32994
	32996	32999						
Mercedes-Benz	41168	41169	41170	41401	41403	41421	41416	
Volvo B10M coach	52215							

Brynmawr (Warwick Road) - Red & White (BR)

Volvo B10M bus	20385	20387	20388	20389	20390	20391	20698	20707
	20709							
Dart SLF	33554	33556	33557	33558	34621	34622	34623	34624
Mercedes-Benz	40541	40567	40568	40570	40571	40712	40715	
Volvo B10M coach	52180	52186	52406	52417	52495	52496	52498	52499
	52500	52501	52502	52503	52504	52273	52275	52276
	52277	52278						

Ancillary	46272

Caerphilly (Bedwas House Ind Est, Bedwas) - Red & White (CL)

Dart	32051	32609	32612	32960	32968	32983	32990	32996
Dart SLF	33559	33561	33609	33610	33611	33612	33613	33614
	33615	33616	33617	33619	33620	34663	34664	34665
	34666	34667	34668	34669	34670	34671	34672	34673
	34674	34675	34676	34677	34678			

Ancillary	41155

Chepstow (Bulwark Road) - Red & White (CW)

Volvo B10M bus	20870	20874	20886	20887	20889
Volvo B10M coach	52397	52399			

Cwmbran (St David's Road) - Red & White (CN)

Titan	10492	10542	10589	10592	10602	10619	10646	10651
	10665	10702	10905					
Leyland Olympian	13606	13610	13611	13619	13624	13627		
Volvo Olympian	16149	16444	16445	16446	16447			
Volvo B10M bus	20370	20392	20403	20404	20405	20420	20421	20869
Dart SLF	34043	34044	34045	34046	34049	34051	34052	34055
	34056	34058	34105	34106	34125	34126	34127	34128
	34139	34130	34131	34132	34136	34137	34138	
Mercedes-Benz	40145	40537	40543	40547	40555	40566	40569	40572
	40573	40574	40575	40577	40578	40579	40580	40581
	40582	40583	40584	40618	40643	40708	40709	40710
	40714	41405	41408	41412	41413	41414	41415	41417
	41420	41423	41425	41430				
Volvo B10M coach	52182	52300	52401	52402	52403	52404		

Ancillary	46273	52059

Merthyr Tydfil (Merthyr Industrial Estate, Dowlais) - Red & White (MR)

Outstation: Brecon

Volvo B10M bus	20354	20355	20356	20357	20359	20360	20361	20362
	20363	20365	20366	20367	20368	20369	20697	20706
	20708	20806	20807	20810	20811	20815	20824	20825
	20826							
Dart	32967	32997						
Dart SLF	34042	34096						
Mercedes-Benz	40552	40556	40562	40563	40564	40565	40723	41402
	41406	41407	41409	41410				
Volvo B10M coach	52281	52299						
Ancillary	52090							

Pontypool (Pontnewynydd Industrial Estate) - (PY)

Mercedes-Benz	40595	41331	41332	41424	42025	42026	42027	42028
Volvo B10M	52015	52016	52019	52025	52152	52153	52154	52221
Leyland Tiger	59002							
Javelin	59101	59102						
Mercedes Sprinter	59601							
Volvo B6R	59701							
Volvo B9M	59801							

Porth (Aberrhondda Road) - Red & White (PT)

Volvo B10M bus	20871	20872	20873	20883	20884	20885	20890	20891
	20892							
MB O405/Prisma	23950	23951						
Dart	32052	32053	32964	32965				
Dart SLF	33606	33607	33608	33621	33622	33623	33624	33625
	33626	33627	34037	34038	34041	34124	34134	34135
	34500	34501	34502	34503	34504	34505	34506	34507
	34508	34509	34510	34511	34512	34513		
Mercedes-Benz	41150	41154	41162	41163	41164	41165	41166	41404
	41411	41418	41419	41422	41426	41427	41428	
Volvo B10M coach	52181	52220						
Ancillary	20001	20406						

Unallocated (Wales & West) - (WX)

Volvo B10M	20364							
Volvo B6	30705	30706						
Dart	32242	32969	32995	32998				
Mercedes-Benz	40144	40205	40539	40544	40557	40576	40644	40713
	41156	41429						
Iveco	46271							
Volvo B10M Interurban	52274							

South West (SW)

Exeter (Belgrave Road) - (EX)

Outstations: Cullompton; Ottery St Mary; Sidmouth and Tiverton

Scania	15322	15323	15324	15325	15326			
Volvo Olympian	16050	16052	16058	16059	16064	16069	16071	16602
	16603	16604						
Trident	17002	17003	17004	17005	17006	17734	17735	17736
	18112	18113	18114	18115	18116	18117	18118	18119
Volvo B10M bus	20347	20616	20621	20630	20651	20801		
Scania N112	28705	28706	28913	28919				
Volvo B6BLE	31701	31702	31704	31705	31706	31707	31708	31709
	31710	31711	31712	31713	31714			
Dart	32139	32140	32141	32163	32164	32165	32251	32252
	32253	32260	32262	09999 (32271)		32410	32411	32431
	32432	32439	32440	32442	32443	32444	32446	32599
Dart SLF	33158	33159	33160	33200	33751	33781	33782	33783
	33803	33804	33805	33807	33823	33824	34115	
Mercedes-Benz	42109	42110	42112	42113	42114	42115	42116	42117
	42118							
Optare Solo	47081	47082	47083	47084	47085	47086	47087	47088
	47089	47090	47091	47092	47093	47094	47095	47096
	47097	47098	47099	47100	47101	47102	47103	47104
	47105	47106	47107	47108	47109	47110		
Volvo B10M coach	52341	52342	52343	52344	52345	52346		
Ancillary	28701	28704	48080	52071				
Special Event Vehicle	19992							

Exmouth (Imperial Road) - (EH)

Volvo Olympian	16017	16069	16137	16164				
Dart	32056	32064	32079	32084	32099	32434	32435	32436
	32437	32438						
Dart SLF	33201	33202	33801	34399				
Mercedes-Benz	40716	40717	40718	40719	40734	42107	42108	

Paignton (Dartmouth Road) - (PN)

Trident	18076	18077	18078	18079	18080	18081		
Dart	32022							
Mercedes-Benz	40511	40513	40545	40549	40551	40560	40506	40507
	40508	40509	40510	40512	40701			

Torquay (Regent Close, Shiphay) - (TQ)

Volvo Olympian	16601							
Trident	18061	18062	18063	18064	18065	18066	18067	18068
	18069	18070	18071	18072	18073	18074	18075	
Volvo B10M bus	20479	20480	20481	20482	20802			
Dart	32014	32015	32016	32017	32018	32019	32020	32021
	32433	32618	32619	32636	32639	32640		
Dart SLF	33774	34077	34095					
Mercedes-Benz	40514	40515	40516	40517	40518	40550	40553	40554
	40704	40705	40706	40707	40711	40732	40978	40979
	40980	40981	40982	42101	42102	42103	42104	42105
Ancillary	26028	40698	40699	40702	46609			

South West unallocated/stored - (SW)

Leyland Olympian	14281							
Scania DD	15327	15328	15329					
Volvo Olympian	16016							
Scania SD	26028	28703						
Volvo B6BLE	31703							
Dart	32991	32993						
Mercedes-Benz	40226	40227	40228	40229	40230	40232	40234	40236
	40237	40239	40240	40241	40242	40243	40244	40245
	40246	40248	40249	40250	40696	40697	40703	
Iveco	46319	46321	46378	46379	46381	46382	46398	46399
	46604	46608						
Volvo B10M coach	52218							

London - (LN)

Barking (Longbridge Road) - BK

Trident	17039	17063	17064	17065	17080	17106	17261	17262
	17263	17264	17265	17266	17267	17269	17270	17271
	17272	17273	17274	17275	17359	17360	17361	17362
	17363	17364	17365	17366	17367	17368	17369	17370
	17371	17372	17373	17374	17375	17376	17377	17378
	17379	17380	17381	17382	17383	17384	17385	17386
	17387	17388	17389	17390	17391	17392	17393	17394
	17855	17856	17857	17858	17859	17860	17861	17862
	17863	17892	17893	17894	17895	17896	17897	17898
	17899	17900	17901	17902				
Dart SLF	34119	34120	34121	34122	34123	34199	34202	34254
	34255	34256	34257	34258	34259	34260	34261	34262
	34263	34264	34265	34266	34267	34268	34269	34270
	34271	34272	34273	34274	34275	34276	34277	34278
	34279	34280	34281	34282	34283	34284	34285	34286
	34287	34288	34289	34290	34291	34292	34293	34294
	34295	34296	34297	34298	34299	34300	34301	34302
	34347	34348	34349	34350	34351	34352	34353	
Ancillary	26012	26025	26027	26031	26032	26033		

Bow (Fairfield Road) - BW

Trident	17537	17538	17539	17540	17541	17542	17543	17544
	17545	17546	17547	17548	17549	17550	17551	17552
	17553	17554	17555	17556	17557	17558	17559	17560
	17750	17751	17752	17753	17754	17755	17756	17757
	17782	17783	17784	17785	17786	17787	17854	17879
	17880	17881	17882	17883	17884	17885	17886	17887
	17888	17909	17910	17911	17912	17913	17914	17915
	17916	17917	17918	17919	17920	17921	17922	17923
	17924	17925	17926	17927	17928	17929	17930	17931
	17932	17933	18201	18202	18203	18204	18205	18206
	18207	18208	18209	18210	18211	18212	18213	18214
	18215	18216	18217	18218	18219	18220	18221	18222
	18223	18224	18225	18226	18227	18228	18229	18230
	18231	18232	18233	18234	18235	18236	18237	18238

Bromley (Hastings Road) - TB

Olympian	16122	16123						
Trident	17230	17279	17280	17281	17282	17283	17284	17285
	17286	17287	17288	17289	17290	17324	17334	17335
	17336	17337	17338	17339	17340	17341	17342	17343
	17344	17345	17346	17347	17348	17349	17351	17352
	17353	17354	17355	17356	17357	17358	17965	17966
	17967	17968	17969	17970	17971	17972	17973	17974
	17975							
Dart SLF	34097	34141	34152	34204	34205	34206	34213	34217
	34218	34219	34220	34221	34222	34223	34224	34225
	34226	34227	34228	34229	34230	34231	34232	34233
	34234	34235	34236	34354	34355	34356	34357	34358
	34359	34360	34361	34362	34363	34364	34365	
Ancillary	26003	26011	26018	26024	26026			

Catford (Bromley Road) - TL

Trident	17139	17143	17148	17150	17151	17152	17153	17154
	17155	17156	17157	17158	17160	17223	17224	17225
	17226	17227	17228	17229	17231	17232	17233	17317
	17318	17319	17320	17321	17322	17323	17325	17326
	17327	17328	17329	17330	17331	17332	17333	17350
	17467	17468	17469	17470	17471	17472	17473	17474
	17475	17476	17477	17478	17479	17480	17481	17482
	17483	17484	17485	17523	17524	17525	17526	17527
	17528	17529	17530	17531	17532	17533	17534	17561
	17562	17567	17568	17569	17570	17571	17572	17573
	17574	17575	17576	17577	17578	17579	17580	17581
	17582	17583	17584	17585	17586	17587	17588	17589
	17590	17591						
Dart	34114	34116	34117	34118	34173	34177	34180	34200
	34201	34203	34237	34238	34239	34241	34242	34243
	34244	34246	34247	34249	34250	34251	34252	34253
	34303	34304	34305	34306	34307	34308	34309	34310
	34311	34312	34313	34314	34315	34316	34317	34318
	34319	34320	34321	34322	34323	34324	34325	34326
	34327	34387	34388	34389	34390	34391	34392	34393
	34394	34395	34396	34397				
Ancillary	26013	26014	26015	26016	26035			

Leyton (High Road) - T

Leyland Olympian	13607	13608	13609	13617	13618	13636		
Trident	17001	17060	17061	17181	17182	17183	17184	17185
	17186	17187	17188	17189	17190	17191	17409	17410
	17411	17412	17413	17414	17415	17416	17417	17418
	17419	17420	17421	17422	17423	17424	17425	17426
	17427	17592	17593	17594	17595	17596	17597	17598
	17599	17600	17601	17602	17603	17604	17605	17606
	17607	17608	17609	17610	17611	17779	17780	17781
	17788	17789	17790	17791	17792	17793	17794	17795
	17796	17797	17798	17799	17800	17801	17802	17803
	17804	17805	17806	17807	17808	17809	17810	17811
	17812	17813	17814	17815	17816	17817	17818	17819
	17820	17821	17822	17823	17824	17825	17826	17827
	17828	17829	17830	17831	17832	17833	18239	18240
	18241	18242	18243	18244	18245	18246	18247	18248
	18249	18250	18251	18252	18253	18254	18255	18256

Plumstead (Pettman Crescent) - PD

Trident	17099	17100	17101	17102	17103	17104	17105	17107
	17108	17109	17110	17112	17113	17115	17116	17117
	17118	17119	17120	17121	17122	17123	17125	17126
	17127	17128	17130	17131	17133	17134	17138	17140
	17141	17142	17145	17149	17159	17161	17162	17163
	17164	17166	17193	17195	17214	17215	17216	17217
	17218	17219	17220	17221	17222	17276	17277	17278
	17302	17303	17304	17305	17306	17307	17308	17309
	17310	17311	17312	17313	17314	17315	17316	17851
	17852	17853	17866	17867	17868	17869	17870	17871
	17872	17873	17874	17875	17876	17877	17878	17905
	17906	17907	17908	17934	17935	17936	17937	17938
	17939	17940	17941	17942	17943	17944	17945	17946
	17947	17948	17949	17950	17951	17952	17953	17954
	17955	17956	17957	17958	17959	17960	17961	17962
	17963	17964						
Citaro Artic	23001	23002	23003	23004	23005	23006	23007	23008
	23009	23010	23011	23012	23013	23014	23015	23016
	23017	23018	23019	23020	23021	23022	23023	23024
	23025	23026	23027	23028	23029	23030	23031	23032
	23033	23034	23035					
Dart SLF	34147	34148	34149	34150	34215	34216	34240	34245
	34248	34366	34367	34368	34369	34370	34371	34372
	34373	34374	34375	34376	34377	34378	34379	34380
	34381	34382	34383	34384	34385	34386	34551	34552
	34553	34554	34555	34556	34557	34558	34559	34560
Ancillary	26010	26034						

Romford (North Street) - NS

Olympian	16001	16002	16003					
Trident	17114	17124	17132	17135	17136	17137	17144	17146
	17192	17194	17210	17211	17212	17213	17235	17236
	17268	17292	17293	17294	17295	17296	17297	17298
	17299	17300	17301	17428	17429	17430	17431	17432
	17433	17434	17435	17436	17437	17438	17439	17440
	17441	17442	17443	17444	17445	17446	17447	17448
	17449	17450	17451	17452	17453	17454	17455	17456
	17457	17458	17459	17460	17461	17462	17463	17464
	17465	17976	17977	17978	17979	17980	17981	17982
	17983	17984	17985	17986	17987	17988	17989	17990
	17991	17992	17993	17994	17995	17996	17997	17998
	17999							
Volvo B10M coach	52022	52023	52217	52219				
Special event vehicle	10001	12760						
Ancillary	26001							

Stratford (Stability Works, Waterden Road) - SD

Trident	17111	17167	17168	17169	17170	17171	17172	17173
	17174	17175	17176	17177	17178	17179	17180	17196
	17197	17198	17199	17200	17201	17202	17237	17238
	17239	17240	17241	17242	17244	17245	17246	17395
	17396	17397	17398	17399	17400	17401	17403	17404
	17405	17406	17407	17408	17466	17486	17502	17503
	17504	17505	17506	17507	17508	17509	17510	17511
	17512	17513	17514	17515	17516	17517	17518	17519
	17520	17521	17522	17563	17564	17565	17566	17731
	17732	17733	17740	17741	17742	17743	17744	17745
	17746	17747	17748	17749	17758	17759	17760	17761
	17762	17763	17764	17765	17766	17767	17768	17769
	17770	17771	17772	17773	17774	17775	17776	17777
	17778							

Dart SLF	34140	34142	34143	34144	34145	34146	34151	34153
	34154	34155	34156	34157	34159	34161	34162	34163
	34164	34165	34166	34167	34168	34169	34170	34171
	34172	34182	34183	34184	34185	34186	34187	34188
	34189	34191	34192	34193	34194	34195	34196	34197
	34207	34208	34209	34210	34211	34212	34214	34328
	32329	32330	32331	32332	32333	32334	32335	32336
	32337	32338	32339	32340	32341	32342	32343	32344
	32345	32346						

Upton Park (Redclyffe Road) - U

Trident	17040	17041	17042	17043	17044	17045	17046	17047
	17048	17049	17062	17081	17082	17083	17084	17085
	17086	17087	17088	17089	17090	17091	17092	17093
	17094	17095	17096	17097	17098	17129	17147	17165
	17203	17204	17205	17206	17207	17208	17209	17234
	17243	17247	17248	17249	17250	17251	17252	17253
	17254	17255	17256	17257	17258	17259	17260	17291
	17487	17488	17489	17490	17491	17492	17493	17494
	17495	17496	17497	17498	17499	17500	17501	17535
	17536	17834	17835	17836	17837	17838	17839	17840
	17841	17842	17843	17844	17845	17846	17847	17848
	17849	17850	17864	17865	17889	17890	17891	17903
	17904	18257	18258	18259	18260	18261	18262	18263
	18264	18265						
Dart	34133	34158	34160	34174	34175	34176	34178	34179
	34181	34190	34198					
Scania N113	28615	28617	28620	28621	28622	28623	28625	28626
	28627	28628	28630					
Ancillary	26002	26020	26021	26023	26029			

Waterden Road (44 Waterden Road, Stratford) - WA

Citaro Artic	23036	23037	23038	23039	23040	23041	23042	23043
	23044	23045	23046	23047	23048	23049	23050	23051
	23052	23053	23054	23055	23056	23057	23058	23059
	23060	23061	23062	23063	23064	23065	23066	23067
	23068	23069	23070	23071	23072	23073	23074	23075
	23076	23077						
Ancillary	28616	28618	28619	28624	28629			

London stored and reserve

Dart SLF	33354	34098	34100	34102	34111	34112	34113	
Trident (Due 3/05)	18266	18267	18268	18269	18270	18271	18272	18273
	18274	18275	18276	18277				

South East - (SE)

Aldershot (Halimote Road) - in Hants and Surrey (AT)

Outstations - Haslemere and Petersfield

Leyland Olympian	14960	14985	14988					
Volvo Olympian	16302	16305	16320	16373	16624	16625	16626	16627
	16628	16629	16630	16631	16632	16633		
Volvo PS	20446	20447	20461	20462	20606	20618		
Dart	32070	32075	32090	32093	32316	32412	32413	32414
	32515	32517	32519	32522	32529	32536	32565	32577
	32578	32585						
Dart SLF	33020	33029	33031	33032	33033	33119	34010	34011
	34013	34014	34016	34017	34020	34629	34630	34631
	34632	34633	34634	34635	34636	34637	34638	34639
	34640							
Mercedes-Benz	40892	40905	40906	40907	40908	40909	40910	40911
	40912	40913	40914	40916	40935	40936	40937	40940
Ancillary	46613	52096	52106					

Andover (Livingstone Road) - in Hampshire (AR)

Leyland Olympian	14974	14986						
Volvo Olympian	16293	16294	16295	16393	16394	16398		
Trident	17067	17068	17070					
Volvo B10M bus	20313	20438	20615	20617	20631	20635		
Dart	32513	32526	32530					
Mercedes-Benz	40726	40730	40731	40733	40901	40902	40915	40920
	40921	40922	40923	40924				
Solo	47040							
Alero	47801	47805						

Ashford (Brunswick Road) - East Kent (AD)

Leyland Olympian	14803	14806	14809	14828	14829	14830
Volvo B10M bus	20645	20659				
MAN	22191	22192	22194			
Dart	32606	32607				
Dart SLF	33018	33019	33021	33022	33024	
Mercedes-Benz	40898	40948	40949	40950	40951	40952
Special event vehicle	19946					
Ancillary	46615	52094				

Basingstoke (Rankine Road, Daneshill) - in Hampshire (BE)

Leyland Olympian	14717	14951	14952	14954	14956	14987	14989	14990
Volvo Olympian	16262	16268	16269	16319	16366	16367	16379	16380
	16399							
Volvo B10M bus	20668	20669	20670					
Dart	32041	32047	32065	32074	32076	32088	32092	32094
	32098	32321	32451	32459	32460	32461	32462	32463
Dart SLF	33014	33015	33016	33017	33030	33034	33035	33036
	33037	33038	33039	33040	34012	34015	34018	34019
	34030	34032	34033	34034	34059	34060	34067	34068
	34072	34073	34092	34107	34108	34109	34110	
Mercedes-Benz	40662	40969						
Solo	47047	47048	47049					
Ancillary	52197							

Canterbury (Bus Station, St Georges Lane) - East Kent (CA)

Outstation - Herne Bay

Leyland Olympian	14807	14808	14976	14977	14978	14980	14982	
Scania N113	15311	15312	15334					
Volvo Olympian	16264	16265	16266	16267	16270	16271	16272	16273
	16274	16275	16283	16284	16296	16297	16298	16299
	16360	16361	16362	16385	16388			
Trident	17402	17689	17690	18160	18161	18162	18163	18164
	18165	18166	18167	18168	18169	18170	18171	18172
	18173	18174	18175	18176				
Volvo B10M bus	20312	20445	20619	20644	20660			
MAN	22004	22005	22006	22007	22008	22009		
Dart	32458							
Mercedes-Benz	40933	40934	40941	40942	40943	40947	40977	
Special event vehicle	11125							
Ancillary	52002							

Chichester (Southgate) - in the South Downs (CR)

Leyland Olympian	14818	14970	14971	14972	14975			
Volvo Citybus	15201	15206						
Volvo Olympian	16278	16281	16282	16348				
Volvo B10M bus	20601	20602	20603	20604	20605	20623	20629	20648
	20662	20663	20664	20665	20667	20829		
Dart	32511	32518	32524	32532	32537	32541	32546	32552
	32553	32555	32556	32562	32580			
Mercedes-Benz	40164	40655	40656	40661	40891	40893	40895	40897
	40903	40904	40917	40918	40945			
Volvo B10M coach	52475	52477	52478	52479	52481			
Special event vehicles	15760	19909						
Ancillary	46614	52081						

Dover (Russell Street) - East Kent (DO)

Leyland Olympian	14979	14981	14983	14984				
Volvo Olympian	16363	16364	16368	16369	16370	16384	16386	16387
	16389	16390						
Volvo B10M bus	20633	20636	20637	20638	20639	20640		
Mercedes-Benz	40953	40954	40955	40957	40958	40959	40960	40962
	40963	40964	40967	40968	40970			
Volvo B10M coach	52621	52657	52658					
Volvo B12M coach	53001	53002	53003	53004	53005	53006	53007	53008
	53009	53010						
Ancillary	25710							

Folkestone (Kent Road, Cheriton) - East Kent (FO)

Leyland Olympian	14811	14812	14813	14814	14821	14822	14825	
Volvo Olympian	16285	16287	16365	16371	16372	16375	16376	16377
	16378							
Volvo B10M bus	20613	20622	20624	20625				
Dart	32311	32467	32601	32608				
Dart SLF	33080							
Solo	47112	47113	47114	47115	47116	47117	47118	47119
	47120							
Ancillary	15751(tree lopper)	26017						

The 2005 Stagecoach Bus Handbook

Hastings (Beaufort Road, Silverhill, St Leonards) - East Kent (HS)

Leyland Olympian	14801	14802	14804	14805			
Volvo Citybus	15205	15207	15208	15209			
Volvo Olympian	16315	16316	16317	16318	16382	16383		
Volvo B10M bus	20190	20612	20614	20620	20641	20646	20647	20650
	20654	20675	20676	20678	20679	20680		
Dart	32457	32464	32465	32466	32602	32603		
Dart SLF	33005	33007	33009	33010	33023	33357	33358	33359
	33360	33361	34064	34065	34066	34071	34074	34075
	34078	34089	34090	34091	34093	34094		
Ancillary	25833	46616						

Lewes (Eastgate Street) - in the South Downs (LS)

Outstations: Eastbourne; Seaford and Uckfield

Leyland Olympian	14138	14714					
Volvo Olympian	16354	16357					
Trident	17066	17069	17071	17072	17073	17075	17077
Volvo B10M bus	20626	20627	20643	20652	20831	20833	20834
Dart	32091	32095	32097	32327	32456		
Dart SLF	34641	34642	34643	34644			
Mercedes-Benz	40729	40971					
Ancillary	25085						

Portsmouth (Langstone Point) - in Portsmouth (PM)

Leyland Olympian	13621						
Volvo Citybus	15202	15203	15204				
Volvo Olympian	16306	16307	16322	16323	16324	16341	16342	16344
	16356	16395					
Volvo B10M bus	20610	20611					
Volvo B6	30141	30142					
Volvo B6LE	31043	31044	31045	31046	31047	31048	31049	31050
	31051	31052					
Dart	32429	32430	32447	32448	32449	32450	32452	32455
Dart SLF	33053	33054	33056	33057	33058	33059	33061	33062
	33063	33064	33065	33066	33067	33068	33069	33071
	33072	33407	34445	34446	34447	34448	34449	34450
	34451	34452	34453	34454	34523	34527	34528	34529
	34531						
Volvo B10M coach	52474	52476	52480				
Ancillary	25825	40894	59014				

Thanet (Margate Road, Westwood) - East Kent (TH)

Leyland Titan	10348						
Leyland Olympian	14715	14716	14810	14815	14819	14823	14824	14826
	14827						
Scania N113	15330	15331	15338	15339	15349	15350	15357	15364
	15366	15367	15369				
Volvo Olympian	16241	16242	16246	16247	16286	16301	16381	
Volvo B10M bus	20311	20608	20609	20642			
Dart	32221	32222	32223				
Dart SLF	34645	34646	34647	34648	34649	34650	34651	34652
	34653	34654	34655	34656	34657	34658	34659	34660
	34661	34662					
Mercedes-Benz	40926	40927	40928	40929	40930	40931	40932	40966
Volvo B10M coach	52654	52655	52656	52659			
Ancillary	46611	52077					

Winchester (The Broadway) - in Hampshire (WI)

Outstations - Alton; Bishop's Waltham and Petersfield

Leyland Olympian	13613	13622	13634	14816	14953	14955	14973
Volvo Olympian	16260	16261	16263	16276	16277	16279	16288	16289
	16290	16291	16292	16303	16304	16374	16396
Volvo B10M bus	20189	20460	20607	20628	20632	20634
Dart	32309	32310	32312	32314	32315	32322	32323	32324
	32325	32326	32453	32454
Dart SLF	33025	33026	33027	33028	34406	34407	34408	34409
	34410	34411	34412	34413	34414	34415	34416	34417
	34418
Mercedes-Benz	40896	40899
Ancillary	46612	52089

Worthing (Library Place) - in the South Downs (WG)

Outstation - Henfield

Leyland Olympian	13612	13620	13635	14817
Volvo Olympian	16308	16309	16310	16311	16312	16313	16314	16346
	16347	16349	16350
Volvo B10M bus	20830	20832	20835	20836
Lance	27404	27405	27406	27407	27408
Dart	32077	32096	32501	32502	32503	32508	32510	32547
	32560	32561
Dart SLF	33002	33003	33004	33006	33008	33011	33012	33013
	34514	34515	34516	34517	34518	34519	34520	34521
	34522	34524	34525
Ancillary	52159

South East unallocated - (SE)

Leyland Olympian	14170
Volvo Olympian	16345
Volvo B10M bus	20198	20649
Dart	32509	32538	32548	32567
Mercedes Benz	40728	40889	40925	40938	40939	40944	40946	40956
	40961	40965	40972	40973	40974	40975	40976
Special event vehicles	19913	19945

Previous UK Registrations

13CLT	P159ASA
83CBD	R559DRP, H1173, WLT528, R559DRP
126ASV	E867RCS
127ASV	E909KSG
128ASV	E910KSG
145CLT	M544RSO
147YFM	M912WJK
283URB	E561UHS
331HWD	(HK)ER8635
400DCD	(HK)GM7642, N977RCD
401DCD	(HK)GM4964, N978RCD
402DCD	(HK)GM6631, N979RCD
403DCD	(HK)GM7558, N24PWV
404DCD	(HK)GM6717, N23PWV
405DCD	R705DNJ
407DCD	(HK)GM7990, N997RCD
408DCD	R118VPU
411DCD	P611SEV
412DCD	R712XAR
413DCD	P613SEV
414DCD	M404OKM
415DCD	M405OKM
417DCD	M407OKM
418DCD	M408OKM
420DCD	R120VPU
421DCD	R115VPU
495FFJ	P973UBV
498FYB	L155LBW
511OHU	(HK)ER7389
527CLT	LX03NGN
630DYE	L158LBW
647DYE	N336HGK
685DYE	N337HGK
703DYE	N620USS
866NHT	J439HDS
3063VC	N129VAO
4012VC	N47MJO
6253VC	N130VAO
9258VC	N131VAO
9737VC	N132VAO
A14RBL	B176FFS
A14SOE	G345FFX
A16SOE	H566MPD, NXI9002, H843AHS
ACZ7490	J740CWT
ACZ7491	J741CWT
BIW4977	(HK)ER9371
BSK744	P625NSE
BSK756	On retention Jan 2005
C38HNF	(HK)DH8689
C42HNF	(HK)DH9398
C43HNF	(HK)DH9707
C44HNF	(HK)DJ714
C45HNF	(HK)DJ3770
C46HNF	(HK)DH9411
C49HNF	(HK)DJ3429
C50HNF	(HK)DH9864
C105DWR	C105DWR, WLT980
C152HBA	(HK)DJ1848
C156HBA	(HK)DH5935
C157HBA	(HK)DH9849
C160HNF	(HK)DH9306
C166HNF	(HK)DH5054
C167HNF	(HK)DJ805
C168HNF	(HK)DH9487
C169HNF	(HK)DJ349
C170HNF	(HK)DH8737
C330DND	C330DND, CSU921
C495LJV	C495LJV, PSU787

CSU920	M532RSO
CSU921	M533RSO
CSU922	M534RSO
CSU923	M535RSO
CSU978	M408BFG
CSU992	M409BFG
D548MVR	D548MVR, TSV780
D553MVR	D553MVR, CSU923
DSV743	N616USS
E644UNE	E644UNE, UOT648
EDS50A	WLT560
ESU435	On retention Jan 2005
FSU739	N619USS
G127WGX	(HK)ES8691
G128WGX	(HK)ET1613
G189YRJ	(HK)EL8119
G280YRG	(HK)EF9412
G344FFX	G344FFX, WLT809
G386PNV	G386PNV, VLT104
GSO1V	C471SSO
GSO6V	D376XRS
GSO7V	D377XRS
GSU341	M107XBW
GSU950	On retention Jan 2005
H41GBD	(HK)ES389
H51SKG	(HK)ET550
H150CVU	H150CVU, WLT830
H406GAV	H406GAV, YSV735
H445EGU	(HK)ER1374
H462EJR	(HK)ET1746
H463EJR	(HK)ET2205
H492LNA	(HK)ET1989
H493LNA	(HK)ES7623
H494LNA	(HK)ES1962
H495LNA	(HK)ET1848
H511FRP	(HK)ES4877
H522FRP	(HK)ER9169
H723KDY	(HK)ER6587
H724KDY	(HK)ER6824
H725KDY	(HK)ES3710
H763KDY	(HK)ET1163
H764KDY	(HK)ET1026
H778VHL	(HK)ET1613
HIL8410	(HK)ET623
HSK760	K910TKP
HSV194	M527RSO
HSV195	E905UNW
HSV196	E315OEG
IIL1321	D51ORH
J166UNH	(HK)EW8584
J167UNH	(HK)EW9231
J515WAX	(HK)EW3034
J688TNF	(HK)EX166
J701HMY	(HK)EW8656
J702HMY	(HK)EW3999
J703HMY	(HK)EW9215
J734HMY	(HK)EWEX441
J909NKP	J909NKP, 927GTA
J925FPS	(HK)EW9357
J938MHC	(HK)EW9757
J939MHC	(HK)EW8815
JPU817	D207LWX
JSK492	(HK)EW9698
K714ASC	K714ASC, YEL4T
K758FYG	J758CWT, K758FYG83CBD
K759FYG	J759CWT, K759FYGVLT255
K921OWV	K921OWV, NDZ3021
K922OWV	K922OWV, NDZ3022

K923OWV	K923OWV, NDZ3023	M614APN	M614APN, 414DCD
K983CBO	NZD3138	M680TDB	Kenya-KAG933E
K985CBO	NDZ3141	M681TDB	Kenya-KAH560B
K986CBO	NDZ3142	M682TDB	Kenya-KAG931E
KSU461	From new	M683TDB	Kenya-KAG544H
KSU462	From new	M684TDB	Kenya-KAG542J
L51CNY	L51CNY, NIL8653	M685TDB	Kenya-KAG770V
L156LBW	L156LBW, VLT225	M686TDB	Kenya-KAG060M
L159LBW	L159LBW, 83CBD	M687TDB	Kenya-KAG292E
L338KCK	L338KCK, 418DCD	M688TDB	Kenya-KAG547J
L345KCK	L345KCK, 415DCD	M689TDB	Kenya-KAG471T
L346KCK	L346KCK, 416DCD	M690TDB	Kenya-KAG522X
L347KCK	L347KCK, 417DCD	M691TDB	Kenya-KAG405W
L392LNA	Kenya-KAG932E	M692TDB	Kenya-KAG025X
L424TJK	L424TJK, 404DCD	M693TDB	Kenya-KAG601M
L425TJK	L425TJK, 405DCD	M694TDB	Kenya-KAG470T
L426TJK	L426TJK, 406DCD	M695TDB	Kenya-KAG544J
L427TJK	L427TJK, 407DCD	M696TDB	Kenya-KAG264R
L608TDY	L608TDY, 408DCD	M699TDB	Kenya-KAG472T
L618TDY	L618TDY, WVT618	MHS4P	C464SSO
L619TDY	L619TDY, 419DCD	MIL4693	G535LWU
L620TDY	L620TDY, 420DCD	MSU463	J430HDS
L621TDY	L621TDY, 421DCD	MSU466	P976UBV
L622TDY	L622TDY, 422DCD	N42MJO	N42MJO, 6253VC
L623TDY	L623TDY, 423DCD	N43MJO	N43MJO, 3063VC
L942RJN	L212YAG	N45MJO	N45MJO, 9258VC
LDS201A	607DYE	N46MJO	N46MJO, 9737VC
LJY145	L125NAO	N48MJO	N48MJO, MSU463
LSK545	M106XBW	N421PWV	(HK)-GU5924
M35LHP	A14GOO, HST11	N422PWV	(HK)-GU5116+H4721
M151FGB	M1ABO	N731XDV	(HK)GM8040
M180XHW	CX53AA	N732XDV	(HK)GM5334
M182XHW	CX54AA	N733XDV	(HK)GM6788
M313YSC	M313YSC, PFN873	N734XDV	(HK)GM9182
M379TJA	Kenya-KAG602M	N735XDV	(HK)GM5431
M406OKM	416DCD	N736XDV	(HK)GM5376
M510FWV	M490BFG, 400DCD	N737XDV	(HK)GM6331
M511FWV	M401BFG, 401DCD	N738XDV	(HK)GM7131
M512FWV	M402BFG, 402DCD, 472YMF	N739XDV	(HK)GM8269
M553FWV	M403BFG, 403DCD, YLJ332	N740XDV	(HK)GM8240
M610APN	M610MPN, 410DCD	N742XDV	(HK)GM6090
M611APN	M611MPN, 411DCD	N743XDV	(HK)GM7606
M612APN	M612APN, 412DCD	N744XDV	(HK)GM5868
M613APN	M613APN, 413DCD	N998RCD	(HK)GM6788, 406DCD

As well as placing British index marks onto imported vehicles, Stagecoach owns many Cherished and Select marks - valuable assets in their own right - and these are detailed here. When three MAN buses were transferred to Ashford for Park and Ride duties they had their plates changed. 22191, NDZ3021, is shown here.
Dave Heath

NDZ3017	W427NFG	TJI4124	F806PSN, 8733CD, F779GNA
NDZ3018	W428NFG	TSU638	(HK)ES3771
NDZ3019	W425NFG	TSU639	R456FCE
NDZ3020	R114VPU	TSU641	K760FYG
NDZ3021	T191MVM	TSU642	K761FYG
NDZ3022	T192MVM	TSV718	On retention Jan 2005
NDZ3023	T194MVM	TSV719	On retention Jan 2005
NFX667	N452PAP	TSV720	On retention Jan 2005
NIB4138	B114WUV	TSV721	On retention Jan 2005
NIB5232	B100WUV	TSV722	On retention Jan 2005
NIB5233	B93WUV	TSV778	M528RSO
NIB5455	B106WUV	TSV779	M529RSO
NIL8646	J115NJT, NIL8647, A11XEL	TSV780	M530RSO
NIL8647	G668TTN, SIA637	TSV781	M531RSO
NIL8656	J114NJT, NIL8655, A10XEL	UIB3076	EGT458T
NSU132	On retention Jan 2005	UIB3543	P671LWB
NSU133	M104XBW	UJI4184	M948JJU
NUF276	L83YBB	UOT648	On retention Jan 2005
OIW5804	WCN543Y	UWP105	J917LEM
OIW7025	GLP427T	VCS376	B24CGA
OSK784	(HK)EX258	VCS391	N562SJF
OWO37X	XPP297X, JSV391, PIL6502	VKB708	B483UNB
P299AYJ,	(HK)HC8802	VLT14	V473KJN
P301AYJ	(HK)HB7989	VLT37	(HK)ER8952
P302AYJ	(HK)HC5075	VLT54	K511ESS
P330AYJ	(HK)HC5122	VLT154	On retention Jan 2005
P343AYJ	(HK)HC9501	VLT245	On retention Jan 2005
P426AYJ	(HK)HC9965	VLT255	N331HGK
P434AYJ	(HK)HC5014	VLT272	On retention Jan 2005
P435AYJ	(HK)HC5778	VRR447	L126NAO
P457AYJ	(HK)HB5013	W426NFG	W426NFG, 424DCD
P458AYJ	(HK)HB8862	WLT415	L583JSA, FSU739
P466AYJ	(HK)HB5506	WLT416	(HK)ER9289
P479AYJ	(HK)HC4904	WLT439	G569ESD
P610SEV	410DCD	WLT447	N617USS
P758FOD	(HK)HB9296	WLT461	V475KJN
P760FOD	(HK)HC5574	WLT491	V474KJN
P762FOD	(HK)HB4996	WLT512	N332HGK
P832FVU	P832FVU, XSU682	WLT526	On retention Jan 2005
PCK335	J121AHH	WLT528	N353HGK
PHH149W	KRM431W	WLT538	S485BWC
PS2743	D550MVR, CSU920	WLT546	TBC1X
PSU443	D547MVR, TSV779	WLT575	X374NNO
PSU764	D549MVR, TSV781	WLT682	N334HGK
PSU787	N314AMC	WLT720	P670LWB
PSU788	M164SCK	WLT727	F201FHH
R71NPN	(HK)HM6567	WLT774	E158XHS
R95NPN	(HK)HM2185	WLT794	F202FHH
R116VPU	R116VPU, 422DCD	WLT809	P199OSE
R117VPU	R117VPU, 423DCD	WLT830	On retention Jan 2005
R119NPN	(HK)HM853	WLT874	G528LWU
R119VPU	R119VPU, 419DCD	WLT890	L157LBW
R132NPN	(HK)HM1895	WLT898	On retention Jan 2005
R133NPN	(HK)HM547	WLT908	N335HGK
R144NPN	(HK)HM8456	WLT978	P198OSE
R177NPN	(HK)HM536	WSU293	N41MJO
R178NPN	(HK)HM2053	WVT618	N455PAP
R196NPN	(HK)HM1495	XIL1284	S464BWC
R270NPN	(HK)HM1748	XIL1286	S466BWC
R706DNJ	BOU6V	XIL1560	S465BWC
RBZ5459	M165SCK	XIL1568	S478BWC
RIB4309	B110WUV	XIL1575	S475BWC
S210WHK	S210WHK, WLT898	XRC487	On retention Jan 2005
SHH124M	SCS355M	XSU612	R812HCD
SJI4558	(HK)ER2467	XSU682	N454PAP
SYC852	M407BFG	XYK976	N451PAP
T614DWL	T40UBE	YDG616	D206LWX
T615DWL	T44UBE	YLJ332	N453PAP
T616DWL	T50UBE	YSV730	N561SJF
T617DWL	T55UBE		
T618DWL	T60UBE		
TJI4123	K61BAX, TJI4124		

Stagecoach SUPERTRAM

South Yorkshire Supertram Ltd, 11 Arundel Gate, Sheffield, S1 2PN.

101-125		Siemens		Duewag		AB88T	1993-94		
101	104	107	110	113	116	118	120	122	124
102	105	108	111	114	117	119	121	123	125
103	106	109	112	115					

Depot: Nunnery, Sheffield

Stagecoach took over the management of tram operations in Sheffield in 1997, and 1998 saw the start of a repaint programme with tram 107 being the first in corporate colours, with additional blue being added following the change in livery to the bus fleet. Tram 117 is seen at Halfway. *Mark Lyons*

STAGECOACH NEW ZEALAND

Stagecoach Wellington, 45 Onepu Road, Kilbirnie, Wellington, New Zealand
Cityline Hutt Valley, Waterloo Interchange, Oxford Terrace, Lower Hutt
Stagecoach Auckland, 451 Mount Eden Road, Mount Eden, Auckland
Runciman Motors, 4 Masefield Street, Upper Hutt

2	NA4281	Isuzu MR113	Coachwork International	B28F	1987
5	NA3943	Isuzu MR113	Coachwork International	BC28F	1987
6	SK700	Isuzu ECR570	Demac	C45F	1986
8	NY58	Isuzu ECR570	Coachwork International	BC45F	1988
9	MQ8716	Isuzu ECR570	Coachwork International	BC49F	1986
10	JR48	Ford R1114	New Zealand Motor Bodies	BC48F	1980
11	ON223	Isuzu ECR570	Austral	B45F	1989
12	PT2685	Hino RG197	Coachwork International	B37D	1991
13	JR47	Ford R1114	New Zealand Motor Bodies	BC48F	1980
15	JZ7041	Ford R1114	New Zealand Motor Bodies	BC48F	1981
16	OB1552	Isuzu ECR570	Coachwork International	BC49F	1988
17	JR2616	Mercedes-Benz 0303	New Zealand Motor Bodies	B41D	1980
18	JW8024	Mercedes-Benz 0303	New Zealand Motor Bodies	B41D	1980
19	LE4641	Hino BX341	New Zealand Motor Bodies	BC48F	1983
21	MC609	Isuzu ECR570	New Zealand Motor Bodies	BC49F	1985

22-26

		Volvo B10M-56	Alexander PS	BC41F	1993	Stagecoach Hong Kong, 1996

22	UO8044	23	UO7966	24	UO7989	25	UO8020	26	UO8000

27-35

		MAN 10-100	Designline	BC28F	1990

27	OU3699	29	OZ8661	31	OZ8664	33	OZ8666	35	OZ8668
28	OZ8699	30	OZ8660	32	OZ8665	34	OZ8667		

37-57

		Mercedes-Benz 709D	Alexander Sprint	B25F	1996

37	UN5515	42	UN5521	46	UO3110	50	UP7144	54	UP8933
38	UN5517	43	UN5522	47	UO3112	51	UP7145	55	UP8934
39	UN5518	44	UO3084	48	UP4829	52	UP8928	56	UP8944
40	UN5519	45	UO3085	49	UP4840	53	UP8929	57	UP8945
41	UN5520								

58	ABT884	Denning Landseer	Austral	C	1988

61-70

		Volvo B6LE	Plaxton Pointer	NC26D	1998	Citybus, Hong Kong, 2002

61	AKS536	63	AKS533	65	AKS534	67	AKS508	69	AKS535
62	AKS504	64	AKS511	66	AKS532	68	AKS510	70	AKS509

71-78

		Volvo B6LE	Plaxton Pointer	NC26D	1996	Citybus, Hong Kong, 2003

71w	BGG705	73w	BGG706	75w	BET890	77w	BET887	78w	BET886
72w	BET891	74w	BET889	76w	BET888				

101	BFZ261	Designline Olympus 2HEV	Designline	N	2003
102	BFZ273	Designline Olympus 2HEV	Designline	N	2003
103	BGS107	Designline Olympus 2HEV	Designline	N	2003

117	ON350	Hino RB145	Coachwork International	1989
121	NN4726	Hino RK76	Coachwork International	1988
122	ND8808	Hino RK176	Coachwork International	1987
130	WA9789	Isuzu LR312J	Isuzu (Japanese)	1988

Stagecoach Auckland's 24, UO7989 is a Volvo B10M with Alexander PS bodywork built for the original Stagecoach operation in Hong Kong. It is seen in Prrie Street, Wellington. *Mark Lyons*

141-170   MAN SL202   Coachwork International   B45D   1987-89

141	NF2109	147	NH2755	153	NL9414	159	NL9540	165	NZ8003
142	NF2117	148	NI5642	154	NL9420	160	NL9566	166	NZ8266
143	BSS626	149	NI5704	155	NL9466	161	OB1550	167	OG8397
144	NH2652	150	NI5718	156	ZP1073	162	NT9387	168	OG8398
145	NH2754	151	NL9377	157	NL9461	163	PA6879	169	OG8399
146	NH2756	152	NL9393	158	NL9531	164	NZ8004	170	OG8551

171-180   MAN 16.200 UOCL   Coachwork International   B39D   1989-91

171	ON525	173	PL5272	175	PL5274	177	PL5823	179	PP5206
172	PL5003	174	PL5273	176	PL5822	178	PL5824	180	PP5205

181	PP5219	MAN 16.240 UOCL	Coachwork International	B41D	1991
206	JY6549	Volvo B58 BBC4EL02002	Designline (2004)	B40D	1981

201-234   Volvo B58 BBC4EL02002   Hawke   B40D   1981-84

201	KA9102	211	KA9110	217	NA87	222	KD7488	227	KH4274
204	JM7127	212	KA9111	218	KA7233	223	KD7485	229	AKW871
207	JY5832	213	KA9184	219	KA7234	224	KD7486	232	KJ8245
208	JY5831	214	KA9185	220	KA7235	225	KH4273	233	KJ8244
209	KA9103	216	KA9192	221	KD7490	226	KD7487	234	LQ2643
210	KA9109								

235-254   Volvo B58 BBC4EL02002   Hawke   B40D   1985

235	LW6465	239	MB7635	243	ME9235	247	MJ2016	251	MJ2168
236	MA8821	240	MB7638	244	ME9236	248	MJ2015	252	MJ2169
237	MA5210	241	MB7636	245	ME2504	249	MJ2014	253	MJ2171
238	MA5209	242	MB7637	246	MJ2012	250	MJ2013	254	MJ2172

The trolleybus operation has received its first rebuilt vehicle, number 206, which now carries a Designline body. One from the main batch is 237, MA5210, shown here. *Mark Lyons*

255-268

| | | | | | | Volvo B58 BBC4ELO2002 | | Hawke | | B40D | 1986 | | |

255	MO1322	258	SC2911	261	MS1706	264	MS1703	267	MS1812
256	MO1321	259	MO1397	262	MS1705	265	MS1814	268	MS1815
257	MO1391	260	MS1707	263	XG2300	266	MS1813		

290	PD1036	Renault S75	Coachwork International	B23F	1990	
294	RM4511	Toyota Hiace	Toyota	M15	1992	Wellington, 1993

401-416

Leyland Leopard PSU3C/2R   Hawke   B40D   1976-77

401	HZ2712	406	HE2656	409	HQ3907	413	IL4518	416	IK7801
402	HI1974								

419-480

Leyland Leopard PSU3E/2R   Hawke   B40D   1978-79

		425	IX3781	442	JA1198	455	JF1910	469	JA1184
419w	IU9432	427	IX3783	444w	JC2568	456	JF1911	474	JD181
		435	IU9931	448	JD183	457	JF1913	476	JD199
423	IX3304	436	IU9932	451	JD197	462	IX7767	478	JF1912
		441	JA1185	452	JF1903	464	ADN679	480	ADS121

501-520

MAN 11.190 HOCL - R   Designline   B39D   1994-95

501	SS5537	505	TB6105	509	SY1641	513	TA2667	517	TB6042
502	SS5538	506	SW4400	510	SY1631	514	TA2691	518	TB6050
503	ST7109	507	SW4435	511	SZ5917	515	TA2714	519	TB6056
504	SX7724	508	SW4436	512	SZ5918	516	TB6023	520	TB6057

521-554 — MAN 11.190 HOCL — Designline — B39D — 1995

521	TB6106	528	TE2325	535	TG5856	542	TG5879	549	TJ2515
522	TB6107	529	TE2326	536	TG5857	543	TG5896	550	TJ2516
523	TD2564	530	TE2327	537	TG5871	544	TG5897	551	TR1643
524	TD2593	531	TF6235	538	TG5872	545	TG5898	552	TR1644
525	TD2594	532	TF6236	539	TG5876	546	TG5899	553	TR1645
526	TD2630	533	TF6237	540	TG5877	547	TH5837	554	TR1646
527	TD2631	534	TG5855	541	TG5878	548	TH5838		

601-626 — MAN 11.190 HOCL — Designline — N39D — 1995-96

601	TJ2541	607	UB490	612	XY8784	617	UB483	622	UF5846
602	TJ2542	608	UB491	613	UB500	618	UB482	623	XT1245
603	UB487	609	UB492	614	UB499	619	UB484	624	UF5850
604	UB488	610	UB497	615	UB498	620	UB485	625	UF5851
605	TU1498	611	UB495	616	UF5845	621	UF5849	626	UF5852
606	UB489								

627-658 — MAN 11.190 HOCL — Designline Ashburton — N39D — 1996-97

627	UF5853	634	UH7205	641	UH7218	647	UL5044	653	UL5060
628	UF5854	635	UH7206	642	UH7212	648	UL5045	654	UL5042
629	UF5855	636	UH7207	643	UH7219	649	UL5046	655	UO9429
630	UF5856	637	UH7208	644	UH7220	650	UL5051	656	UO9427
631	UF5857	638	UH7215	645	UH7213	651	UL5052	657	UO9433
632	UF5858	639	UH7216	646	UH7214	652	UL5053	658	UT5625
633	UH7204	640	UH7217						

701-740 — MAN 11.190 HOCL — Designline Ashburton — N39D — 1998

701	XG2082	709	XI9041	717	XJ5244	725	XL3262	733	XL9778
702	XG2081	710	XI9042	718	XJ5245	726	XL3264	734	XL9779
703	XG2083	711	XI9043	719	XJ5246	727	XL3265	735	XN4432
704	XG2084	712	XI9044	720	ZD6442	728	XL3266	736	XN4433
705	XG2085	713	XI9045	721	XJ5247	729	XL9773	737	XN4436
706	XG2087	714	XJ5241	722	XJ5249	730	XL9774	738	XN4437
707	XG2088	715	XJ5242	723	XJ5250	731	XL9775	739	XN4438
708	XG2089	716	XJ5243	724	XL3261	732	XL9777	740	XN4439

741-780 — MAN 11.190 HOCL — Designline Ashburton — N39D — 1998-99

741	XN8101	749	XO7306	757	XS4093	765	XT7869	773	XW4119
742	XN8102	750	ZE2402	758	XS4094	766	XT7870	774	XY1872
743	XN8103	751	XP6952	759	XS4097	767	XW4111	775	XY1873
744	XN8106	752	XP6953	760	XS4098	768	XW4112	776	XY1874
745	XN8107	753	XP6954	761	XS4100	769	XW4113	777	XY1875
746	XN8108	754	XP6955	762	XT7864	770	XW4114	778	XY1877
747	XO7305	755	XP6958	763	XT7867	771	XW4115	779	XY1878
748	XO7304	756	XP6959	764	XT7868	772	XW4118	780	XY1880

781	ZR8220	MAN 11.220 HOCL	Designline Ashburton	B51D	2000
782	ZR8221	MAN 11.220 HOCL	Designline Ashburton	B51D	2000
783	ZR8222	MAN 11.220 HOCL	Designline Ashburton	B51D	2001
784	ZR8223	MAN 11.220 HOCL	Designline Ashburton	B51D	2001

801-835 — MAN 16.230 HOCL — Fairfax Industries — N51D — 2000

801	ZI7441	808	ZI7448	815	ZI7455	822	ZI7462	829	ZI7469
802	ZI7442	809	ZI7449	816	ZI7456	823	ZI7463	830	ZI7470
803	ZI7443	810	ZI7450	817	ZI7457	824	ZI7464	831	ZI7471
804	ZI7444	811	ZI7451	818	ZI7458	825	ZI7465	832	ZI7472
805	ZI7445	812	ZI7452	819	ZI7459	826	ZI7466	833	ZI7473
806	ZI7446	813	ZI7453	820	ZI7460	827	AGR422	834	BFS522
807	ZI7447	814	ZI7454	821	ZI7461	828	ZI7468	835	ZI7475

Illustrating the batch of Fairfax Industries' bodies on MAN chassis from 2000 is 830, ZI7470. It is shown with Stagecoach Auckland markings. *Garth Stewart*

901-920

		MAN 15.223 HOCL		Designline Ashburton		N45D	2004			
901	CDN359	**905**	CFY844	**909**	CHW258	**913**	CJJ618	**917**	CJZ401
902	CDN360	**906**	CFY855	**910**	CHW259	**914**	CJJ619	**918**	CJZ420
903	CER435	**907**	CFY858	**911**	CJJ609	**915**	CJP97	**919**	CJZ402
904	CFA182	**908**	CHW255	**912**	CJJ611	**916**	CJP98	**920**	CFH436

1012	IX3950	Mercedes-Benz O303	NZ Motor Bodies	B51D	1978
1033	JD616	Mercedes-Benz O303	NZ Motor Bodies	B51D	1979
1036	JD800	Mercedes-Benz O303	NZ Motor Bodies	B51D	1979
1040	JD1323	Mercedes-Benz O303	NZ Motor Bodies	B51D	1979
1070	NY9392	Mercedes-Benz O303	NZ Motor Bodies	B51D	1980
1074	JQ9731	Mercedes-Benz O303	NZ Motor Bodies	B51D	1980
1096	LA5164	Mercedes-Benz O303	NZ Motor Bodies	B51D	1980

1101-1139

		MAN 22.240		Coachwork International		B53D	1998			
1101	PG8701	**1109**	PI9549	**1117**	PS2953	**1125**	YY8717	**1133**	PX3611
1102	PG8702	**1110**	PM772	**1118**	PS2954	**1126**	PT7114	**1134**	TD2660
1103	PG8703	**1111**	PM773	**1119**	PS2955	**1127**	PT7115	**1135**	PX3613
1104	PG8704	**1112**	PM774	**1120**	PS2956	**1128**	PT7116	**1136**	PX3614
1105	PG8705	**1113**	PM775	**1121**	PT6621	**1129**	PT7117	**1137**	PX3615
1106	PG8706	**1114**	PN8766	**1122**	PT6849	**1130**	PT7118	**1138**	PX3616
1107	PI9547	**1115**	PS3379	**1123**	PT6850	**1131**	PX3609	**1139**	PX3617
1108	SR1039	**1116**	PS3380	**1124**	PT6851	**1132**	PX3610		

1140	WR2559	Mercedes-Benz O305	Fairfax Industries	BC53D	1997
1141	XU8299	Mercedes-Benz O305	Fairfax Industries	BC53D	1999
1142	YC6102	Mercedes-Benz O305	Fairfax Industries	BC53D	1998
1143	YE4656	Mercedes-Benz O305	Fairfax Industries	BC53D	1999
1144	YE4658	Mercedes-Benz O305	Fairfax Industries	BC53D	1999
1145	YH5811	Mercedes-Benz O305	Fairfax Industries	BC53D	1999
1146	YS5352	Mercedes-Benz O305	Designline Ashburton	BC53D	2000
1147	YP8055	Mercedes-Benz O305	Designline Ashburton	BC53D	2000
1200	ST7217	MAN 11.190	Fairfax Industries	B41F	1994
1201	SN7897	MAN 11.190	Coachwork Auckland	B39F	1994

1202-1241 — Nissan Scorpion SBR180 — Fairfax Industries — N41D — 1995-96

1202	SP4125	1210	TE8727	1218	TK2701	1226	TO2604	1234	TY882
1203	SR7404	1211	TE8775	1219	TK2732	1227	TP3843	1235	TY8997
1204	SR7403	1212	TE8776	1220	TK2731	1228	TS119	1236	TY8998
1205	ZE5673	1213	TG2853	1221	TM8033	1229	TS118	1237	UA8873
1206	SZ8401	1214	TI3484	1222	TM8050	1230	ZO3592	1238	UA8872
1207	TB6204	1215	TI3485	1223	TM8049	1231	TU7223	1239	UD4659
1208	TD2659	1216	TI3511	1224	TM7788	1232	TU7222	1240	UE3261
1209	TE8726	1217	TI3540	1225	TO2605	1233	TU7221	1241	UE3262

1296	WP7444	MAN 10.160	Designline Ashburton	N37F	1997
1297	WP7445	MAN 10.160	Designline Ashburton	N37F	1997
1299	MF7517	Volvo B10M	Coachwork Auckland	B46D	1985
1300	MF7516	Volvo B10M	Coachwork Auckland	B46D	1985

1301-1360 — MAN 12.223 — Coachwork International — N53D — 2002

1301	AMT745	1313	ATK361	1325	AWZ519	1337	AQL357	1349	ATZ473
1302	ANF929	1314	ATK362	1326	AQB435	1338	ATP945	1350	AUM732
1303	APP362	1315	ATK364	1327	AQB436	1339	ARR725	1351	AUM734
1304	APP365	1316	ATK365	1328	AQB438	1340	ARR728	1352	AUW481
1305	APP366	1317	ATK366	1329	AQL344	1341	ARD600	1353	AUW486
1306	APP369	1318	APT947	1330	AQL345	1342	ARR730	1354	AUW487
1307	ASJ557	1319	AZE116	1331	AQL352	1343	ASA164	1355	AUW491
1308	ASH467	1320	AZE115	1332	AQL351	1344	ASA165	1356	AUW497
1309	ASU457	1321	AZE112	1333	AQL356	1345	ASA168	1357	AWZ508
1310	ASU458	1322	AYP208	1334	ARD190	1346	ASA170	1358	AWZ509
1311	ATB792	1323	AYP204	1335	ARD196	1347	ATZ463	1359	AWZ511
1312	ATB794	1324	AWZ520	1336	ARD197	1348	ATZ472	1360	AWZ512

1401-1480 — MAN 17.223 HOCL-R — Coachwork International — N53D — 2002-04

1401	BAW608	1417	BFZ266	1433	BJY879	1449	BNK105	1465	BRM886
1402	BAW609	1418	BFZ267	1434	BKR301	1450	BNK111	1466	BRM899
1403	BAW618	1419	BFZ277	1435	BKR304	1451	BNK114	1467	BSA601
1404	BBL543	1420	BGS116	1436	BKR306	1452	BNK117	1468	BSA602
1405	BBL544	1421	BFG911	1437	BKR311	1453	BQF941	1469	BSA604
1406	BBL546	1422	BFG912	1438	BKR314	1454	BQF942	1470	BSJ161
1407	BBL558	1423	BGS117	1439	BKR315	1455	BQF957	1471	BSJ164
1408	BBY262	1424	BGS118	1440	BKR316	1456	BQF960	1472	BSJ165
1409	BBY263	1425	BHL726	1441	BKR317	1457	BQU522	1473	BSJ166
1410	BCW231	1426	BHL728	1442	BKR318	1458	BQU531	1474	BSJ176
1411	BCW232	1427	BHL729	1443	BLD741	1459	BQU530	1475	BSJ180
1412	BCW239	1428	BHL731	1444	BLD742	1460	BQU534	1476	BSY613
1413	BCW718	1429	BHL732	1445	BLD749	1461	BQU537	1477	BSY616
1414	BCW716	1430	BJY870	1446	BMZ538	1462	BRC550	1478	BSY617
1415	BCW717	1431	BJY874	1447	BNK101	1463	BRC551	1479	BTL962
1416	BFZ265	1432	BJY878	1448	BNK103	1464	BRC552	1480	BTL968

1509-1551 — Mercedes-Benz O305 — NZ Motor Bodies — B45D — 1978

1509	IU3476	1527	IU8160	1539	XC8762	1544	IX4153	1549	JA2161
1511	IU3478	1534	TD2661	1540	IX3955	1545	IX4154	1550	JA2162
1512	IU3479	1535	IX2562	1543	IX4152	1547	JA1474	1551	NR8964
1521	IU7096	1538	IX3260						

1552-1600 — Mercedes-Benz O305 — NZ Motor Bodies — B45D — 1979

1552	RE7374	1561	JD795	1572	IB8098	1579	JG6298	1591	PE1593
1553	JD140	1562	JD796	1573	IB8099	1582	JQ3496	1592	JL2163
1554	JD241	1565	JD1678	1574	JB8100	1584	JL879	1593	SJ1700
1555	JD612	1566	PS2957	1575	JG5928	1585	JL1404	1594	TC5184
1556	JD790	1567	MF7509	1576	JG5929	1587	JL1406	1595	JN1685
1557	JD791	1568	JG4613	1577	JG5930	1588	JL1407	1599	JN2205
1558	JD792	1569	JG4614	1578	UK5492	1589	JL1408	1600	JN2206
1559	JD793	1570	YL6611						

While **MAN** chassis now dominate the New Zealand fleet, during the mid-1990s two batches of Nissan Scorpions were supplied. Seen in Custom Street, Auckland, is 1237, UA8873, with Fairfax Industries bodywork. *Garth Stewart*

1601-1661   MAN SL200   Hawke Coachwork   B45D   1981-83

1601	KI6723	**1613**	KN4858	**1626**	KQ1183	**1638**	KT8186	**1650**	KT9106
1602	KI6724	**1614**	KN4859	**1627**	KQ1184	**1639**	KT8187	**1651**	KX8648
1603	KI6725	**1615**	KN4860			**1640**	KD3568	**1652**	KX8647
1604	KI6726	**1616**	KN4881	**1629**	KQ1186	**1641**	KD3569	**1653**	KX8646
1605	KI6727	**1617**	KN4882	**1630**	KS1252	**1642**	KD3570	**1654**	KX8645
1606	KJ1587	**1618**	KN5551	**1631**	KS1253	**1643**	KD3571	**1655**	KX8644
1607	KJ1588	**1620**	KN5547	**1632**	KS1254	**1644**	KD3572	**1656**	KX9350
1608	KJ1589	**1621**	KN5548	**1633**	KS1255	**1645**	KT8916	**1657**	KX9351
1609	KJ1590	**1622**	KN5549	**1634**	KS1256	**1646**	KT8917	**1658**	KX9352
1610	KJ1591	**1623**	KN5550	**1635**	KS1257	**1647**	RE7408	**1659**	KX9353
1611	KJ1592	**1624**	KQ1181	**1636**	KT8184	**1648**	KT8919	**1660**	KX9394
		1625	KQ1182	**1637**	KT8185	**1649**	KT8920	**1661**	KD9603

1662	RD5280	MAN SL200	Coachwork International	B45 D	1985

1663-1670   MAN SL200   Hawke Coachwork   B45D   1984

1663	LT964	**1665**	LX1166	**1667**	LX4260	**1669**	LX4258	**1670**	LX4257
1664	LT965	**1666**	LX1165	**1668**	LX4259				

1671-1688   MAN SL200   Coachwork International   B45D   1985

1671	MA6604	**1675**	MD1200	**1678**	MD1203	**1681**	MF7341	**1686**	MH6117
1672	MA7121	**1676**	MD1201	**1679**	MF7339	**1682**	MF7607	**1687**	MH6118
1673	MA7122	**1677**	MD1202	**1680**	MF7340	**1685**	MH6116	**1688**	MH6119
1674	MA7123								

Fleet number 784, ZR8223, is allocated to one of four MAN 11.220s from 2001 with Designline Ashburton bodywork. *Garth Stewart*

1689-1757

MAN SL202   Coachwork International   B45D   1986-89

1689	MA6224	1703	CCK250	1717	CCK259	1731	NS2855	1745	OC4045
1690	MT7457	1704	MW3306	1718	NF6909	1732	NS2853	1746	OC4046
1691	WN5440	1705	MW3307	1719	CCK258	1733	NS3202	1747	OD3724
1692	OC4173	1706	MY4759	1720	NK9509	1734	NS3201	1748	NX1748
1693	MJ8299	1707	CCK991	1721	CCK257	1735	NO3078	1749	NY8741
1694	CCK239	1708	CCK994	1722	NL528	1736	NO3081	1750	NX1750
1695	MW2339	1709	CCK993	1723	YW9657	1737	NO3079	1751	NY8742
1696	CCK238	1710	CCK992	1724	NL530	1738	NX1738	1752	OF313
1697	CCK234	1711	MU3568	1725	CCK235	1739	NX1739	1753	OF314
1698	CCK237	1712	NF2699	1726	NF5887	1740	NY9889	1754	OF315
1699	ZK8188	1713	CCK236	1727	NF5885	1741	NY9890	1755	OF316
1700	MW2382	1714	NF1525	1728	NS1647	1742	OC4042	1756	OD3725
1701	ZE2405	1715	NF4958	1729	NS1648	1743	OC5480	1757	OD3726
1702	MW3304	1716	NF6911	1730	YY8711	1744	OC4044		

1801-1867

Nissan Scorpion SLF180   Fairfax Industries   N35D   1996-97

1801	UN7501	1814	WK5488	1832	UZ3649	1844	WD4127	1856	WG1059
1802	UN7502	1821	US7577	1833	UZ7785	1845	WD4126	1857	WG8781
1803	UN7503	1822	UU3597	1834	UZ7786	1846	WD4185	1858	WG8782
1804	UN7504	1823	US7576	1835	UZ7787	1847	WD4187	1859	WJ3305
1805	UN7505	1824	UW6598	1836	WA4292	1848	WD4186	1860	WJ3304
1806	UN7506	1825	UW6597	1837	WA4291	1849	WE6195	1861	WJ3302
1807	UN7507	1826	UX2881	1838	WA4290	1850	WE6196	1862	WJ3301
1808	UN7508	1827	UX2882	1839	WA4289	1851	WE6197	1863	WJ9156
1809	UN7509	1828	UX9327	1840	WA2443	1852	WE6198	1864	CHQ73
1810	UN7510	1829	UX9328	1841	WA2445	1853	WG5359	1865	WK8984
1811	UN7511	1830	UX9330	1842	WA2444	1854	WF6426	1866	XQ2361
1812	ZK1561	1831	UZ3648	1843	WA2442	1855	WG5360	1867	WK8986
1813	UN7513								

1868-1892   Nissan Scorpion SLF180   Fairfax Industries   N38D   1997-98

1868	WM5722	1873	WO2149	1878	WO2145	1883	WU6684	1888	WG8922
1869	WM5723	1874	WO2148	1879	WR2862	1884	WW3947	1889	WI9316
1870	WM5724	1875	WT657	1880	WS696	1885	WX4593	1890	WL5655
1871	WM5725	1876	WO2147	1881	WS697	1886	WX7647	1891	XM9633
1872	WO2150	1877	WO2146	1882	WT9909	1887	WX7648	1892	XN7643

2001-2020   MAN SG220   Hawke   AB76D   1983

2001	KS1258	2005	LC7015	2009	LC7936	2013	KL6812	2017	KD9596
2002	LA5936	2006	LC7016	2010	KL6786	2014	KD4078	2018	KD9597
2003	LA5937	2007	LC7017	2011	KL6787	2015	KD4077	2019	KD9598
2004	KR6018	2008	LC7018	2012	KL6788	2016	KD9594	2020	PE1592

2021-2034   MAN SG240   Coachwork International   AB76D   1988-90

2021	NY8743	2024	NY9893	2027	OW6753	2030	OT6354	2033	OT6350
2022	NY9891	2025	OW6752	2028	OT6352	2031	OT6351	2034	OT6349
2023	NY9892	2026	PB8184	2029	OT6353	2032	OW6754		

2401-2096   MAN 17.223   Designline, Ashburton   B51D   2004 and on order

2401	CDG911	2421	CGQ812	2440		2459		2478	
2402	CDG914	2422	CGQ813	2441		2460		2479	
2403	CCR712	2423	CGQ815	2442		2461		2480	
2404	CEK69	2424	CHE847	2443		2462		2481	
2405	CEK70	2425	CHE858	2444		2463		2482	
2406	CEK71	2426	CKJ348	2445		2464		2483	
2407	CER429	2427	CKJ349	2446		2465		2484	
2408	CER430	2428		2447		2466		2485	
2409	CER438	2429		2448		2467		2486	
2410	CFA184	2430		2449		2478		2487	
2411	CFA196	2431		2450		2479		2488	
2412	CFH401	2432		2451		2470		2489	
2413	CFH413	2433		2452		2471		2490	
2414	CFH417	2434		2453		2472		2491	
2415	CGF518	2435		2454		2473		2492	
2416	CGF520	2436		2455		2474		2493	
2417	CGL207	2437		2456		2475		2494	
2418	CGL219	2438		2457		2476		2495	
2419	CGQ801	2439		2458		2477		2496	
2420	CGQ804								

5907	1055IC	Hino BG300	Emslie	C41F	1980
6890	MI8415	Hino RK176	NZ Motor Bodies	B45D	1985

7193-7253   Hino RK176   Coachwork International   B47D*   1987-88   *several are B45D

7193	NA6078	7201w	NK8507	7237	NA7358	7246	NL7827	7250	NL7831
7197w	NA6060	7231	NA7353	7238	NA7359	7247	NL7828	7251	NA7832
7198	NA6947	7232	NA7350	7239	NA7361	7248	NL7829	7252	NA7833
7199w	NA6946	7233w	NA7351	7244	NL7825	7249	NL7830	7253	NL7834
7200	NA6945	7236	NA7357	7245	NL7826				

7255-7556   Hino RK177   Coachwork International   B47D   1988-89

7255	NL7823	7267	NL7793	7278	NX9487	7538	OB4207	7547	OE7912
7256	NL7790	7268	NL8264	7279	NX9488	7539	OB4208	7548	OE7917
7259	NL7797	7269	NL8265	7532	NX9510	7540	OB4215	7549	OG5328
7260	NL7799	7270	NL8266	7533	NX9509	7542	OB4213	7551	OG5327
7261	NL7794	7271	NL8273	7534	NX9507	7543	OB4212	7553	OG5341
7264	NL7792	7273	NL8267	7535	NX9508	7544	OB4214	7554	OG5342
7265	NL7798	7274	NL8268	7536	NX9516	7545	OE7913	7556	OG5344
7266	NL8272	7276	NX9485	7537	NX9517	7546	OE7916		

Ancillary vehicles

480	ADS121	Leyland Leopard PSU3E/2R	Hawke	B49D	1978	Arts Festival promotion
1368	HL6982	Mercedes-Benz O305	NZ Motor Bodies	B--D	1975	

Coach USA

The acquisition of Coach USA was completed on 26th July 1999 with regulatory approval confirmed on 7th September. Operating in 35 US states and Canada, Coach USA is the largest provider of charter, tour and sightseeing services in North America, with some 6500 coaches and 3000 taxicabs with an average fleet age of less than five years.

New vehicles included almost 100 of the Van Hool T2145 delivered during 1999 along with twenty Prevost H345. Around a hundred Thompson International school buses are operated by the Wisconsin Coach Lines. The oldest vehicle from the special event buses is a 1947 Chevrolet that operates with Powder River, while Gray Line San Francisco operates seven Leyland double-decks and Shortline of Mahwah in New Jersey runs a fleet of thirty Bristol VRs, with new double-deck buses from the UK expected shortly.

Stagecoach is a major provider of transport services in North America, where around 5000 people are employed and a fleet of 3500 coaches operated. The businesses are focused mainly on commuter services, although they also include tour and charter, sightseeing and school bus operations.

Three specific geographic areas are involved: the North East and North central regions of the United States, and Canada. Stagecoach's operations have a share of around 1% of the highly-fragmented North American transport market, where there are around 5,000 operators.

Coach Canada livery is shown on MCI coach 53343. *Ken MacKenzie*

The Grey-Line motif is included on their Coach USA-liveried coach. A picture of the New York double-deck Tridents is included in the 2004 edition of this book. *Ken MacKenzie*

The North East business covers the states of New York, New Jersey and Pennsylvania. It includes significant commuter and local bus services, express links to Newark Airport and other destinations, charter business and contract work on behalf of transit authorities and private sector organisations. The North East also operate New York Sightseeing, which offers the Big Apple's premier sightseeing tours.

The North Central region operates in seven states in the northern Midwest of the United States, serving major cities such as Chicago, Milwaukee, Pittsburgh and Syracuse. There are significant contract and charter operations, as well as sightseeing buses in Chicago, scheduled services to Chicago Airport and a growing school-bus business in Milwaukee.

In Canada, Stagecoach operates in the provinces of Quebec and Ontario, providing services in the main centres such as Toronto, Montreal, Kingston, and Niagara Falls. The division is mainly a mix of scheduled services and charter operations, with additional income from transit, school contracts and sightseeing tours.

The North American trade had a turnover for the six months to 31 October 2004 of US$224.1m (2003 - US$382.0m). On a like for like basis, turnover was up by 12.7%. Operating profit was US$26.1m (2003 - US$26.0m), resulting in an improved operating margin of 11.7%, up from 6.8%. Converted to sterling, turnover for the six months to 31 October 2004 was £123.6m (2003 - £234.0m). Operating profit for the six months was £14.4m (2003 - £15.9m).

The New York Sightseeing business, which has a leading market share, continues to achieve both passenger volume and turnover growth as it added more tours to the product portfolio. Expected for delivery in the spring of 2005 is a fleet of 20 new open-top Alexander Dennis double-decker vehicles, which will allow a more frequent service for visitors and provide even more upper-deck seats.

Index to UK Vehicles

Reg	No	Region	Reg	No	Region	Reg	No	Region
13CLT	52359	West Scotland	A999SYE	10999	West Scotland	B357LSO	14457	East Scotland
126ASV	15250	East Scotland	ACZ7490	52108	Eastern	B358LSO	14458	East Scotland
127ASV	15260	East Scotland	ACZ7491	52109	Eastern	B625DWF	25825	South East
128ASV	15259	East Scotland	AE51RXW	22301	Eastern	B629DWF	25829	East Midlands
145CLT	52244	East Scotland	AE51RXX	22302	Eastern	B630DWF	25830	East Midlands
147YFM	52272	East Scotland	AE51RXY	22303	Eastern	B631DWF	25831	East Midlands
283URB	52058	East Scotland	AE51RXZ	22304	Eastern	B632DWF	25832	East Midlands
331HWD	13604	South Wales	AE51RYA	22305	Eastern	B633DWF	25833	South East
400DCD	32448	South East	AE51RYB	22306	Eastern	B900WRN	25800	North West
401DCD	32449	South East	AE51RYC	22307	Eastern	B909TVR	15009	East Midlands
402DCD	32450	South East	AE51RYD	22308	Eastern	B911TVR	15011	Manchester
403DCD	32429	South East	AE51RYF	22309	Eastern	B912ODU	14932	South Midlands
404DCD	32430	South East	AE51RYG	22310	Eastern	B916JVK	48007	North East
405DCD	33005	South East	AE51RYH	22311	Eastern	B916TVR	15016	Manchester
407DCD	32447	South East	AE51RYK	22312	Eastern	BIW4977	13601	South Wales
408DCD	34018	South East	AE51RYN	22313	Eastern	BMS222	59922	East Scotland
409DCD	19909	South East	AE51RYO	22314	Eastern	BSJ917T	25797	West Scotland
411DCD	34011	South East	AE51RYP	22315	Eastern	BSK744	52385	East Scotland
412DCD	34012	South East	AE51RYR	22316	Eastern	C38HNF	13513	Manchester
413DCD	34013	South East	AE51RYT	22317	Eastern	C42HNF	13503	Manchester
414DCD	27404	South East	AE51RYU	22318	Eastern	C43HNF	13504	Manchester
415DCD	27405	South East	AE51RYV	22319	Eastern	C44HNF	13505	Manchester
417DCD	27407	South East	AE51RYW	22320	Eastern	C45HNF	13509	Manchester
418DCD	27408	South East	AE51RYX	22321	Eastern	C46HNF	13510	Manchester
420DCD	34020	South East	AE51RYY	22322	Eastern	C49HNF	13519	Manchester
421DCD	34015	South East	AE51RYZ	22323	Eastern	C50HNF	13517	Manchester
495FFJ	51073	West Scotland	AE51RZA	22324	Eastern	C105DWR	52072	North West
498FYB	52020	South Midlands	AE51RZB	22325	Eastern	C112CHM	14367	West
511OHU	13619	South Wales	AE51RZC	22326	Eastern	C119CHM	14369	South Midlands
527CLT	17879	London	AE51RZF	22327	Eastern	C121CHM	14371	South Midlands
630DYE	52023	London	AE51RZG	22328	Eastern	C152HBA	13512	Manchester
647DYE	16436	North East	AE51RZH	22329	Eastern	C156HBA	13516	Manchester
685DYE	16437	North East	AE51RZJ	22330	Eastern	C157HBA	13514	Manchester
703DYE	52392	East Scotland	AE51RZK	22331	Eastern	C158HBA	13518	Manchester
866NHT	52104	East Scotland	AE51RZL	22332	Eastern	C160HBA	13502	Manchester
3063VC	52329	Eastern	AE51RZM	22333	Eastern	C165YBA	13165	Manchester
4012VC	52037	South Midlands	AE51RZN	22334	Eastern	C166HBA	13515	Manchester
6253VC	52330	Eastern	AE51RZO	22335	Eastern	C166YBA	13166	Manchester
9258VC	52331	Eastern	AE51RZP	22336	Eastern	C167HBA	13511	Manchester
9737VC	52332	Eastern	AE51RZR	22337	Eastern	C168HBA	13508	Manchester
A14RBL	20001	South Wales	AE51RZS	22338	Eastern	C169HBA	13507	Manchester
A16SOE	52089	South East	AE51RZT	22339	Eastern	C170ECK	14170	South East
A22HNC	13022	North West	AE51RZU	22340	Eastern	C170HBA	13506	Manchester
A23HNC	13023	North East	AE53TZJ	18057	Eastern	C170YBA	13170	Manchester
A26ORJ	13026	Eastern	AE53TZK	18058	Eastern	C173YBA	13173	Manchester
A27ORJ	13027	Manchester	AE53TZL	18059	Eastern	C174YBA	13174	Manchester
A28ORJ	13028	Manchester	AE53TZM	18060	Eastern	C176YBA	13176	Manchester
A44FRS	14444	East Scotland	ARP605X	14005	Eastern	C178YBA	13178	Manchester
A66THX	11066	East Scotland	B23TVU	15023	Manchester	C179ECK	14179	Eastern
A76THX	11076	West Scotland	B53DWJ	59060	East Midlands	C181YBA	13181	Manchester
A138MRN	14138	South East	B81WUV	11081	North West	C185YBA	13185	Manchester
A314XWG	14314	East Scotland	B83WUV	11083	West Scotland	C191YBA	13191	Manchester
A319XWG	14319	East Midlands	B84WUV	11084	East Scotland	C193YBA	13193	Manchester
A324AKU	14324	East Midlands	B91WUV	11091	North West	C195YBA	13195	Manchester
A542HAC	14942	South Midlands	B92WUV	11092	West Scotland	C198YBA	13198	Manchester
A543HAC	14943	South Midlands	B116WUV	11116	East Scotland	C205CBU	13205	Manchester
A544HAC	14944	South Midlands	B119WUV	11119	East Scotland	C207CBU	13207	Manchester
A547HAC	14947	Eastern	B121TVU	13121	Manchester	C208CBU	13208	Manchester
A632THV	11032	West Scotland	B122WUV	11122	East Scotland	C210CBU	13210	Manchester
A645THV	11045	West Scotland	B125WUV	11125	South East	C212CBU	13212	Manchester
A825SUL	10825	East Scotland	B180FFS	15280	West Scotland	C214CBU	13214	Manchester
A843SUL	10843	West Scotland	B181FFS	15281	West Scotland	C215CBU	13215	Manchester
A855SUL	10855	North West	B182FFS	15282	West Scotland	C221CBU	13221	Manchester
A858SUL	10858	East Scotland	B183FFS	15283	West Scotland	C224CBU	13224	Manchester
A866SUL	10866	West Scotland	B184FFS	15284	West Scotland	C226ENE	13226	Manchester
A874SUL	10874	West Scotland	B185FFS	15285	West Scotland	C234ENE	13234	Manchester
A905SYE	10905	South Wales	B186FFS	15286	East Scotland	C236EVU	13236	Manchester
A921SYE	10921	East Scotland	B348LSO	14448	East Scotland	C255FRJ	13255	Manchester
A922SYE	10922	East Scotland	B352LSO	14452	East Scotland	C330DND	52004	East Scotland
A950SYE	10950	West Scotland	B354LSO	14454	West Scotland	C335HWJ	14335	East Midlands
A976SYE	10976	West Scotland	B355LSO	14455	East Scotland	C462SSO	14462	West Scotland
A996SYE	10996	East Scotland	B356LSO	14456	East Scotland	C467SSO	14467	East Scotland

The 2005 Stagecoach Bus Handbook

C468SSO	14468	East Scotland	C805USG	15275	West Scotland	D553MVR	52011	East Scotland
C469SSO	14469	East Scotland	C806USG	15276	East Scotland	D560RCK	41998	Eastern
C472SSO	14472	Eastern	C807USG	15269	East Scotland	D918KPT	48047	North East
C495LJV	59014	South East	C962XVC	14935	Eastern	DGS625	39925	East Scotland
C601LFT	14601	West Scotland	C963XVC	14936	South Midlands	DSV743	52306	East Scotland
C602LFT	14602	West Scotland	C964XVC	14937	Eastern	E32RNV	48061	Eastern
C603LFT	14603	West Scotland	CD7045	19945	South East	E61JFV	20401	South Midlands
C605LFT	14605	North East	CN04JDK	34513	South Wales	E62JFV	20402	South Midlands
C608LFT	14608	West Scotland	CN04VJV	34621	South Wales	E63JFV	20403	South Wales
C609LFT	14609	West	CN04VJX	34622	South Wales	E64JFV	20404	South Wales
C610LFT	14610	West	CN04VJY	34623	South Wales	E65JFV	20405	South Wales
C611LFT	14611	North East	CN04VJZ	34624	South Wales	E66JFV	20406	South Wales
C612LFT	14612	West Scotland	CN53HWO	34504	South Wales	E131ORP	52061	North West
C613LFT	14613	North East	CN53HWP	34505	South Wales	E132ORP	52062	North West
C614LFT	14614	North East	CN53HWR	34506	South Wales	E133ORP	52063	North West
C615LFT	14615	North East	CN53HWU	34507	South Wales	E134ORP	52064	North West
C616LFT	14616	West Scotland	CN53HWV	34508	South Wales	E135ORP	52065	North West
C617LFT	14617	North East	CN53HWW	34509	South Wales	E500EFL	14500	West
C618LFT	14618	North East	CN53HWX	34510	South Wales	E501EFL	14501	West
C619LFT	14619	West Scotland	CN53HWY	34511	South Wales	E502EFL	14502	West
C621LFT	14621	East Midlands	CN53HWZ	34500	South Wales	E644UNE	52014	East Scotland
C622LFT	14622	West Scotland	CN53HXA	34501	South Wales	E864RCS	15247	West Scotland
C623LFT	14623	West Scotland	CN53HXB	34502	South Wales	E865RCS	15248	East Scotland
C624LFT	14624	West	CN53HXC	34503	South Wales	E866RCS	15249	West Scotland
C625LFT	14625	West Scotland	CN53UZG	34512	South Wales	E875GRG	48065	North East
C626LFT	14626	West Scotland	CN54ECT	34673	South Wales	E901KYR	14901	East Midlands
C627LFT	14627	West Scotland	CN54ECV	34674	South Wales	E908KYR	14908	East Midlands
C628LFT	14628	West Scotland	CN54ECW	34675	South Wales	E909KYR	14909	East Midlands
C629LFT	14629	West Scotland	CN54ECX	34676	South Wales	E912KYR	14912	East Midlands
C630LFT	14630	East Midlands	CN54ECY	34677	South Wales	E918KYR	14918	East Midlands
C631LFT	14631	Eastern	CN54ECZ	34678	South Wales	E920HCD	48071	South East
C632LFT	14632	East Midlands	CN54EDC	34663	South Wales	E922KYR	14922	East Midlands
C633LFT	14633	North East	CN54EDF	34664	South Wales	E924KYR	14924	East Midlands
C634LFT	14634	East Midlands	CN54EDJ	34665	South Wales	E925KYR	14925	East Midlands
C635LFT	14635	East Midlands	CN54EDK	34666	South Wales	EDS50A	12060	West Scotland
C636LFT	14636	North East	CN54EDL	34667	South Wales	EGB53T	25753	North West
C638LFT	14638	West Scotland	CN54EDO	34668	South Wales	EJV34Y	27034	West
C639LFT	14639	North East	CN54EDP	34669	South Wales	ETC310W	25710	South East
C640LFT	14640	West Scotland	CN54EDR	34670	South Wales	EWS751W	15763	South East
C641LFT	14641	West Scotland	CN54EDU	34671	South Wales	EYE236V	10236	West Scotland
C642LFT	14642	West Scotland	CN54EDV	34672	South Wales	EYE246V	10246	West Scotland
C643LFT	14643	East Midlands	CSU920	52232	East Scotland	F41XCS	14520	Eastern
C644LFT	14644	East Midlands	CSU921	52233	East Scotland	F76TFU	15076	East Midlands
C645LFT	14645	North East	CSU922	52234	East Scotland	F77TFU	15077	East Midlands
C646LFT	14646	North East	CSU923	52235	East Scotland	F105HVK	29105	West
C647LFT	14647	West Scotland	CSU978	52218	West	F107HVK	29107	North East
C648LFT	14648	North East	CSU992	52219	London	F108HVK	29108	South Midlands
C649LFT	14649	East Midlands	CUL179V	10179	North West	F110NES	14000	Eastern
C650LFT	14650	West Scotland	CUL208V	10208	West Scotland	F111HVK	29111	Eastern
C651LFT	14651	North East	CUL209V	10209	West Scotland	F115HVK	29115	Eastern
C653LFT	14653	West Scotland	CUV286C	12286	East Midlands	F116HVK	29116	West
C654LFT	14654	West Scotland	CUV303C	12303	East Midlands	F122HVK	29122	North East
C655LFT	14655	North East	D123FYM	14373	South Midlands	F135SPX	27035	North West
C656LFT	14656	West Scotland	D124FYM	14374	South Midlands	F136SPX	27036	North West
C657LFT	14657	West Scotland	D125FYM	14375	South Midlands	F137SPX	27037	North West
C658LFT	14658	North East	D127FYM	14377	South Midlands	F144BKH	15044	East Midlands
C659LFT	14659	West Scotland	D128FYM	14378	South Midlands	F146BKH	15046	East Midlands
C661LFT	14661	North East	D131FYM	14381	South Midlands	F147BKH	15047	East Midlands
C662LFT	14662	West Scotland	D132FYM	14382	South Midlands	F148BKH	15048	East Midlands
C663LFT	14663	West Scotland	D136FYM	14386	South Midlands	F149BKH	15049	East Midlands
C664LFT	14664	East Midlands	D137FYM	14387	South Midlands	F149XCS	14522	West Scotland
C665LFT	14665	East Midlands	D142FYM	14392	West Scotland	F151BKH	15051	East Midlands
C787USG	15287	East Scotland	D157HHN	48022	North East	F251JRM	29541	North East
C788USG	15288	East Scotland	D235MEA	48023	South East	F252OFP	52069	West Scotland
C789USG	15289	East Scotland	D260JVR	13260	Manchester	F282DRJ	13282	Manchester
C790USG	15290	East Scotland	D272JVR	13272	Manchester	F283DRJ	13283	Manchester
C792USG	15292	East Scotland	D277JVR	13277	Manchester	F285DRJ	13285	Manchester
C793USG	15293	East Scotland	D375DCK	48029	North West	F289DRJ	13289	Manchester
C795USG	15295	East Scotland	D379XRS	14479	Eastern	F291DRJ	13291	Manchester
C796USG	15296	West Scotland	D382XRS	14482	Eastern	F294DRJ	13294	Manchester
C797USG	15297	East Scotland	D383XRS	14483	Eastern	F295DRJ	13295	Manchester
C799USG	15299	West Scotland	D384XRS	14484	Eastern	F296DRJ	13296	North West
C800HCS	14412	West Scotland	D385XRS	14485	West Scotland	F297DRJ	13297	North West
C800USG	15270	East Scotland	D386XRS	14486	East Scotland	F298DRJ	13298	Manchester
C801USG	15271	East Scotland	D387XRS	14487	East Scotland	F300DRJ	13300	Manchester
C802USG	15272	East Scotland	D388XRS	14488	East Scotland	F301DRJ	13301	Manchester
C803USG	15273	East Scotland	D443GAV	48034	Eastern	F301MYJ	15201	South East
C804USG	15274	East Scotland	D548MVR	52006	East Scotland	F302MYJ	15202	South East

Reg	No	Area
F303MYJ	15203	South East
F304DRJ	13304	Manchester
F304MYJ	15204	South East
F305MYJ	15205	South East
F306MYJ	15206	South East
F307MYJ	15207	South East
F308MYJ	15208	South East
F309MYJ	15209	South East
F310MYJ	15210	East Scotland
F311MYJ	15211	East Scotland
F312MYJ	15212	East Scotland
F344ECK	48074	North West
F392DHL	40205	South Wales
F506NJE	14506	Eastern
F507NJE	14507	Eastern
F508NJE	14508	Eastern
F509NJE	14509	Eastern
F510NJE	14510	Eastern
F511NJE	14511	Eastern
F512NJE	14512	Eastern
F513NJE	14513	Eastern
F514NJE	14514	Eastern
F515NJE	14515	South Midlands
F516NJE	14516	South Midlands
F517NJE	14517	South Midlands
F524WSJ	14521	West Scotland
F601MSL	14951	South East
F601UVN	29601	North East
F602MSL	14952	South East
F603MSL	14953	South East
F604MSL	14954	South East
F605MSL	14955	South East
F606MSL	14956	South East
F608UVN	29608	Eastern
F609UVN	29609	Eastern
F610UVN	29610	North East
F620MSL	14020	Eastern
F621MSL	14021	Eastern
F622MSL	14022	Eastern
F623MSL	14023	Eastern
F624MSL	14024	Eastern
F625MSL	14025	Eastern
F626MSL	14026	Eastern
F627MSL	14027	Eastern
F628MSL	14028	Eastern
F629MSL	14029	Eastern
F630MSL	14030	Eastern
F632MSL	14032	Eastern
F633MSL	14033	Eastern
F634MSP	14034	Eastern
F635YRP	14035	Eastern
F636YRP	14036	Eastern
F638YRP	14038	Eastern
F701BAT	28701	Devon
F703BAT	28703	Devon
F704BAT	28704	Devon
F705BAT	28705	Devon
F706CAG	28706	Devon
F781KKP	15311	South East
F782KKP	15312	South East
F803FAO	14243	North West
F804FAO	14244	North West
F805FAO	14245	North West
F806FAO	14246	North West
F807FAO	14247	North West
F808FAO	14248	North West
F809FAO	14249	North West
F810FAO	14250	North West
F811FAO	14251	North West
F901JRG	28901	North East
F902JRG	28902	North East
F903JRG	28903	North East
F905JRG	28905	North East
F906JRG	28906	North East
F907JRG	28907	North East
F908JRG	28908	North East
F910JRG	28910	West Scotland
F911JRG	28911	North East
F912JRG	28912	North East
F913JRG	28913	Devon
F914JRG	28914	North East
F915JRG	28915	North East
F917JRG	28917	North East
F918JRG	28918	North East
F919JRG	28919	Devon
FES831W	59931	East Scotland
FSU739	52386	East Scotland
G49TGW	32349	East Scotland
G67PFR	20407	South Wales
G68PFR	20408	South Wales
G79VFW	15079	East Midlands
G80VFW	15080	East Midlands
G81VFW	15081	East Midlands
G101AAD	14271	West
G102AAD	14272	West
G103AAD	14273	West
G104AAD	14274	West
G105AAD	14275	West
G108CEH	28938	North East
G113SKX	28927	North East
G127WGX	13633	London
G128WGX	13636	London
G180JHG	14180	North East
G181JHG	14181	North East
G182JHG	14182	North East
G183JHG	14183	North East
G184JHG	14184	North East
G185JHG	14185	North East
G186JHG	14186	North East
G187JHG	14187	North West
G188JHG	14188	North West
G189JHG	14189	North East
G189YRJ	13616	Manchester
G192PAO	40192	North West
G194PAO	40194	East Scotland
G195PAO	40195	East Scotland
G197PAO	40197	East Scotland
G198PAO	40198	East Scotland
G203PAO	40203	East Scotland
G210SSL	14960	South East
G211SSL	14961	South East
G212SSL	14962	East Scotland
G213SSL	14963	East Scotland
G214SSL	14964	East Scotland
G251TSL	40251	West Scotland
G277TSL	40277	West Scotland
G280YRG	13643	Manchester
G283TSL	40283	North East
G337KKW	14337	West Scotland
G338KKW	14338	East Scotland
G339KKW	14339	East Midlands
G340KKW	14340	East Midlands
G341KKW	14341	East Midlands
G342KKW	14342	East Midlands
G343KKW	14343	East Midlands
G344FFX	52073	East Scotland
G345FFX	52085	South East
G386PNV	52075	North West
G387PNV	52076	West Scotland
G520LWU	52077	South East
G525LWU	52078	East Midlands
G530LWU	52081	South East
G531LWU	52082	East Scotland
G570PRM	40670	West Scotland
G571PRM	40671	West Scotland
G578PRM	40678	North East
G611CEF	29611	North East
G612CEF	29612	West
G613CEF	29613	West
G614CEF	29614	West
G615CEF	29615	South Midlands
G616CEF	29616	North East
G617CEF	29617	South Midlands
G620CEF	29620	North East
G640EVV	14040	Eastern
G642EVV	14042	Eastern
G643EVV	14043	Eastern
G645EVV	14045	Eastern
G646EVV	14046	Eastern
G647EVV	14047	Eastern
G648EVV	14048	Eastern
G649EVV	14049	Eastern
G675XTN	48078	North East
G684KNW	26010	London
G701TCD	14981	South East
G702TCD	14982	South East
G703TCD	14983	South East
G704TCD	14984	South East
G705TCD	14975	South East
G706TCD	14976	South East
G707TCD	14977	South East
G708TCD	14978	South East
G709TCD	14979	South East
G710TCD	14980	South East
G806YTA	48080	Devon
G807RTS	14957	East Scotland
G808RTS	14958	West
G809RTS	14959	East Scotland
G921TCU	28921	North East
G923TCU	28923	North East
G924TCU	28924	West Scotland
G926TCU	28926	North East
GAZ4381	47900	Eastern
GAZ4382	47901	Eastern
GCS69V	25769	West Scotland
GRS343E	59943	East Scotland
GSO1V	14471	East Scotland
GSO6V	14476	Eastern
GSO7V	14477	Eastern
GSU341	52030	North West
GSU839T	25739	East Scotland
GSU859T	25759	North West
GU52WSX	53001	South East
GU52WSY	53002	South East
GU52WSZ	53003	South East
GU52WTA	53004	South East
GU52WTC	53005	South East
GU52WTD	53006	South East
GU52WTE	53007	South East
GU52WTF	53008	South East
GU52WTG	53009	South East
GU52WTJ	53010	South East
GX04EXH	34514	South East
GX04EXJ	34515	South East
GX04EXK	34516	South East
GX04EXL	34517	South East
GX04EXM	34518	South East
GX04EXN	34519	South East
GX04EXP	34520	South East
GX04EXR	34521	South East
GX04EXS	34522	South East
GX04EXT	34523	South East
GX04EXU	34524	South East
GX04EXV	34525	South East
GX04EXW	34526	Eastern
GX04EXZ	34527	South East
GX04EYA	34528	South East
GX04EYB	34529	South East
GX04EYC	34530	Eastern
GX04EYD	34531	South East
GX04EYF	34532	Eastern
GX04EYG	34533	Eastern
GX04EYH	34534	Eastern
GX04EYJ	34535	Eastern
GX04EYK	34536	Eastern
GX04EYL	34537	Eastern
GX04EYM	34538	Eastern
GX04EYP	34539	Eastern
GX04EYR	34540	Eastern
GX04EYS	34541	Eastern
GX04EYT	34542	Eastern
GX04EYU	34543	Eastern
GX04EYV	34544	Eastern
GX04EYW	34545	Eastern

Reg	No	Location	Reg	No	Location	Reg	No	Location
GX04EYY	34546	Eastern	GX54DXO	47115	South East	H437EFT	28937	North East
GX04EYZ	34547	Eastern	GX54DXP	47116	South East	H445EGU	13617	London
GX04EZA	34548	Eastern	GX54DXR	47117	South East	H462EJR	13652	North East
GX04EZB	34549	Eastern	GX54DXT	47118	South East	H463EJR	13646	North East
GX51PUJ	22009	South East	GX54DXU	47119	South East	H463GVM	15313	Manchester
GX53MVU	34406	South East	GX54DXV	47120	South East	H464GVM	15314	Manchester
GX53MVV	34407	South East	GX54FVU	34659	South East	H465GVM	15315	Manchester
GX53MVW	34408	South East	GX54FVV	34660	South East	H466GVM	15316	Manchester
GX53MVY	34409	South East	GX54FVW	34661	South East	H467GVM	15317	Manchester
GX53MVZ	34410	South East	GX54FVY	34662	South East	H473CEG	14523	Eastern
GX53MWA	34411	South East	GYE252W	10252	West Scotland	H474CEG	14524	Eastern
GX53MWC	34412	South East	GYE254W	10254	North West	H475CEG	14525	Eastern
GX53MWD	34413	South East	GYE281W	10281	North West	H484BEE	15084	East Midlands
GX53MWE	34414	South East	GYN285X	10285	North West	H485BEE	15085	East Midlands
GX53MWF	34415	South East	H41GBD	13626	South Midlands	H492LNA	13631	North East
GX53MWG	34416	South East	H51SKG	13645	West	H493LNA	13630	North East
GX53MWJ	34417	South East	H71MOB	32347	East Scotland	H494LNA	13623	Manchester
GX53MWK	34418	South East	H112SAO	14252	North West	H495LNA	13629	Manchester
GX53MWL	34445	South East	H113SAO	14253	North West	H511FRP	13625	South Midlands
GX53MWM	34446	South East	H114SAO	14254	North West	H522FRP	13618	London
GX53MWN	34447	South East	H115SAO	14255	North West	H617ACK	20417	South Midlands
GX53MWO	34448	South East	H116SAO	14256	North West	H618ACK	20418	East Midlands
GX53MWP	34449	South East	H117SAO	14257	North West	H619ACK	20419	East Midlands
GX53MWU	34450	South East	H118SAO	14258	North West	H620ACK	20420	South Wales
GX53MWV	34451	South East	H119SAO	14259	North West	H621ACK	20421	South Wales
GX53MWW	34452	South East	H127ACU	29127	South Midlands	H622ACK	20422	West Scotland
GX53MWY	34453	South East	H131GVM	15031	Manchester	H623ACK	20423	South Midlands
GX53MWZ	34454	South East	H132GVM	15032	Manchester	H640UWR	52094	South East
GX54DVA	18160	South East	H133GVM	15033	Manchester	H654VVV	14054	Eastern
GX54DVB	18161	South East	H134GVM	15034	Manchester	H667BNL	14667	North East
GX54DVC	18162	South East	H135GVM	15035	Manchester	H668BNL	14668	North East
GX54DVF	18163	South East	H136GVM	15036	Manchester	H669BNL	14669	North East
GX54DVG	18164	South East	H137GVM	15037	Manchester	H670BNL	14670	North East
GX54DVH	18165	South East	H138GVM	15038	Manchester	H671BNL	14671	North East
GX54DVJ	18166	South East	H139GVM	15039	Manchester	H672BNL	14672	North East
GX54DVK	18167	South East	H140GVM	15040	Manchester	H673BNL	14673	North East
GX54DVL	18168	South East	H146MOB	32346	East Scotland	H674BNL	14674	North East
GX54DVM	18169	South East	H149CVU	52086	West Scotland	H675BNL	14675	North East
GX54DVN	18170	South East	H150HVU	52087	East Scotland	H676BNL	14676	North East
GX54DVO	18171	South East	H154MOB	32344	East Scotland	H723KDY	13620	South East
GX54DVP	18172	South East	H162NON	32342	East Scotland	H724KDY	13621	South East
GX54DVR	18173	South East	H181EGU	52091	East Midlands	H725KDY	13622	South East
GX54DVT	18174	South East	H182EGU	52092	East Midlands	H763KDY	13635	South East
GX54DVU	18175	South East	H191WFR	14191	North East	H764KDY	13634	South East
GX54DVV	18176	South East	H192WFR	14192	North East	H778VHL	13632	East Midlands
GX54DVW	34629	South East	H193WFR	14193	North West	H801BKK	14801	South East
GX54DVY	34630	South East	H194WFR	14194	North East	H802BKK	14802	South East
GX54DVZ	34631	South East	H195WFR	14195	North West	H803BKK	14803	South East
GX54DWA	34632	South East	H196WFR	14196	North West	H804BKK	14804	South East
GX54DWC	34633	South East	H197WFR	14197	North West	H805BKK	14805	South East
GX54DWD	34634	South East	H344SWA	14344	East Midlands	H806BKK	14806	South East
GX54DWE	34635	South East	H345SWA	14345	East Midlands	H807BKK	14807	South East
GX54DWF	34636	South East	H346SWA	14346	East Midlands	H808BKK	14808	South East
GX54DWG	34637	South East	H347SWA	14347	East Midlands	H809BKK	14809	South East
GX54DWJ	34638	South East	H348SWA	14348	East Midlands	H810BKK	14810	South East
GX54DWK	34639	South East	H402DEG	52090	South Wales	H815CBP	14815	South East
GX54DWL	34640	South East	H405PRW	41505	South Midlands	H816CBP	14816	South East
GX54DWM	34641	South East	H406GAV	52088	West Scotland	H817CBP	14817	South East
GX54DWN	34642	South East	H406PRW	41506	South Midlands	H818CBP	14818	South East
GX54DWO	34643	South East	H421BNL	15301	North East	H819CBP	14819	South East
GX54DWP	34644	South East	H422BNL	15302	North East	H838GLD	41983	Eastern
GX54DWU	34645	South East	H423BNL	15303	North East	HDV639E	59939	East Scotland
GX54DWV	34646	South East	H424BNL	15304	North East	HGM335E	19935	East Scotland
GX54DWW	34647	South East	H425BNL	15305	North East	HIL6075	48083	West
GX54DWY	34648	South East	H426BNL	15306	North East	HIL8410	13627	South Wales
GX54DWZ	34649	South East	H427BNL	15307	North East	HSK760	52130	East Scotland
GX54DXA	34650	South East	H428BNL	15308	North East	HSV194	52227	East Scotland
GX54DXB	34651	South East	H428EFT	28928	West Scotland	HSV195	52071	Devon
GX54DXC	34652	South East	H429BNL	15309	North East	HSV196	52059	South Wales
GX54DXD	34653	South East	H429EFT	28929	North East	IIL1321	52051	East Midlands
GX54DXE	34654	South East	H430BNL	15310	North East	J24MCW	20424	West Scotland
GX54DXF	34655	South East	H430EFT	28930	North East	J25MCW	20425	West Scotland
GX54DXG	34656	South East	H431EFT	28931	North East	J92DJV	15092	East Midlands
GX54DXH	34657	South East	H432EFT	28932	North East	J93DJV	15093	East Midlands
GX54DXJ	34658	South East	H433EFT	28933	North East	J94DJV	15094	East Midlands
GX54DXK	47112	South East	H434EFT	28934	North East	J120AAO	14260	North West
GX54DXL	47113	South East	H435EFT	28935	North East	J120XHH	14490	East Scotland
GX54DXM	47114	South East	H436EFT	28936	North East	J121AAO	14261	North West

Reg	No.	Area	Reg	No.	Area	Reg	No.	Area
J121XHH	14491	East Scotland	J509GCD	32509	South East	J824HMC	15324	Devon
J122AAO	14262	Manchester	J510FPS	32810	East Scotland	J825HMC	15325	Devon
J122XHH	14492	East Scotland	J510GCD	32510	South East	J826HMC	15326	Devon
J123XHH	14263	West	J511FPS	32811	East Scotland	J827HMC	15327	Devon
J124XHH	14264	West	J511GCD	32511	South East	J828HMC	15328	Devon
J125XHH	14265	North West	J512FPS	32812	East Scotland	J829HMC	15329	Devon
J126XHH	14266	North West	J513GCD	32513	South East	J901UKV	29621	North East
J127XHH	14267	North West	J515GCD	32515	South East	J909NKP	52115	Manchester
J132HMT	15332	Manchester	J515WAX	13648	West	J925FPS	13653	West Scotland
J133HMT	15333	Manchester	J517GCD	32517	South East	J938MHC	13612	South East
J134HMT	15334	South East	J518GCD	32518	South East	J939MHC	13613	South East
J135HMT	15335	Manchester	J519GCD	32519	South East	JAH552D	19952	Eastern
J136HMT	15336	Manchester	J522GCD	32522	South East	JAH553D	19953	Eastern
J137HMT	15337	Manchester	J524GCD	32524	South East	JDZ2360	32260	Devon
J138HMT	15338	South East	J526GCD	32526	South East	JDZ2362	32262	Devon
J139HMT	15339	South East	J529GCD	32529	South East	JDZ2371	09999	Devon
J140HMT	15340	Manchester	J530GCD	32530	South East	JHU899X	14282	West
J141HMT	15341	Manchester	J532GCD	32532	South East	JJD392D	12392	London
J142HMT	15342	Manchester	J536GCD	32536	South East	JJD399D	12399	East Midlands
J143HMT	15343	Manchester	J537GCD	32537	South East	JJD429D	12429	North West
J144HMT	15344	Manchester	J538GCD	32538	South East	JJD435D	12435	East Midlands
J145HMT	15345	Manchester	J541GCD	32541	South East	JJD437D	12437	East Midlands
J166UNH	13614	South Midlands	J542GCD	32542	Eastern	JJD444D	12444	West Scotland
J167UNH	13615	South Midlands	J546GCD	32546	Eastern	JJD450D	12450	East Midlands
J196YSS	14496	East Scotland	J547GCD	32547	South East	JJD451D	12451	North West
J197YSS	14497	East Scotland	J548GCD	32548	South East	JJD462D	12462	East Midlands
J198HFR	14198	North East	J550GCD	32550	Eastern	JJD470D	12470	North West
J198YSS	14498	West Scotland	J552GCD	32552	South East	JJD481D	12481	East Midlands
J199HFR	14199	North West	J620GCR	14493	Eastern	JJD488D	12488	North West
J199YSS	14499	East Scotland	J621GCR	14494	Eastern	JJD493D	12493	North West
J201HFR	14201	North West	J622GCR	14495	Eastern	JJD495D	12495	North West
J202HFR	14202	North West	J623GCR	14973	South East	JJD496D	12496	East Midlands
J203HFR	14203	North West	J624GCR	14974	South East	JJD550D	12550	West Scotland
J204HFR	14204	North West	J688TNF	13654	Manchester	JJD592D	12592	North West
J205HFR	14205	North West	J701HMY	13609	London	JOU160P	15760	South East
J206HFR	14206	North West	J701KCU	32701	North West	JPU817	52057	North West
J207HFR	14207	North West	J702CWT	52106	South East	JSK492	13610	South Wales
J208HFR	14208	North West	J702HMY	13606	London	JWV251W	15751	South East
J209HFR	14209	North West	J702KCU	32702	North West	K91BNY	32991	Devon
J210HFR	14210	North West	J702YRM	32582	Eastern	K92BNY	32992	South Wales
J214AET	41714	East Midlands	J703HMY	13607	London	K93BNY	32993	Devon
J215AET	41715	East Midlands	J711CYG	26011	London	K94AAX	32994	South Wales
J216AET	41716	East Midlands	J712CYG	26012	London	K95AAX	32995	South Wales
J217AET	41717	East Midlands	J713DAP	26013	London	K96AAX	32996	South Wales
J217XKY	40525	West Scotland	J714CYG	26014	London	K97XNY	32997	South Wales
J219AET	41719	East Midlands	J715DAP	26015	London	K98XNY	32998	West
J230XKY	15330	South East	J716CYG	26016	London	K101JWJ	16471	East Midlands
J231XKY	15331	South East	J717CYG	26017	South East	K101XHG	32101	East Scotland
J304UKG	41304	East Scotland	J718CYG	26018	London	K102JWJ	16472	East Midlands
J349XET	14349	East Midlands	J719CYG	26019	West	K102XHG	32102	East Scotland
J350XET	14350	East Midlands	J720CYG	26020	London	K103JWJ	16473	East Midlands
J351XET	14351	East Midlands	J720GAP	14970	South East	K104JWJ	16474	East Midlands
J352XET	14352	East Midlands	J721CYG	26021	London	K104XHG	32104	East Scotland
J353XET	14353	East Midlands	J721GAP	14971	South East	K105JWJ	16475	East Midlands
J401LKO	26001	London	J722CYG	26022	East Scotland	K105XHG	32105	East Scotland
J402LKO	26002	London	J722GAP	14972	South East	K106JWJ	16476	East Midlands
J403LKO	26003	London	J723CYG	26023	London	K106XHG	32106	East Scotland
J407PRW	41507	East Scotland	J724CYG	26024	London	K107JWJ	16477	East Midlands
J409PRW	41509	East Scotland	J725CYG	26025	London	K107XHG	32107	South East
J411PRW	41511	East Scotland	J726CYG	26026	London	K109SRH	32147	East Midlands
J412PRW	41512	East Scotland	J727CYG	26027	London	K110SRH	32148	East Midlands
J413PRW	41513	East Scotland	J728CYG	26028	Devon	K110XHG	32110	East Scotland
J417PRW	41517	East Scotland	J729CYG	26029	London	K112SRH	32112	North East
J454JRH	32999	South Wales	J734HMY	13608	London	K113SRH	32113	East Midlands
J456FSR	52095	East Midlands	J801WFS	14701	East Scotland	K114SRH	32114	East Midlands
J501FPS	32801	East Scotland	J802WFS	14702	East Scotland	K115SRH	32115	East Midlands
J501GCD	32501	South East	J803WFS	14703	East Scotland	K116SRH	32116	East Midlands
J502FPS	32802	East Scotland	J804WFS	14704	East Scotland	K117SRH	32117	North East
J502GCD	32502	South East	J805WFS	14705	East Scotland	K117XHG	40417	North West
J503FPS	32803	East Scotland	J806WFS	14706	East Scotland	K118SRH	32118	East Midlands
J503GCD	32503	South East	J807WFS	14707	East Scotland	K120SRH	32120	West Scotland
J504FPS	32804	East Scotland	J808WFS	14708	Eastern	K121SRH	32121	North East
J505FPS	32805	East Scotland	J811NKK	14811	South East	K122SRH	32122	East Scotland
J506FPS	32806	East Midlands	J812NKK	14812	South East	K123SRH	32123	East Midlands
J507FPS	32807	East Midlands	J813NKK	14813	South East	K124SRH	32124	North East
J508FPS	32808	East Scotland	J814NKK	14814	South East	K124XHG	40424	North West
J508GCD	32508	South East	J822HMC	15322	Devon	K125SRH	32125	North East
J509FPS	32809	East Scotland	J823HMC	15323	Devon	K126SRH	32126	W

Reg	No	Area	Reg	No	Area	Reg	No	Area
K127SRH	32127	North East	K569GSA	52139	East Scotland	K707DAO	20707	South Wales
K128DAO	14268	North West	K569NHC	32569	North East	K708DAO	20708	South Wales
K128SRH	32128	North East	K570GSA	52140	East Scotland	K709ASC	14709	Eastern
K129DAO	14229	North West	K571DFS	52141	West Scotland	K709DAO	20709	South Wales
K129SRH	32129	North East	K571LTS	20171	East Scotland	K709PCN	32709	North East
K130DAO	14230	North West	K572DFS	52142	East Scotland	K710ASC	14710	Eastern
K130SRH	32130	W	K572LTS	20172	East Scotland	K710DAO	20710	North West
K131DAO	14231	North West	K573DFS	52143	East Scotland	K710PCN	32710	North East
K132DAO	14232	North West	K573LTS	20173	East Scotland	K711DAO	20711	North West
K132SRH	32132	W	K574DFS	52144	West Scotland	K711PCN	32711	North East
K133DAO	14233	North West	K574LTS	20174	East Scotland	K712DAO	20712	North West
K133SRH	32133	North East	K575DFS	52145	East Midlands	K712PCN	32712	North East
K134DAO	14234	North West	K575LTS	20175	East Scotland	K713ASC	14713	Eastern
K134SRH	32134	North East	K575NHC	32575	Eastern	K713DAO	20713	North West
K135DAO	14235	North West	K576DFS	52146	East Midlands	K713PCN	32713	East Midlands
K150DNV	52120	Eastern	K576LTS	20176	East Scotland	K714ASC	14714	South East
K151DNV	52121	Eastern	K577DFS	52147	East Midlands	K714DAO	20714	North East
K153DNV	52123	Eastern	K577LTS	20177	East Scotland	K714PCN	32714	North East
K154DNV	52124	Eastern	K577NHC	32577	South East	K715ASC	14715	South East
K211SRH	32111	East Midlands	K578LTS	20178	East Scotland	K715DAO	20715	West Scotland
K235NHC	14985	South East	K578NHC	32578	South East	K715PCN	32715	North East
K236NHC	14986	South East	K579NHC	32579	North East	K716ASC	14716	South East
K237NHC	14987	South East	K580NHC	32580	South East	K716DAO	20716	North East
K238NHC	14988	South East	K585ODY	32585	South East	K717ASC	14717	South East
K239NHC	14989	South East	K601ESH	32201	East Scotland	K717DAO	20717	North West
K240NHC	14990	South East	K602ESH	32202	East Scotland	K717PCN	32717	North East
K315YKG	41315	East Scotland	K603ESH	32203	East Scotland	K718ASC	14718	East Scotland
K320YKG	40593	East Scotland	K604ESH	32204	East Scotland	K718DAO	20718	West Scotland
K321YKG	40594	East Scotland	K605ESH	32205	East Scotland	K718PCN	32718	North East
K350ANV	40350	Eastern	K610UFR	40810	East Scotland	K719ASC	14719	East Scotland
K351ANV	40351	Eastern	K622UFR	40822	North West	K719DAO	20719	North West
K352ANV	40352	Eastern	K622YVN	29622	North East	K720ASC	14720	East Scotland
K353ANV	40353	East Scotland	K623UFR	40823	North West	K720DAO	20720	East Midlands
K354DWJ	14354	East Midlands	K623YVN	29623	North East	K720PCN	32720	North East
K355DWJ	14355	East Midlands	K624YVN	29624	North East	K721ASC	14721	East Scotland
K356ANV	40356	Eastern	K625YVN	29625	North East	K721DAO	20721	North West
K356DWJ	14356	East Midlands	K626YVN	29626	North East	K721PCN	32721	North East
K357DWJ	14357	East Midlands	K627YVN	29627	North East	K722ASC	14722	East Scotland
K358DWJ	14358	East Midlands	K628YVN	29628	North East	K722DAO	20722	North East
K359ANV	40359	Eastern	K629YVN	29629	North East	K722PCN	32722	North East
K359DWJ	14359	East Midlands	K630HWX	26030	East Scotland	K723ASC	14723	East Scotland
K360DWJ	14360	East Midlands	K630YVN	29630	North East	K723DAO	20723	North East
K361DWJ	14361	East Midlands	K631HWX	26031	London	K723PNL	32723	North East
K362DWJ	14362	East Midlands	K632HWX	26032	London	K724ASC	14724	East Scotland
K363DWJ	14363	East Midlands	K633HWX	26033	London	K724DAO	20724	North East
K402EDT	32990	South Wales	K634HWX	26034	London	K724PNL	32724	North East
K420ARW	41520	East Scotland	K635HWX	26035	London	K725ASC	14725	East Scotland
K487FFS	40087	East Scotland	K655NHC	32555	South East	K725DAO	20725	North West
K489FFS	40089	East Scotland	K655UNH	14055	Eastern	K725PNL	32725	North East
K490FFS	40090	East Scotland	K656UNH	14056	Eastern	K726DAO	20726	North East
K491FFS	40091	East Scotland	K657UNH	14057	Eastern	K726PNL	32726	North East
K492FFS	40092	North East	K658UNH	14058	Eastern	K727DAO	20727	North West
K493FFS	40093	North East	K659UNH	14059	Eastern	K727PNL	32727	North East
K508ESS	14408	East Scotland	K660UNH	14060	Eastern	K728DAO	20728	North West
K509ESS	14409	East Scotland	K661UNH	14061	Eastern	K728PNL	32728	North East
K510ESS	14410	East Scotland	K662UNH	14062	Eastern	K729DAO	20729	North East
K511ESS	14411	West Scotland	K663UNH	14063	Eastern	K730DAO	20730	North East
K515ESS	14415	West Scotland	K664UNH	14064	Eastern	K731DAO	20731	North West
K518ESS	14418	East Scotland	K667UNH	14067	Eastern	K732DAO	20732	North West
K553NHC	32553	South East	K668UNH	14068	Eastern	K733DAO	20733	North West
K554NHC	32554	South East	K669UNH	14069	Eastern	K734DAO	20734	North West
K556NHC	32556	South East	K670UNH	14070	Eastern	K735DAO	20735	North West
K560NHC	32560	South East	K699ERM	20699	North West	K736DAO	20736	North West
K561GSA	52131	East Scotland	K700DAO	20700	North West	K737DAO	20737	North West
K561NHC	32561	South East	K701DAO	20701	North West	K738DAO	20738	North West
K562GSA	52132	East Scotland	K701NDO	27701	East Midlands	K739DAO	20739	North West
K562NHC	32562	South East	K702DAO	20702	North West	K741DAO	20741	North West
K563GSA	52133	East Scotland	K702NDO	27702	East Midlands	K742DAO	20742	North West
K563NHC	32563	North East	K703DAO	20703	North East	K743DAO	20743	North West
K564GSA	52134	East Scotland	K703NDO	27703	East Midlands	K744DAO	20744	East Midlands
K564NHC	32564	North East	K703PCN	32703	North East	K745DAO	20745	North West
K565GSA	52135	East Scotland	K704ERM	20704	South Midlands	K746DAO	20746	North West
K565NHC	32565	South East	K704NDO	27704	East Midlands	K748DAO	20748	North West
K566GSA	52136	East Scotland	K704PCN	32704	South Midlands	K749DAO	20749	North West
K567GSA	52137	West Scotland	K705DAO	20705	North West	K750DAO	20750	North West
K567NHC	32567	South East	K705PCN	32705	South Midlands	K751DAO	20751	North West
K568GSA	52138	East Scotland	K706DAO	20706	South Wales	K752DAO	20752	North West
K568NHC	32568	North East	K706PCN	32706	South Midlands	K753DAO	20753	North West

Reg	No	Region	Reg	No	Region	Reg	No	Region
K754DAO	20754	North West	K922OWV	32222	South East	KV53EZL	34434	Eastern
K755DAO	20755	North West	K923OWV	32223	South East	KV53EZM	34435	Eastern
K756DAO	20756	North West	K972HUB	47972	Eastern	KV53EZN	34436	Eastern
K757DAO	20757	North West	K983CBO	32238	South Wales	KV53EZO	34437	Eastern
K758DAO	20758	North West	K986CBO	32241	West	KV53EZP	34438	Eastern
K758FYG	52116	East Scotland	K987CBO	32242	South Wales	KV53EZR	34439	Eastern
K759DAO	20759	North West	KN04XCT	34398	South Midlands	KV53EZT	34440	Eastern
K759FYG	52117	East Scotland	KN04XJB	18127	South Midlands	KV53EZU	34441	Eastern
K760DAO	20760	North West	KN04XJC	18128	South Midlands	KV53EZW	34442	Eastern
K761DAO	20761	North West	KN04XJD	18129	South Midlands	KV53EZX	34443	Eastern
K762DAO	20762	North West	KN04XJE	18130	South Midlands	KV53EZZ	34444	Eastern
K763DAO	20763	North West	KN04XJF	18131	South Midlands	KV53FAA	22057	South Midlands
K764DAO	20764	North West	KN04XJG	18132	South Midlands	KV53FAF	22058	Eastern
K765DAO	20765	North West	KN04XJH	18133	South Midlands	KV53FAJ	22059	Eastern
K766DAO	20766	North West	KN04XJJ	18134	South Midlands	KV53FAK	22060	Eastern
K767DAO	20767	North West	KN04XJK	18135	South Midlands	KV53NHA	34466	South Midlands
K768DAO	20768	North West	KN04XJL	18136	South Midlands	KV53NHB	34467	South Midlands
K769DAO	20769	North West	KN04XJM	18137	South Midlands	KV53NHC	34468	South Midlands
K770DAO	20770	North West	KN04XKC	47069	South Midlands	KV53NHD	34469	South Midlands
K771DAO	20771	North West	KN04XKD	47070	South Midlands	KV53NHE	34470	South Midlands
K772DAO	20772	North West	KN04XKE	47071	South Midlands	KV53NHF	34471	South Midlands
K773DAO	20773	North West	KN04XKF	47072	South Midlands	KV53NHG	34472	South Midlands
K774DAO	20774	North West	KN04XKG	47073	South Midlands	KV53NHH	34491	South Midlands
K775DAO	20775	North West	KN04XKH	47074	South Midlands	KV53NHJ	34492	South Midlands
K776DAO	20776	North West	KN04XKJ	47075	South Midlands	KV53NHK	34493	South Midlands
K777DAO	20777	North West	KN04XKK	47076	South Midlands	KV53NHL	34494	South Midlands
K778DAO	20778	North West	KN04XKL	47077	South Midlands	KV53NHM	34495	South Midlands
K779DAO	20779	North West	KN54XYP	47123	Eastern	KV53NHN	34496	South Midlands
K780DAO	20780	North West	KN54XYR	47124	Eastern	KV53NHO	34497	South Midlands
K782DAO	20781	North West	KN54XYT	47125	Eastern	KV53NHP	34498	South Midlands
K783DAO	20783	West Scotland	KN54XYU	47126	Eastern	KX03KYS	47029	Eastern
K784DAO	20784	North West	KN54XYV	47127	Eastern	KX03KYT	47030	Eastern
K785DAO	20785	East Midlands	KN54XYW	47128	Eastern	KX03KYU	47031	Eastern
K786DAO	20786	North West	KN54XYX	47129	Eastern	KX03KYV	47032	Eastern
K787DAO	20787	North West	KN54ZXK	18195	South Midlands	KX03KYW	47033	Eastern
K788DAO	20788	North West	KN54ZXL	18196	South Midlands	KX03KYY	47034	Eastern
K789DAO	20659	South East	KN54ZXM	18197	South Midlands	KX03KYZ	47035	Eastern
K790DAO	20660	South East	KN54ZXO	18198	South Midlands	KX03KZA	47036	Eastern
K791DAO	20661	East Midlands	KN54ZXP	18199	South Midlands	KX03KZB	47037	Eastern
K801OMW	41801	East Scotland	KP04GJA	50111	South Midlands	KX03KZC	47038	Eastern
K802OMW	41802	East Scotland	KP04GJC	50112	South Midlands	KX03KZD	47039	Eastern
K821TKP	14821	South East	KP04GJE	50101	South Midlands	KX04GZL	34591	Eastern
K822TKP	14822	South East	KP04GJF	50102	South Midlands	KX04GZM	34592	Eastern
K823TKP	14823	South East	KP04GJG	50103	South Midlands	KX04GZN	34593	Eastern
K824TKP	14824	South East	KP04GJJ	50104	South Midlands	KX04GZR	34594	Eastern
K825TKP	14825	South East	KP04GJK	50105	South Midlands	KX04GZS	34595	Eastern
K846LMK	15346	Manchester	KP04GJU	50106	South Midlands	KX04RBV	47042	Eastern
K847LMK	15347	Manchester	KP04GJV	50107	South Midlands	KX04RBY	47043	Eastern
K848LMK	15348	Manchester	KP04GJX	50108	South Midlands	KX04RBZ	47044	Eastern
K849LMK	15349	South East	KP04GJY	50109	South Midlands	KX04RCF	47045	Eastern
K850LMK	15350	South East	KP04GJZ	50110	South Midlands	KX04RCU	47046	Eastern
K851LMK	15351	Manchester	KP04GKD	50113	South Midlands	KX04RCV	15401	Eastern
K852LMK	15352	Manchester	KP04GKE	50114	South Midlands	KX04RCY	15402	Eastern
K853LMK	15353	Manchester	KP04GKF	50115	South Midlands	KX04RCZ	15403	Eastern
K854LMK	15354	Manchester	KP04GKG	50116	South Midlands	KX04RDU	15404	Eastern
K855LMK	15355	Manchester	KP04GKJ	50117	South Midlands	KX04RDV	15405	Eastern
K856LMK	15356	Manchester	KP04GKK	50118	South Midlands	KX04RDY	18101	Eastern
K857LMK	15357	South East	KP04GKL	50119	South Midlands	KX04RDZ	18102	Eastern
K858LMK	15358	Manchester	KP04GKN	50120	South Midlands	KX04REU	18103	Eastern
K859LMK	15359	Manchester	KP04HVR	47050	Eastern	KX04RFE	18104	Eastern
K860LMK	15360	Manchester	KS03HNC	48203	Eastern	KX04RFF	18105	Eastern
K861LMK	15361	Manchester	KSU461	52644	East Midlands	KX04RUW	34585	Eastern
K862LMK	15362	Manchester	KSU462	52645	South Midlands	KX04RUY	34586	Eastern
K863LMK	15363	Manchester	KV53EYU	34419	Eastern	KX04RVA	34587	Eastern
K864LMK	15364	South East	KV53EYW	34420	Eastern	KX04RVC	34588	Eastern
K865LMK	15365	Manchester	KV53EYX	34421	Eastern	KX04RVE	34589	Eastern
K866LMK	15366	South East	KV53EYY	34422	Eastern	KX04RVF	18106	Eastern
K867LMK	15367	South East	KV53EYZ	34423	Eastern	KX04RVJ	18107	Eastern
K868LMK	15368	Manchester	KV53EZA	34424	Eastern	KX04RVK	18108	Eastern
K869LMK	15369	South East	KV53EZB	34425	Eastern	KX04RVL	18109	Eastern
K870LMK	15370	Manchester	KV53EZC	34426	Eastern	KX04RVM	18110	Eastern
K871LMK	15371	Manchester	KV53EZD	34427	Eastern	KX04RVN	18111	Eastern
K873GHH	40036	East Scotland	KV53EZE	34428	Eastern	KX04RVP	34590	Eastern
K875GHH	40038	East Scotland	KV53EZF	34429	Eastern	KX51CRU	47001	South Midlands
K876GHH	40039	North West	KV53EZG	34430	Eastern	KX51CRV	47002	South Midlands
K877GHH	40040	North West	KV53EZH	34431	Eastern	KX51CRZ	47003	South Midlands
K878GHH	40081	North West	KV53EZJ	34432	Eastern	KX51CSF	47004	South Midlands
K921OWV	32221	South East	KV53EZK	34433	Eastern	KX51CSO	47005	South Midlands

Reg	No	Area	Reg	No	Area	Reg	No	Area
KX51CSU	47006	South Midlands	L203YAG	27203	North West	L347KCK	20447	South East
KX51CSV	47007	South Midlands	L204YAG	27204	North West	L362JBD	40362	East Scotland
KX51CSY	47008	South Midlands	L205YAG	27205	North West	L365JBD	40365	East Scotland
KX51CSZ	47009	South Midlands	L206YAG	27206	North West	L366JBD	40366	East Scotland
KX51CTE	47010	South Midlands	L207YAG	27207	North West	L371JBD	40371	Eastern
KX51CTF	47011	South Midlands	L208PSB	32382	West Scotland	L373JBD	40373	Eastern
KX51CTK	47012	South Midlands	L208YAG	27208	North West	L374JBD	40374	Eastern
KX51CTO	47013	South Midlands	L209YAG	27209	North West	L375JBD	40375	Eastern
KX51CTU	47014	South Midlands	L210YAG	27210	North West	L376JBD	40376	Eastern
KX51CTV	47015	South Midlands	L211YAG	27211	North West	L377JBD	40377	Eastern
KX53VNB	18051	South Midlands	L241CCK	30241	North West	L378JBD	40378	Eastern
KX53VNC	18052	South Midlands	L241SDY	16241	South East	L379JBD	40379	Eastern
KX53VND	18053	South Midlands	L242SDY	16242	South East	L380JBD	40380	Eastern
KX53VNE	18054	South Midlands	L243SDY	16243	Eastern	L381JBD	40381	Eastern
KX53VNF	18055	South Midlands	L244SDY	16244	Eastern	L382JBD	40382	Eastern
KX53VNG	18056	South Midlands	L245SDY	16245	Eastern	L383JBD	40383	Eastern
KX53VNH	22052	South Midlands	L246SDY	16246	South East	L392LNA	15198	Manchester
KX53VNJ	22053	South Midlands	L247SDY	16247	South East	L414SFL	32960	South Wales
KX53VNK	22054	South Midlands	L248SDY	16248	East Scotland	L423MVV	30429	East Scotland
KX53VNL	34499	South Midlands	L249SDY	16249	East Scotland	L424MVV	30430	East Scotland
KX54DPA	34626	South Midlands	L250SDY	16250	East Scotland	L424TJK	20604	South East
KX54DPB	34627	South Midlands	L267CCK	30267	East Scotland	L425MVV	30431	East Scotland
KX54DPC	34628	South Midlands	L268CCK	30268	East Scotland	L425TJK	20605	South East
KX54HJK	34625	South Midlands	L270EHB	32988	South Wales	L426MVV	30426	East Scotland
KYV311X	10311	North West	L270LHH	30270	North West	L426TJK	20606	South East
KYV334X	10334	North West	L271LHH	30271	North West	L427MVV	30427	East Scotland
KYV340X	10340	North West	L272LHH	30272	North West	L427TJK	20607	South East
KYV348X	10348	South East	L273LHH	30273	North West	L428MVV	30428	East Scotland
KYV410X	10410	West Scotland	L274LHH	30274	North West	L578HSG	52178	West Scotland
KYV462X	10462	West Scotland	L275JAO	30275	North West	L579HSG	52179	Eastern
KYV469X	10469	West Scotland	L276JAO	30276	North West	L579JSA	52169	East Scotland
KYV473X	10473	West Scotland	L277JAO	30277	North West	L580HSG	52180	South Wales
KYV492X	10492	South Wales	L278JAO	30278	North West	L580JSA	52170	East Scotland
KYV512X	10512	North West	L281JAO	30281	North West	L581HSG	52181	South Wales
KYV542X	10542	South Wales	L282JAO	30282	North West	L581JSA	52171	East Scotland
L26JSA	16198	East Scotland	L283JAO	30283	North West	L582HSG	52182	South Wales
L27JSA	16199	East Scotland	L301JSA	40101	West Scotland	L582JSA	52172	Eastern
L28JSA	16200	East Scotland	L301PSC	20301	East Scotland	L583HSG	52183	East Scotland
L31HHN	21031	North East	L302JSA	40102	East Scotland	L584HSG	52184	East Scotland
L32HHN	21032	North East	L302PSC	20302	East Scotland	L584JSA	52174	East Scotland
L33HHN	21033	North East	L303JSA	40103	East Scotland	L585HSG	52185	East Scotland
L34HHN	21034	North East	L303PSC	20303	East Scotland	L585JSA	52175	East Scotland
L35HHN	21035	North East	L304PSC	20304	East Scotland	L586HSG	52186	South Wales
L36HHN	21036	North East	L305PSC	20305	East Scotland	L586JSA	52176	East Scotland
L37HHN	21037	North East	L306PSC	20306	East Scotland	L587HSG	52187	East Scotland
L51CNY	52152	South Wales	L307PSC	20307	East Scotland	L587JSA	52177	East Scotland
L81YBB	52193	East Scotland	L308PSC	20308	West Scotland	L588HSG	52188	East Scotland
L83CWO	32983	South Wales	L308YDU	40108	South Midlands	L588JSA	52168	East Scotland
L84CWO	32984	South Wales	L309PSC	20309	East Scotland	L589HSG	52189	Eastern
L85CWO	32985	South Wales	L310PSC	20310	East Scotland	L590HSG	52190	Eastern
L86CWO	32986	South Wales	L310YDU	40110	South Midlands	L601VCD	20601	South East
L89CWO	32989	South Wales	L315JSA	40585	East Scotland	L602VCD	20602	South East
L100JLB	16610	East Scotland	L316JSA	40586	East Scotland	L603VCD	20603	South East
L101JSA	16201	East Scotland	L317YDU	40117	South East	L608TDY	20608	South East
L102JSA	16202	East Scotland	L320YDU	40120	South East	L609TDY	20609	South East
L108LHL	16478	East Midlands	L323YDU	40123	South East	L616TDY	20616	Devon
L109LHL	16479	East Midlands	L325YDU	40125	South East	L617TDY	20617	South East
L119DRN	40419	East Scotland	L330CHB	41330	West	L618TDY	20618	South East
L127DRN	40427	North West	L330YKV	40130	South East	L619TDY	20619	South East
L127NAO	52197	South East	L334FWO	40534	East Scotland	L620TDY	20620	South East
L137VRH	32137	West Scotland	L335FWO	40535	East Scotland	L621TDY	20621	Devon
L138VRH	32138	West Scotland	L336FWO	40536	East Scotland	L622TDY	20622	South East
L139VRH	32139	Devon	L337FWO	40537	South Wales	L623TDY	20623	South East
L140VRH	32140	Devon	L338FWO	40538	East Scotland	L624TDY	20624	South East
L141VRH	32141	Devon	L338KCK	20438	South East	L625TDY	20625	South East
L145VRH	32145	West Scotland	L339FWO	40539	South Wales	L626TDY	20626	South East
L155JNH	52155	Eastern	L339KCK	20439	East Midlands	L627TDY	20627	South East
L156JNH	52156	Eastern	L340FWO	40540	East Scotland	L628TDY	20628	South East
L156LBW	52021	Eastern	L340KCK	20440	East Midlands	L629TDY	20629	South East
L157JNH	52157	West	L341FWO	40541	South Wales	L630TDY	20630	Devon
L158JNH	52158	West	L341KCK	20441	East Midlands	L631TDY	20631	South East
L159JNH	52159	South East	L342FWO	40542	East Scotland	L632TDY	20632	South East
L159LBW	52024	Eastern	L342KCK	20442	East Midlands	L633TDY	20633	South East
L160JNH	52160	Eastern	L343FWO	40543	South Wales	L634BFV	40834	North West
L161JNH	52161	Eastern	L343KCK	20443	East Midlands	L634TDY	20634	South East
L162JNH	52162	Eastern	L344KCK	20444	East Midlands	L635TDY	20635	South East
L201YAG	27201	North West	L345KCK	20445	South East	L637LDT	52207	East Midlands
L202YAG	27202	North West	L346KCK	20446	South East	L638LDT	52208	West Scotland

Reg	No	Region	Reg	No	Region	Reg	No	Region
L639LDT	52209	East Midlands	L742VNL	32742	North East	LV52HGK	34372	London
L640LDT	52210	East Midlands	L743VNL	32743	North East	LV52HGL	34373	London
L641LDT	52211	East Midlands	L744VNL	32744	North East	LV52HGM	34374	London
L642LDT	52212	East Midlands	L745VNL	32745	North East	LV52HGN	34375	London
L643LDT	52213	East Midlands	L746VNL	32746	North East	LV52HGO	34376	London
L651HKS	30651	East Scotland	L748VNL	32748	North East	LV52HHA	17592	London
L652HKS	30652	East Scotland	L749VNL	32749	North East	LV52HHB	17593	London
L653HKS	30653	East Scotland	L750VNL	32750	North East	LV52HHC	17594	London
L655HKS	30655	East Scotland	L751VNL	32751	North East	LV52HHD	17595	London
L656HKS	30656	East Scotland	L752VNL	32752	North East	LV52HHE	17596	London
L657HKS	30657	East Scotland	L753VNL	32753	North East	LV52HHF	17597	London
L658HKS	30658	East Scotland	L757VNL	32757	Eastern	LV52HHG	17598	London
L659HKS	30659	East Scotland	L758VNL	32758	Eastern	LV52HHJ	17599	London
L665MSF	30665	North West	L759VNL	32759	North East	LV52HHK	17600	London
L668MSF	30668	North West	L760ARG	32760	North East	LV52HHL	17601	London
L671HNV	16671	Eastern	L761ARG	32761	North East	LV52HHM	17602	London
L672HNV	16672	Eastern	L762ARG	32762	North East	LV52HHN	17603	London
L673HNV	16673	Eastern	L763ARG	32763	North East	LV52HHO	17604	London
L674HNV	16674	Eastern	L764ARG	32764	North East	LV52HHP	17605	London
L675HNV	16675	Eastern	L765ARG	32765	North East	LV52HHR	17606	London
L676HNV	16676	Eastern	L803XDG	41803	West	LV52HHS	17607	London
L677HNV	16677	Eastern	L804XDG	41804	West	LV52HHT	17608	London
L678HNV	16678	Eastern	L805XDG	41805	West	LV52HHU	17609	London
L679HNV	16679	Eastern	L806XDG	41806	West	LV52HHW	17610	London
L680HNV	16680	Eastern	L826BKK	14826	South East	LV52HHX	17611	London
L681HNV	16681	Eastern	L827BKK	14827	South East	LV52HHY	17731	London
L682HNV	16682	Eastern	L828BKK	14828	South East	LV52HHZ	17732	London
L683HNV	16683	Eastern	L829BKK	14829	South East	LV52HJA	17733	London
L684HNV	16684	Eastern	L830BKK	14830	South East	LV52HJY	34347	London
L685CDD	40685	Devon	L831CDG	30831	West	LV52HJZ	34348	London
L685JBD	16685	Eastern	L832CDG	30832	West	LV52HKA	34349	London
L689CDD	40689	East Scotland	L882SDY	40882	North West	LV52HKB	34350	London
L691CDD	40691	Devon	L883SDY	40883	North West	LV52HKC	34351	London
L692CDD	40692	Devon	L885SDY	40885	North West	LV52HKD	34352	London
L693CDD	40693	Devon	L886SDY	40886	North West	LV52HKE	34353	London
L694CDD	40694	Devon	L942RJN	27212	North West	LV52HKF	34354	London
L695CDD	40695	Devon	LCU112	19912	North East	LV52HKG	34355	London
L696CDD	40696	Devon	LDS201A	12107	East Scotland	LV52HKH	34356	London
L705FWO	30705	South Wales	LJY145	52195	East Midlands	LV52HKJ	34357	London
L705HFU	27705	East Midlands	LK51FPJ	34300	London	LV52HKK	34358	London
L706FWO	30706	South Wales	LRV992	19992	Devon	LV52HKL	34359	London
L706HFU	27706	East Midlands	LSK545	52029	East Scotland	LV52HKM	34360	London
L707HFU	27707	East Midlands	LV52HDO	17562	London	LV52HKN	34361	London
L708HFU	27708	East Midlands	LV52HDU	17563	London	LV52HKO	34362	London
L709FWO	30709	West	LV52HDX	17564	London	LV52HKP	34363	London
L709HFU	27709	East Midlands	LV52HDY	17565	London	LV52HKT	34364	London
L711FWO	30711	West	LV52HDZ	17566	London	LV52HKU	34365	London
L712FWO	30712	West	LV52HEJ	17567	London	LV52USF	17561	London
L714JUD	32014	Devon	LV52HEU	17568	London	LV52VFW	23001	London
L715JUD	32015	Devon	LV52HFA	17569	London	LV52VFX	23002	London
L716JUD	32016	Devon	LV52HFB	17570	London	LV52VFY	23003	London
L717JUD	32017	Devon	LV52HFC	17571	London	LV52VFZ	23004	London
L718JUD	32018	Devon	LV52HFD	17572	London	LV52VGA	23005	London
L719JUD	32019	Devon	LV52HFE	17573	London	LWS34Y	14286	West
L720JUD	32020	Devon	LV52HFF	17574	London	LWS35Y	14287	West
L721JUD	32021	Devon	LV52HFH	17575	London	LWS36Y	14288	West
L722JUD	32022	Devon	LV52HFJ	17576	London	LWS37Y	14289	West
L729VNL	32729	North East	LV52HFK	17577	London	LWS39Y	14291	West
L730VNL	32730	North East	LV52HFL	17578	London	LWS40Y	14292	West
L731LWA	40777	East Midlands	LV52HFM	17579	London	LWS41Y	14293	West
L731VNL	32731	North East	LV52HFN	17580	London	LX03BTE	17750	London
L732LWA	40778	East Midlands	LV52HFO	17581	London	LX03BTF	17751	London
L732VNL	32732	North East	LV52HFP	17582	London	LX03BTU	17752	London
L733LWA	40779	East Midlands	LV52HFR	17583	London	LX03BTV	17753	London
L733VNL	32733	North East	LV52HFS	17584	London	LX03BTY	17754	London
L734LWA	40780	East Midlands	LV52HFT	17585	London	LX03BTZ	17755	London
L734VNL	32734	North East	LV52HFU	17586	London	LX03BUA	17756	London
L735LWA	40781	East Midlands	LV52HFW	17587	London	LX03BUE	17757	London
L735VNL	32735	North East	LV52HFX	17588	London	LX03BUF	17758	London
L736LWA	40736	East Midlands	LV52HFY	17589	London	LX03BUH	17759	London
L736VNL	32736	North East	LV52HFZ	17590	London	LX03BUJ	17760	London
L737VNL	32737	North East	LV52HGA	17591	London	LX03BUP	17761	London
L738VNL	32738	North East	LV52HGC	34366	London	LX03BUU	17762	London
L739LWA	40739	East Midlands	LV52HGD	34367	London	LX03BUV	17763	London
L739VNL	32739	North East	LV52HGE	34368	London	LX03BUW	17764	London
L740VNL	32740	North East	LV52HGF	34369	London	LX03BVA	17765	London
L741VNL	32741	North East	LV52HGG	34370	London	LX03BVB	17766	London
L742LWA	40742	East Midlands	LV52HGJ	34371	London	LX03BVC	17767	London

Reg	No	Loc	Reg	No	Loc	Reg	No	Loc
LX03BVD	17768	London	LX03BYZ	17846	London	LX03NFV	17873	London
LX03BVE	17769	London	LX03BZA	17847	London	LX03NFX	17874	London
LX03BVF	17770	London	LX03BZB	17848	London	LX03NFY	17875	London
LX03BVG	17771	London	LX03BZC	17849	London	LX03NGE	17876	London
LX03BVH	17772	London	LX03BZD	17850	London	LX03NGF	17877	London
LX03BVJ	17773	London	LX03BZE	17851	London	LX03NGJ	17878	London
LX03BVK	17774	London	LX03BZF	17852	London	LX03NGU	17880	London
LX03BVL	17775	London	LX03BZG	17853	London	LX03NGV	17881	London
LX03BVM	17776	London	LX03BZH	17854	London	LX03NGY	17882	London
LX03BVN	17777	London	LX03BZJ	34377	London	LX03NGZ	17883	London
LX03BVP	17778	London	LX03BZK	34378	London	LX03NHA	17884	London
LX03BVR	17779	London	LX03BZL	34379	London	LX03OPT	17885	London
LX03BVS	17780	London	LX03BZM	34380	London	LX03OPU	17886	London
LX03BVT	17781	London	LX03BZN	34381	London	LX03OPV	17887	London
LX03BVU	17782	London	LX03BZP	34382	London	LX03OPW	17888	London
LX03BVV	17783	London	LX03BZR	34383	London	LX03OPY	17889	London
LX03BVW	17784	London	LX03BZS	34384	London	LX03OPZ	17890	London
LX03BVY	17785	London	LX03BZT	34385	London	LX03ORA	17891	London
LX03BVZ	17786	London	LX03BZU	34386	London	LX03ORC	17892	London
LX03BWA	17787	London	LX03BZV	34387	London	LX03ORF	17893	London
LX03BWB	17788	London	LX03BZW	34388	London	LX03ORG	17894	London
LX03BWC	17789	London	LX03BZY	34389	London	LX03ORH	17895	London
LX03BWD	17790	London	LX03CAA	34390	London	LX03ORJ	17896	London
LX03BWE	17791	London	LX03CAE	34391	London	LX03ORK	17897	London
LX03BWF	17792	London	LX03CAU	34392	London	LX03ORN	17898	London
LX03BWG	17793	London	LX03CAV	34393	London	LX03ORP	17899	London
LX03BWH	17794	London	LX03CBF	34394	London	LX03ORS	17900	London
LX03BWJ	17795	London	LX03CBU	34395	London	LX03ORT	17901	London
LX03BWK	17796	London	LX03CBV	34396	London	LX03ORU	17902	London
LX03BWL	17797	London	LX03CBY	34397	London	LX03ORV	17903	London
LX03BWM	17798	London	LX03HCE	23006	London	LX03ORW	17904	London
LX03BWN	17799	London	LX03HCF	23007	London	LX03ORY	17905	London
LX03BWP	17800	London	LX03HCG	23008	London	LX03ORZ	17906	London
LX03BWU	17801	London	LX03HCH	23009	London	LX03OSA	17907	London
LX03BWV	17802	London	LX03HCJ	23010	London	LX03OSB	17908	London
LX03BWW	17803	London	LX03HCK	23011	London	LX03OSC	17909	London
LX03BWY	17804	London	LX03HCL	23012	London	LX03OSD	17910	London
LX03BWZ	17805	London	LX03HCN	23013	London	LX03OSE	17911	London
LX03BXA	17806	London	LX03HCP	23014	London	LX03OSG	17912	London
LX03BXB	17807	London	LX03HCU	23015	London	LX03OSJ	17913	London
LX03BXC	17808	London	LX03HCV	23016	London	LX03OSK	17914	London
LX03BXD	17809	London	LX03HCY	23017	London	LX03OSL	17915	London
LX03BXE	17810	London	LX03HCZ	23018	London	LX03OSM	17916	London
LX03BXF	17811	London	LX03HDC	23019	London	LX03OSN	17917	London
LX03BXG	17812	London	LX03HDD	23020	London	LX03OSP	17918	London
LX03BXH	17813	London	LX03HDE	23021	London	LX03OSR	17919	London
LX03BXJ	17814	London	LX03HDF	23022	London	LX03OSU	17920	London
LX03BXK	17815	London	LX03HDG	23023	London	LX03OSV	17921	London
LX03BXL	17816	London	LX03HDH	23024	London	LX03OSW	17922	London
LX03BXM	17817	London	LX03HDJ	23025	London	LX03OSY	17923	London
LX03BXN	17818	London	LX03HDK	23026	London	LX03OSZ	17924	London
LX03BXP	17819	London	LX03HDL	23027	London	LX03OTA	17925	London
LX03BXR	17820	London	LX03HDN	23028	London	LX03OTB	17926	London
LX03BXS	17821	London	LX03HDU	23029	London	LX03OTC	17927	London
LX03BXU	17822	London	LX03HDV	23030	London	LX03OTD	17928	London
LX03BXV	17823	London	LX03HDY	23031	London	LX03OTE	17929	London
LX03BXW	17824	London	LX03HDZ	23032	London	LX03OTF	17930	London
LX03BXY	17825	London	LX03HEJ	23033	London	LX03OTG	17931	London
LX03BXZ	17826	London	LX03HEU	23034	London	LX03OTH	17932	London
LX03BYA	17827	London	LX03HEV	23035	London	LX03OTJ	17933	London
LX03BYB	17828	London	LX03NEU	17855	London	LX04FWL	18201	London
LX03BYC	17829	London	LX03NEY	17856	London	LX04FWM	18202	London
LX03BYD	17830	London	LX03NFA	17857	London	LX04FWN	18203	London
LX03BYF	17831	London	LX03NFC	17858	London	LX04FWP	18204	London
LX03BYG	17832	London	LX03NFD	17859	London	LX04FWR	18205	London
LX03BYH	17833	London	LX03NFE	17860	London	LX04FWS	18206	London
LX03BYJ	17834	London	LX03NFF	17861	London	LX04FWT	18207	London
LX03BYL	17835	London	LX03NFG	17862	London	LX04FWU	18208	London
LX03BYM	17836	London	LX03NFH	17863	London	LX04FWV	18209	London
LX03BYN	17837	London	LX03NFJ	17864	London	LX04FWW	18210	London
LX03BYP	17838	London	LX03NFK	17865	London	LX04FWY	18211	London
LX03BYR	17839	London	LX03NFL	17866	London	LX04FWZ	18212	London
LX03BYS	17840	London	LX03NFM	17867	London	LX04FXA	18213	London
LX03BYT	17841	London	LX03NFN	17868	London	LX04FXB	18214	London
LX03BYU	17842	London	LX03NFP	17869	London	LX04FXC	18215	London
LX03BYV	17843	London	LX03NFR	17870	London	LX04FXD	18216	London
LX03BYW	17844	London	LX03NFT	17871	London	LX04FXE	18217	London
LX03BYY	17845	London	LX03NFU	17872	London	LX04FXF	18218	London

LX04FXG	18219	London	LX04LCF	23067	London	LX51FLC	17466	London
LX04FXH	18220	London	LX04LCG	23068	London	LX51FLD	17467	London
LX04FXJ	18221	London	LX04LCJ	23069	London	LX51FLE	17468	London
LX04FXK	18222	London	LX04LCK	23070	London	LX51FLF	17469	London
LX04FXL	18223	London	LX04LCM	23071	London	LX51FLG	17471	London
LX04FXM	18224	London	LX04LCN	23072	London	LX51FLH	17472	London
LX04FXP	18225	London	LX04LCP	23073	London	LX51FLJ	17473	London
LX04FXR	18226	London	LX04LCT	23074	London	LX51FLK	17474	London
LX04FXS	18227	London	LX04LCU	23075	London	LX51FLL	17475	London
LX04FXT	18228	London	LX04LCV	23076	London	LX51FLM	17476	London
LX04FXU	18229	London	LX04LCW	23077	London	LX51FLN	17477	London
LX04FXV	18230	London	LX43JYF	17943	London	LX51FLP	17478	London
LX04FXW	18231	London	LX43JYK	17947	London	LX51FLR	17479	London
LX04FXY	18232	London	LX51FFO	34341	London	LX51FLV	17480	London
LX04FXZ	18233	London	LX51FFW	34290	London	LX51FLW	17481	London
LX04FYA	18234	London	LX51FGA	34303	London	LX51FLZ	17482	London
LX04FYB	18235	London	LX51FGD	34306	London	LX51FMA	17483	London
LX04FYC	18236	London	LX51FGE	34305	London	LX51FMC	17484	London
LX04FYD	18237	London	LX51FGF	34304	London	LX51FMD	17485	London
LX04FYE	18238	London	LX51FGG	34307	London	LX51FME	17486	London
LX04FYF	18239	London	LX51FGJ	34311	London	LX51FMF	17487	London
LX04FYG	18240	London	LX51FGK	34309	London	LX51FMG	17488	London
LX04FYH	18241	London	LX51FGM	34308	London	LX51FMJ	17489	London
LX04FYJ	18242	London	LX51FGN	34312	London	LX51FMK	17490	London
LX04FYK	18243	London	LX51FGO	34313	London	LX51FML	17491	London
LX04FYL	18244	London	LX51FGP	34314	London	LX51FMM	17492	London
LX04FYM	18245	London	LX51FGU	34315	London	LX51FMO	17493	London
LX04FYN	18246	London	LX51FGV	34310	London	LX51FMP	17494	London
LX04FYP	18247	London	LX51FGZ	34316	London	LX51FMU	17495	London
LX04FYR	18248	London	LX51FHA	34319	London	LX51FMV	17496	London
LX04FYS	18249	London	LX51FHB	34318	London	LX51FMY	17497	London
LX04FYT	18250	London	LX51FHC	34320	London	LX51FMZ	17498	London
LX04FYU	18251	London	LX51FHD	34321	London	LX51FNA	17499	London
LX04FYV	18252	London	LX51FHE	34322	London	LX51FNC	17500	London
LX04FYW	18253	London	LX51FHF	34323	London	LX51FND	17501	London
LX04FYY	18254	London	LX51FHG	34317	London	LX51FNE	17502	London
LX04FYZ	18255	London	LX51FHH	34326	London	LX51FNF	17503	London
LX04FZA	18256	London	LX51FHJ	34327	London	LX51FNG	17504	London
LX04FZB	18257	London	LX51FHK	34324	London	LX51FNH	17505	London
LX04FZC	18258	London	LX51FHL	34325	London	LX51FNJ	17506	London
LX04FZD	18259	London	LX51FHN	17394	London	LX51FNK	17507	London
LX04FZE	18260	London	LX51FHO	17396	London	LX51FNL	17508	London
LX04FZF	18261	London	LX51FHP	17399	London	LX51FNM	17509	London
LX04FZG	18262	London	LX51FHS	17403	London	LX51FNN	17510	London
LX04FZH	18263	London	LX51FHT	17405	London	LX51FNO	17511	London
LX04FZJ	18264	London	LX51FHU	17408	London	LX51FNP	17512	London
LX04FZK	18265	London	LX51FHV	17410	London	LX51FNR	17513	London
LX04GCU	17999	London	LX51FHW	17411	London	LX51FNS	17514	London
LX04KZG	23036	London	LX51FHY	17412	London	LX51FNT	17515	London
LX04KZJ	23037	London	LX51FHZ	17413	London	LX51FNU	17516	London
LX04KZK	23038	London	LX51FJA	17414	London	LX51FNV	17517	London
LX04KZL	23039	London	LX51FJC	17415	London	LX51FNW	17518	London
LX04KZM	23040	London	LX51FJD	17416	London	LX51FNY	17519	London
LX04KZN	23041	London	LX51FJE	17417	London	LX51FNZ	17520	London
LX04KZP	23042	London	LX51FJF	17418	London	LX51FOA	17521	London
LX04KZR	23043	London	LX51FJJ	17419	London	LX51FOC	17522	London
LX04KZS	23044	London	LX51FJK	17420	London	LX51FOD	17523	London
LX04KZT	23045	London	LX51FJN	17421	London	LX51FOF	17524	London
LX04KZV	23047	London	LX51FJO	17422	London	LX51FOH	17525	London
LX04KZW	23048	London	LX51FJP	17423	London	LX51FOJ	17526	London
LX04KZY	23049	London	LX51FJV	17424	London	LX51FOK	17527	London
LX04KZZ	23050	London	LX51FJY	17426	London	LX51FOM	17528	London
LX04LBA	23051	London	LX51FJZ	17425	London	LX51FON	17529	London
LX04LBE	23052	London	LX51FKA	17427	London	LX51FOP	17530	London
LX04LBF	23053	London	LX51FKB	17428	London	LX51FOT	17531	London
LX04LBG	23054	London	LX51FKD	17430	London	LX51FOU	17532	London
LX04LBJ	23055	London	LX51FKE	17431	London	LX51FOV	17533	London
LX04LBK	23056	London	LX51FKF	17432	London	LX51FPA	17534	London
LX04LBL	23057	London	LX51FKG	17433	London	LX51FPC	17387	London
LX04LBN	23058	London	LX51FKJ	17435	London	LX51FPD	17390	London
LX04LBP	23059	London	LX51FKL	17439	London	LX51FPE	34278	London
LX04LBU	23060	London	LX51FKO	17444	London	LX51FPF	17383	London
LX04LBV	23061	London	LX51FKR	17451	London	LX53JXU	17934	London
LX04LBY	23062	London	LX51FKT	17457	London	LX53JXV	17935	London
LX04LBZ	23063	London	LX51FKU	17459	London	LX53JXW	17936	London
LX04LCA	23064	London	LX51FKW	17461	London	LX53JXY	17937	London
LX04LCC	23065	London	LX51FKZ	17463	London	LX53JYA	17938	London
LX04LCE	23066	London	LX51FLB	17465	London	LX53JYB	17939	London

Reg	Fleet	Area	Reg	Fleet	Area	Reg	Fleet	Area
LX53JYC	17940	London	LY02OAU	17545	London	M151FGB	21051	West Scotland
LX53JYD	17941	London	LY02OAV	17546	London	M160CCD	52260	East Scotland
LX53JYE	17942	London	LY02OAW	17547	London	M161CCD	52261	West Scotland
LX53JYG	17944	London	LY02OAX	17548	London	M162CCD	52262	West Scotland
LX53JYH	17945	London	LY02OAZ	17549	London	M163CCD	52263	West Scotland
LX53JYJ	17946	London	LY02OBB	17550	London	M164CCD	52264	West Scotland
LX53JYL	17948	London	LY02OBC	17551	London	M165CCD	52265	West
LX53JYN	17949	London	LY02OBD	17552	London	M166CCD	52266	North West
LX53JYO	17950	London	LY02OBE	17553	London	M180XHW	59101	South Wales
LX53JYP	17951	London	LY02OBF	17554	London	M182XHW	59102	South Wales
LX53JYR	17952	London	LY02OBG	17555	London	M201DRG	27301	East Midlands
LX53JYT	17953	London	LY02OBH	17556	London	M201LHP	20201	South Midlands
LX53JYU	17954	London	LY02OBJ	17557	London	M202DRG	27302	East Midlands
LX53JYV	17955	London	LY02OBK	17558	London	M202LHP	20202	South Midlands
LX53JYW	17956	London	LY02OBL	17559	London	M203DRG	27303	East Midlands
LX53JYY	17957	London	LY02OBM	17560	London	M203LHP	20203	South Midlands
LX53JYZ	17958	London	LY52ZDX	17740	London	M204DRG	27304	East Midlands
LX53JZA	17959	London	LY52ZDZ	17741	London	M204LHP	20204	South Midlands
LX53JZC	17960	London	LY52ZFA	17742	London	M205LHP	20205	South Midlands
LX53JZD	17961	London	LY52ZFB	17743	London	M209LHP	20209	South Midlands
LX53JZE	17962	London	LY52ZFC	17744	London	M210LHP	20210	South Midlands
LX53JZF	17963	London	LY52ZFD	17745	London	M223SVN	16823	East Midlands
LX53JZG	17964	London	LY52ZFE	17746	London	M224SVN	16824	East Midlands
LX53JZH	17965	London	LY52ZFF	17747	London	M225SVN	16825	East Midlands
LX53JZJ	17966	London	LY52ZFG	17748	London	M226SVN	16826	East Midlands
LX53JZK	17967	London	LY52ZFH	17749	London	M226UTM	40226	Devon
LX53JZL	17968	London	M38PVN	21038	North East	M227SVN	16827	East Midlands
LX53JZM	17969	London	M39PVN	21039	North East	M227UTM	40227	Devon
LX53JZN	17970	London	M40PVN	21040	North East	M228UTM	40228	Devon
LX53JZO	17971	London	M41PVN	21041	North East	M229UTM	40229	Devon
LX53JZP	17972	London	M42PVN	21042	North East	M230TBV	20430	North West
LX53JZR	17973	London	M59VJO	32066	East Midlands	M230UTM	40230	Devon
LX53JZT	17974	London	M61VJO	32041	South East	M232UTM	40232	Devon
LX53JZU	17975	London	M62VJO	32070	South East	M234UTM	40234	Devon
LX53JZV	17976	London	M63VJO	32077	South East	M235TBV	20435	North West
LX53JZW	17977	London	M64HHB	32964	South Wales	M236TBV	20436	North West
LX53KAE	17978	London	M64VJO	32080	East Midlands	M236UTM	40236	Devon
LX53KAJ	17979	London	M65HHB	32965	South Wales	M237UTM	40237	Devon
LX53KAK	17980	London	M65VJO	32065	South East	M239UTM	40239	Devon
LX53KAO	17981	London	M67HHB	32967	South Wales	M240UTM	40240	Devon
LX53KAU	17982	London	M67VJO	32067	East Midlands	M241UTM	40241	Devon
LX53KBE	17983	London	M68HHB	32968	South Wales	M242UTM	40242	Devon
LX53KBF	17984	London	M68VJO	32068	East Midlands	M243UTM	40243	Devon
LX53KBJ	17985	London	M69HHB	32969	West	M244UTM	40244	Devon
LX53KBK	17986	London	M69VJO	32069	East Midlands	M245UTM	40245	Devon
LX53KBN	17987	London	M71VJO	32071	East Midlands	M246UTM	40246	Devon
LX53KBO	17988	London	M73HHB	30723	West	M247UTM	40247	Devon
LX53KBP	17989	London	M73VJO	32073	East Midlands	M248UTM	40248	Devon
LX53KBV	17990	London	M74HHB	30724	North West	M249UTM	40249	Devon
LX53KBW	17991	London	M74VJO	32074	South East	M250UTM	40250	Devon
LX53KBZ	17992	London	M75VJO	32075	South East	M301DGP	16401	East Scotland
LX53KCA	17993	London	M76HHB	30726	North West	M302DGP	16402	East Scotland
LX53KCC	17994	London	M76VJO	32076	South East	M303DGP	16403	East Scotland
LX53KCE	17995	London	M78VJO	32078	South Wales	M304DGP	16404	East Scotland
LX53KCF	17996	London	M79VJO	32079	Devon	M305DGP	16405	East Scotland
LX53KCG	17997	London	M84WBW	32084	Devon	M306DGP	16406	East Scotland
LX53KCJ	17998	London	M85DEW	32936	West	M307DGP	16407	East Scotland
LX53LGF	34551	London	M85WBW	32085	West	M308DGP	16408	East Scotland
LX53LGG	34552	London	M86DEW	32937	West	M309DGP	16409	East Scotland
LX53LGJ	34553	London	M86WBW	32086	West	M310DGP	16410	East Scotland
LX53LGK	34554	London	M87WBW	32087	East Midlands	M311DGP	16411	West
LX53LGL	34555	London	M89WBW	32089	East Midlands	M311YSC	20311	South East
LX53LGN	34556	London	M91WBW	32091	South East	M312DGP	16412	East Scotland
LX53LGO	34557	London	M92JHB	40595	South Wales	M312YSC	20312	South East
LX53LGU	34558	London	M92WBW	32092	South East	M313DGP	16413	East Scotland
LX53LGV	34559	London	M93WBW	32093	South East	M313YSC	20313	South East
LX53LGW	34560	London	M94WBW	32094	South East	M314DGP	16414	East Scotland
LXO4KZU	23046	London	M95WBW	32095	South East	M314PKS	20314	East Scotland
LY02OAA	17535	London	M96WBW	32096	South East	M315DGP	16415	East Scotland
LY02OAB	17536	London	M97WBW	32097	South East	M315PKS	20315	East Scotland
LY02OAC	17537	London	M98WBW	32098	South East	M316DGP	16416	East Scotland
LY02OAD	17538	London	M100AAB	28955	West Scotland	M317DGP	16417	East Scotland
LY02OAE	17539	London	M101WBW	32088	South East	M317RSO	40587	East Scotland
LY02OAG	17540	London	M102WBW	32090	South East	M318DGP	16418	East Scotland
LY02OAN	17541	London	M103WBW	32099	Devon	M318RSO	40588	East Scotland
LY02OAO	17542	London	M103XBW	52026	West Scotland	M319DGP	16419	East Scotland
LY02OAP	17543	London	M134SKY	52015	South Wales	M319RSO	40589	East Scotland
LY02OAS	17544	London	M135SKY	52016	South Wales	M320DGP	16420	East Scotland

Reg	Fleet	Region	Reg	Fleet	Region	Reg	Fleet	Region
M320RSO	40590	East Scotland	M409SPY	20299	North East	M545SPY	20245	North East
M321KRY	52025	South Wales	M410BFG	52220	South Wales	M546SPY	20246	North East
M321RSO	40591	East Scotland	M410SPY	20300	North East	M547SPY	20247	North East
M331LHP	40131	South East	M411RRN	20411	East Midlands	M548SPY	20248	North East
M332DRP	40332	Eastern	M412RRN	20412	East Midlands	M549SPY	20249	North East
M332LHP	40132	South East	M413RRN	20413	East Midlands	M550MTG	23950	South Wales
M334DRP	40334	Eastern	M414RRN	20414	East Midlands	M550SPY	20250	North East
M334LHP	40134	East Scotland	M415MBW	32415	East Midlands	M551MTG	23951	South Wales
M335DRP	40335	Eastern	M416MBW	32416	East Midlands	M551SPY	20251	North East
M335LHP	40135	East Scotland	M417MBW	32417	East Midlands	M552SPY	20252	North East
M336DRP	40336	Eastern	M418MBW	32418	East Midlands	M553FWV	30803	East Scotland
M336LHP	40136	East Scotland	M419MBW	32419	East Midlands	M562JTG	32966	South Wales
M337DRP	40337	Eastern	M420MBW	32420	East Midlands	M589OSO	20189	South East
M337LHP	40137	Eastern	M421MBW	32421	East Midlands	M590OSO	20190	South East
M338DRP	40338	Eastern	M422MBW	32422	East Midlands	M591OSO	20191	East Scotland
M338LHP	40138	East Scotland	M423MBW	32423	East Midlands	M592OSO	20192	East Scotland
M339DRP	40339	Eastern	M424MBW	32424	East Midlands	M593OSO	20193	East Scotland
M339LHP	40139	Eastern	M425MBW	32425	East Midlands	M594OSO	20194	East Scotland
M340DRP	40340	Eastern	M426MBW	32426	East Midlands	M595OSO	20195	East Scotland
M340LHP	40140	Eastern	M427MBW	32427	East Midlands	M596OSO	20196	East Scotland
M341DRP	40341	Eastern	M451VCW	20451	North West	M597OSO	20197	East Scotland
M341LHP	40141	East Scotland	M452VCW	20452	North West	M597SSB	32795	North East
M342DRP	40342	Eastern	M454VCW	20454	North West	M598OSO	20198	South East
M342LHP	40142	South Midlands	M454VHE	30454	North West	M601VHE	20491	East Midlands
M343DRP	40343	Eastern	M455VCW	20455	North West	M602VHE	20492	East Midlands
M343LHP	40143	South Midlands	M455VHE	30455	North West	M603VHE	20493	East Midlands
M344DRP	40344	Eastern	M456VCW	20456	North West	M604VHE	20494	East Midlands
M344JBO	40544	South Wales	M456VHE	30456	North West	M605VHE	20495	East Midlands
M344LHP	40144	South Wales	M457VCW	20457	North West	M606VHE	20496	East Midlands
M345DRP	40345	Eastern	M457VHE	30457	North West	M607VHE	20497	East Midlands
M345JBO	40545	Devon	M458VCW	20458	North West	M608WET	20498	East Midlands
M345LHP	40145	South Wales	M458VHE	30458	North West	M609WET	20499	East Midlands
M346DRP	40346	Eastern	M459VCW	20459	North West	M610APN	20610	South East
M346KWK	40146	South Midlands	M460VCW	20460	South East	M611APN	20611	South East
M347DRP	40347	Eastern	M460VHE	30460	North West	M612APN	20612	South East
M347JBO	40547	South Wales	M461VCW	20461	South East	M613APN	20613	South East
M348DRP	40348	Eastern	M461VHE	30461	North West	M614APN	20614	South East
M348JBO	40548	East Scotland	M462VCW	20462	South East	M615APN	20615	South East
M349DRP	40349	Eastern	M463VCW	20463	North West	M615XLG	41332	South Wales
M349JBO	40549	Devon	M466ASW	20583	West Scotland	M624HDV	46321	Devon
M350JBO	40550	Devon	M467ASW	20594	West Scotland	M625KKG	32970	West
M351JBO	40551	Devon	M468ASW	20512	West Scotland	M636BCD	20636	South East
M352JBO	40552	South Wales	M469ASW	20509	West Scotland	M637BCD	20637	South East
M353JBO	40553	Devon	M470ASW	20570	West Scotland	M638BCD	20638	South East
M354JBO	40554	Devon	M471ASW	20571	West Scotland	M639BCD	20639	South East
M355JBO	40555	South Wales	M472ASW	20572	West Scotland	M639HDV	46319	Devon
M356JBO	40556	South Wales	M473ASW	20573	West Scotland	M648FYS	40098	West Scotland
M357JBO	40557	South Wales	M474ASW	20574	West Scotland	M649FYS	40099	West Scotland
M358JBO	40558	East Scotland	M475ASW	20575	West Scotland	M650BCD	20650	South East
M35LHP	52221	South Wales	M476ASW	20576	West Scotland	M650FYS	40100	West Scotland
M360JBO	40560	Devon	M477ASW	20577	West Scotland	M651BCD	20651	Devon
M362LAX	40562	South Wales	M478ASW	20578	West Scotland	M651FYS	40066	West Scotland
M363LAX	40563	South Wales	M479ASW	20579	West Scotland	M652BCD	20652	South East
M364LAX	40564	South Wales	M480ASW	20565	West Scotland	M652FYS	40069	West Scotland
M365LAX	40565	South Wales	M481ASW	20510	West Scotland	M653FYS	40053	West Scotland
M366LAX	40566	South Wales	M482ASW	20569	West Scotland	M654FYS	40054	West Scotland
M367LAX	40567	South Wales	M483ASW	20511	West Scotland	M655FYS	40055	West Scotland
M368LAX	40568	South Wales	M484ASW	20581	West Scotland	M656FYS	40056	West Scotland
M369LAX	40569	South Wales	M486ASW	20566	West Scotland	M657FYS	40057	West Scotland
M370LAX	40570	South Wales	M487ASW	20567	West Scotland	M658FYS	40058	West Scotland
M371LAX	40571	South Wales	M488ASW	20505	West Scotland	M659FYS	40059	West Scotland
M379TJA	15197	Manchester	M489ASW	20568	West Scotland	M660FYS	40060	West Scotland
M387KVR	32794	North East	M490ASW	16846	East Scotland	M661FYS	40061	West Scotland
M395KVR	40985	West Scotland	M491ASW	16847	East Scotland	M662ECD	20662	South East
M396KVR	40986	West Scotland	M492ASW	16848	East Scotland	M662FYS	40062	West Scotland
M397KVR	40987	West Scotland	M510FWV	30800	East Scotland	M663ECD	20663	South East
M401SPY	20291	North East	M511FWV	30801	East Scotland	M663FYS	40063	West Scotland
M402SPY	20292	North East	M512FWV	30802	East Scotland	M664ECD	20664	South East
M403SPY	20293	North East	M536RSO	52236	East Scotland	M664FYS	40064	West Scotland
M404BFG	52214	East Scotland	M537RSO	52237	East Scotland	M665ECD	20665	South East
M404SPY	20294	North East	M538RSO	52238	East Scotland	M665FYS	40065	West Scotland
M405BFG	52215	South Wales	M539RSO	52239	East Scotland	M667ECD	20667	South East
M405SPY	20295	North East	M540RSO	52240	East Scotland	M667FYS	40067	West Scotland
M406BFG	52216	West Scotland	M541RSO	52241	East Scotland	M668ECD	20668	South East
M406OKM	27406	South East	M542SPY	20242	North East	M668FYS	40068	West Scotland
M406SPY	20296	North East	M543RSO	52243	East Scotland	M669ECD	20669	South East
M407SPY	20297	North East	M543SPY	20243	North East	M670ECD	20670	South East
M408SPY	20298	North East	M544SPY	20244	North East	M670SSX	30670	East Scotland

Reg	No.	Location	Reg	No.	Location	Reg	No.	Location
M671SSX	30671	East Scotland	M750PRS	30310	North West	M944TSX	52258	East Scotland
M672SSX	30672	East Scotland	M751LAX	20351	South Wales	M945TSX	52245	East Scotland
M673SSX	30673	East Scotland	M752LAX	20352	South Wales	M946TSX	52246	East Scotland
M674SSX	30674	West Scotland	M753LAX	20353	South Wales	M948TSX	52248	East Scotland
M675SSX	30675	West Scotland	M754LAX	20354	South Wales	M949EGE	32380	West Scotland
M679SSX	30679	East Scotland	M755LAX	20355	South Wales	M949TSX	52249	East Scotland
M680SSX	30680	East Scotland	M756LAX	20356	South Wales	M950EGE	32381	West Scotland
M680TDB	15180	Manchester	M757LAX	20357	South Wales	M950TSX	52250	East Scotland
M681SSX	30681	East Scotland	M758LAX	20358	South Wales	M951DRG	28951	West Scotland
M681TDB	15181	Manchester	M759LAX	20359	South Wales	M951TSX	52251	East Scotland
M682TDB	15182	Manchester	M760LAX	20360	South Wales	M952DRG	28952	West Scotland
M683TDB	15183	Manchester	M761LAX	20361	South Wales	M952TSX	52252	East Scotland
M684TDB	15184	Manchester	M762LAX	20362	South Wales	M953DRG	28953	West Scotland
M685TDB	15185	Manchester	M763LAX	20363	South Wales	M953TSX	52253	East Scotland
M686TDB	15186	Manchester	M764LAX	20364	South Wales	M954DRG	28954	West Scotland
M687TDB	15187	Manchester	M765LAX	20365	South Wales	M954TSX	52254	East Scotland
M688TDB	15188	Manchester	M766DRG	32766	North East	M955TSX	52255	East Scotland
M689FJF	41331	South Wales	M766LAX	20366	South Wales	M956TSX	52256	East Scotland
M689TDB	15189	Manchester	M767DRG	32767	North East	M959VWY	47979	Eastern
M690TDB	15190	Manchester	M767LAX	20367	South Wales	M975WWR	47975	Eastern
M691TDB	15191	Manchester	M768DRG	32768	North East	M976WWR	47976	Eastern
M692TDB	15192	Manchester	M768LAX	20368	South Wales	M977WWR	47977	Eastern
M693TDB	15193	Manchester	M769DRG	32769	North East	M978WWR	47978	Eastern
M694TDB	15194	Manchester	M769LAX	20369	South Wales	MBE613R	15513	East Midlands
M695TDB	15195	Manchester	M770DRG	32770	North East	MFN946F	19946	South East
M696TDB	15196	Manchester	M770LAX	20370	South Wales	MHS4P	14464	West
M697EDD	40697	Devon	M770TFS	40070	East Scotland	MIL4693	52084	North West
M698EDD	40698	Devon	M771DRG	32771	Eastern	MK02EGD	17722	West
M699EDD	40699	Devon	M771TFS	40071	East Scotland	MK02EGX	17728	West
M699TDB	15199	Manchester	M772BCS	30312	West Scotland	MK02EGY	17729	West
M701EDD	40701	Devon	M772TFS	40072	East Scotland	ML02EFU	17715	Manchester
M702EDD	40702	Devon	M773TFS	40073	East Scotland	ML02EFV	17716	Manchester
M703EDD	40703	Devon	M774TFS	40074	East Scotland	ML02EFW	17717	Manchester
M704JDG	40704	Devon	M775TFS	40075	East Scotland	ML02EFX	17718	Manchester
M705JDG	40705	Devon	M776TFS	40076	East Scotland	ML02EFY	17719	Manchester
M706JDG	40706	Devon	M778TFS	40078	East Scotland	ML02EFZ	17720	Manchester
M707JDG	40707	Devon	M779TFS	40079	East Scotland	ML02EGC	17721	Manchester
M707KRH	20267	North East	M780TFS	40080	East Scotland	ML02EGE	17723	Manchester
M708JDG	40708	South Wales	M784PRS	20584	West Scotland	ML02EGF	17724	Manchester
M708KRH	20268	North East	M785PRS	20585	West Scotland	ML02EGJ	17725	Manchester
M709JDG	40709	South Wales	M786PRS	20586	West Scotland	ML02EGU	17726	Manchester
M709KRH	20269	North East	M787PRS	20587	West Scotland	ML02EGV	17727	Manchester
M710JDG	40710	South Wales	M788PRS	20588	West Scotland	ML02EGZ	17730	Manchester
M710KRH	20270	North East	M789PRS	20589	West Scotland	ML02EHC	17710	Manchester
M711FMR	40711	Devon	M790PRS	20590	West Scotland	ML02EHD	17711	Manchester
M711KRH	20271	North East	M791PRS	20591	West Scotland	ML02KCO	17703	Manchester
M712FMR	40712	South Wales	M792PRS	20592	West Scotland	ML02KCU	17706	Manchester
M712KRH	20272	North East	M793PRS	20593	West Scotland	ML02KCV	17709	Manchester
M713FMR	40713	South Wales	M808JTY	52269	East Scotland	ML02KNO	17704	Manchester
M713KRH	20273	North East	M808WWR	47988	Eastern	ML02RWJ	17712	Manchester
M714FMR	40714	South Wales	M809WWR	47989	Eastern	ML02RWK	17713	Manchester
M714KRH	20274	East Midlands	M810WWR	47990	Eastern	ML02RWN	17714	Manchester
M715FMR	40715	South Wales	M817KRH	16817	East Midlands	ML02RWO	17701	Manchester
M715KRH	20275	East Midlands	M818KRH	16818	East Midlands	ML02RWU	17702	Manchester
M716KRH	20276	East Midlands	M819KRH	16819	East Midlands	ML02RWV	17705	Manchester
M717KRH	20277	East Midlands	M81WBW	32081	East Midlands	ML02RWW	17707	Manchester
M718BCS	30318	West Scotland	M82WBW	32082	East Midlands	ML02RWX	17708	Manchester
M718KRH	20278	East Midlands	M83WBW	32083	East Midlands	MSU463	52103	East Scotland
M722BCS	30322	West Scotland	M846HDF	30846	North West	MSU466	51076	West Scotland
M723BCS	30323	West Scotland	M847PRS	30307	North West	MX04VLN	47151	Devon
M724BCS	30324	West Scotland	M866LNY	41150	South Wales	MX04VLP	47152	Devon
M725BCS	30325	West Scotland	M869ASW	20506	West Scotland	MX04VLR	47153	Devon
M726BCS	30326	West Scotland	M870ASW	20580	West Scotland	MX04VLS	47154	Devon
M732BSJ	30332	West Scotland	M871ASW	20507	West Scotland	MX04VLT	47155	Devon
M734BSJ	30334	North West	M872ASW	20582	West Scotland	MX04XFV	18177	Manchester
M735BSJ	30335	West Scotland	M889ECD	40889	South East	MX04XFW	18178	Manchester
M737BSJ	30337	West Scotland	M890ECD	40890	South East	MX53FLA	18021	Manchester
M738BSJ	30338	West Scotland	M901DRG	21001	North East	MX53FLB	18022	Manchester
M739BSJ	30339	West Scotland	M902DRG	21002	North East	MX53FLC	18023	Manchester
M740BSJ	30340	West Scotland	M911WJK	52271	East Scotland	MX53FLD	18024	Manchester
M741PRS	30301	North West	M913WJK	52273	South Wales	MX53FLE	18025	Manchester
M743PRS	30303	North West	M914WJK	52274	South Wales	MX53FLF	18026	Manchester
M744PRS	30304	North West	M915WJK	52275	South Wales	MX53FLG	18027	Manchester
M745PRS	30305	North West	M916WJK	52276	South Wales	MX53FLH	18028	Manchester
M746PRS	30306	North West	M917WJK	52277	South Wales	MX53FLJ	18029	Manchester
M748PRS	30308	North West	M918WJK	52278	South Wales	MX53FLK	18030	Manchester
M749PRS	30309	North West	M942TSX	52259	East Midlands	MX53FLL	18031	Manchester
M750LAX	20350	South Wales	M943TSX	52257	East Midlands	MX53FLM	18032	Manchester

Reg	No	Location	Reg	No	Location	Reg	No	Location
MX53FLN	18033	Manchester	N117YHH	40017	North West	N203LTN	20103	North East
MX53FLP	18034	Manchester	N118YHH	40018	North West	N203UHH	40003	North West
MX53FLR	18035	Manchester	N119YHH	40019	North West	N204LPN	40904	South East
MX53FLV	18036	Manchester	N120YHH	40020	North West	N204LTN	20104	North East
MX53FLZ	18037	Manchester	N121YHH	40021	North West	N204UHH	40004	North West
MX53FMA	18038	Manchester	N122YHH	40022	North West	N205LTN	20105	North East
MX53FMC	18039	Manchester	N123YHH	40023	North West	N205UHH	40005	North West
MX53FME	18040	Manchester	N124YHH	40024	North West	N206LTN	20106	North East
MX53FMF	18041	Manchester	N125YHH	40025	North West	N206TDU	20206	South Midlands
MX53FMG	18042	Manchester	N126YRM	40026	North West	N206UHH	40006	North West
MX53FMJ	18043	Manchester	N127YRM	40027	North West	N207LCK	35016	West Scotland
MX53FMK	18044	Manchester	N128VAO	52328	West Scotland	N207LTN	20107	East Scotland
MX53FML	18045	Manchester	N128YRM	40028	North West	N207TDU	20207	South Midlands
MX53FMM	18046	Manchester	N129YRM	40029	North West	N207UHH	40007	North West
MX53FMP	18047	Manchester	N130AET	16480	East Midlands	N208LCK	35017	West Scotland
MX53FMU	18048	Manchester	N130YRM	40030	North West	N208LTN	20108	East Scotland
MX53FMV	18049	Manchester	N131AET	16481	East Midlands	N208TDU	20208	South Midlands
MX53FMZ	18050	Manchester	N131YRM	40031	North West	N208UHH	40008	North West
MX53FNA	22055	Manchester	N132AET	16482	East Midlands	N209LTN	20109	West Scotland
MX53FNC	22056	Manchester	N133AET	16483	East Midlands	N209UHH	40009	North West
MX53VHO	29801	Manchester	N133YRM	40033	North West	N210LTN	20110	West Scotland
MX53VHP	29802	Manchester	N134AET	16484	East Midlands	N210UHH	40010	North West
MX54LPA	18179	Manchester	N135AET	16485	East Midlands	N211LTN	20111	East Scotland
MX54LPC	18180	Manchester	N136AET	16486	East Midlands	N211TDU	20211	South Midlands
MX54LPE	18181	Manchester	N137AET	16487	East Midlands	N211UHH	40011	North West
MX54LPF	18182	Manchester	N138AET	16488	East Midlands	N212LTN	20112	East Scotland
MX54LPJ	18183	Manchester	N139AET	16489	East Midlands	N212TDU	20212	South Midlands
MX54LPK	18184	Manchester	N140AET	16490	East Midlands	N212UHH	40012	North West
MX54LPL	18185	Manchester	N141AET	16491	East Midlands	N213LTN	20113	East Scotland
MX54LPN	18186	Manchester	N142AET	16492	East Midlands	N213TDU	20213	South Midlands
MX54LPO	18187	Manchester	N142XSA	52282	West Scotland	N213UHH	40013	North West
MX54LPP	18188	Manchester	N143AET	16493	East Midlands	N214LTN	20114	West Scotland
MX54LPU	18189	Manchester	N143XSA	52283	West Scotland	N214TDU	20214	South Midlands
MX54LPV	18190	Manchester	N144AET	16494	East Midlands	N214UHH	40014	North West
MX54LPY	18191	Manchester	N144XSA	52284	West Scotland	N215LTN	20115	North East
MX54LPZ	18192	Manchester	N145XSA	52285	West Scotland	N215TDU	20215	South Midlands
MX54LRA	18193	Manchester	N148XSA	52288	East Scotland	N215UHH	40015	North West
MX54LRE	18194	Manchester	N149XSA	52289	East Scotland	N216LTN	20116	North East
MX54LRF	22083	Manchester	N150XSA	52290	East Scotland	N216TDU	20216	South Midlands
MX54LRJ	22084	Manchester	N151XSA	52291	East Scotland	N217LTN	20117	North East
MX54LRK	22085	Manchester	N152MTG	41152	West	N247XSA	52287	West Scotland
MX54LRL	22086	Manchester	N152XSA	52292	East Scotland	N301AMC	32301	North East
MX54LRN	22087	Manchester	N153MTG	41153	West	N301XRP	40301	Eastern
MX54LRO	22088	Manchester	N153XSA	52293	East Scotland	N302AMC	32302	North East
MX54LRU	22089	Manchester	N154MTG	41154	South Wales	N302XRP	40302	Eastern
MX54LRV	22090	Manchester	N154XSA	52294	East Scotland	N303AMC	32303	North East
MX54LRY	22091	Manchester	N155MTG	41155	South Wales	N303XRP	40303	Eastern
MX54LRZ	22092	Manchester	N156MTG	41156	South Wales	N304AMC	32304	East Scotland
MX54LSC	22093	Manchester	N158MTG	41158	West	N304XRP	40304	Eastern
MX54LSD	22094	Manchester	N159MTG	41159	West	N305AMC	32305	North East
MX54LSE	22095	Manchester	N182CMJ	46378	Devon	N305XRP	40305	Eastern
MX54XLB	22096	Manchester	N183CMJ	46379	Devon	N306AMC	32306	East Scotland
MX54XLC	22097	Manchester	N188GFR	46398	Devon	N306XRP	40306	Eastern
MX54XLD	22098	Manchester	N190GFR	46381	Devon	N307AMC	32307	East Scotland
MX54XLE	22099	Manchester	N191LPN	40891	South East	N307XRP	40307	Eastern
MX54XLF	22100	Manchester	N192LPN	40892	South East	N308AMC	32308	East Scotland
N45MJO	52035	Eastern	N193LPN	40893	South East	N308XRP	40308	Eastern
N46MJO	52036	Eastern	N194LFV	40394	North West	N309AMC	32309	South East
N48EJO	32048	Manchester	N194LPN	40894	South East	N309XRP	40309	Eastern
N48MJO	52038	East Scotland	N195LFV	40395	North West	N310AMC	32310	South East
N51KBW	32051	South Wales	N195LPN	40895	South East	N310XRP	40310	Eastern
N52KBW	32052	South Wales	N196LFV	40396	North West	N311AMC	32311	South East
N53KBW	32053	South Wales	N196LPN	40896	South East	N311XRP	40311	Eastern
N54KBW	32054	West Scotland	N197LFV	40397	North West	N312AMC	32312	South East
N56KBW	32056	Devon	N197LPN	40897	South East	N312XRP	40312	Eastern
N57KBW	32057	West Scotland	N198LFV	40398	North West	N313AMC	32313	West
N58KBW	32058	West Scotland	N198LPN	40898	South East	N313XRP	40313	Eastern
N61KBW	32061	West Scotland	N199LFV	40399	North West	N314XRP	40314	Eastern
N62KBW	32062	West Scotland	N199LPN	40899	South East	N315AMC	32315	South East
N62MTG	32962	West	N201LFV	40401	North West	N315XRP	40315	Eastern
N63KBW	32063	West Scotland	N201LPN	40901	South East	N316AMC	32316	South East
N63MTG	32963	West	N201LTN	20101	North East	N316VMS	20316	East Scotland
N64KBW	32064	Devon	N201UHH	40001	North West	N316XRP	40316	Eastern
N91RVK	52281	South Wales	N202LFV	40402	North West	N317AMC	32317	West
N95ALS	40095	East Scotland	N202LPN	40902	South East	N317VMS	20317	East Scotland
N96ALS	40096	East Scotland	N202LTN	20102	North East	N317XRP	40317	Eastern
N97ALS	40097	East Scotland	N202UHH	40002	North West	N318NMC	32318	West
N116YHH	40016	North West	N203LPN	40903	South East	N318VMS	20318	East Scotland

Reg	No	Region	Reg	No	Region	Reg	No	Region
N318XRP	40318	Eastern	N347KKH	40797	East Midlands	N382LPN	16382	South East
N319AMC	32319	West	N347MPN	16347	South East	N382PNY	40582	South Wales
N319VMS	20319	East Scotland	N348AVV	40148	South Midlands	N383LPN	16383	South East
N319XRP	40319	Eastern	N348HGK	16448	West	N383PNY	40583	South Wales
N320AMC	32320	West	N348KKH	40798	East Midlands	N384LPN	16384	South East
N320VMS	20320	East Scotland	N348MPN	16348	South East	N384PNY	40584	South Wales
N320XRP	40320	Eastern	N349AVV	40149	South Midlands	N385LPN	16385	South East
N321AMC	32321	South East	N349HGK	16449	West	N386LPN	16386	South East
N321HGK	16421	East Scotland	N349MPN	16349	South East	N387LPN	16387	South East
N321VMS	20321	East Scotland	N350AVV	40150	South Midlands	N388LPN	16388	South East
N321XRP	40321	Eastern	N350HGK	16450	East Scotland	N389LPN	16389	South East
N322AMC	32322	South East	N350MPN	16350	South East	N390LPN	16390	South East
N322HGK	16422	East Scotland	N350YFL	32650	North East	N391LPN	16391	North West
N322VMS	20322	East Scotland	N351MPN	16351	North West	N392LPN	16392	North West
N322XRP	40322	Eastern	N351YFL	32651	North East	N393LPN	16393	South East
N323AMC	32323	South East	N352AVV	40152	South Midlands	N394LPN	16394	South East
N323HGK	16423	East Scotland	N352HGK	16452	West	N395LPN	16395	South East
N323VMS	20323	East Scotland	N352MPN	16352	North West	N396LPN	16396	South East
N323XRP	40323	Eastern	N352YFL	32652	North East	N397LPN	16397	North West
N324AMC	32324	South East	N353AVV	40153	South Midlands	N398LPN	16398	South East
N324HGK	16424	East Scotland	N353MPN	16353	North West	N399LPN	16399	South East
N324VMS	20324	East Scotland	N354AVV	40154	South Midlands	N401LDF	20681	West
N324XRP	40324	Eastern	N354MPN	16354	South East	N401WVR	41401	South Wales
N325AMC	32325	South East	N355AVV	40155	South Midlands	N402LDF	20682	West
N325HGK	16425	East Scotland	N355MPN	16355	North West	N402WVR	41402	South Wales
N325MPN	16325	North West	N356AVV	40156	South Midlands	N403LDF	20683	West
N325VMS	20325	East Scotland	N356MPN	16356	South East	N403WVR	41403	South Wales
N326AMC	32326	South East	N357AVV	40157	East Scotland	N404LDF	20684	West
N326HGK	16426	East Scotland	N357MPN	16357	North West	N404WVR	41404	South Wales
N326MPN	16326	North West	N358AVV	40158	South Midlands	N405LDF	20685	West
N326VMS	20326	East Scotland	N358MPN	16358	North West	N405WVR	41405	South Wales
N327AMC	32327	South East	N359AVV	40159	South Midlands	N406LDF	20686	West
N327HGK	16427	East Scotland	N359MPN	16359	North West	N406WVR	41406	South Wales
N327MPN	16327	North West	N360AVV	40160	South Midlands	N407LDF	20687	West
N327VMS	20327	East Scotland	N360LPN	16360	South East	N407WVR	41407	South Wales
N327XRP	40327	North West	N361AVV	40161	East Scotland	N408LDF	20688	West
N328HGK	16428	East Scotland	N361LPN	16361	South East	N408WVR	41408	South Wales
N328MPN	16328	North West	N362AVV	40162	South Midlands	N409LDF	20689	West
N328VMS	20328	East Scotland	N362LPN	16362	South East	N409WVR	41409	South Wales
N328XRP	40328	North West	N363AVV	40163	South Midlands	N410MBW	32410	Devon
N329HGK	16429	East Scotland	N363LPN	16363	South East	N410WVR	41410	South Wales
N329MPN	16329	North West	N364AVV	40164	South East	N411MBW	32411	Devon
N329VMS	20329	East Scotland	N364LPN	16364	South East	N411WVR	41411	South Wales
N329XRP	40329	North West	N365AVV	40165	East Scotland	N412MBW	32412	South East
N330HGK	16430	East Scotland	N365LPN	16365	South East	N412WVR	41412	South Wales
N330MPN	16330	North West	N366AVV	40166	East Scotland	N413MBW	32413	South East
N331MPN	16331	North West	N366LPN	16366	South East	N413WVR	41413	South Wales
N332MPN	16332	North West	N367AVV	40167	East Scotland	N414MBW	32414	South East
N334MPN	16334	North West	N367LPN	16367	South East	N414WVR	41414	South Wales
N335MPN	16335	North West	N368AVV	40168	East Scotland	N415WVR	41415	South Wales
N336MPN	16336	North West	N368LPN	16368	South East	N416KPS	30342	West Scotland
N337MPN	16337	North West	N369AVV	40169	East Scotland	N416WVR	41416	South Wales
N338HGK	16438	East Scotland	N369LPN	16369	South East	N417WVR	41417	South Wales
N338MPN	16338	North West	N370AVV	40170	East Scotland	N418WVR	41418	South Wales
N339HGK	16439	East Scotland	N370LPN	16370	South East	N419WVR	41419	South Wales
N339MPN	16339	North West	N371AVV	40171	East Scotland	N420WVR	41420	South Wales
N340HGK	16440	East Scotland	N371LPN	16371	South East	N421PWV	30141	South East
N340MPN	16340	North West	N372AVV	40172	South Midlands	N421WVR	41421	South Wales
N341HGK	16441	West	N372LPN	16372	South East	N422PWV	30142	South East
N341KKH	40791	North East	N372PNY	40572	South Wales	N422WVR	41422	South Wales
N341MPN	16341	South East	N373LPN	16373	South East	N423WVR	41423	South Wales
N342HGK	16442	West	N373PNY	40573	South Wales	N424WVR	41424	South Wales
N342KKH	40792	North East	N374LPN	16374	South East	N425WVR	41425	South Wales
N342MPN	16342	South East	N374PNY	40574	South Wales	N426WVR	41426	South Wales
N343HGK	16443	West	N375LPN	16375	South East	N427WVR	41427	South Wales
N343KKH	40793	East Scotland	N375PNY	40575	South Wales	N428WVR	41428	South Wales
N343MPN	16343	North West	N376LPN	16376	South East	N429WVR	41429	South Wales
N344HGK	16444	South Wales	N376PNY	40576	South Wales	N42MJO	52032	Eastern
N344KKH	40794	East Scotland	N377LPN	16377	South East	N430WVR	41430	South Wales
N344MPN	16344	South East	N377PNY	40577	South Wales	N43MJO	52033	Eastern
N345HGK	16445	South Wales	N378LPN	16378	South East	N445XVA	52295	West Scotland
N345KKH	40795	East Scotland	N378PNY	40578	South Wales	N446TOS	40530	West Scotland
N345MPN	16345	South East	N379LPN	16379	South East	N446XVA	52296	West Scotland
N346HGK	16446	South Wales	N379PNY	40579	South Wales	N447XVA	52297	West Scotland
N346KKH	40796	North East	N380LPN	16380	South East	N448XVA	52298	London
N346MPN	16346	North West	N380PNY	40580	South Wales	N449XVA	52299	South Wales
N347AVV	40147	South Midlands	N381LPN	16381	South East	N450XVA	52300	South Wales
N347HGK	16447	South Wales	N381PNY	40581	South Wales	N451XVA	52301	Eastern

Reg	No.	Location	Reg	No.	Location	Reg	No.	Location
N452VOD	40452	North West	N520BJA	40520	North West	N650VSS	40650	North West
N455VOD	40455	North West	N520XER	16600	South Midlands	N651VSS	40651	North West
N456PAP	32456	South East	N551VDC	20261	North East	N652VSS	40652	North West
N457PAP	32457	South East	N552VDC	20262	North East	N653VSS	40653	South Midlands
N458PAP	32458	South East	N553VDC	20263	North East	N654VSS	40654	South Midlands
N459PAP	32459	South East	N582XSA	52312	East Scotland	N655VSS	40655	South East
N460PAP	32460	South East	N583XSA	52313	East Scotland	N656VSS	40656	South East
N461PAP	32461	South East	N584XSA	52314	East Scotland	N657VSS	40657	South Midlands
N461RVK	40461	North East	N599DWY	32599	Devon	N658VSS	40658	South Midlands
N461VOD	40441	North West	N601KGF	32601	South East	N659VSS	40659	South Midlands
N462PAP	32462	South East	N601VSS	40601	West Scotland	N660VSS	40660	Manchester
N462RVK	40462	North East	N602KGF	32602	South East	N661VSS	40661	South East
N462VOD	40442	North West	N602VSS	40602	West Scotland	N662VSS	40662	South East
N463HRN	46382	Devon	N603KGF	32603	South East	N663VSS	40663	Manchester
N463PAP	32463	South East	N604KGF	32604	South East	N664VSS	40664	Manchester
N463RVK	40463	North East	N604VSS	40604	West Scotland	N665VSS	40665	Manchester
N463VOD	40443	North West	N605KGF	32605	South East	N701LTN	16701	North East
N464HRN	46399	Devon	N605VSS	40605	West Scotland	N702LTN	16702	North East
N464PAP	32464	South East	N606KGF	32606	South East	N703LTN	16703	North East
N464RVK	40464	North East	N606VSS	40606	West Scotland	N704LTN	16704	North East
N465PAP	32465	South East	N607KGF	32607	South East	N705LTN	16705	North East
N465RVK	40465	North East	N607VSS	40607	West Scotland	N706LTN	16706	North East
N465VOD	40445	North West	N608KGF	32608	South East	N707LTN	16707	North East
N466PAP	32466	South East	N608VSS	40608	West Scotland	N708LTN	16708	North East
N466RVK	40466	North East	N609KGF	32609	South Wales	N709LTN	16709	North East
N466VOD	40446	North West	N609VSS	40609	West Scotland	N710LTN	16710	North East
N467PAP	32467	South East	N610KGF	32610	South Wales	N711LTN	16711	North East
N467RVK	40467	North East	N610VSS	40610	West Scotland	N712LTN	16712	North East
N467VOD	40447	North West	N611LGC	32611	South Wales	N713LTN	16713	North East
N468RVK	40468	East Scotland	N611VSS	40611	West Scotland	N714LTN	16714	North East
N469RVK	40469	North East	N612LGC	32612	South Wales	N715LTN	16715	North East
N470RVK	40470	North East	N612VSS	40612	West Scotland	N716KAM	40716	Devon
N471RVK	40471	North East	N613LGC	32613	South Midlands	N716LTN	16716	Devon
N472RVK	40472	North East	N613VSS	40613	North West	N717KAM	40717	Devon
N473RVK	40473	North East	N614LGC	32614	South Midlands	N717LTN	16717	North East
N474RVK	40474	North East	N614VSS	40614	North West	N718LTN	16718	North East
N475RVK	40475	North East	N615VSS	40615	North West	N718RDD	40718	Devon
N476RVK	40476	North East	N616VSS	40616	North West	N719LTN	16719	North East
N477RVK	40477	North East	N617VSS	40617	North West	N719RDD	40719	Devon
N478RVK	40478	North East	N618USS	52308	South Midlands	N720LTN	16720	North East
N479RVK	40479	North East	N618VSS	40618	South Wales	N720RDD	40720	West
N47EJO	32047	South East	N619USS	52309	East Scotland	N721LTN	16721	North East
N480RVK	40480	North East	N619VSS	40619	South Wales	N722LTN	16722	North East
N481RVK	40481	North East	N620USS	52310	East Scotland	N723LTN	16723	North East
N482RVK	40482	North East	N620VSS	40620	North East	N723RDD	40723	South Wales
N483RVK	40483	North East	N621VSS	40621	West Scotland	N724LTN	16724	North East
N484RVK	40484	North East	N622VSS	40622	West Scotland	N725LTN	16725	North East
N485RVK	40485	North East	N624VSS	40624	West Scotland	N725RDD	40725	West
N486RVK	40486	North East	N625VSS	40625	West Scotland	N726LTN	16726	North East
N487RVK	40487	North East	N626VSS	40626	West Scotland	N726RDD	40726	South East
N488RVK	40488	East Scotland	N627VSS	40627	West Scotland	N727LTN	16727	North East
N489RVK	40489	North East	N628VSS	40628	West Scotland	N727RDD	40727	West
N491RVK	40491	North East	N630VSS	40630	West Scotland	N728LTN	16728	North East
N492RVK	40492	North East	N631VSS	40631	West Scotland	N728RDD	40728	South East
N493RVK	40493	North East	N632VSS	40632	West Scotland	N729LTN	16729	North East
N494RVK	40494	North East	N633VSS	40633	West Scotland	N729RDD	40729	South East
N495RVK	40495	North East	N634VSS	40634	West Scotland	N730LTN	16730	North East
N496RVK	40496	East Scotland	N635VSS	40635	West Scotland	N730RDD	40730	South East
N497RVK	40497	North East	N636VSS	40636	East Scotland	N731LTN	16731	North East
N498RVK	40498	North East	N637VSS	40637	East Scotland	N731RDD	40731	South East
N499RVK	40499	North East	N638VSS	40638	West Scotland	N731XDV	32431	Devon
N501RVK	40501	North East	N639VSS	40639	West Scotland	N732LTN	16732	North East
N506BJA	40506	Devon	N640LPN	20640	South East	N732RDD	40732	Devon
N507BJA	40507	Devon	N640VSS	40640	East Scotland	N732XDV	32432	Devon
N508BJA	40508	Devon	N641LPN	20641	South East	N733LTN	16733	North East
N509BJA	40509	Devon	N641VSS	40641	North West	N733RDD	40733	South East
N510BJA	40510	Devon	N642LPN	20642	South East	N733XDV	32433	Devon
N511BJA	40511	Devon	N642VSS	40642	East Scotland	N734LTN	16734	North East
N512BJA	40512	Devon	N643LPN	20643	South East	N734RDD	40734	Devon
N513BJA	40513	Devon	N643VSS	40643	South Wales	N734XDV	32434	Devon
N514BJA	40514	Devon	N644LPN	20644	South East	N735LTN	16735	North East
N515BJA	40515	Devon	N644VSS	40644	South Wales	N735RDD	40735	West
N516BJA	40516	Devon	N645LPN	20645	South East	N735XDV	32435	Devon
N517BJA	40517	Devon	N645VSS	40645	North West	N736LTN	16736	North East
N518BJA	40518	Devon	N646VSS	40646	North West	N736XDV	32436	Devon
N518XER	16598	South Midlands	N647VSS	40647	North West	N737LTN	16737	North East
N519BJA	40519	North West	N648VSS	40648	North West	N737XDV	32437	Devon
N519XER	16599	South Midlands	N649VSS	40649	North West	N738LTN	16738	North East

Reg	No.	Location	Reg	No.	Location	Reg	No.	Location
N738XDV	32438	Devon	N880AVV	40430	Manchester	N975NAP	40975	South East
N739LTN	16739	North East	N881AVV	40431	Manchester	N976NAP	40976	South East
N739XDV	32439	Devon	N882AVV	40432	Manchester	N977NAP	40977	South East
N740LTN	16740	North East	N883AVV	40433	Manchester	N978NAP	40978	Devon
N740XDV	32440	Devon	N884AVV	40434	Manchester	N979NAP	40979	Devon
N742XDV	32442	Devon	N885AVV	40435	North West	N980NAP	40980	Devon
N743XDV	32443	Devon	N901PFC	27901	North West	N981NAP	40981	Devon
N744XDV	32444	Devon	N902PFC	27902	North West	N982NAP	40982	Devon
N752CKU	40752	East Midlands	N903PFC	27903	North West	N998RCD	32446	Devon
N754CKU	40754	East Midlands	N905NAP	40905	South East	NDZ3017	33027	South East
N755CKU	40755	East Midlands	N906NAP	40906	South East	NDZ3018	33028	South East
N756CKU	40756	East Midlands	N907NAP	40907	South East	NDZ3019	33025	South East
N757CKU	40757	East Midlands	N908NAP	40908	South East	NDZ3020	34014	South East
N758CKU	40758	East Midlands	N909NAP	40909	South East	NDZ3021	22191	South East
N759CKU	40759	East Midlands	N910NAP	40910	South East	NDZ3022	22192	South East
N760CKU	40760	East Midlands	N911NAP	40911	South East	NDZ3023	22194	South East
N761CKU	40761	East Midlands	N912NAP	40912	South East	NDZ3134	32234	West
N762EWG	40762	East Midlands	N913NAP	40913	South East	NDZ3136	32236	West
N763EWG	40763	East Midlands	N914NAP	40914	South East	NDZ3151	32251	Devon
N764EWG	40764	East Midlands	N915NAP	40915	South East	NDZ3152	32252	Devon
N765EWG	40765	East Midlands	N916NAP	40916	South East	NDZ3153	32253	Devon
N767EWG	40767	East Midlands	N917NAP	40917	South East	NDZ3157	32257	West
N769EWG	40769	East Midlands	N918NAP	40918	South East	NFX667	32452	South East
N770EWG	40770	East Midlands	N920NAP	40920	South East	NHL303X	14303	East Midlands
N771EWG	40771	East Midlands	N921NAP	40921	South East	NIB4138	11114	East Scotland
N772EWG	40772	East Midlands	N922NAP	40922	South East	NIB5232	11100	North West
N772RVK	32772	Eastern	N923NAP	40923	South East	NIB5233	11093	East Scotland
N773EWG	40773	East Midlands	N924NAP	40924	South East	NIB5455	11106	East Scotland
N773RVK	32773	North East	N925NAP	40925	South East	NIL8646	52153	South Wales
N774EWG	40774	East Midlands	N926NAP	40926	South East	NIL8647	59801	South Wales
N774RVK	32774	North East	N927NAP	40927	South East	NIL8656	52154	South Wales
N775EWG	40775	East Midlands	N928NAP	40928	South East	NK03XJA	22011	North East
N775RVK	32775	North East	N929NAP	40929	South East	NK03XJB	22012	North East
N776EWG	40776	East Midlands	N930NAP	40930	South East	NK03XJC	22013	North East
N776RVK	32776	North East	N931NAP	40931	South East	NK03XJD	22014	North East
N778RVK	32777	North East	N932NAP	40932	South East	NK03XJE	22015	North East
N779RVK	32778	North East	N933NAP	40933	South East	NK03XJF	22016	North East
N780RVK	32779	North East	N934NAP	40934	South East	NK03XJG	22017	North East
N789YRM	20789	North West	N935NAP	40935	South East	NK03XJH	22018	North East
N790YRM	20790	North West	N936NAP	40936	South East	NK03XJJ	22019	North East
N801DNE	20801	Devon	N937NAP	40937	South East	NK03XJL	22020	North East
N802DNE	20802	Devon	N938NAP	40938	South East	NK03XJM	22021	North East
N803DNE	20803	South Midlands	N939NAP	40939	South East	NK03XJN	22022	North East
N804DNE	20804	South Midlands	N940NAP	40940	South East	NK03XJP	22023	North East
N805DNE	20805	South Midlands	N941NAP	40941	South East	NK03XJT	22024	North East
N806DNE	20806	South Wales	N942NAP	40942	South East	NK03XJU	22025	North East
N807DNE	20807	South Wales	N943NAP	40943	South East	NK03XJV	22026	North East
N808DNE	20808	South Midlands	N944NAP	40944	South East	NK03XJW	22027	North East
N809DNE	20809	South Midlands	N945NAP	40945	South East	NK03XJX	22028	North East
N810DNE	20810	South Wales	N946NAP	40946	South East	NK03XJY	22029	North East
N811DNE	20811	South Wales	N947NAP	40947	South East	NK03XJZ	22030	North East
N812DNE	20812	South Midlands	N948NAP	40948	South East	NK03XKA	22031	North East
N813DNE	20813	South Midlands	N949NAP	40949	South East	NK03XKB	22032	North East
N814DNE	20814	South Midlands	N950NAP	40950	South East	NK03XKC	22033	North East
N815DNE	20815	South Wales	N951NAP	40951	South East	NK04KZT	34550	North East
N816DNE	20816	South Midlands	N952NAP	40952	South East	NK04KZU	34561	North East
N817DNE	20817	West	N953NAP	40953	South East	NK04KZV	34562	North East
N818DNE	20818	West	N954NAP	40954	South East	NK04KZW	34563	North East
N849VHH	16849	East Scotland	N955NAP	40955	South East	NK04KZX	34564	North East
N850VHH	16850	East Scotland	N956NAP	40956	South East	NK04KZY	34565	North East
N851VHH	16851	East Scotland	N957NAP	40957	South East	NK04KZZ	34566	North East
N852VHH	16852	West Scotland	N958NAP	40958	South East	NK04LBA	34567	North East
N853VHH	16853	West Scotland	N959NAP	40959	South East	NK04LBE	34568	North East
N854VHH	16854	West Scotland	N960NAP	40960	South East	NK04NPE	34569	North East
N855VHH	16855	East Scotland	N961NAP	40961	South East	NK04NPF	34605	North East
N856VHH	16856	East Scotland	N962NAP	40962	South East	NK04NPJ	34606	North East
N857VHH	16857	East Scotland	N963NAP	40963	South East	NK04NPN	34607	North East
N858VHH	16858	East Scotland	N964NAP	40964	South East	NK04NPP	34608	North East
N859VHH	16859	West Scotland	N965NAP	40965	South East	NK04NPU	34609	North East
N860VHH	16860	East Scotland	N966NAP	40966	South East	NK04NPV	34610	North East
N861VHH	16861	West Scotland	N967NAP	40967	South East	NK04NPX	34611	North East
N862VHH	16862	West Scotland	N968NAP	40968	South East	NK04NPY	34612	North East
N863VHH	16863	West Scotland	N969NAP	40969	South East	NK04NPZ	34613	North East
N864VHH	16864	West Scotland	N970NAP	40970	South East	NK04NRE	34614	North East
N865VHH	16865	East Scotland	N971NAP	40971	South East	NK04NRF	34615	North East
N866VHH	16866	East Scotland	N972NAP	40972	South East	NK53KDZ	22034	North East
N871MSU	52279	West Scotland	N973NAP	40973	South East	NK53KEJ	22035	North East
N879AVV	40429	Manchester	N974NAP	40974	South East	NK53KEU	22036	North East

Reg	Fleet No	Region
NK53KFA	22037	North East
NK53KFC	22038	North East
NK53KFD	22039	North East
NK53KFE	22040	North East
NK53KFF	22041	North East
NK53KFG	22042	North East
NK53KFJ	22043	North East
NK53KFL	22044	North East
NK53KFN	22045	North East
NK53KFO	22046	North East
NK53KFP	22047	North East
NK53KFR	22048	North East
NK53KFT	22049	North East
NK53KFU	22050	North East
NK53KFV	22051	North East
NK53KFW	34401	North East
NK54BFE	22061	North East
NK54BFF	22062	North East
NK54BFJ	22063	North East
NK54BFL	22064	North East
NK54BFM	22065	North East
NK54BFN	22066	North East
NK54BFO	22067	North East
NK54BFP	22068	North East
NK54BFU	22069	North East
NK54BFV	22070	North East
NK54BFX	22071	North East
NK54BFY	22072	North East
NK54BFZ	22073	North East
NK54BGE	22074	North East
NK54BGF	22075	North East
NK54BGO	22076	North East
NK54BGU	22077	North East
NK54BGV	22078	North East
NK54BGX	22079	North East
NK54BGY	22080	North East
NK54BGZ	22081	North East
NK54BHA	22082	North East
NML607E	12607	East Midlands
NML624E	12624	North West
NML639E	12639	East Midlands
NML641E	12641	North West
NML642E	12642	North West
NML657E	12657	North West
NOE602R	25402	South Midlands
NSU133	52027	North West
NTC132Y	14294	West
NUF276	52194	Manchester
NUW555Y	10555	East Scotland
NUW560Y	10560	East Scotland
NUW562Y	10562	East Scotland
NUW571Y	10571	East Scotland
NUW577Y	10577	East Scotland
NUW585Y	10585	West Scotland
NUW586Y	10586	East Scotland
NUW587Y	10587	East Scotland
NUW589Y	10589	South Wales
NUW591Y	10591	East Scotland
NUW592Y	10592	South Wales
NUW593Y	10593	East Scotland
NUW601Y	10601	East Scotland
NUW602Y	10602	South Wales
NUW615Y	10615	South Wales
NUW619Y	10619	South Wales
NUW622Y	10622	South Wales
NUW626Y	10626	East Scotland
NUW646Y	10646	South Wales
NUW651Y	10651	South Wales
NUW665Y	10665	South Wales
OHV684Y	10684	North West
OHV686Y	10686	North West
OHV699Y	10699	North West
OHV700Y	10700	West Scotland
OHV702Y	10702	South Wales
OHV728Y	10728	North West
OHV729Y	10729	North West
OHV738Y	10738	North West
OHV751Y	10751	East Scotland
OHV762Y	10762	West Scotland
OHV802Y	10802	East Scotland
OIW5804	52001	North West
OIW7025	25475	West Scotland
OSK784	13611	South Wales
OU51KAE	22945	South Midlands
OU51KAG	22946	South Midlands
OU51KAK	22947	South Midlands
OU51KAO	22948	South Midlands
OU51WLK	22942	South Midlands
OU51WLL	22943	South Midlands
OU51WLN	22944	South Midlands
OWO37X	59001	W
P21HMF	34001	East Midlands
P23HMF	34003	East Midlands
P24HMF	34004	East Midlands
P25HMF	34005	East Midlands
P26HMF	34006	East Midlands
P27HMF	34007	East Midlands
P28HMF	34008	East Midlands
P29HMF	34009	East Midlands
P31HMF	34002	East Midlands
P54XBO	33554	South Wales
P56XBO	33556	South Wales
P57XBO	33557	South Wales
P58XBO	33558	South Wales
P59VTG	33559	South Wales
P101HNH	32001	South Midlands
P102HNH	32002	South Midlands
P103HNH	32003	South Midlands
P104HNH	32004	South Midlands
P105HNH	32005	West Scotland
P107FRS	52397	South Wales
P108DCW	52408	North West
P108FRS	52398	Eastern
P109DCW	52409	North West
P109FRS	52399	South Wales
P110DCW	52410	North West
P112DCW	52412	North West
P113DCW	52413	North West
P114DCW	52414	North West
P118XCN	20118	East Scotland
P119XCN	20119	West Scotland
P120XCN	20120	North West
P121XCN	20121	North East
P122XCN	20122	North East
P123XCN	20123	North East
P124XCN	20124	North East
P125XCN	20125	North East
P126XCN	20126	North East
P127XCN	20127	North East
P128XCN	20128	North East
P129XCN	20129	North East
P130XCN	20130	North East
P131XCN	20131	North East
P132XCN	20132	North East
P133XCN	20133	North East
P134XCN	20134	North East
P135XCN	20135	North East
P145KWJ	16495	East Midlands
P146KWJ	16496	East Midlands
P148ASA	52348	West Scotland
P148KWJ	16498	East Midlands
P149ASA	52349	West Scotland
P149KWJ	16499	East Midlands
P150ASA	52350	West Scotland
P150KWJ	16500	East Midlands
P151ASA	52351	East Midlands
P151KWJ	16455	East Midlands
P152ASA	52352	East Scotland
P152KWJ	16497	East Midlands
P153ASA	52353	East Scotland
P153KWJ	16453	East Midlands
P154ASA	52354	East Scotland
P154KWJ	16454	East Midlands
P156ASA	52356	East Scotland
P156KWJ	16456	East Midlands
P157ASA	52357	East Midlands
P157KWJ	16457	East Midlands
P158ASA	52358	West Scotland
P158KWJ	16458	East Midlands
P159KAK	16459	East Midlands
P160ASA	52360	West Scotland
P160KAK	16460	East Midlands
P161TDW	41161	West
P162TDW	41162	South Wales
P163TNY	41163	South Wales
P164TNY	41164	South Wales
P165TNY	41165	South Wales
P166TNY	41166	South Wales
P167TNY	41167	West
P168KBD	52368	Eastern
P168TNY	41168	South Wales
P169KBD	52369	Eastern
P169TNY	41169	South Wales
P170KBD	52370	Eastern
P170TNY	41170	South Wales
P171KBD	52371	Eastern
P171TNY	41171	West
P172KBD	52372	Eastern
P173KBD	52373	Eastern
P178PRH	52378	East Midlands
P179PRH	52379	East Midlands
P180PRH	52380	East Scotland
P181PRH	52381	East Midlands
P198OSE	51098	West Scotland
P199OSE	51099	West Scotland
P217HBD	20217	South Midlands
P218HBD	20218	South Midlands
P219HBD	20219	South Midlands
P220HBD	20220	South Midlands
P224VCK	16624	South East
P225VCK	16625	South East
P226VCK	16626	South East
P227VCK	16627	South East
P228VCK	16628	South East
P229VCK	16629	South East
P230VCK	16630	South East
P231VCK	16631	South East
P232VCK	16632	South East
P233VCK	16633	South East
P234VCK	16634	North West
P235VCK	16635	North West
P255ASA	52355	West Scotland
P260VPN	16636	North West
P260WPN	16260	South East
P261VPN	16637	North West
P261WPN	16261	South East
P262VPN	16638	North West
P262WPN	16262	South East
P263VPN	16639	North West
P263WPN	16263	South East
P264VPN	16264	South East
P265VPN	16265	South East
P266VPN	16266	South East
P267VPN	16267	South East
P268VPN	16268	South East
P269VPN	16269	South East
P270VPN	16640	North West
P271VPN	16641	North West
P272VPN	16642	North West
P273VPN	16643	North West
P274VPN	16644	North West
P275VPN	16645	North West
P276VPN	16276	South East
P277VPN	16277	South East
P278VPN	16278	South East
P279VPN	16279	South East
P281VPN	16281	South East
P281XYS	52396	West
P282VPN	16282	South East
P283VPN	16283	South East
P284VPN	16284	South East
P285VPN	16285	South East
P286VPN	16286	South East
P287VPN	16287	South East

Reg	No	Region	Reg	No	Region	Reg	No	Region
P288VPN	16288	South East	P377DSA	31377	West Scotland	P541ESA	20541	South Midlands
P289VPN	16289	South East	P378DSA	31378	West Scotland	P541PNE	42541	Manchester
P290VPN	16290	South East	P379DSA	31379	West Scotland	P542EFL	16542	Eastern
P299AYJ	33029	South East	P380DSA	31380	West Scotland	P542ESA	20542	South Midlands
P301AYJ	33031	South East	P381DSA	31381	West Scotland	P542PNE	42542	Manchester
P301JBU	21101	North East	P382DSA	31382	West Scotland	P543EFL	16543	Eastern
P302AYJ	33032	South East	P383DSA	31383	West Scotland	P543ESA	20543	South Midlands
P302JBU	21102	North East	P384DSA	31384	West Scotland	P543PNE	42543	Manchester
P303JBU	21103	North East	P385DSA	31385	West Scotland	P544EFL	16544	Eastern
P304JBU	21104	North East	P386DSA	31386	West Scotland	P544ESA	20544	North West
P305JBU	21105	North East	P390LPS	32390	West Scotland	P544PNE	42544	Manchester
P315EFL	20695	North East	P391LPS	32391	West Scotland	P545EFL	16545	Eastern
P316EFL	20696	North East	P392LPS	32392	West Scotland	P545ESA	20545	North West
P317EFL	20697	South Wales	P393LPS	32393	West Scotland	P545PNE	42545	Manchester
P318EFL	20698	South Wales	P394LPS	32394	West Scotland	P546ESA	20546	North West
P319EFL	20694	South Midlands	P395BRS	32395	West Scotland	P546PNE	42546	Manchester
P320EFL	31320	South Midlands	P396BRS	32396	West Scotland	P547ESA	20547	North West
P321EFL	31319	South Midlands	P397BRS	32397	West Scotland	P547PNE	42547	Manchester
P321JND	31321	South Midlands	P398BRS	32398	West Scotland	P548ESA	20548	West Scotland
P322EFL	33322	Eastern	P418KWF	32818	East Midlands	P548PNE	42548	Manchester
P322JND	31322	South Midlands	P419KWF	32819	East Midlands	P549ESA	20549	West Scotland
P323EFL	33323	Eastern	P420KWF	32820	East Midlands	P549PNE	42549	North West
P323JND	31323	South Midlands	P426AYJ	33036	South East	P550ESA	20550	North East
P324EFL	33324	Eastern	P434AYJ	33034	South East	P550PNE	42550	North West
P324JND	31324	South Midlands	P435AYJ	33035	South East	P551ESA	20551	North East
P325JND	31325	South Midlands	P450KRP	32006	South Midlands	P551PNE	42551	Manchester
P326JND	31326	South Midlands	P451KRP	32007	South Midlands	P552ESA	20552	North East
P327JND	31327	South Midlands	P452KRP	32008	South Midlands	P552PNE	42552	Manchester
P328JND	31328	South Midlands	P455EEF	32655	North East	P553ESA	20553	North East
P329JND	31329	South Midlands	P456EEF	32656	North East	P553PNE	42553	North West
P330AYJ	33030	South East	P457AYJ	33037	South East	P554ESA	20554	North East
P330JND	31330	South Midlands	P457EEF	32657	North East	P554PNE	42554	Manchester
P331JND	31331	South Midlands	P458AYJ	33038	South East	P556ESA	20556	West Scotland
P332JND	31332	South Midlands	P458EEF	32658	North East	P556PNE	42556	Manchester
P334JND	31334	South Midlands	P459EEF	32659	North East	P557ESA	20557	South Midlands
P341ASO	40041	East Scotland	P460EEF	32660	North East	P557PNE	42557	East Midlands
P342ASO	40042	East Scotland	P461EEF	32661	North East	P558ESA	20558	South Midlands
P343ASO	40043	East Scotland	P466AYJ	33040	South East	P558PNE	42558	Manchester
P343AYJ	33033	South East	P479AYJ	33039	South East	P559ESA	20559	South Midlands
P344ASO	40044	East Scotland	P491BRS	31491	East Scotland	P559PNE	42559	Manchester
P345ASO	40045	East Scotland	P492BRS	31492	East Scotland	P560ESA	20560	South Midlands
P346ASO	40046	East Scotland	P493BRS	31493	East Scotland	P562PNE	42562	North West
P347ASO	40047	East Scotland	P494BRS	31494	East Scotland	P563MSX	51063	West Scotland
P348ASO	40048	East Scotland	P495BRS	31495	East Scotland	P563PNE	42563	Manchester
P349ASO	40049	East Scotland	P496BRS	31496	East Scotland	P564APM	33397	Eastern
P349NKH	40799	East Midlands	P497BRS	31497	East Scotland	P564MSX	51064	West Scotland
P350ASO	40050	East Scotland	P498BRS	31498	East Scotland	P564PNE	42564	Manchester
P350JND	31350	South Midlands	P499BRS	31499	East Scotland	P565MSX	52365	East Scotland
P350NKH	40800	East Midlands	P526EFL	16555	Eastern	P565PNE	42565	North West
P351ASO	40051	East Scotland	P527EFL	16527	Eastern	P566MSX	52366	East Scotland
P351JND	31351	South Midlands	P528EFL	16528	Eastern	P566PNE	42566	North West
P351NKH	40801	East Midlands	P530ESA	20530	West Scotland	P567MSX	52367	East Scotland
P352ASO	40052	East Scotland	P530PNE	42530	Manchester	P568MSX	52361	East Scotland
P352JND	31352	South Midlands	P531ESA	20531	West Scotland	P569MSX	52362	East Scotland
P352NKH	40802	East Midlands	P531PNE	42531	North West	P606CMS	32206	East Scotland
P353JND	31353	South Midlands	P532ESA	20532	West Scotland	P607CMS	32207	East Scotland
P353NKH	40803	East Midlands	P532PNE	42532	East Midlands	P608CMS	32208	East Scotland
P354JND	31354	South Midlands	P533ESA	20533	West Scotland	P609CMS	32209	East Scotland
P354NKH	40804	East Midlands	P533PNE	42533	North West	P610CMS	32210	East Scotland
P355JND	31355	South Midlands	P534EFL	16534	Eastern	P610SEV	34010	South East
P356JND	31356	South Midlands	P534ESA	20534	West Scotland	P611CMS	32211	East Scotland
P357JND	31357	South Midlands	P534PNE	42534	North West	P612CMS	32212	East Scotland
P361DSA	31361	South Midlands	P535ESA	20535	West Scotland	P613CMS	32213	East Scotland
P362DSA	31362	South Midlands	P535PNE	42535	North West	P615PGP	32615	North East
P363DSA	31363	South Midlands	P536ESA	20536	West Scotland	P616PGP	32616	North East
P364DSA	31364	South Midlands	P536PNE	42536	Manchester	P617PGP	32617	North East
P365DSA	31365	South Midlands	P537EFL	16537	Eastern	P618PGP	32618	Devon
P366DSA	31366	West Scotland	P537ESA	20537	West Scotland	P619PGP	32619	Devon
P367DSA	31367	West Scotland	P537PNE	42537	Manchester	P61VTG	33561	South Wales
P368DSA	31368	West Scotland	P538EFL	16538	Eastern	P620PGP	32620	North East
P369DSA	31369	West Scotland	P538ESA	20538	West Scotland	P621PGP	32621	North East
P370DSA	31370	West Scotland	P538PNE	42538	North West	P622ESO	52382	Eastern
P371DSA	31371	West Scotland	P539EFL	16539	Eastern	P622PGP	32622	North East
P372DSA	31372	West Scotland	P539ESA	20539	West Scotland	P623PGP	32623	North East
P373DSA	31373	West Scotland	P539PNE	42539	Manchester	P624PGP	32624	North East
P374DSA	31374	West Scotland	P540ESA	20540	North West	P625PGP	32625	South Midlands
P375DSA	31375	West Scotland	P540PNE	42540	Manchester	P626PGP	32626	South Midlands
P376DSA	31376	West Scotland	P541EFL	16541	Eastern	P627ESO	52387	Eastern

Reg	No	Region	Reg	No	Region	Reg	No	Region
P627PGP	32627	South Midlands	P802NJN	33352	London	P859GND	20859	Manchester
P628PGP	32628	South Midlands	P802XTA	52342	Devon	P860GND	20860	Manchester
P629PGP	32629	South Midlands	P803GMU	16003	London	P861GND	20861	Manchester
P630PGP	32630	South Midlands	P803NJN	33353	London	P862GND	20862	Manchester
P631PGP	32631	North East	P803XTA	52343	Devon	P863GND	20863	Manchester
P632PGP	32632	North East	P804GMU	16004	Eastern	P864GND	20864	Manchester
P633PGP	32633	North East	P804NJN	33354	London	P865GND	20865	Manchester
P634PGP	32634	North East	P804XTA	52344	Devon	P866GND	20866	Manchester
P636PGP	32636	Devon	P805GMU	16005	Eastern	P867GND	20867	Manchester
P637PGP	32637	North East	P805NJN	33355	London	P868GND	20868	Manchester
P638PGP	32638	North East	P805XTA	52345	Devon	P869MNE	20869	South Wales
P639PGP	32639	Devon	P806GMU	16006	Eastern	P870MNE	20870	South Wales
P640PGP	32640	Devon	P806NJN	33356	London	P871MNE	20871	South Wales
P644SEV	16044	West	P806XTA	52346	Devon	P872MNE	20872	South Wales
P645SEV	16045	East Scotland	P807GMU	16007	Eastern	P873MNE	20873	South Wales
P646SEV	16046	East Scotland	P807NJN	33357	South East	P874MNE	20874	South Wales
P677NOJ	31333	South Midlands	P808GMU	16008	Eastern	P875MNE	20875	Manchester
P686JBD	16686	Eastern	P809GMU	16009	Eastern	P876MNE	20876	Manchester
P687JBD	16687	Eastern	P810GMU	16010	Eastern	P877MNE	20877	Manchester
P688JBD	16688	Eastern	P811GMU	16011	Eastern	P878MNE	20878	Manchester
P689JBD	16689	Eastern	P812GMU	16012	Eastern	P879MNE	20879	Manchester
P690JBD	16690	Eastern	P813GMU	16013	Eastern	P880MNE	20880	Manchester
P691JBD	16691	Eastern	P814GMU	16014	Eastern	P881MNE	20881	Manchester
P692JBD	16692	Eastern	P815GMU	16015	Eastern	P882MNE	20882	Manchester
P701PTA	31701	Devon	P816GMU	16016	Devon	P883MNE	20883	South Wales
P702PTA	31702	Devon	P817GMU	16017	Devon	P884MNE	20884	South Wales
P703PTA	31703	Devon	P818GMU	16018	Eastern	P885MNE	20885	South Wales
P704PTA	31704	Devon	P819GMU	16019	Eastern	P886MNE	20886	South Wales
P705PTA	31705	Devon	P819GNC	20819	West	P887MNE	20887	South Wales
P706PTA	31706	Devon	P820GMU	16020	Eastern	P889MNE	20889	South Wales
P707PTA	31707	Devon	P820GNC	20820	South Midlands	P890MNE	20890	South Wales
P708PTA	31708	Devon	P821FVU	20821	South Midlands	P891MNE	20891	South Wales
P709PTA	31709	Devon	P821GMU	16021	Eastern	P892MNE	20892	South Wales
P710PTA	31710	Devon	P822FVU	20822	South Midlands	P893MNE	20893	Manchester
P711PTA	31711	Devon	P822GMU	16022	Eastern	P894MNE	20894	Manchester
P712PTA	31712	Devon	P823FVU	20823	South Midlands	P901SMR	32901	West
P713PTA	31713	Devon	P823GMU	16023	Eastern	P902SMR	32902	West
P714PTA	31714	Devon	P824FVU	20824	South Wales	P903SMR	32903	West
P716GND	16786	Manchester	P824GMU	16024	Eastern	P904SMR	33904	West
P717GND	16787	Manchester	P825FVU	20825	South Wales	P905SMR	33905	West
P718GND	16788	Manchester	P825GMU	16025	Eastern	P906SMR	33906	West
P719GND	16789	Manchester	P826FVU	20826	South Wales	P907SMR	33907	West
P720GND	16790	Manchester	P826GMU	16026	Eastern	P908SMR	33908	West
P721GND	16791	Manchester	P827FVU	20827	West	P909SMR	33909	West
P722GND	16792	Manchester	P828FVU	20828	West	P910SMR	33910	West
P723GND	16793	Manchester	P829FVU	20829	South East	P911SMR	33911	West
P724GND	16794	Manchester	P830FVU	20830	South East	P912SMR	33912	West
P725GND	16795	Manchester	P831FVU	20831	South East	P913SMR	33913	West
P726GND	16796	Manchester	P832FVU	20832	South East	P914SMR	33914	West
P727GND	16797	Manchester	P833FVU	20833	South East	P969UKG	46271	South Wales
P728GND	16798	Manchester	P834FVU	20834	South East	P970UKG	46272	South Wales
P729GND	16799	Manchester	P835FVU	20835	South East	P971UKG	46273	South Wales
P730GND	16800	Manchester	P836GND	20836	South East	P977UBV	52405	North West
P758FOD	33158	Devon	P837GND	20837	North East	P978UBV	52406	North West
P760FOD	33160	Devon	P838GND	20838	North East	P979UBV	52407	West Scotland
P762FOD	33159	Devon	P839GND	20839	North East	P988AFV	33080	South East
P771TTG	52401	South Wales	P840GND	20840	North East	PCK335	52099	North West
P772TTG	52402	South Wales	P841GND	20841	North East	PHH149W	15731	North West
P773TTG	52403	South Wales	P842GND	20842	North East	PO51WLF	47016	North West
P774TTG	52404	South Wales	P843GND	20843	North East	PO51WLG	47017	North West
P780WCN	32780	North East	P844GND	20844	North East	PO51WLH	47018	North West
P781WCN	32781	North East	P845GND	20845	Manchester	PO51WLJ	47019	North West
P782WCN	32782	North East	P846GND	20846	Manchester	PO51WLK	47020	North West
P783WCN	32783	North East	P847GND	20847	Manchester	PO51WLL	47021	North West
P784WCN	32784	North East	P848GND	20848	Manchester	PO51WLN	47022	North West
P785WCN	32785	North East	P849GND	20849	Manchester	PO51WLP	47023	North West
P786WCN	32786	North East	P850GND	20850	Manchester	PO51WLR	47024	North West
P787WCN	32787	North East	P851GND	20851	Manchester	PS2743	52008	East Midlands
P788WCN	32788	North East	P852GND	20852	Manchester	PSU443	52005	East Midlands
P789WCN	32789	North East	P852SMR	31852	South Midlands	PSU764	52007	East Midlands
P790WCN	32790	North East	P853GND	20853	Manchester	PSU787	32314	South East
P791WCN	32791	North East	P853SMR	31853	South Midlands	PSU788	52267	East Scotland
P792WCN	32792	North East	P854GND	20854	Manchester	PX03KCN	53018	North West
P793WCN	32793	North East	P854SMR	31854	South Midlands	PX03KCU	53019	North West
P801GMU	16001	London	P855GND	20855	Manchester	PX03KCV	53020	North West
P801NJN	33351	London	P856GND	20856	Manchester	PX03KCY	53021	North West
P801XTA	52341	Devon	P857GND	20857	Manchester	PX04DLV	47055	North West
P802GMU	16002	London	P858GND	20858	Manchester	PX04DLY	47056	North West

Reg	No	Region	Reg	No	Region	Reg	No	Region
PX04DLZ	47057	North West	R65UFC	32165	Devon	R118OPS	52418	West Scotland
PX04DME	47058	North West	R71NPN	31051	South East	R118XNO	16118	East Scotland
PX04DMF	47059	North West	R82SEF	52462	East Scotland	R119KRG	33119	South East
PX04DMU	47060	North West	R82XNO	16082	South Wales	R119NPN	31049	South East
PX04DMV	47061	North West	R83SEF	52463	East Scotland	R119OPS	52419	West Scotland
PX04DMY	47062	North West	R83XNO	16083	Eastern	R119VPU	34019	South East
PX04DMZ	18138	North West	R84SEF	52464	West Scotland	R119XNO	16119	East Scotland
PX04DND	18139	North West	R84XNO	16084	East Scotland	R120KRG	33120	North East
PX04DNE	18140	North West	R85SEF	52465	West Scotland	R120OPS	52420	East Scotland
PX04DNF	18141	North West	R85XNO	16085	Manchester	R120VFR	52490	North West
PX04DNJ	18142	North West	R86XNO	16086	Eastern	R120XNO	16120	East Scotland
PX04DNN	18143	North West	R87XNO	16087	Manchester	R121KRG	33121	North East
PX04DNU	18144	North West	R89XNO	16089	Eastern	R121OPS	52421	West Scotland
PX04DNV	18145	North West	R91XNO	16091	Eastern	R121VPU	34021	West Scotland
PX04DNY	18146	North West	R92XNO	16092	East Scotland	R121XNO	16121	East Scotland
PX04DOA	18147	North West	R93XNO	16093	East Midlands	R122EVX	16122	London
PX04DOH	18148	North West	R94XNO	16094	East Midlands	R122KRG	33122	North East
PX04DOJ	18149	North West	R95NPN	31045	South East	R122VPU	34022	East Scotland
PX04DOU	18150	North West	R95XNO	16095	Eastern	R123EVX	16123	London
PX04DPE	18151	North West	R96XNO	16096	East Midlands	R123KRG	33123	North East
PX04DPF	18152	North West	R97XNO	16097	Eastern	R123VPU	34023	East Scotland
PX04DPJ	18153	North West	R98XNO	16098	East Scotland	R124EVX	16124	Eastern
PX04DPN	18154	North West	R101KRG	33101	North East	R124KRG	33124	North East
PX04DPU	18155	North West	R101NTA	42101	Devon	R124VPU	34024	West Scotland
PX04DPV	18156	North West	R101XNO	16101	East Scotland	R125EVX	16125	Eastern
PX04DRZ	34579	North West	R102KRG	33102	North East	R125KRG	33125	North East
PX04DSE	34580	North West	R102NTA	42102	Devon	R125VPU	34025	West Scotland
PX04HTT	34616	North West	R102XNO	16102	Eastern	R126EVX	16126	West
PX04HTU	34617	North West	R103KRG	33103	East Midlands	R126KRG	33126	North East
PX04HTV	34618	North West	R103LSO	52425	West Scotland	R126VPU	34026	West Scotland
PX04HTY	34619	North West	R103NTA	42103	Devon	R127EVX	16127	West
PX04HTZ	34620	North West	R103XNO	16103	Manchester	R127KRG	33127	North East
PX53DJV	34473	North West	R104KRG	33104	East Midlands	R127VPU	34027	West Scotland
PX53DJY	34474	North West	R104LSO	52426	West Scotland	R128EVX	16128	West
PX53DJZ	34475	North West	R104NTA	42104	Devon	R128KRG	33128	North East
PX53DKA	34476	North West	R104XNO	16104	East Scotland	R128VPU	34028	East Scotland
PX53DKD	34477	North West	R105KRG	33105	East Midlands	R129EVX	16129	West
PX53DKE	34478	North West	R105LSO	52427	West Scotland	R129VPU	34029	East Scotland
PX53DKF	34479	North West	R105NTA	42105	Devon	R130EVX	16130	Eastern
PX53DKJ	34480	North West	R105XNO	16105	East Midlands	R131EVX	16131	East Midlands
PX53DKK	34481	North West	R107KRG	33107	East Midlands	R132EVX	16132	East Midlands
PX54AWU	18157	North West	R107NTA	42107	Devon	R132NPN	31052	South East
PX54AWV	18158	North West	R107XNO	16107	East Scotland	R133EVX	16133	East Midlands
PX54AWW	18159	North West	R108KRG	33108	East Midlands	R133NPN	31043	South East
PX54E0Z	47141	North West	R108NTA	42108	Devon	R134EVX	16134	East Midlands
PX54EJO	34679	North West	R108XNO	16108	East Scotland	R135EVX	16135	West
PX54EJU	34680	North West	R109KRG	33109	East Midlands	R136EVX	16136	East Midlands
PX54EOY	47140	North West	R109NTA	42109	Devon	R137EVX	16137	Devon
PX54EPA	47142	North West	R109XNO	16109	Eastern	R138EVX	16138	East Scotland
PX54EPC	47143	North West	R110FRS	52400	West	R139EVX	16139	Eastern
PX54EPD	47144	North West	R110KRG	33110	East Midlands	R140EVX	16140	East Scotland
PX54EPE	47145	North West	R110NTA	42110	Devon	R141EVX	16141	East Scotland
PX54EPF	47146	North West	R112KRG	33112	East Midlands	R142EVX	16142	West
PX54EPJ	47147	North West	R112NTA	42112	Devon	R143EVX	16143	East Midlands
PX54EPK	47130	North West	R112OPS	52422	East Scotland	R144EVX	16144	East Scotland
PX54EPL	47131	North West	R112XNO	16112	East Scotland	R144NPN	31044	South East
PX54EPN	47132	North West	R113KRG	33113	East Midlands	R145EVX	16145	East Midlands
PX54EPO	47133	North West	R113NTA	42113	Devon	R146EVX	16146	Eastern
PX54EPP	47134	North West	R113OPS	52423	East Scotland	R147EVX	16147	East Midlands
PX54EPU	47135	North West	R113XNO	16113	Eastern	R148EVX	16148	East Midlands
PX54EPV	47136	North West	R114KRG	33114	East Midlands	R148VPU	16048	East Midlands
PX54EPY	47137	North West	R114NTA	42114	Devon	R149HHK	16149	South Wales
PX54EPZ	47138	North West	R114OPS	52424	East Scotland	R149VPU	16049	Eastern
PX54ERJ	47139	North West	R114XNO	16114	East Scotland	R150CRW	33650	South Midlands
PX54EXM	47148	North West	R115KRG	33115	East Midlands	R150HHK	16150	East Scotland
PX54EXN	47149	North West	R115NTA	42115	Devon	R150VPU	16050	Devon
PY02KTO	33078	West Scotland	R115OPS	52415	Eastern	R151CRW	33651	South Midlands
PY02KTP	33079	West Scotland	R115XNO	16115	East Scotland	R151HHK	16151	East Midlands
PYE841Y	59087	East Midlands	R116KRG	33116	East Midlands	R151VPU	16051	East Midlands
R34AKV	52434	Eastern	R116NTA	42116	Devon	R152CRW	33652	South Midlands
R35AKV	52435	Eastern	R116OPS	52416	West Scotland	R152HHK	16152	East Scotland
R36AKV	52436	Eastern	R116VPU	34016	South East	R152VPU	16052	Devon
R36LSO	42000	North West	R116XNO	16116	East Scotland	R153CRW	33653	South Midlands
R37AKV	52437	Eastern	R117KRG	33117	East Midlands	R153HHK	16153	East Midlands
R38AKV	52438	Eastern	R117OPS	52417	South Wales	R153VPU	16053	East Midlands
R39AKV	52439	Eastern	R117VPU	34017	South East	R154CRW	33654	South Midlands
R63UFC	32163	Devon	R117XNO	16117	East Scotland	R154HHK	16154	East Scotland
R64UFC	32164	Devon	R118KRG	33118	North East	R154VPU	16054	East Scotland

Reg	No	Region	Reg	No	Region	Reg	No	Region
R155CRW	33655	South Midlands	R208XNO	33358	South East	R339HFS	20339	East Scotland
R155HHK	16155	East Scotland	R209XNO	33359	South East	R340HFS	20340	East Scotland
R155VPU	16055	West	R210XNO	16100	East Scotland	R341HFS	20341	East Scotland
R156HHK	16156	East Scotland	R221CRW	20221	South Midlands	R342HFS	20342	East Scotland
R156VPU	16056	Eastern	R223CRW	20223	South Midlands	R353LER	33393	Eastern
R157HHK	16157	East Scotland	R224CRW	20224	South Midlands	R354LER	33394	Eastern
R157VPU	16057	East Scotland	R225CRW	20225	South Midlands	R355LER	33395	Eastern
R158HHK	16158	East Scotland	R226CRW	20226	South Midlands	R356LER	33396	Eastern
R158VPU	16058	Devon	R227CRW	20227	South Midlands	R365JVA	33398	Eastern
R159HHK	16159	East Scotland	R228CRW	20228	South Midlands	R366JVA	33400	Eastern
R159VPU	16059	Devon	R236KRG	21136	North East	R414XFC	16514	South Midlands
R160HHK	16160	East Scotland	R237KRG	21137	North East	R415XFC	16515	South Midlands
R160VPU	16060	East Scotland	R238KRG	21138	North East	R416XFC	16516	South Midlands
R161HHK	16161	East Scotland	R239KRG	21139	North East	R417XFC	16517	South Midlands
R161VPU	16061	East Midlands	R240KRG	21140	North East	R418XFC	16518	South Midlands
R162HHK	16162	Eastern	R241KRG	21141	North East	R419XFC	16519	South Midlands
R162VPU	16062	Devon	R242KRG	21142	North East	R420XFC	16520	South Midlands
R163HHK	16163	East Scotland	R243KRG	21143	North East	R421XFC	16521	South Midlands
R163VPU	16063	East Midlands	R244KRG	21144	North East	R422XFC	16522	South Midlands
R164HHK	16164	Devon	R245KRG	21145	North East	R423XFC	16523	South Midlands
R164VPU	16064	Devon	R246KRG	21146	North East	R424XFC	16524	South Midlands
R165HHK	16165	East Scotland	R246NBV	16646	North West	R425XFC	16525	South Midlands
R165VPU	16065	East Scotland	R247KRG	21147	North East	R426XFC	16526	South Midlands
R166HHK	16166	East Scotland	R247NBV	16647	North West	R446YNF	42569	Manchester
R166VPU	16066	East Midlands	R248KRG	21148	North East	R447YNF	42570	Manchester
R167HHK	16167	Eastern	R248NBV	16648	North West	R451FVX	34051	South Wales
R167VPU	16067	East Scotland	R249KRG	21149	North East	R452FVX	34052	South Wales
R168HHK	16168	East Midlands	R249NBV	16649	North West	R453FCE	52447	Eastern
R168VPU	16068	West Scotland	R250KRG	21150	North East	R453FVX	34053	Manchester
R169HHK	16169	East Midlands	R250NBV	16650	North West	R454FCE	52444	Eastern
R169VPU	16069	Devon	R251KRG	21151	North East	R454FVX	34054	Manchester
R170HHK	16170	East Scotland	R251NBV	16651	North West	R455FCE	52445	Eastern
R170VPU	16070	Eastern	R252KRG	21152	North East	R455FVX	34055	South Wales
R171HHK	16171	East Scotland	R252NBV	16652	North West	R456FVX	34056	South Wales
R171VPU	16071	Devon	R253KRG	21153	North East	R457FVX	34057	Manchester
R172HHK	16172	East Scotland	R253NBV	16653	North West	R458FVX	34058	South Wales
R172VPU	16072	South Midlands	R254KRG	21154	North East	R460LSO	33760	East Midlands
R173HHK	16173	East Scotland	R254NBV	16654	North West	R461LSO	33761	East Midlands
R173VPU	16073	East Scotland	R255KRG	21155	North East	R462LSO	33762	East Midlands
R174DNH	52474	South East	R255NBV	16655	North West	R462SEF	33482	North East
R174HHK	16174	Eastern	R256KRG	21156	North East	R463LSO	33763	South Midlands
R174VPU	16074	West Scotland	R256NBV	16656	North West	R463SEF	33483	North East
R175DNH	52475	South East	R257KRG	21157	North East	R464LSO	33764	East Midlands
R175HHK	16175	Eastern	R257NBV	16657	North West	R464SEF	33484	North East
R175VPU	16075	East Scotland	R258KRG	21158	North East	R465LSO	33765	East Midlands
R176DNH	52476	South East	R258NBV	16658	North West	R465SEF	33485	North East
R176HHK	16176	East Scotland	R259NBV	16659	North West	R466LSO	33766	East Midlands
R176VPU	16076	South Midlands	R260NBV	16660	North West	R466SEF	33486	North East
R177DNH	52477	South East	R261NBV	16661	North West	R467LSO	33767	East Midlands
R177HHK	16177	East Scotland	R262NBV	16662	North West	R467SEF	33487	North East
R177NPN	31047	South East	R263NBV	16663	North West	R468LSO	33768	East Midlands
R177VPU	16077	East Scotland	R264NBV	16664	North West	R468SEF	33488	North East
R178DNH	52478	South East	R265NBV	16665	North West	R469LSO	33769	East Midlands
R178HHK	16178	East Scotland	R266NBV	16666	North West	R469MVN	33489	North East
R178NPN	31048	South East	R267NBV	16667	North West	R470LSO	33770	East Midlands
R178VPU	16078	South Midlands	R268NBV	16668	North West	R470MVN	33490	North East
R179DNH	52479	South East	R270NPN	31050	South East	R471LSO	33771	East Midlands
R179VPU	16079	South Midlands	R276CBU	42567	Manchester	R471MVN	33491	North East
R180DNH	52480	South East	R277CBU	42568	Manchester	R472MVN	33492	North East
R180VPU	16080	West	R291HCD	16291	South East	R473MCW	20473	North West
R181DNH	52481	South East	R292HCD	16292	South East	R474MCW	20474	North West
R181VPU	16081	West	R293HCD	16293	South East	R475MCW	20475	North West
R182DNH	52482	Eastern	R294HCD	16294	South East	R476MCW	20476	North West
R183DNH	52483	Eastern	R295HCD	16295	South East	R477MCW	20477	North West
R184DNH	52484	Eastern	R296HCD	16296	South East	R478MCW	20478	North West
R185DNH	52485	Eastern	R297HCD	16297	South East	R479MCW	20479	Devon
R186DNH	52486	Eastern	R298HCD	16298	South East	R480MCW	20480	Devon
R188XNO	16088	East Midlands	R299HCD	16299	South East	R481MCW	20481	Devon
R190XNO	16090	Manchester	R301HCD	16301	South East	R482MCW	20482	Devon
R196NPN	31046	South East	R311XNO	16111	East Scotland	R501UWL	16501	Manchester
R203DHB	16203	West	R330HFS	20330	East Scotland	R501YWC	42001	Manchester
R204DHB	16204	West	R331HFS	20331	East Scotland	R502KSA	20502	West Scotland
R205DHB	16205	West	R332HFS	20332	East Scotland	R502UWL	16502	Manchester
R206DHB	16206	West	R334HFS	20334	East Scotland	R502YWC	42002	Manchester
R206XNO	16106	Eastern	R335HFS	20335	East Scotland	R503KSA	20503	West Scotland
R207DHB	16207	West	R336HFS	20336	East Scotland	R503UWL	16503	Manchester
R207XNO	16099	West	R337HFS	20337	East Scotland	R503YWC	42003	Manchester
R208DHB	16208	West	R338HFS	20338	East Scotland	R504KSA	20504	West Scotland

Reg	No	Location	Reg	No	Location	Reg	No	Location
R504UWL	16504	Manchester	R609KDD	46609	Devon	R703DNJ	33003	South East
R504YWC	42004	Manchester	R609SWO	33609	South Wales	R703YWC	32353	Manchester
R505UWL	16505	Manchester	R609XAO	47932	West Scotland	R704DNJ	33004	South East
R505YWC	42005	Manchester	R610KDD	46610	West	R704YWC	32354	Manchester
R506UWL	16506	Manchester	R610SWO	33610	South Wales	R705YWC	32355	Manchester
R506YWC	42006	Manchester	R611KDD	46611	South East	R706DNJ	33006	South East
R507UWL	16507	Manchester	R611SWO	33611	South Wales	R706YUD	33806	Eastern
R507YWC	42007	Manchester	R612KDD	46612	South East	R706YWC	32356	Manchester
R508UWL	16508	Manchester	R612SWO	33612	South Wales	R707DNJ	33007	South East
R508YWC	42008	Manchester	R613KDD	46613	South East	R707YWC	32357	Manchester
R509UWL	16509	Manchester	R613SWO	33613	South Wales	R708DNJ	33008	South East
R509YWC	42009	Manchester	R614GFS	33414	East Scotland	R708YWC	32358	Manchester
R510UWL	16510	Manchester	R614KDD	46614	South East	R709DNJ	33009	South East
R510YWC	42010	Manchester	R614SWO	33614	South Wales	R709YWC	32359	Manchester
R511UWL	16511	Manchester	R615KDD	46615	South East	R710DNJ	33010	South East
R511YWC	42011	Manchester	R615SWO	33615	South Wales	R710YWC	32360	Manchester
R512UWL	16512	Manchester	R616KDD	46616	South East	R711DNJ	33011	South East
R512YWC	42012	Manchester	R616SWO	33616	South Wales	R711YWC	32361	Manchester
R513KSA	20513	West Scotland	R617SWO	33617	South Wales	R712YWC	32362	Manchester
R513UWL	16513	Manchester	R618SWO	33618	South Wales	R713YWC	32363	Manchester
R513YWC	42013	Manchester	R619SWO	33619	South Wales	R714YWC	32364	Manchester
R514KSA	20514	West Scotland	R620SWO	33620	South Wales	R715YWC	32365	Manchester
R514YWC	42014	Manchester	R621SWO	33621	South Wales	R716YWC	32366	Manchester
R515KSA	20515	West Scotland	R624CTX	42624	South Midlands	R717YWC	32367	Manchester
R515YWC	42015	Manchester	R636RSE	52456	West Scotland	R718YWC	32368	Manchester
R516VSE	20516	West Scotland	R637RSE	52457	East Scotland	R719RPY	20279	East Midlands
R516YWC	42016	Manchester	R638RSE	52458	East Scotland	R720RPY	20280	East Midlands
R517VSE	20517	West Scotland	R639RSE	52459	East Scotland	R720YUD	33820	Eastern
R517YWC	42017	Manchester	R640RSE	52460	East Scotland	R721RPY	20281	East Midlands
R518VSE	20518	West Scotland	R641LSO	20141	East Scotland	R722RPY	20282	East Midlands
R518YWC	42018	Manchester	R642LSO	20142	East Scotland	R723RPY	20283	East Midlands
R519VSE	20519	West Scotland	R643LSO	20143	East Scotland	R724RPY	20284	East Midlands
R521VSE	20521	West Scotland	R644LSO	20144	East Scotland	R725RPY	20285	East Midlands
R522VSE	20522	West Scotland	R645LSO	20145	West Scotland	R726RPY	20286	East Midlands
R524VSE	20524	West Scotland	R646HCD	20646	South East	R744DRJ	16744	Manchester
R526VSE	20526	West Scotland	R646LSO	20146	West Scotland	R745DRJ	16745	Manchester
R539GSF	52440	East Scotland	R647HCD	20647	South East	R746DRJ	16746	Manchester
R541GSF	52441	East Scotland	R647LSO	20147	East Scotland	R747DRJ	16747	Manchester
R542GSF	52442	East Scotland	R648HCD	20648	South East	R747XAR	16047	East Midlands
R543GSF	52443	East Scotland	R648LSO	20148	East Scotland	R748DRJ	16748	Manchester
R550JDF	52450	Eastern	R649HCD	20649	South East	R749DRJ	16749	Manchester
R551JDF	52451	Eastern	R649LSO	20149	East Scotland	R751BDV	33751	Devon
R552JDF	52452	Eastern	R650LSO	20150	East Scotland	R751DRJ	16751	Manchester
R553JDF	52453	Eastern	R651VSE	20151	East Scotland	R752DRJ	16752	Manchester
R554JDF	52454	Eastern	R652VSE	20152	West Scotland	R753DRJ	16753	Manchester
R554RPY	20264	North East	R653HCD	20653	Manchester	R754DRJ	16754	Manchester
R556RPY	20256	North East	R653RPY	20253	North East	R755DRJ	16755	Manchester
R557RPY	20257	North East	R653VSE	20153	East Scotland	R755RPY	20265	North East
R558RPY	20258	North East	R654HCD	20654	South East	R756DRJ	16756	Manchester
R560DRP	16210	Eastern	R654RPY	20254	North East	R757DRJ	16757	Manchester
R562DRP	16212	Eastern	R654VSE	20154	East Scotland	R758DRJ	16758	Manchester
R563DRP	16213	Eastern	R655RPY	20255	North East	R759DRJ	16759	Manchester
R564DRP	16214	Eastern	R663TKU	52493	Eastern	R760DRJ	16760	Manchester
R565DRP	16215	Eastern	R664TKU	52494	Eastern	R761DRJ	16761	Manchester
R566DRP	16216	Eastern	R670LFV	42670	North West	R762DRJ	16762	Manchester
R567DRP	16217	Eastern	R672LFV	42672	North West	R763DRJ	16763	Manchester
R568DRP	16218	Eastern	R674HCD	20674	Manchester	R765DRJ	16765	Manchester
R580JVA	16580	Eastern	R675HCD	20675	South East	R775CDW	52495	South Wales
R581JVA	16581	Eastern	R676HCD	20676	South East	R776CDW	52496	South Wales
R582JVA	16582	Eastern	R677HCD	20677	Manchester	R778CDW	52498	South Wales
R583JVA	16583	Eastern	R678HCD	20678	South East	R779CDW	52499	South Wales
R584JVA	16584	Eastern	R679HCD	20679	South East	R780CDW	52500	South Wales
R586JVA	16586	Eastern	R680HCD	20680	South East	R781CDW	52501	South Wales
R595LSO	20595	West Scotland	R691PAO	52491	North West	R782CDW	52502	South Wales
R596LSO	20596	West Scotland	R692PAO	52492	North West	R783CDW	52503	South Wales
R601SWO	33601	West	R693DNH	16693	Eastern	R784CDW	52504	South Wales
R602KDD	46602	North West	R694DNH	16694	Eastern	R785DHB	20385	South Wales
R602SWO	33602	West	R695DNH	16695	Eastern	R787DHB	20387	South Wales
R603KDD	46603	North West	R696DNH	16696	Eastern	R788DHB	20388	South Wales
R603SWO	33603	West	R697DNH	16697	Eastern	R789DHB	20389	South Wales
R604KDD	46604	Devon	R698DNH	16698	Eastern	R790DHB	20390	South Wales
R604SWO	33604	Eastern	R699DNH	16699	Eastern	R791DHB	20391	South Wales
R606KDD	46606	West	R701DNH	16221	Eastern	R792DHB	20392	South Wales
R606SWO	33606	South Wales	R701DNJ	33001	East Midlands	R793URM	20793	North West
R607KDD	46607	West	R701YWC	32351	Manchester	R794URM	20794	North West
R607SWO	33607	South Wales	R702DNH	16222	Eastern	R795URM	20795	North West
R608KDD	46608	Devon	R702DNJ	33002	South East	R801YUD	33801	Devon
R608SWO	33608	South Wales	R702YWC	32352	Manchester	R802YUD	33802	Eastern

Reg	Fleet	Location	Reg	Fleet	Location	Reg	Fleet	Location
R803YUD	33803	Devon	R912XVM	20912	Manchester	R965XVM	20965	Manchester
R804YUD	33804	Devon	R913XVM	20913	Manchester	R966XVM	20966	Manchester
R805YUD	33805	Devon	R914XVM	20914	Manchester	R967XVM	20967	Manchester
R807JDV	20347	Devon	R915GMW	33915	West	R968XVM	20968	Manchester
R807YUD	33807	Devon	R915XVM	20915	Manchester	R969XVM	20969	Manchester
R808YUD	33808	West	R916GMW	33916	West	R970XVM	20970	Manchester
R809YUD	33809	West	R916XVM	20916	Manchester	R971XVM	20971	Manchester
R810YUD	33810	West	R917GMW	33917	West	R972XVM	20972	Manchester
R811YUD	33811	West	R917XVM	20917	Manchester	R973XVM	20973	Manchester
R812YUD	33812	West	R918GMW	33918	West	R974XVM	20974	Manchester
R813HCD	33013	South East	R918XVM	20918	Manchester	R975XVM	20975	Manchester
R813YUD	33813	Eastern	R919XVM	20919	Manchester	R976XVM	20976	Manchester
R814HCD	33014	South East	R920XVM	20920	Manchester	R977XVM	20977	Manchester
R814YUD	33814	Eastern	R921XVM	20921	Manchester	R978XVM	20978	Manchester
R815HCD	33015	South East	R922XVM	20922	Manchester	R979XVM	20979	Manchester
R815YUD	33815	Eastern	R923XVM	20923	Manchester	R980XVM	20980	Manchester
R816HCD	33016	South East	R924XVM	20924	Manchester	R981XVM	20981	Manchester
R816YUD	33816	Eastern	R925XVM	20925	Manchester	R982XVM	20982	Manchester
R817HCD	33017	South East	R926XVM	20926	Manchester	R983XVM	20983	Manchester
R817YUD	33817	Eastern	R927XVM	20927	Manchester	R984XVM	20984	Manchester
R818HCD	33018	South East	R928XVM	20928	Manchester	R985XVM	20985	Manchester
R818YUD	33818	Eastern	R929XVM	20929	Manchester	R986XVM	20986	Manchester
R819HCD	33019	South East	R930FOO	34030	South East	R987XVM	20987	Manchester
R819YUD	33819	Eastern	R930XVM	20930	Manchester	R988XVM	20988	Manchester
R821HCD	33021	South East	R931FOO	34031	South East	R989XVM	20989	Manchester
R821YUD	33821	South Midlands	R931XVM	20931	Manchester	R990XVM	20990	Manchester
R822HCD	33022	South East	R932FOO	34032	South East	R991XVM	20991	Manchester
R822YUD	33822	South Midlands	R932XVM	20932	Manchester	R992XVM	20992	Manchester
R823HCD	33023	South East	R933FOO	34033	South East	R993XVM	20993	Manchester
R823YUD	33823	Devon	R933XVM	20933	Manchester	R994XVM	20994	Manchester
R824HCD	33024	South East	R934FOO	34034	South East	R995XVM	20995	Manchester
R824YUD	33824	Devon	R934XVM	20934	Manchester	R996XVM	20996	Manchester
R825YUD	33825	North East	R935FOO	34035	South East	RBZ5459	52268	North West
R826YUD	33826	North East	R935XVM	20935	Manchester	RCS382	19982	West Scotland
R827YUD	33827	North East	R936FOO	34036	East Scotland	RDZ6115	28615	London
R828YUD	33828	North East	R936XVM	20936	Manchester	RDZ6116	28616	London
R829YUD	33829	North East	R937FOO	34037	South Wales	RDZ6117	28617	London
R831OVN	16831	North East	R937XVM	20937	Manchester	RDZ6118	28618	London
R832OVN	16832	North East	R938FOO	34038	South Wales	RDZ6119	28619	London
R833OVN	16833	North East	R938XVM	20938	Manchester	RDZ6120	28620	London
R834OVN	16834	North East	R939FOO	34039	East Scotland	RDZ6121	28621	London
R835OVN	16835	North East	R939XVM	20939	Manchester	RDZ6122	28622	London
R836OVN	16836	North East	R940FOO	34040	East Scotland	RDZ6123	28623	London
R837OVN	16837	North East	R940XVM	20940	Manchester	RDZ6124	28624	London
R838OVN	16838	North East	R941FOO	34041	South Wales	RDZ6125	28625	London
R839OVN	16839	North East	R941XVM	20941	Manchester	RDZ6126	28626	London
R840OVN	16840	North East	R942FOO	34042	South Wales	RDZ6127	28627	London
R895XVM	20895	Manchester	R942XVM	20942	Manchester	RDZ6128	28628	London
R896XVM	20896	Manchester	R943FOO	34043	South Wales	RDZ6129	28629	London
R897XVM	20897	Manchester	R943XVM	20943	Manchester	RDZ6130	28630	London
R898AVM	42572	Manchester	R944FOO	34044	South Wales	RIB4309	11110	North West
R898XVM	20898	Manchester	R944XVM	20944	Manchester	RV52OGL	27501	Manchester
R899AVM	42571	Manchester	R945FOO	34045	South Wales	S101TRJ	22101	Manchester
R899XVM	20899	Manchester	R945XVM	20945	Manchester	S101WHK	34101	London
R901AVM	42573	Manchester	R946FOO	34046	South Wales	S102TRJ	22102	Manchester
R901FDV	16601	Devon	R946XVM	20946	Manchester	S102WHK	34102	London
R901XVM	20901	Manchester	R947FOO	34047	Manchester	S103TRJ	22103	Manchester
R902JDV	16602	Devon	R947XVM	20947	Manchester	S103WHK	34103	London
R902XVM	20902	Manchester	R948FOO	34048	Manchester	S104TRJ	22104	Manchester
R903JDV	16603	Devon	R948XVM	20948	Manchester	S104WHK	34104	East Scotland
R903XVM	20903	Manchester	R949FOO	34049	South Wales	S105TRJ	22105	Manchester
R904JDV	16604	Devon	R949XVM	20949	Manchester	S105WHK	34105	South Wales
R904XFC	20004	South Midlands	R950FOO	34050	South Wales	S106TRJ	22106	Manchester
R904XVM	20904	Manchester	R950XVM	20950	Manchester	S106WHK	34106	South Wales
R905XFC	20005	South Midlands	R951XVM	20951	Manchester	S107TRJ	22107	Manchester
R905XVM	20905	Manchester	R952XVM	20952	Manchester	S108TRJ	22108	Manchester
R906XFC	20006	South Midlands	R953XVM	20953	Manchester	S109TRJ	22109	East Scotland
R906XVM	20906	Manchester	R954XVM	20954	Manchester	S110SHJ	16110	West
R907XFC	20007	South Midlands	R955XVM	20955	Manchester	S110TRJ	22110	East Scotland
R907XVM	20907	Manchester	R956XVM	20956	Manchester	S112TRJ	22112	East Scotland
R908XFC	20008	South Midlands	R957XVM	20957	Manchester	S113TRJ	22113	Manchester
R908XVM	20908	Manchester	R958XVM	20958	Manchester	S114TRJ	22114	Manchester
R909XFC	20009	South Midlands	R959XVM	20959	Manchester	S115TRJ	22115	Manchester
R909XVM	20909	Manchester	R960XVM	20960	Manchester	S116TRJ	22116	Manchester
R910XFC	20010	South Midlands	R961XVM	20961	Manchester	S117JFJ	42117	Devon
R910XVM	20910	Manchester	R962XVM	20962	Manchester	S117TRJ	22117	Manchester
R911XFC	20011	South Midlands	R963XVM	20963	Manchester	S118JFJ	42118	Devon
R912XFC	20012	South Midlands	R964XVM	20964	Manchester	S118TRJ	22118	Manchester

Reg	Fleet	Location	Reg	Fleet	Location	Reg	Fleet	Location
S119TRJ	22119	Manchester	S312CCD	16312	South East	S478JSE	33478	East Scotland
S120TRJ	22120	Manchester	S313CCD	16313	South East	S479BWC	34079	Manchester
S121TRJ	22121	Manchester	S314CCD	16314	South East	S479JSE	33479	East Scotland
S122TRJ	22122	Manchester	S315CCD	16315	South East	S480BWC	34080	Manchester
S124KRM	22124	Manchester	S316CCD	16316	South East	S481BWC	34081	Manchester
S125TRJ	22125	Manchester	S317CCD	16317	South East	S482BWC	34082	East Scotland
S126TRJ	22126	Manchester	S318CCD	16318	South East	S483BWC	34083	London
S127TRJ	22127	Manchester	S319CCD	16319	South East	S484BWC	34084	East Scotland
S128TRJ	22128	Manchester	S320CCD	16320	South East	S486BWC	34086	East Scotland
S129TRJ	22129	Manchester	S322CCD	16322	South East	S487BWC	34087	East Scotland
S130TRJ	22130	Manchester	S323CCD	16323	South East	S488BWC	34088	London
S131TRJ	22131	Manchester	S324CCD	16324	South East	S489BWC	34089	South East
S132TRJ	22132	Manchester	S355SEF	42355	East Midlands	S490BWC	34090	South East
S133KRM	52603	South Midlands	S356SEF	42356	East Midlands	S491BWC	34091	South East
S133TRJ	22133	Manchester	S357SEF	42357	East Midlands	S492BWC	34092	South East
S134KRM	52604	South Midlands	S358SEF	42358	East Midlands	S493BWC	34093	South East
S134TRJ	22134	Manchester	S371DFC	42371	South Midlands	S494BWC	34094	South East
S135TRJ	22135	Manchester	S372DFC	42372	South Midlands	S495BWC	34095	Devon
S136TRJ	22136	Manchester	S373DFC	42373	South Midlands	S496BWC	34096	South Wales
S137TRJ	22137	Manchester	S374DFC	42374	South Midlands	S497BWC	34097	London
S138TRJ	22138	Manchester	S375DFC	42375	South Midlands	S498BWC	34098	London
S139TRJ	22139	Manchester	S376DFC	42376	South Midlands	S499BWC	34099	London
S140TRJ	22140	Manchester	S377DFC	42377	South Midlands	S587BCE	16587	Eastern
S141TRJ	22141	Manchester	S378DFC	42378	South Midlands	S588BCE	16588	Eastern
S142TRJ	22142	Manchester	S379DFC	42379	South Midlands	S589BCE	16589	Eastern
S143TRJ	22143	Manchester	S380DFC	42380	South Midlands	S590BCE	16590	Eastern
S144TRJ	22144	Manchester	S381DFC	42381	South Midlands	S591BCE	16591	Eastern
S145TRJ	22145	Manchester	S382DFC	42382	South Midlands	S592BCE	16592	Eastern
S146TRJ	22146	Manchester	S383DFC	42383	South Midlands	S593BCE	16593	Eastern
S147TRJ	22147	Manchester	S401SDT	33404	East Midlands	S615CSC	33415	East Scotland
S148TRJ	22148	Manchester	S402SDT	33405	East Midlands	S616CSC	33416	East Scotland
S149TRJ	22149	Manchester	S403SDT	33406	East Midlands	S617CSC	33417	East Scotland
S150TRJ	22150	Manchester	S410TNO	33360	South East	S618CSC	33418	East Scotland
S151TRJ	22151	Manchester	S411TNO	33361	South East	S619CSC	33419	East Scotland
S152TRJ	22152	Manchester	S451OFT	22451	North East	S622TDW	33622	South Wales
S153TRJ	22153	Manchester	S452OFT	22452	North East	S623TDW	33623	South Wales
S154TRJ	22154	Manchester	S453CVV	33453	Eastern	S624TDW	33624	South Wales
S156TRJ	22156	Manchester	S453OFT	22453	North East	S625TDW	33625	South Wales
S157TRJ	22157	Manchester	S454CVV	33454	Eastern	S626TDW	33626	South Wales
S158TRJ	22158	Manchester	S454OFT	22454	North East	S627TDW	33627	South Wales
S159TRJ	22159	Manchester	S455CVV	33455	Eastern	S638MGA	42025	South Wales
S161RET	16461	East Midlands	S455OFT	22455	North East	S655JSE	52605	East Scotland
S162RET	16462	East Midlands	S456CVV	33456	Eastern	S656JSE	52606	East Scotland
S163RET	16463	East Midlands	S456OFT	22456	North East	S657JSE	52607	East Scotland
S164RET	16464	East Midlands	S457BCE	52617	Eastern	S658JSE	52608	East Scotland
S165RET	16465	East Midlands	S457CVV	33457	Eastern	S659JSE	52609	East Scotland
S166RET	16466	East Midlands	S457OFT	22457	Eastern	S660JSE	52610	East Scotland
S167RET	16467	East Midlands	S458BCE	52618	Eastern	S661JSE	52611	East Scotland
S168RET	16468	East Midlands	S458CVV	33458	Eastern	S662JSE	52612	East Scotland
S169RET	16469	East Midlands	S458OFT	22458	Eastern	S665SDT	52635	East Midlands
S173SVK	52601	East Midlands	S459BCE	52619	Eastern	S670RWJ	52630	East Midlands
S174BLG	59601	South Wales	S459BWC	34059	South East	S671RWJ	52631	East Midlands
S174SVK	52602	East Midlands	S459CVV	33459	Eastern	S672RWJ	52632	East Midlands
S190RAO	42090	North West	S459OFT	22459	Eastern	S673RWJ	52633	East Midlands
S191RAO	42091	North West	S460BCE	52620	Eastern	S753DRP	16223	Eastern
S192RAO	42092	North West	S460BWC	34060	South East	S754DRP	16224	Eastern
S193RAO	42093	North West	S460CVV	33460	Eastern	S755DRP	16225	Eastern
S194RAO	42094	North West	S460OFT	22460	Eastern	S756DRP	16226	Eastern
S195RAO	42095	North West	S461BWC	34061	East Scotland	S757DRP	16227	Eastern
S196RAO	42096	North West	S461CVV	33461	Eastern	S758DRP	16228	Eastern
S269KHG	52613	North West	S462BWC	34062	East Scotland	S759DRP	16229	Eastern
S270CCD	16270	South East	S463BWC	34063	West Scotland	S760DRP	16230	Eastern
S270KHG	52614	North West	S467BWC	34067	South East	S761DRP	16231	Eastern
S271CCD	16271	South East	S468BWC	34068	South East	S762DRP	16232	Eastern
S272CCD	16272	South East	S469BWC	34069	East Scotland	S764SVU	16764	Manchester
S273CCD	16273	South East	S470BWC	34070	East Scotland	S766SVU	16766	Manchester
S274CCD	16274	South East	S471BWC	34071	South East	S767SVU	16767	Manchester
S275CCD	16275	South East	S472BWC	34072	South East	S768SVU	16768	Manchester
S302CCD	16302	South East	S472JSE	33472	East Scotland	S769RVU	16769	Manchester
S303CCD	16303	South East	S473BWC	34073	South East	S770RVU	16770	Manchester
S304CCD	16304	South East	S473JSE	33473	East Scotland	S771RVU	16771	Manchester
S305CCD	16305	South East	S474BWC	34074	South East	S772RVU	16772	Manchester
S306CCD	16306	South East	S474JSE	33474	East Scotland	S773RVU	16773	Manchester
S307CCD	16307	South East	S475JSE	33475	East Scotland	S774RVU	16774	Manchester
S308CCD	16308	South East	S476BWC	34076	East Scotland	S775RVU	16775	Manchester
S309CCD	16309	South East	S476JSE	33476	East Scotland	S776RVU	16776	Manchester
S310CCD	16310	South East	S477BWC	34077	Devon	S778RVU	16778	Manchester
S311CCD	16311	South East	S477JSE	33477	East Scotland	S779RVU	16779	Manchester

Reg	No.	Location	Reg	No.	Location	Reg	No.	Location
S780RVU	16780	Manchester	S926PDD	33926	West	SP04DBY	18094	East Scotland
S781RVU	16781	Manchester	S927CFC	22927	South Midlands	SP04DBZ	18095	East Scotland
S782RVU	16782	Manchester	S927PDD	33927	West	SP04DCE	18096	East Scotland
S796KRM	52626	North West	S928CFC	22928	South Midlands	SP04DCF	18097	East Scotland
S797KRM	52627	North West	S928PDD	33928	West	SP04DCU	18098	East Scotland
S798KRM	52628	North West	S929CFC	22929	South Midlands	SP04DCV	18099	East Scotland
S799KRM	52629	North West	S929PDD	33929	West	SP04DCX	18100	East Scotland
S801BWC	17001	London	S930CFC	22930	South Midlands	SP51AMK	22278	Eastern
S802BWC	17002	Devon	S930PDD	33930	West	SP51AMO	22279	South Midlands
S803BWC	17003	Devon	S931CFC	22931	South Midlands	SV04DVK	47051	East Scotland
S804BWC	17004	Devon	S932CFC	22932	South Midlands	SV04DVL	47052	East Scotland
S805BWC	17005	Devon	S933CFC	22933	South Midlands	SV04DVM	47053	East Scotland
S806BWC	17006	Devon	S934CFC	22934	South Midlands	SV04DVN	47054	East Scotland
S807BWC	17007	Eastern	S935CFC	22935	South Midlands	SV04HLM	47078	East Scotland
S808BTT	52638	East Scotland	S936CFC	22936	South Midlands	SV04HLN	47079	East Scotland
S808BWC	17008	Eastern	S937CFC	22937	South Midlands	SV04HLP	47080	East Scotland
S809BWC	17009	Eastern	S938CFC	22938	South Midlands	SV53DDJ	34482	East Scotland
S810BWC	17010	Eastern	S940CFC	22940	South Midlands	SV53DDK	34483	East Scotland
S811BWC	17011	Eastern	S941CFC	22941	South Midlands	SV53DDL	34484	East Scotland
S812BWC	17012	North West	SF03ZXU	47041	West Scotland	SV53DDN	34485	East Scotland
S813BWC	17013	North West	SF04SKD	47063	West Scotland	SV53DDO	34486	East Scotland
S814BWC	17014	North West	SF04SKE	47064	West Scotland	SV53DDU	34487	East Scotland
S815BWC	17015	North West	SF04SKJ	47065	West Scotland	SV53DDX	34489	East Scotland
S816BWC	17016	North West	SF04SKK	47066	West Scotland	SV53DDY	34490	East Scotland
S817BWC	17017	North West	SF04SKN	47067	West Scotland	SV53DDZ	34488	East Scotland
S818BWC	17018	North West	SF04VSV	34596	West Scotland	SV54BYM	47111	East Scotland
S819BWC	17019	North West	SF04VSX	34597	West Scotland	SV54BYN	47807	East Scotland
S820BWC	17020	North West	SF04VSY	34598	West Scotland	SV54BYO	53201	East Scotland
S821BWC	17021	North West	SF04VSZ	34599	West Scotland	SV54BYP	53202	East Scotland
S822BWC	17022	North West	SF04VTA	34600	West Scotland	SV54BYR	53203	East Scotland
S823BWC	17023	North West	SF04VTC	34601	West Scotland	SV54BYT	53204	East Scotland
S824BWC	17024	North West	SF04VTD	34602	West Scotland	SV54BYU	53205	East Scotland
S825BWC	17025	East Midlands	SF04VTE	34603	West Scotland	SV54BYW	53206	East Scotland
S826BWC	17026	East Midlands	SF04VTG	34604	West Scotland	SV54BYY	53207	East Scotland
S827BWC	17027	East Midlands	SF53BYL	18013	West Scotland	SV54BYZ	53208	East Scotland
S828BWC	17028	East Midlands	SF53BYM	18014	West Scotland	SV54EKP	53209	East Scotland
S829BWC	17029	East Midlands	SF53BYN	18015	West Scotland	SV54EKR	53210	East Scotland
S830BWC	17030	East Midlands	SF53BYO	18016	West Scotland	SV54EKT	53211	East Scotland
S831BWC	17031	East Midlands	SF53BYP	18017	West Scotland	SV54EKU	53212	East Scotland
S832BWC	17032	East Midlands	SF53BYR	18018	West Scotland	SV54EKW	53213	East Scotland
S833BWC	17033	East Midlands	SF53BYT	18019	West Scotland	SV54EKX	53214	East Scotland
S834BWC	17034	East Midlands	SF53BYU	18020	West Scotland	SV54EKY	53215	East Scotland
S835BWC	17035	East Midlands	SF53BYV	18003	West Scotland	SV54EKZ	53216	East Scotland
S836BWC	17036	Eastern	SF53BYW	18004	West Scotland	SV54ELC	50126	East Scotland
S837BWC	17037	Eastern	SF53BYX	18005	West Scotland	SV54ELH	50127	East Scotland
S838BWC	17038	Eastern	SF53BYY	18006	West Scotland	SV54ELJ	50128	East Scotland
S839BWC	17039	London	SF53BYZ	18007	West Scotland	SV54ELO	50129	East Scotland
S860VAT	52510	West Scotland	SF53BZA	18008	West Scotland	SV54ELU	50130	East Scotland
S901CCD	52621	Eastern	SF53BZB	18009	West Scotland	SV54ELW	50131	East Scotland
S902CCD	52622	North West	SF53BZC	18010	West Scotland	SV54ELX	50132	East Scotland
S903CCD	52623	North West	SF53BZD	18011	West Scotland	SV54EMF	53217	East Scotland
S903JHG	16669	North West	SF53BZE	18012	West Scotland	SV54EMJ	53218	East Scotland
S904JHG	16670	North West	SF53BZG	18000	West Scotland	SV54EMK	53219	East Scotland
S905JHG	52615	North West	SF53BZH	18001	West Scotland	SV54ENC	53220	East Scotland
S906JHG	52616	North West	SF53BZJ	18002	West Scotland	SW03OYA	60001	South East
S913CFC	22913	South Midlands	SF54RJU	47150	West Scotland	SW03OYB	60002	South East
S914ANH	16614	South Midlands	SHH124M	25704	North West	SW03OYC	60003	South East
S914CFC	22914	South Midlands	SJI4558	13605	North East	SW03OYD	60004	East Scotland
S915ANH	16615	South Midlands	SK04VFS	47068	West Scotland	SW03OYE	60005	East Scotland
S915CFC	22915	South Midlands	SK52USN	17734	Devon	SW03OYF	60006	East Scotland
S916ANH	16616	South Midlands	SK52USO	17735	Devon	SW03OYG	60007	East Scotland
S916CFC	22916	South Midlands	SK52USP	17736	Devon	SW03OYJ	60008	East Scotland
S917ANH	16617	South Midlands	SMK665F	12665	London	SW03OYK	60009	East Scotland
S917CFC	22917	South Midlands	SMK671F	12671	North West	SW03OYL	60010	East Scotland
S918ANH	16618	South Midlands	SMK709F	12709	North West	SW03OYM	60011	East Scotland
S918CFC	22918	South Midlands	SMK738F	12738	East Midlands	SW03OYP	60013	East Scotland
S919ANH	16619	South Midlands	SMK748F	12748	North West	SWO3OYN	60012	East Scotland
S919CFC	22919	South Midlands	SMK749F	12749	North West	SYC852	52217	London
S920ANH	16620	South Midlands	SMK760F	12760	London	T34DFC	50034	West Scotland
S920CFC	22920	South Midlands	SN03FHK	42022	West Scotland	T35DFC	50035	West Scotland
S921CFC	22921	South Midlands	SN03FHL	42023	West Scotland	T35VCS	33088	West Scotland
S922CFC	22922	South Midlands	SN03FHM	42024	West Scotland	T36DFC	50036	West Scotland
S923CFC	22923	South Midlands	SN04EFS	27502	South Midlands	T36VCS	33089	West Scotland
S924CFC	22924	South Midlands	SN04EFT	27503	South Midlands	T37BBW	50037	West Scotland
S924PDD	33924	West	SN04EFU	27504	South Midlands	T38BBW	50038	West Scotland
S925CFC	22925	South Midlands	SN04EFV	27505	South Midlands	T38PKG	42579	East Midlands
S925PDD	33925	West	SP04DBV	18092	East Scotland	T39BBW	50039	West Scotland
S926CFC	22926	South Midlands	SP04DBX	18093	East Scotland	T40UBE	50121	South Midlands

The 2005 Stagecoach Bus Handbook

Reg	No.	Region	Reg	No.	Region	Reg	No.	Region
T41BBW	50041	West Scotland	T373FUG	17673	East Midlands	T651KPU	17051	Eastern
T42BBW	50042	East Scotland	T374FUG	17674	East Midlands	T652KPU	17052	Eastern
T43BBW	50043	West Scotland	T375FUG	17675	East Midlands	T653KPU	17053	Eastern
T44UBE	50122	South Midlands	T376FUG	17676	East Midlands	T654KPU	17054	Eastern
T45BBW	50045	West Scotland	T377FUG	17677	East Midlands	T655KPU	17055	Eastern
T46BBW	50046	East Scotland	T402UCS	33772	West Scotland	T656KPU	17056	Eastern
T47BBW	50047	East Scotland	T403UCS	33773	West Scotland	T656OEF	22656	North East
T48BBW	50048	East Scotland	T404UCS	33774	Devon	T657KPU	17057	Eastern
T49BBW	50049	West Scotland	T461BNL	22461	Eastern	T657OEF	22657	North East
T50UBE	50123	South Midlands	T462BNL	22462	North East	T658KPU	17058	Eastern
T51BBW	50051	West Scotland	T463BNL	22463	North East	T658OEF	22658	North East
T52BBW	50052	West Scotland	T464BNL	22464	North East	T659KPU	17059	Eastern
T53BBW	50053	West Scotland	T465BNL	22465	North East	T659OEF	22659	North East
T54BBW	50054	West Scotland	T466BNL	22466	North East	T660KPU	17060	London
T55UBE	50124	South Midlands	T467BNL	22467	North East	T660OEF	22660	North East
T56BBW	50056	West Scotland	T468BNL	22468	North East	T661KPU	17061	London
T56JKG	42576	East Midlands	T469BNL	22469	North East	T661OBD	52641	South Midlands
T57BBW	50057	West Scotland	T469GPS	33469	East Scotland	T661OEF	22661	North East
T57JKG	42577	East Midlands	T470BNL	22470	North East	T662KPU	17062	London
T58BBW	50058	East Scotland	T470GPS	33470	East Scotland	T662OBD	52642	South Midlands
T58JKG	42578	East Midlands	T471BNL	22471	North East	T662OEF	22662	North East
T59BBW	50059	West Scotland	T471GPS	33471	East Scotland	T663KPU	17063	London
T60UBE	50125	South Midlands	T472BNL	22472	North East	T663OBD	52643	South Midlands
T95JHN	51095	West Scotland	T473BNL	22473	North East	T663OEF	22663	North East
T96JHN	51096	West Scotland	T474BNL	22474	North East	T664KPU	17064	London
T97JHN	51097	West Scotland	T475BNL	22475	North East	T664OEF	22664	North East
T131MGB	33782	Devon	T476BNL	22476	North East	T665KPU	17065	London
T132MGB	33783	Devon	T477BNL	22477	North East	T665OEF	22665	North East
T160MVM	22160	Manchester	T478BNL	22478	North East	T667KPU	17067	South East
T161MVM	22161	Manchester	T479BNL	22479	North East	T667RET	42026	South Wales
T162MVM	22162	Manchester	T480BNL	22480	North East	T667XTV	52647	South Midlands
T163MVM	22163	Manchester	T481BNL	22481	North East	T668KPU	17068	South East
T164MVM	22164	Manchester	T482BNL	22482	North East	T668XTV	52648	South Midlands
T165MVM	22165	Manchester	T483BNL	22483	North East	T669KPU	17069	South East
T166MVM	22166	Manchester	T484BNL	22484	North East	T669XTV	52649	South Midlands
T167MVM	22167	Manchester	T485BNL	22485	North East	T670KPU	17070	South East
T168MVM	22168	Manchester	T486BNL	22486	North East	T671KPU	17071	South East
T169MVM	22169	Manchester	T487BNL	22487	North East	T672KPU	17072	South East
T172MVM	22172	North East	T488BNL	22488	North East	T673KPU	17073	South East
T173MVM	22173	Manchester	T489BNL	22489	North East	T675KPU	17075	South East
T174MVM	22174	North East	T490BNL	22490	North East	T676KPU	17076	Eastern
T178MVM	22178	Manchester	T491BNL	22491	North East	T677KPU	17077	South East
T179MVM	22179	Manchester	T492BNL	22492	North East	T678KPU	17078	Eastern
T180MVM	22180	Manchester	T493BNL	22493	North East	T679KPU	17079	Eastern
T181MVM	22181	Manchester	T494BNL	22494	North East	T680KPU	17080	London
T182MVM	22182	Manchester	T495BNL	22495	North East	T681KPU	17081	London
T183MVM	22183	Manchester	T575KGB	33781	Devon	T682KPU	17082	London
T184MVM	22184	Manchester	T582SKG	42582	East Midlands	T683KPU	17083	London
T185MVM	22185	Manchester	T583SKG	42583	East Midlands	T684KPU	17084	London
T186MVM	22186	Manchester	T584SKG	42584	East Midlands	T685KPU	17085	London
T187MVM	22187	Manchester	T585SKG	42585	East Midlands	T686KPU	17086	London
T188MVM	22188	Manchester	T586SKG	42586	South Midlands	T687KPU	17087	London
T189MVM	22189	Manchester	T587SKG	42587	South Midlands	T688KPU	17088	London
T190MVM	22190	North East	T588SKG	42588	South Midlands	T689KPU	17089	London
T193MVM	22193	North East	T589SKG	42589	South Midlands	T690KPU	17090	London
T195MVM	22195	North East	T590SKG	42590	East Midlands	T691KPU	17091	London
T196MVM	22196	North East	T593CGT	33020	South East	T692KPU	17092	London
T197MVM	22197	North East	T612MNF	17612	Manchester	T693KPU	17093	London
T198MVM	22198	North East	T613MNF	17613	Manchester	T694KPU	17094	London
T199TND	22199	North East	T614DWL	50040	South Midlands	T695KPU	17095	London
T201TND	22201	North East	T615DWL	50044	West Scotland	T696KPU	17096	London
T202TND	22202	North East	T616DWL	50050	West Scotland	T697KPU	17097	London
T203TND	22203	South Midlands	T617DWL	50055	East Scotland	T698KPU	17098	London
T204TND	22204	North East	T618DWL	50060	West Scotland	T699KVX	17066	South East
T205TND	22205	South Midlands	T640KCS	51092	West Scotland	T727OEF	22727	North East
T206TND	22206	North East	T640KPU	17040	London	T728OEF	22728	North East
T207TND	22207	South Midlands	T641KCS	51093	West Scotland	T729OEF	22729	North East
T208TND	22208	North East	T641KPU	17041	London	T730OEF	22730	North East
T209TND	22209	South Midlands	T642KCS	51094	West Scotland	T731OEF	22731	North East
T210TND	22210	North East	T642KPU	17042	London	T732OEF	22732	North East
T211TND	22211	North East	T643KPU	17043	London	T733OEF	22733	North East
T212TND	22212	Manchester	T644KPU	17044	London	T734OEF	22734	North East
T213TND	22213	Manchester	T645KPU	17045	London	T735OEF	22735	North East
T214TND	22214	North East	T646KPU	17046	London	T736OEF	22736	North East
T215TND	22215	North East	T647KPU	17047	London	T801OHL	33401	East Midlands
T370FUG	17686	East Midlands	T648KPU	17048	London	T802OHL	33402	East Midlands
T371FUG	17687	East Midlands	T649KPU	17049	London	T803OHL	33403	East Midlands
T372FUG	17688	East Midlands	T650KPU	17050	Eastern	T905XCD	33407	South East

Reg	Fleet	Area		Reg	Fleet	Area		Reg	Fleet	Area
THX401S	10001	London		V136MVX	34136	South Wales		V167DFT	17667	Manchester
TJI4123	52019	South Wales		V137MEV	17137	London		V167MEV	17167	London
TJI4124	59002	South Wales		V137MVX	34137	South Wales		V167MVX	34167	London
TSJ71S	25771	West Scotland		V138MEV	17138	London		V168DFT	17668	Manchester
TSU638	13624	South Wales		V138MVX	34138	South Wales		V168MEV	17168	London
TSU639	52446	Eastern		V139MEV	17139	London		V168MVX	34168	London
TSU641	52118	East Scotland		V139MVX	34139	London		V169DFT	17669	Manchester
TSU642	52119	East Scotland		V140MEV	17140	London		V169MEV	17169	London
TSV778	52228	East Scotland		V140MVX	34140	London		V169MVX	34169	London
TSV779	52229	East Scotland		V141MEV	17141	London		V170DFT	17670	Manchester
TSV780	52230	East Scotland		V141MVX	34141	London		V170MEV	17170	London
TSV781	52231	East Scotland		V142MEV	17142	London		V170MVX	34170	London
UCS659	19959	West Scotland		V142MVX	34142	London		V171DFT	17671	Manchester
UF4813	19913	South East		V143MEV	17143	London		V171MEV	17171	London
UIB3076	25476	West Scotland		V143MVX	34143	London		V171MVX	34171	London
UIB3543	51071	West Scotland		V144MEV	17144	London		V172DFT	17672	Manchester
UJI4184	59701	South Wales		V144MVX	34144	London		V172MEV	17172	London
UWP105	52096	South East		V145MEV	17145	London		V172MVX	34172	London
UWW3X	14281	Devon		V145MVX	34145	London		V173MEV	17173	London
UWW7X	14283	West		V146MEV	17146	London		V173MVX	34111	London
V102MEV	17102	London		V146MVX	34146	London		V174MEV	17174	London
V103MEV	17103	London		V147MEV	17147	London		V174MVX	34121	London
V104MEV	17104	London		V147MVX	34147	London		V175MEV	17175	London
V105MEV	17105	London		V148MEV	17148	London		V176MEV	17176	London
V106MEV	17106	London		V148MVX	34148	London		V177MEV	17177	London
V107MEV	17107	London		V149MEV	17149	London		V178MEV	17178	London
V107MVX	34107	South East		V149MVX	34149	London		V179MEV	17179	London
V108MEV	17108	London		V150MEV	17150	London		V181MEV	17181	London
V108MVX	34108	South East		V150MVX	34150	London		V182MEV	17182	London
V109MEV	17109	London		V151DFT	17651	Manchester		V183MEV	17183	London
V109MVX	34109	South East		V151MEV	17151	London		V184MEV	17184	London
V110MVX	34110	South East		V151MVX	34151	London		V185MEV	17185	London
V112MEV	17112	London		V152DFT	17652	Manchester		V186MEV	17186	London
V112MVX	34112	London		V152MEV	17152	London		V188MEV	17188	London
V113MEV	17113	London		V152MVX	34152	London		V189MEV	17189	London
V113MVX	34113	London		V153DFT	17653	Manchester		V190MEV	17190	London
V114MEV	17114	London		V153MEV	17153	London		V191MEV	17191	London
V114MVX	34114	London		V153MVX	34153	London		V192MEV	17192	London
V115MEV	17115	London		V154DFT	17654	Manchester		V193MEV	17193	London
V115MVX	34115	Devon		V154MEV	17154	London		V194MEV	17194	London
V116MEV	17116	London		V154MVX	34154	London		V195MEV	17195	London
V116MVX	34116	London		V155DFT	17655	Manchester		V196MEV	17196	London
V117MEV	17117	London		V155MEV	17155	London		V197MEV	17197	London
V117MVX	34117	London		V155MVX	34155	London		V198MEV	17198	London
V118MEV	17118	London		V156DFT	17656	Manchester		V199MEV	17199	London
V118MVX	34118	London		V156MEV	17156	London		V201MEV	17201	London
V119MEV	17119	London		V156MVX	34156	London		V202MEV	17202	London
V119MVX	34119	London		V157DFT	17657	Manchester		V203MEV	17203	London
V120MEV	17120	London		V157MEV	17157	London		V204MEV	17204	London
V120MVX	34120	London		V157MVX	34157	London		V205MEV	17205	London
V122MEV	17122	London		V158DFT	17658	Manchester		V206MEV	17206	London
V122MVX	34122	London		V158MEV	17158	London		V207MEV	17207	London
V123MVX	34123	London		V158MVX	34158	London		V208MEV	17208	London
V124MEV	17124	London		V159DFT	17659	Manchester		V209MEV	17209	London
V124MVX	34124	South Wales		V159MEV	17159	London		V210MEV	17210	London
V125MEV	17125	London		V159MVX	34159	London		V211MEV	17211	London
V125MVX	34125	South Wales		V160DFT	17660	Manchester		V212MEV	17212	London
V126MEV	17126	London		V160MEV	17160	London		V213MEV	17213	London
V126MVX	34126	South Wales		V160MVX	34160	London		V214MEV	17214	London
V127MEV	17127	London		V161DFT	17661	Manchester		V215MEV	17215	London
V127MVX	34127	South Wales		V161MEV	17161	London		V216MEV	17216	London
V128MEV	17128	London		V161MVX	34161	London		V217MEV	17217	London
V128MVX	34128	South Wales		V162DFT	17662	Manchester		V218MEV	17218	London
V129MEV	17129	London		V162MEV	17162	London		V219MEV	17219	London
V129MVX	34129	South Wales		V162MVX	34162	London		V220MEV	17220	London
V130MEV	17130	London		V163DFT	17663	Manchester		V221MEV	17221	London
V130MVX	34130	South Wales		V163MEV	17163	London		V252ESX	22252	East Scotland
V131MEV	17131	London		V163MVX	34163	London		V253ESX	22253	East Scotland
V131MVX	34131	South Wales		V164DFT	17664	Manchester		V254ESX	22254	East Scotland
V132MEV	17132	London		V164MEV	17164	London		V255ESX	22255	East Scotland
V132MVX	34132	South Wales		V164MVX	34164	London		V256ESX	22256	East Scotland
V133MEV	17133	London		V165DFT	17665	Manchester		V257ESX	22257	East Scotland
V133MVX	34133	London		V165MEV	17165	London		V258ESX	22258	East Scotland
V134MEV	17134	London		V165MVX	34165	London		V259ESX	22259	East Scotland
V134MVX	34134	South Wales		V166DEF	22666	North East		V260ESX	22260	East Scotland
V135MEV	17135	London		V166DFT	17666	Manchester		V261ESX	22261	East Scotland
V135MVX	34135	South Wales		V166MEV	17166	London		V262ESX	22262	East Scotland
V136MEV	17136	London		V166MVX	34166	London		V263ESX	22263	East Scotland

The 2005 Stagecoach Bus Handbook

Reg	No	Region	Reg	No	Region	Reg	No	Region
V264ESX	22264	East Scotland	V907DDY	52657	South East	W186DNO	34186	London
V265ESX	22265	East Scotland	V908DDY	52658	South East	W187CNO	17180	London
V266ESX	22266	East Scotland	V909DDY	52659	South East	W187DNO	34187	London
V267ESX	22267	East Scotland	V938DFH	33938	West	W188DNO	34188	London
V268ESX	22268	East Scotland	V939DFH	33939	West	W189DNO	34189	London
V362OWC	17187	London	V940DFH	33940	West	W191DNO	34191	London
V362OWC	17200	London	V941DFH	33941	West	W192DNO	34192	London
V364OWC	17222	London	V942DFH	33942	West	W193DNO	34193	London
V378EWE	17678	East Midlands	V943DFH	33943	West	W194DNO	34194	London
V379EWE	17679	East Midlands	V944DFH	33944	West	W195DNO	34195	London
V380EWE	17680	East Midlands	V945DFH	33945	West	W196DNO	34196	London
V381EWE	17681	East Midlands	V946DFH	33946	West	W197DNO	34197	London
V382EWE	17682	East Midlands	V947DFH	33947	West	W198DNO	34198	London
V383EWE	17683	East Midlands	V948DDG	33948	West	W199DNO	34199	London
V384EWE	17684	East Midlands	V949DDG	33949	West	W201DNO	34201	London
V385EWE	17685	East Midlands	V950DDG	33950	West	W202DNO	34202	London
V462TVV	33462	Eastern	V951DDG	33951	West	W203DNO	34203	London
V463TVV	33463	Eastern	V952DDG	33952	West	W204DNO	34204	London
V464TVV	33464	Eastern	V953DDG	33953	West	W207DNO	34207	London
V476KJN	17110	London	V954DDG	33954	West	W208DNO	34208	London
V477KJN	17111	London	V955DDG	33955	West	W209DNO	34209	London
V478KJN	17121	London	V956DDG	33956	West	W211DNO	34211	London
V479KJN	17123	London	V957DDG	33957	West	W212DNO	34212	London
V601GCS	22601	West Scotland	V958DDG	33958	West	W213DNO	34213	London
V602GCS	22602	West Scotland	V959DDG	33959	West	W214DNO	34214	London
V603GCS	22603	West Scotland	V960DDG	33960	West	W215DNO	34215	London
V604GCS	22604	West Scotland	V961DDG	33961	West	W216DNO	34216	London
V605GCS	22605	West Scotland	V962DDG	33962	West	W218DNO	34218	London
V606GCS	22606	West Scotland	V972DRM	33076	North West	W219DNO	34219	London
V614DJA	17614	Manchester	V973DRM	33073	West Scotland	W221DNO	34221	London
V615DJA	17615	Manchester	V974DRM	33074	West Scotland	W223DNO	34223	London
V616DJA	17616	Manchester	V975DRM	33075	West Scotland	W224DNO	34175	London
V617DJA	17617	Manchester	VA53LCV	34402	West	W226DNO	34179	London
V618DJA	17618	Manchester	VA53LCW	34403	West	W227DNO	34180	London
V619DJA	17619	Manchester	VA53LCY	34404	West	W228DNO	34205	London
V620DJA	17620	Manchester	VA53LCZ	34405	West	W229DNO	34206	London
V621DJA	17621	Manchester	VCS376	15246	West Scotland	W231DNO	34190	London
V622DJA	17622	Manchester	VCS391	51062	East Scotland	W232DNO	34210	London
V623DJA	17623	Manchester	VKB708	52002	South East	W233DNO	34200	London
V624DJA	17624	Manchester	VLT14	17099	London	W234DNO	34217	London
V667DDC	22667	North East	VLT37	13603	East Scotland	W235DNO	34220	London
V668DDC	22668	North East	VLT255	16431	North East	W236DNO	34222	London
V669DDC	22669	North East	VRR447	52196	North West	W426NFG	33026	South East
V670DDC	22670	North East	VU03VVW	53012	North West	W501VDD	33501	West
V671DDC	22671	North East	VU03VVX	53013	North West	W504VDD	33504	West
V672DDC	22672	North East	VU03VVY	53014	North West	W508VDD	33508	West
V673DDC	22673	North East	VU03VVZ	53015	North West	W509VDD	33509	West
V674DDC	22674	North East	VU03VWA	53016	North West	W626RND	17626	Manchester
V675DDC	22675	North East	VU03VWB	53017	North West	W627RND	17627	Manchester
V701DSA	22701	East Scotland	VX04GHF	18082	West	W628RND	17628	Manchester
V702DSA	22702	East Scotland	VX04GHG	18083	West	W629RND	17629	Manchester
V703DSA	22703	East Scotland	VX04GHH	18084	West	W631RND	17631	Manchester
V704DSA	22704	East Scotland	VX04GHJ	18085	West	W632RND	17632	Manchester
V705DSA	22705	East Scotland	VX04GHK	18086	West	W633RND	17633	Manchester
V706DSA	22706	East Scotland	VX04GHN	18087	West	W634RND	17634	Manchester
V707DSA	22707	East Scotland	VX04GHU	18088	West	W635RND	17635	Manchester
V708DSA	22708	East Scotland	VX04GHV	18089	West	W636RND	17636	Manchester
V709DSA	22709	East Scotland	VX04GHY	18090	West	W637RND	17637	Manchester
V710DSA	22710	East Scotland	VX04GHZ	18091	West	W638RND	17638	Manchester
V711DSA	22711	East Scotland	VX04MZG	80009	North East	W639RND	17639	Manchester
V712DSA	22712	East Scotland	VX51NXR	33978	West	W641RND	17641	Manchester
V713DSA	22713	East Scotland	VX51NXS	33979	West	W642RND	17642	Manchester
V772GCS	42019	West Scotland	VX51NXT	33980	West	W643RND	17643	Manchester
V773GCS	42020	West Scotland	VX54LMJ	47121	West	W644RND	17644	Manchester
V774GCS	42021	West Scotland	VX54LMK	47122	West	W645RND	17645	Manchester
V801DFV	22801	North West	VX54NNK	18200	West	W646RND	17646	Manchester
V802DFV	22802	North West	W66BBW	50066	West Scotland	W647RND	17647	Manchester
V803DFV	22803	North West	W102PMS	33200	Devon	W805VDD	33505	West
V804DFV	22804	North West	W173DNO	34173	London	W851TBC	42027	South Wales
V806DFV	22806	North West	W174DNO	34174	London	W852TBC	42028	South Wales
V807DFV	22807	North West	W176DNO	34176	London	WA03WWZ	34399	Devon
V808DFV	22808	North West	W177DNO	34177	London	WA04CPY	18061	Devon
V809DFV	22809	North West	W178DNO	34178	London	WA04CPZ	18062	Devon
V811DFV	22811	North West	W181DNO	34181	London	WA04CRF	18063	Devon
V812DFV	22812	North West	W182DNO	34182	London	WA04CRJ	18064	Devon
V904DPN	52654	South Midlands	W183DNO	34183	London	WA04CRK	18065	Devon
V905DPN	52655	South East	W184DNO	34184	London	WA04CRU	18066	Devon
V906DPN	52656	South East	W185DNO	34185	London	WA04CRV	18067	Devon

Reg	No	Depot	Reg	No	Depot	Reg	No	Depot
WA04CRX	18068	Devon	WYV56T	10056	North West	X272NNO	17272	London
WA04CRZ	18069	Devon	X59RCS	33780	West Scotland	X273MTS	22273	East Scotland
WA04CSF	18070	Devon	X216BNE	22216	Manchester	X273NNO	17273	London
WA04CSU	18071	Devon	X217BNE	22217	Manchester	X274MTS	22274	East Scotland
WA04CSV	18072	Devon	X218BNE	22218	Manchester	X274NNO	17274	London
WA04CSX	18073	Devon	X219BNE	22219	Manchester	X276MTS	22276	East Scotland
WA04CSY	18074	Devon	X221BNE	22221	Manchester	X276NNO	17276	London
WA04CSZ	18075	Devon	X223BNE	22223	Manchester	X277MTS	22277	East Scotland
WA04CTE	18076	Devon	X224BNE	22224	Manchester	X277NNO	17277	London
WA04CTF	18077	Devon	X224WNO	34224	London	X278NNO	17278	London
WA04CTK	18078	Devon	X226BNE	22226	Manchester	X279NNO	17279	London
WA04CTU	18079	Devon	X226WNO	34226	London	X281NNO	17281	London
WA04CTV	18080	Devon	X227BNE	22227	Manchester	X282NNO	17282	London
WA04CTX	18081	Devon	X227WNO	34227	London	X283NNO	17283	London
WA04FNZ	18112	Devon	X228BNE	22228	Manchester	X284NNO	17284	London
WA04FOC	18113	Devon	X228WNO	34228	London	X285NNO	17285	London
WA04FOD	18114	Devon	X229BNE	22229	Manchester	X286NNO	17286	London
WA04FOF	18115	Devon	X229NNO	17229	London	X287NNO	17287	London
WA04FOH	18116	Devon	X229WNO	34229	London	X288NNO	17288	London
WA04FOJ	18117	Devon	X231BNE	22231	Manchester	X289NNO	17289	London
WA04FOK	18118	Devon	X231NNO	17231	London	X291NNO	17291	London
WA04FOM	18119	Devon	X231WNO	34231	London	X292NNO	17292	London
WA04TWU	47081	Devon	X232BNE	22232	Manchester	X293NNO	17293	London
WA04TWV	47082	Devon	X232NNO	17232	London	X294NNO	17294	London
WA04TWW	47083	Devon	X232WNO	34232	London	X295NNO	17295	London
WA04TWX	47084	Devon	X233BNE	22233	Manchester	X296NNO	17296	London
WA04TWY	47085	Devon	X233NNO	17233	London	X297NNO	17297	London
WA04TWZ	47086	Devon	X233WNO	34233	London	X298NNO	17298	London
WA04TXB	47087	Devon	X234BNE	22234	Manchester	X299NNO	17299	London
WA04TXC	47088	Devon	X234NNO	17234	London	X301NNO	17301	London
WA04TXD	47089	Devon	X234WNO	34234	London	X302NNO	17302	London
WA04TXE	47090	Devon	X235BNE	22235	Manchester	X303NNO	17303	London
WA04TXF	47091	Devon	X235NNO	17235	London	X304NNO	17304	London
WA04TXG	47092	Devon	X235WNO	34235	London	X307NNO	17307	London
WA04TXH	47093	Devon	X236BNE	22236	Manchester	X308NNO	17308	London
WA04TXJ	47094	Devon	X236NNO	17236	London	X309NNO	17309	London
WA04TXK	47095	Devon	X236WNO	34236	London	X311NNO	17311	London
WA04TXL	47096	Devon	X237BNE	22237	Manchester	X312NNO	17312	London
WA04TXM	47097	Devon	X237NNO	17237	London	X313NNO	17313	London
WA04TXN	47098	Devon	X237WNO	34225	London	X314NNO	17314	London
WA04TXP	47099	Devon	X238BNE	22238	Manchester	X315NNO	17315	London
WA04TXR	47100	Devon	X238NNO	17238	London	X317NNO	17317	London
WA04TXS	47101	Devon	X238WNO	34230	London	X319NNO	17319	London
WA04TXT	47102	Devon	X239BNE	22239	Manchester	X322NNO	17322	London
WA04TXU	47103	Devon	X239NNO	17239	London	X324NNO	17324	London
WA04TXV	47104	Devon	X241ATD	22241	Manchester	X326NNO	17326	London
WA04TXW	47105	Devon	X241NNO	17241	London	X327NNO	17327	London
WA04TXX	47106	Devon	X242ATD	22242	Manchester	X329NNO	17329	London
WA04TXY	47107	Devon	X242NNO	17242	London	X331NNO	17331	London
WA04TXZ	47108	Devon	X243ATD	22243	Manchester	X332NNO	17332	London
WA04TYB	47109	Devon	X243NNO	17243	London	X334NNO	17334	London
WA04TYC	47110	Devon	X244ATD	22244	Manchester	X335NNO	17335	London
WA51OSE	33201	Devon	X246ATD	22246	Manchester	X336NNO	17336	London
WA51OSF	33202	Devon	X246NNO	17246	London	X337NNO	17337	London
WLT415	52173	East Scotland	X247NNO	17247	London	X338NNO	17338	London
WLT416	13602	East Scotland	X248NNO	17248	London	X339NNO	17339	London
WLT439	20599	East Scotland	X249NNO	17249	London	X341NNO	17341	London
WLT447	52307	East Scotland	X251NNO	17251	London	X342NNO	17342	London
WLT461	17101	London	X252NNO	17252	London	X343NNO	17343	London
WLT491	17100	London	X253NNO	17253	London	X344NNO	17344	London
WLT512	16432	North East	X254NNO	17254	London	X346NNO	17346	London
WLT528	16433	North East	X256NNO	17256	London	X347NNO	17347	London
WLT538	34085	East Scotland	X257NNO	17257	London	X348NNO	17348	London
WLT546	25728	West Scotland	X258NNO	17258	London	X349NNO	17349	London
WLT575	17260	London	X259NNO	17259	London	X351NNO	17351	London
WLT682	16434	North East	X261NNO	17261	London	X352NNO	17352	London
WLT720	51070	East Scotland	X262NNO	17262	London	X353NNO	17353	London
WLT727	14239	East Scotland	X263NNO	17263	London	X354NNO	17354	London
WLT774	20597	East Scotland	X264NNO	17264	London	X356NNO	17356	London
WLT794	14240	East Scotland	X265NNO	17265	London	X357NNO	17357	London
WLT874	52079	East Midlands	X266NNO	17266	London	X358NNO	17358	London
WLT890	52022	London	X267NNO	17267	London	X361NNO	17223	London
WLT898	34100	London	X268NNO	17268	London	X362NNO	17224	London
WLT908	16435	North East	X269MTS	22269	East Scotland	X363NNO	17225	London
WSU293	52031	South Midlands	X269NNO	17269	London	X364NNO	17226	London
WVT618	32455	South East	X271MTS	22271	East Scotland	X365NNO	17227	London
WYV5T	10005	West Scotland	X271NNO	17271	London	X366NNO	17228	London
WYV29T	10029	West Scotland	X272MTS	22272	East Scotland	X367NNO	17230	London

The 2005 Stagecoach Bus Handbook

Reg	No	Region	Reg	No	Region	Reg	No	Region
X368NNO	17240	London	X741JCS	33776	West Scotland	Y244FJN	34244	London
X369NNO	17244	London	X742JCS	33777	West Scotland	Y246FJN	34246	London
X371NNO	17245	London	X743JCS	33778	West Scotland	Y247FJN	34247	London
X372NNO	17250	London	X744JCS	33779	West Scotland	Y248FJN	34248	London
X373NNO	17255	London	X805SRM	22805	North West	Y249FJN	34249	London
X376NNO	17270	London	X813SRM	22813	North West	Y251FJN	34251	London
X377NNO	17275	London	X814SRM	22814	North West	Y252FJN	34252	London
X378NNO	17280	London	X815SRM	22815	North West	Y253FJN	34253	London
X379NNO	17290	London	X816SRM	22816	North West	Y254FJN	34254	London
X381NNO	17300	London	X817SRM	22817	North West	Y256FJN	34256	London
X382NNO	17305	London	X818SRM	22818	North West	Y257FJN	34257	London
X383NNO	17306	London	X819SRM	22819	North West	Y258FJN	34258	London
X384NNO	17310	London	X821SRM	22821	North West	Y259FJN	34259	London
X385NNO	17316	London	X822SRM	22822	North West	Y261FJN	34261	London
X386NNO	17318	London	X823SRM	22823	North West	Y262FJN	34262	London
X387NNO	17320	London	X824SRM	22824	North West	Y263FJN	34263	London
X388NNO	17321	London	X825SRM	22825	North West	Y264FJN	34264	London
X389NNO	17323	London	X826SRM	22826	North West	Y265FJN	34265	London
X391NNO	17325	London	X827AKW	33847	East Midlands	Y266FJN	34266	London
X392NNO	17328	London	X827SRM	22827	North West	Y267FJN	34267	London
X393NNO	17330	London	X828AKW	33848	East Midlands	Y268FJN	34268	London
X394NNO	17333	London	X829AKW	33849	East Midlands	Y269FJN	34269	London
X395NNO	17340	London	X831AKW	33831	East Midlands	Y271FJN	34271	London
X396NNO	17345	London	X832AKW	33832	East Midlands	Y272FJN	34272	London
X397NNO	17350	London	X833AKW	33833	East Midlands	Y273FJN	34273	London
X398NNO	17355	London	X834AKW	33834	East Midlands	Y274FJN	34274	London
X428NSE	33428	East Scotland	X835AKW	33835	East Midlands	Y276FJN	34276	London
X429NSE	33429	East Scotland	X836AKW	33836	East Midlands	Y277FJN	34277	London
X431NSE	33431	East Scotland	X837AKW	33837	East Midlands	Y279FJN	34279	London
X432NSE	33432	East Scotland	X838AKW	33838	East Midlands	Y281FJN	34281	London
X433NSE	33433	East Scotland	X839AKW	33839	East Midlands	Y282FJN	34282	London
X434NSE	33434	East Scotland	X840AKW	33840	East Midlands	Y283FJN	34283	London
X435NSE	33435	East Scotland	X841AKW	33841	East Midlands	Y284FJN	34284	London
X436NSE	33436	East Scotland	X948VAP	22008	South East	Y285FJN	34285	London
X437NSE	33437	East Scotland	X953VAP	33053	South East	Y286FJN	34286	London
X438NSE	33438	East Scotland	X954VAP	33054	South East	Y287FJN	34287	London
X439NSE	33439	East Scotland	X956VAP	33056	South East	Y289FJN	34289	London
X441NSE	33430	East Scotland	X957VAP	33057	South East	Y291FJN	34291	London
X502ADF	33502	West	X958VAP	33058	South East	Y292FJN	34292	London
X503ADF	33503	West	X959VAP	33059	South East	Y293FJN	34293	London
X506ADF	33506	West	X961VAP	33061	South East	Y294FJN	34294	London
X507ADF	33507	West	X962VAP	33062	South East	Y295FJN	34295	London
X511ADF	33511	West	X963VAP	33063	South East	Y296FJN	34296	London
X512ADF	33512	West	X964VAP	33064	South East	Y297FJN	34297	London
X513ADF	33513	West	X965VAP	33065	South East	Y298FJN	34298	London
X518ADF	33510	West	X966AFH	33966	West	Y299FJN	34299	London
X523SHH	33077	West Scotland	X966VAP	33066	South East	Y301FJN	34301	London
X601VDY	17689	South East	X967AFH	33967	West	Y302FJN	34302	London
X602VDY	17690	South East	X967VAP	33067	South East	Y329FJN	34329	London
X604VDY	22004	South East	X968AFH	33968	West	Y331FJN	34331	London
X605VDY	22005	South East	X968VAP	33068	South East	Y332FJN	34332	London
X606VDY	22006	South East	X969AFH	33969	West	Y334FJN	34334	London
X607VDY	22007	South East	X969VAP	33069	South East	Y335FJN	34335	London
X613JCS	33443	West Scotland	X971AFH	33971	West	Y336FJN	34336	London
X614JCS	33444	West Scotland	X971VAP	33071	South East	Y337FJN	34337	London
X615JCS	33445	West Scotland	X972AFH	33972	West	Y338FJN	34338	London
X616JCS	33446	West Scotland	X972VAP	33072	South East	Y339FJN	34339	London
X617JCS	33447	West Scotland	X973AFH	33973	West	Y342FJN	34342	London
X676NSE	52666	East Scotland	X974AFH	33974	West	Y343FJN	34343	London
X677NSE	52667	East Scotland	X975AFH	33975	West	Y344FJN	34344	London
X678NSE	52668	East Scotland	X976AFH	33976	West	Y346FJN	34346	London
X679NSE	52669	East Scotland	X977AFH	33977	West	Y347FJN	34240	London
X701JVV	17691	Eastern	X978AFH	33970	West	Y348FJN	34245	London
X702JVV	17692	Eastern	XIL1284	34064	South East	Y349FJN	34250	London
X703JVV	17693	Eastern	XIL1286	34066	South East	Y351FJN	34255	London
X704JVV	17694	Eastern	XIL1560	34065	South East	Y352FJN	34260	London
X705JVV	17695	Eastern	XIL1568	34078	South East	Y353FJN	34270	London
X706JVV	17696	Eastern	XIL1575	34075	South East	Y354FJN	34275	London
X707JVV	17697	Eastern	XSU612	33012	South East	Y356FJN	34280	London
X714NSE	22714	East Scotland	XSU682	32454	South East	Y359NHK	17359	London
X715NSE	22715	East Scotland	XYK976	32451	South East	Y361NHK	17361	London
X716NSE	22716	East Scotland	Y103GHC	17402	South East	Y362NHK	17362	London
X717NSE	22717	East Scotland	Y237FJN	34237	London	Y363NHK	17363	London
X718NSE	22718	East Scotland	Y238FJN	34238	London	Y364NHK	17364	London
X719NSE	22719	East Scotland	Y239FJN	34239	London	Y365NHK	17365	London
X721NSE	22721	North West	Y241FJN	34241	London	Y366NHK	17366	London
X722NSO	22722	East Scotland	Y242FJN	34242	London	Y367NHK	17367	London
X739JCS	33775	West Scotland	Y243FJN	34243	London	Y368NHK	17368	London

Reg	Fleet No	Region	Reg	Fleet No	Region	Reg	Fleet No	Region
Y369NHK	17369	London	Y453NHK	17453	London	YN04YXV	34571	East Midlands
Y371FJN	34328	London	Y454NHK	17454	London	YN04YXW	34572	East Midlands
Y371NHK	17371	London	Y458NHK	17458	London	YN04YXX	34573	East Midlands
Y372FJN	34330	London	Y462NHK	17462	London	YN04YXY	34574	East Midlands
Y372NHK	17372	London	Y464NHK	17464	London	YN04YXZ	34575	East Midlands
Y373FJN	34333	London	Y508NHK	17360	London	YN04YYA	34576	East Midlands
Y373NHK	17373	London	Y509NHK	17370	London	YN04YYB	34577	East Midlands
Y374FJN	34340	London	Y511NHK	17375	London	YN04YYC	34578	East Midlands
Y374NHK	17374	London	Y512NHK	17380	London	YN04YYD	34581	East Midlands
Y376FJN	34345	London	Y514NHK	17400	London	YN51VHH	35000	East Midlands
Y376NHK	17376	London	Y517NHK	17406	London	YN51VHJ	35001	East Midlands
Y377NHK	17377	London	Y522NHK	17440	London	YN51VHK	35002	East Midlands
Y378NHK	17378	London	Y524NHK	17450	London	YN51VHL	35003	East Midlands
Y379NHK	17379	London	Y526NHK	17455	London	YN51VHM	35004	East Midlands
Y381NHK	17381	London	Y527NHK	17456	London	YN51VHN	35005	East Midlands
Y382NHK	17382	London	Y529NHK	17460	London	YN51VHP	35006	East Midlands
Y384NHK	17384	London	Y531NHK	17470	London	YN51VHR	35007	East Midlands
Y385NHK	17385	London	Y601TSD	31387	West Scotland	YN51VHT	35008	East Midlands
Y386NHK	17386	London	Y601TSD	31388	West Scotland	YN51VHU	35009	East Midlands
Y388NHK	17388	London	Y671JSG	34288	London	YN51VHV	35010	East Midlands
Y389NHK	17389	London	YA02YRO	47040	South East	YN51VHW	35011	East Midlands
Y391NHK	17391	London	YDG616	52056	North West	YN51VHX	35012	East Midlands
Y392NHK	17392	London	YG52DFZ	47028	South Midlands	YN51VHY	35013	East Midlands
Y393NHK	17393	London	YG52DHM	47026	South Midlands	YN51VHZ	35014	East Midlands
Y395NHK	17395	London	YG52DHY	47027	South Midlands	YN51VJA	35015	East Midlands
Y397NHK	17397	London	YK04KVU	47047	South East	YN53ZRT	34457	East Midlands
Y398NHK	17398	London	YK04KVV	47048	South East	YN53ZRU	34458	East Midlands
Y401NHK	17401	London	YK04KVW	47049	South East	YN53ZRV	34459	East Midlands
Y404NHK	17404	London	YL02FKY	47025	North East	YN53ZRX	34460	East Midlands
Y407NHK	17407	London	YLJ332	32453	South East	YN53ZRY	34461	East Midlands
Y409NHK	17409	London	YM52UOU	17737	East Midlands	YN53ZRZ	34462	East Midlands
Y429NHK	17429	London	YM52UOV	17738	East Midlands	YN53ZSD	34463	East Midlands
Y434NHK	17434	London	YM52UOW	17739	East Midlands	YN53ZSE	34464	East Midlands
Y436NHK	17436	London	YN03UXY	47805	South East	YN53ZSF	34465	East Midlands
Y437NHK	17437	London	YN03WNA	53011	South Midlands	YN53ZSG	34455	East Midlands
Y438NHK	17438	London	YN04KGA	18120	East Midlands	YN53ZSJ	34456	East Midlands
Y441NHK	17441	London	YN04KGE	18121	East Midlands	YNO4KGG	18123	East Midlands
Y442NHK	17442	London	YN04KGF	18122	East Midlands	YR02YRY	47801	South East
Y443NHK	17443	London	YN04KGJ	18124	East Midlands	YR02YTA	47802	South East
Y445NHK	17445	London	YN04KGK	18125	East Midlands	YSD350L	59950	West Scotland
Y446NHK	17446	London	YN04KGP	18126	East Midlands	YSV730	51061	East Scotland
Y447NHK	17447	London	YN04YXR	34582	East Midlands	YU02GRK	47803	North East
Y448NHK	17448	London	YN04YXS	34583	East Midlands	YU02GRX	47804	North East
Y449NHK	17449	London	YN04YXT	34584	East Midlands	YV03TZN	53022	South Midlands
Y452NHK	17452	London	YN04YXU	34570	East Midlands			

ISBN 1 904875 05 X

© Published by *British Bus Publishing Ltd* , February .02005

**British Bus Publishing Ltd, 16 St Margaret's Drive, Telford, TF1 3PH
Telephone: 01952 255669 - Facsimile: 01952 222397**